Cuba, the United States, and the Helms-Burton Doctrine

CONTEMPORARY
CUBA

Contemporary Cuba

Edited by John M. Kirk

A multidisciplinary series focusing on balanced, current, and provocative aspects of Cuban history, culture, society, and politics. Of special interest are works that examine the dramatic changes in Cuba since 1959, such as the role of the military, the nature of economic reforms, and the impact of foreign investments, human rights treaties, and tourism on the island.

Afro-Cuban Voices: On Race and Identity in Contemporary Cuba, by Pedro Pérez-Sarduy and Jean Stubbs (2000)

Cuba, the United States, and the Helms-Burton Doctrine: International Reactions, by Joaquín Roy (2000)

Cuba, the United States, and the Helms-Burton Doctrine

International Reactions

Joaquín Roy

University Press of Florida

Gainesville · Tallahassee · Tampa · Boca Raton
Pensacola · Orlando · Miami · Jacksonville

05 04 03 02 01 00 6 5 4 3 2 1

Library of Congress Cataloging-in-Publication Data
Roy, Joaquín, 1943–
Cuba, the United States, and the Helms-Burton Doctrine: international
reactions / Joaquín Roy
p. m.— (Contemporary Cuba)
ISBN 0-8130-1760-2 (alk. paper)
1. Economic sanctions, American—Cuba. I. Title. II. Series
KF4678.R69 2000
327.7307291'09'049—dc21   99-059526

The University Press of Florida is the scholarly publishing agency for
the State University System of Florida, comprising Florida A&M
University, Florida Atlantic University, Florida International University,
Florida State University, University of Central Florida, University of
Florida, University of North Florida, University of South Florida, and
University of West Florida.

University Press of Florida
15 Northwest 15th Street
Gainesville, FL 32611–2079
http://www.upf.com

To
Richard P. Kinkade
Robert Kirsner
David Lagmanovich
Ambler H. Moss, Jr.
Evelyn Stevens
and
Clarence Stuckwisch
and to the memory of
Ludlow Baldwin
for their help
in decisive stages
of my professional life
in the United States of America

"*The American continents are not to be considered a subject for future colonization by any European power. . . . We would not view any intervention for the purpose of oppressing the former colonies, or controlling in any other manner their destiny by any European power in any other light than as a manifestation of an unfriendly disposition toward the U.S.*"
James Monroe, 1823

"*We will oppose, with all of our means, the forcible interposition of any other power, as auxiliary, stipendiary, or under any other form or pretext, and most especially, [Cuba's] transfer to any power by conquest, cession, or acquisition in any other way.*"
Thomas Jefferson, 1823

"*Should you have reason to suspect any design on the part of Spain to transfer voluntarily her title to the island, whether of ownership or possession, and whether permanent or temporary, to . . . any other power, you will distinctly state that the U.S. will prevent it, at all hazard.*"
Secretary of State John Forsyth, 1840

"*The government is resolutely determined that the island of Cuba, shall never be ceded by Spain to any other power than the United States . . . the news of the cession of Cuba to any other foreign power would, in the United States, be the instant signal for war.*"
Secretary of State John Clayton, 1850

CONTENTS

List of Tables and Figures   x

Foreword by John M. Kirk, series editor   xi

Preface   xiii

Acknowledgments   xviii

List of Acronyms and Abbreviations   xxi

1. Background and Development   1

2. Getting Their Act Together: Content and Initial Perception   28

3. Lawyers Meet the Law: U.S. Voices Critical of Helms-Burton   61

4. The World's Response: Protest in the Americas   84

5. The Washington-Havana Feud as Seen from Brussels: Perceptions and Reactions of the European Union   105

6. The Ever Faithful Island: Spain's Relations with Havana under U.S. Policy   130

7. Disproportionate Influence Still Creates Outsized Problems   151

8. Conclusion   182

Appendix: Biographical Sketches   203

Notes   207

Bibliography   241

Index   265

TABLES AND FIGURES

Tables

1. European Union direct investment flows to Cuba, 1990–96   13
2. Foreign investment in Cuba   13
3. Certified claims   16
4. Mexican-Cuban bilateral trade, 1994–97   91
5. UN vote on resolution against the U.S. embargo on Cuba   103

Figures

1. European Union trade with Cuba, 1980–96   86
2. Canadian-Cuban merchandise trade: Exports to and imports from Cuba, 1985–97   108
3. Spanish-Cuban trade relations, 1975–98   144

FOREWORD

Few countries raise the ire in Washington as rapidly as revolutionary Cuba—and this has been the case for four decades. Little wonder, then, that a piece of legislation as draconian as the "Cuban Liberty and Democratic Solidarity (LIBERTAD) Act," popularly known as Helms-Burton, should have been introduced. The 1996 legislation was clearly intended to choke off the oxygen to Cuba—that is, foreign investment—at a time when Havana was reeling from the demise of the Soviet Union, and had decided as a last resort to open the doors to entrepreneurs from around the world.

Debate continues about the success of the legislation. It is clear that, while some major investors have been scared off, some 360 others have flocked to Cuba, keen to take advantage of the absence of U.S. competition. Of these, about half have invested since the passing of Helms-Burton. (Ironically, the law has also been used by Havana, in part to rationalize its disappointing economic growth in recent years, and to justify the hardening of political attitudes among some Cuban politicians.)

What is not as widely appreciated, at least outside the Washington, D.C., Beltway, is the reaction of the international community to the Helms-Burton Law. Some may recall former president Jimmy Carter's emotional criticism of it, but most observers are unaware of the depth of feelings outside the United States.

It is clear, in the wake of threats by the European Union to take the United States before the World Trade Organization over Helms-Burton, as well as complaints from both NAFTA partners, that Helms-Burton was a clear violation of international law. Indeed, the legislation had few supporters outside the United States. In his book, Joaquín Roy examines in detail the reaction of the international community, both at large and in specific cases. Significantly, not one nation has stood up to support the U.S. position.

Roy argues, and argues convincingly, that this legislation is but the latest stage in a hostile U.S. policy toward revolutionary Cuba. His analysis of the background to the actual passage of the legislation also reveals the single-minded approach of Washington to Cuba all these years. The initial goal of U.S. policy toward Cuba in this legislation had been to isolate that country. How strange, then, that history has come full circle and now—as witnessed eloquently by the international reaction to this legislation—it is the United States that is largely isolated in its Cuba policy.

This study of Helms-Burton offers a fascinating analysis of how U.S. policy on Cuba is formulated and what its impact is—in seeking both to punish Cuba and to influence the international community. The book will undoubtedly add sparks to the necessary debate both on the validity of this law and on the larger issue of U.S.-Cuban relations. And well it might—for the new millennium is very distant from the Cold War of the 1950s and 1960s, as the international community has known for several decades.

John M. Kirk, series editor

PREFACE

Clarification

The customary disclaimer appended to the preceding note of thanks should suffice. A distinction is necessary between the content of this book and the opinions of the people who have helped me in developing this and other projects related to Cuba.

This is not a book to praise Castro, but his political survival over forty years does not permit us to come and bury him. However, as the conclusion will confirm and elaborate, we render unto Caesar the things which are his. The same is true of the United States. Both share part of the blame as well as credit for the survival of the Cuban regime.

On one hand, the evidence is that Cuba has been presided over by a personalistic, dictatorial, Marxist-Leninist system that denies most of the fundamental rights that are the common legacy of liberal democracy. On the other hand, sovereign nations have the right to govern themselves as they see fit. Personally, I would prefer that Cuba rejoin, as quickly and peacefully as possible, the family of states guided by one form or another of liberal democracy, but my wish is not the central subject of this book.

Before deciding to invest considerable time into this project, I hesitated in view of the apparent lack of real consequences anticipated by the "Cuban Liberty and Democratic Solidarity (LIBERTAD) Act of 1996 (22 U.S.C 6021 et Seq.)," a.k.a. "the Helms-Burton Law," or H-B for short. From an empirical, social scientific, practical point of view, the record shows that little has in fact happened since the law's passage. In essence, the collapse of the Castro regime (as the ultimate primary objective of the law) has not happened, in spite of the impact of the U.S. embargo on the Cuban economy. Moreover, due to the suspension of Title III (the most important part of this legislation concerning its international reverberations), no legal proceedings against foreign investors in Cuba have been filed. Why then study a non-event? Experts on the Cuban missile crisis of 1962 have faced the same question. Nothing actually happened then either, except for intense speculation by the United States and the Soviet Union about one another's moves. Still, hundreds of books and essays have been written on the subject. If one accepts the thesis of non-events in the case of Helms-Burton, then surely the law deserves consideration for the extraordinary *waste* of energies it represents.

A tally of the staff time invested by U.S. and foreign government agencies and organizations in the actions and counteractions of H-B would reveal a figure as high as the bill for the Kenneth Starr investigation, another example of a non-result if the objective was the removal of a president from office. Helms-Burton must have intrinsic value since it has commanded the attention of such high government officials as the president of the United States, the entire U.S. Congress, and prime ministers and presidents of Canada and of numerous Latin American and Caribbean countries, as well as the top ranks of the main institutions of the European Union and the United Nations. It has revealed unusual dimensions of foreign policies of states with special relations with Cuba, such as the obvious case of Spain.

In any event, the fact remains that much has happened since the initial idea of H-B was put into practice. The record constitutes a lesson on the mechanisms of government, international relations, political perceptions, and simple human imperfection. One positive result of the experience is that we may be able to know more about democracy, government, and commercial ambitions in general than before. Or at least this is one of the purposes of the book.

What initially attracted my attention to the topic was the level of disagreement between official U.S. policy and the perception of most of the rest of the world regarding the Castro regime. The U.S. government tried to dictate to its allies and partners the way to deal with Cuba, potentially expanding a bilateral dispute into a worldwide conflict. At the same time, the most perturbing move of the U.S. legislators was their insistence on imposing *political* conditions on the lifting of the embargo, conditions to be met by a future Cuban government. In addition to the threat of legal suits against foreign investors in Cuba (Title III), Title II of the law imposed specific democratic and economic conditions to be met by any future Cuban government to allow the discontinuation of the U.S. embargo. A close reading of Title II of the Helms-Burton Act, which was for a brief time destined to be the sole text of the law, reveals that the U.S. Congress had managed to be more demanding than previous examples of U.S.-imposed conditions on Cuba, such as the Platt Amendment. A tentative explanation is that the law is more than a policy—it is an amorphous (although historically coherent) tool for updating the Monroe Doctrine. It is the *Helms-Burton Doctrine*.

This perception confirmed my early impression of how little things had changed since 1823, when President James Monroe issued his famous warning to the European states wishing to return to the Americas. It also appears that nothing has changed since 1898, when the United States intervened into what was basically a family quarrel between Spaniards and Cubans—or Spaniards from Spain and Spanish settlers in Cuba. My interest in the relationship between Spain and Cuba through this century has finally found a necessary new dimension—the missing link with the United States. Spain is a member of the European Union, so when Washington denounced all countries trading with Cuba, the subject was expanded. This book and my earlier writings are the result.

In any event, in view of the historical failure of the embargo, a tentative conclusion is that U.S. policy has contributed a great deal to the continuation of the Castro regime, especially after the disappearance of the Soviet Union. While it seems that I am in good company (an impressive number of scholars share this assessment), I have tried here to avoid editorializing. Instead, I elected to let multiple voices speak through the texts of various pieces of legislation, as well as declarations, studies, and papers. If some of these sound sarcastic or ironic at times, the intention is not to be disrespectful but rather to offer a sort of balancing perspective and commentary on what is basically a sad episode in the history of relations among the United States, Cuba, and the rest of the world.

Methodology

Following my initial interest in the subject and preliminary attempts to publish a few articles clarifying the most important developments, I began to consider undertaking a wider study. At first I contemplated a method based on interviews, but many of the main players were at very high levels of governance, and for that reason unlikely to be accessible, not to mention fully frank and forthcoming.

An early attempt at interviewing second-tier staff members revealed that many had a partisan agenda. Nevertheless, a selective number of secondary players were interviewed, and they contributed details on particular aspects of Helms-Burton. I have shared my own drafts and related writings with U.S. congressional staff, as well as with representatives of the European Union Commission and the governments of Spain, Mexico, and Cuba. I have respected the wish of some that their identities be protected. The editors and referees of the journals where parts of this research have been published since 1997 also offered generous comments, corrections, and additional data.

What became obvious, once the systematic interview method was discarded, is that the principal players in this drama had already spoken through the basic documents that are main corpus of the study. In addition to the Helms-Burton Act itself are the subsequent decisions, declarations, motions, and positions taken by different governments and organizations. Then come the speeches and press conferences given by the main and secondary actors. Finally, since the topic belongs to an interdisciplinary field, I have relied heavily on the analysis of different experts in international law, political science, history, and economics. At all times, I have resisted the temptation to editorialize, and I elected to let the main and secondary voices speak.

Aims and Audience

In this volume I seek to analyze and explain the three principal aspects of Helms-Burton—that is, in terms of U.S. domestic politics, the U.S.-Cuba relationship, and the wider international picture. The global dimension is my principal focus, deriving from the internationalization of the original feud between Havana and Washington. The other two aspects are secondary, but they are reviewed when Helms-Burton has contributed unique dimensions to the perennial problem between the United States and the Castro government.

Coming from academic experience and training in a combination of different disciplines (law, history, humanities, politics), I have tried to produce a study that would be useful, first of all, to readers who are broadly interested in international affairs. The expansion of what was in essence a bilateral relationship between the United States and Cuba has converted Helms-Burton into a subject to be closely followed by scholars in the field of U.S.–Latin American relations. It is also an excellent case study of how unilateral sanctions applied by one country (that is, the United States) can ripple beyond their main target (Cuba) to generate serious complications in its international relations. The extraterritorial aims of the law have placed the controversial measure at the center of two triangular relationships: one is the United States' economic relations with Mexico and Canada, in the North American Free Trade Area (NAFTA); the other is the triangle formed by the United States, Latin America (Cuba), and the European Union (E.U.) and its member states.

In the domestic sphere, interest groups with a role in designing foreign policy have converted Helms-Burton into a case study for experts on congressional procedures, the U.S. lobby system, and constitutional law. Most important, H-B has revealed that a well-organized and dedicated group may not simply influence but in some respects actually seize control of certain aspects of U.S. foreign policy. The Cuban-American exile community (especially the Cuban-American National Foundation) has become a major player in determining a portion of U.S. foreign activities. This core of the Cuban-American community has demonstrated an acute understanding of the making of a *policy* attached to the survival of a *doctrine*, still solidly anchored to the political psyche of the U.S. elite.

Relations between the U.S. Congress and the White House have shown signs of strain over Cuba, tilting the initiative and management of foreign policy toward key players at the highest legislative level. With the law temporarily and partially suspended, the courts, the third main arm of government, still have not entered into action directly derived from Helms-Burton. However, as we will see, courts in Miami and New York have issued collateral judgments indirectly related to H-B. On its own, the legal community has intervened with an impressive level of activity. Besides reviewing the analyses given by attorneys to potential clients, this study has aimed to examine the scholarly contributions made by legal experts. The legal dimension may be one of the most important positive results of the Helms-Burton experience.

Miami–Barcelona,
August 1999

ACKNOWLEDGMENTS

I must recognize, above all, the generous and unconditional encouragement of my colleague and friend Enrique Baloyra in what probably was his last editing project before his untimely death in July 1997. His kind response to a simple request for comments on a draft paper was to put it through the customary review process, leading to the eventual publication of my article "The Helms-Burton Law: Development, Consequences, and Legacy for Inter-American and U.S.-European Relations" in the *Journal of Inter-American Studies and World Affairs*. Enrique's objectivity and scholarly integrity encouraged me to proceed with this line of research. With the intention of partially repaying his support in this and other ventures, I decided to expand on the original text, and to develop some aspects that space limitations in the original piece had forced me to set aside.

My next attempt to address this topic, in view of the latest moves from Washington toward Cuba, was in a brief article in Spanish in the *Anuario Iberoamericano '96* of the Spanish News Agency EFE, for which I would like to recognize the confidence demonstrated by its director, Paloma Rupérez. This paper was then developed in Spanish as a short essay titled "Auge y caída de la ley Helms-Burton" (Rise and fall of the Helms-Burton Law), which was published in *Leviatán* (Madrid, edited by Manuel Ortuño), *Archivos del Presente* (Buenos Aires, headed by Aníbal Jozami), and *Encuentro de la Cultura Cubana* (Madrid, edited by Jesús Díaz). The basic themes were elaborated and expanded in English as a paper presented at the biannual conference of the European Community Studies Association (ECSA) held in Seattle, Washington (May 27–June 1, 1997). In the Catalan language, the main points of the central theme were presented in July 1997 as a lecture at the Law School of the University Pompeu Fabra of Barcelona, thanks to the generous invitation of Oriol Casanovas. A portion of the section on Spain was presented at the conference on "U.S. Policy Toward Cuba: Means and Ends," held in Miami on October 16–17, 1997, by the

Center for International Policy, under the coordination of Wayne Smith. The basic facts of the chapters on Spain and the European Union, and some of the concluding ideas, were presented at the conference titled "Transatlantic Tensions: The Challenge of Difficult Countries," organized by the Brookings Institution in Washington, D.C., March 9–10, 1998; I would like to express my thanks to Wolfgang Reinicke and Richard Haass for inviting me to speak. I reviewed changes in the Spanish-Cuban relationship in a paper for the Latin American Studies Association congress held in Chicago on September 24–26, 1998, and also for a symposium organized by the Cuba Project of Queens College of the City University of New York (CUNY) on September 28, 1998, for which I would like to acknowledge the invitations of Michael Erisman and Mauricio Font. As I prepared the final draft of this volume, updates, expansions, and redactions of basic themes were published in *Papel Político* (Universidad Javeriana of Bogotá, edited by Javier Sanín), *Estudios Internacionales* (Universidad de Chile, Santiago, edited by Pilar Alamos), *Ibero-Amerikansches Archiv* (Berlin, edited by Günter Vollmer), *Relaciones Internacionales* (National University of Mexico, Mexico City, edited by Consuelo Dávila), *The European Union Review* (Pavia, Italy, edited by Dario Velo), *Revista de Derecho Comunitario* (University of Salamanca, edited by Araceli Mangas), and *Collegium* (College of Europe, Bruges, Belgium, edited by Marc Vuijlsteke).

During the course of my research and writing of this and other pieces on specific aspects of Helms-Burton, a number of colleagues, officials, and assistants have made generous contributions of various sorts. First, I should thank Ambler H. Moss, Jr., for his continuous support, comments, and corrections, and for his knowledge of sources. I am grateful to Ángel Viñas for sharing his research materials, for his commentaries on an early version of a preliminary paper, and for facilitating contacts in the European Commission. To Luis Ortiz Monasterio, consul general of Mexico in Miami, I owe the initial access to the texts of Mexican legislation and government documents. Wolf Grabendorff and the staff of the Instituto de Relationes Europeo-Latinoamericanas (IRELA) should be recognized for the continuous production of unique materials on European–Latin American relations. Robert Kirsner has contributed editorial assistance with this and other manuscripts on Helms-Burton. Ramón Mestre of *El Nuevo Herald* in Miami has offered corrections and linguistic suggestions. Steve Ralph and Annette Kmetz have always been instrumental with their technological and administrative support. The staffs of at least four libraries should receive proper credit for facilitating my use of difficult-to-find sources: the Richter Library and the Law School Library of the University of Miami, the Law School Library of the University of Barcelona, and the CIDOB Foundation of Barcelona. I would like to recognize the support of Dean Roger Kanet in making possible my fall 1998 sabbatical from the University of Miami, during which I was able to review an advance draft of the book. Simultaneously, and thanks to a grant awarded by the Generalitat de Catalunya and an appointment as visiting professor, I presented most of its findings in a seminar organized by the Jean Monnet Chair of European Integration and the Department of International Law at the University of Lleida, under the direction of Albert Galinsoga.

As in the case of all my previous publications on the relationship between the European Union, Spain, and Cuba, I would like to acknowledge my appreciation for the continuous supply of information, comments, and travel and research opportunities offered by the staff of the Directorate-General I and Directorate-General VIII of the European Commission and its delegation in Washington, D.C. (especially Isabel Auger, Manel Camós, Mendel Goldstein, Francesc Granell, and Carmen Ortiz), and Manuel Medina and Carlos Gasóliba, members of the European Parliament. Special thanks should be reserved for Inocencio Arias and the staff of the Oficina de Información Diplomática (the public information service of the Ministry of Foreign Affairs) and the Consulate of Spain in Miami for the systematic supply of press materials. To Ion de la Riva I owe the opportunity of spending a few days in Havana and giving a lecture under the auspices of the Embassy of Spain.

Above all the contributions made by these individuals and institutions, I would like to recognize most especially my research assistant, Anna Krift, for her invaluable help in editing the complete text of this volume as it evolved from draft into its final form, and also for turning trade and aid data into more convincing tables and graphs.

Finally, recognition should be given to John Kirk for his trust and confidence during the arduous process of revision and editing of the text for inclusion in the series of books on Cuba published by the University Press of Florida. Susan Fernández should be commended for her patience in the coordination of efforts. The generous and constructive anonymous referees deserve the status of joint authors for their advice, corrections, and suggestions. Indeed, credit should be given to my wife, Barbara, my children, Núria and Alex, and my mother, Asunción, for support and understanding beyond the call of duty.

However, the opinions and errors included in the book are the sole responsibility of the author.

ACRONYMS AND ABBREVIATIONS

ACP	African-Caribbean-Pacific
ACS	Association of Caribbean States
AFP	Agence France Press
AIPAC	American-Israel Political Action Committee
ALADI	Asociación Latinoamericana de Integración
AP	Associated Press
ASCE	Association for the Study of the Cuban Economy
BBV	Banco de Bilbao-Vizcaya
CANF	Cuban-American National Foundation
CARICOM	Caribbean Community and Common Market
CARIFORUM	Caribbean Forum
CDA	Cuban Democracy Act of 1992; "Torricelli Law"
CEMEX	Cementos Mexicanos
CFSP	Common Foreign and Security Policy
CNN	Cable News Network
COMECON (CMEA)	Council of Mutual Economic Assistance
CONACEX	Consejo Nacional de Comercio Exterior
COPARMEX	Confederación Patronal de la República Mexicana
COREPER	Committee of Permanent Representatives
ECHO	European Community Humanitarian Office
ECU	European currency unit
EFE	Spanish news agency
ETECSA	Empresa de Telecomunicaciones de Cuba, S.A.
EU	European Union
FAO	Food and Agriculture Organization
FEMA	Foreign Extra-Territorial Measures Act
FBIS	Foreign Broadcast Information Service
GATT	General Agreement on Tariffs and Trade
GRD	German Democratic Republic

H-B	Cuban Liberty and Democratic Solidarity (LIBERTAD) Act of 1996, also known as the Helms-Burton Law
IDB	Inter-American Development Bank
ILSA	Iran-Libya Sanctions Act of 1996
IMF	International Monetary Fund
ITT	International Telephone and Telegraph Corporation
MAI	Multilateral Agreement on Investment
NAFTA	North American Free Trade Area
NATO	North Atlantic Treaty Organization
OAS	Organization of American States
OECD	Organization for Economic Cooperation and Development
PAN	Partido de Acción Nacional
PARLATINO	Latin American Parliament
PP	Partido Popular
PSOE	Partido Socialista Obrero Español
SECOFI	Secretaría de Comercio y Fomento Internacional
SELA	Sistema Económico de América Latina
SINTEL	Sistemas e Instalaciones de Telecomunicación
STET	Società Telefònica e Telegràfica
UCD	Unión de Centro Democrático
UK	United Kingdom of Britain and Northern Ireland
UNESCO	United Nations Education, Scientific and Cultural Organization
USAID	United States Agency for International Development
USIA	United States Information Agency
WB	World Bank
WHO	World Health Organization
WTO	World Trade Organization

1

Background and Development

Acceptance of a practical protectorate over Cuba seems to me very
like the assumption of the responsible care of a madhouse.
Steward Woodford, U.S. Ambassador to Spain, 1898

The government of Cuba consents that the United States may exercise
the right to intervene for the preservation of Cuban independence,
the maintenance of a government adequate for the protection of life,
property, and individual liberty.
Platt Amendment, 1901

I am not interested in power nor do I envisage assuming it at any time.
Fidel Castro, January 1, 1959

The Context and Origins of the Helms-Burton Act

In mid-March of 1996, President Bill Clinton reluctantly signed into law an
act of Congress that had been debated for months in the House and Senate.
In the context of the overall domestic and international commitments of the
U.S. government, Cuba (the cause of the law) was not of much concern,
considering the restructuring of the world at the end of the Cold War. The
new law basically reinforced the more than three decades' long U.S. embargo against Cuba, a failed policy in view of the survival of the regime of
Fidel Castro. The act was seen as a triumph of the Cuban-American exile
community in the United States, which was credited with mastering the
lobby system.

What was new, however, were the international repercussions of this new
attempt to pressure Cuba. And what was particularly alarming was a provision of the law allowing U.S. citizens to sue foreign nationals in U.S.
courts for dealing with properties in Cuba that allegedly were confiscated
improperly by the Castro regime in the early sixties. The rest of the world

had until then considered the U.S.-Cuba dispute as an exclusively bilateral quarrel, and tended to regard the U.S. obsession with Castro with disdain.

The act, known as the Helms-Burton Law, would be the object of controversy and criticism not only from the Cuban government but from the rest of the world, including such traditional allies of the United States as the United Kingdom and Canada, and trade partners such as the European Union and Mexico. U.S. legal scholars and legislators formed part of a coalition that opposed the law as a violation of international law, a mistake, and an embarrassment.

The full impact of the Helms-Burton Law on U.S. international relations and domestic politics cannot yet be evaluated. Since late in 1995, when the U.S. Senate and House made a number of adjustments to the Helms-Burton bill, some major developments have influenced the course of U.S.-Cuban and international relations.

These events are complex, and they affect dozens of states and international organizations, and concern hundreds of companies in many nations. They have raised the hopes of thousands of Cuban-Americans, have consumed thousands of column inches in newspapers and news weeklies in three continents, and have engaged the energies of hundreds of public officers and scholars. Some events are well known publicly. Some have remained confined to board rooms or the pages of academic journals. All have a common origin: the Cuban Revolution and Cuba's confrontation with the United States. This latest chapter of the U.S.-Cuban friction has some unique features, and they are the subject here.

The first event is Cuba's intentional downing of two airplanes belonging to Cuban exiles a few miles off Havana on February 24, 1996. The incident shattered any near-term possibility of rapprochement between the United States and Cuba. As a result, President Clinton, at first ambivalent but under pressure by the Cuban lobby, appeared compelled to sign the Helms-Burton bill into law on March 12. Then, as an example of the world opposition to the law, the European Union (E.U.) decided in the fall of 1996 to enact a regulation (complemented by a joint action) to block U.S. moves, and announced its intent to place this issue in the framework of the World Trade Organization (WTO). As a confirmation of its standing policy of putting conditions on cooperation aid packages, the E.U. also issued a common position detailing the requirements Cuba had to meet in order to become a beneficiary of a cooperation aid agreement.

Next, out of mutual concern for the looming confrontation between close economic and political partners, the E.U. responded on April 11, 1997, to the partial suspension of the law and the promises to extend its neutralization by agreeing with the United States on a pact that would in essence freeze its impact. This compromise was subsequently confirmed by another, more elaborate agreement on May 18, 1998. The next key event was the death of prominent Cuban exile leader Jorge Mas Canosa, a major force behind Helms-Burton, in Miami on November 23, 1997. His death raised many questions about U.S.-Cuban relations and the future of his many involvements, among them the Cuban-American National Foundation, Radio and TV Martí, and the overall exiles' political lobby in Washington. Finally, the visit of Pope John Paul II to Cuba in January 1998 dramatized the U.S. isolation regarding Cuba and the need for a fresher, more pragmatic approach. All these events transpired as the fortieth anniversary of the Cuban Revolution of January 1959 was approaching.

The Cuban political transition, a final decisive development, will be the closing chapter of the recent stormy relationship between the United States and Cuba. Whether it is done with the presence of Fidel Castro or without him (as the advocates of the embargo wished) is irrelevant for this analysis. This discussion is limited to the origin, development, and consequences (especially foreign) of the Helms-Burton Law *while* Cuba is still ruled by a dictatorial, Marxist-Leninist regime, moderately alleviated by a series of openings in its economic policies.

With the law partially neutralized by President Clinton through subsequent suspensions of its most thorny part (Title III), in addition to compromises signed with the E.U., a serious international confrontation has been defused. However, the legacy of the law is the consequences of its simple enactment. At least several by-products can be considered. First is the impressive unanimity among U.S. commercial partners and political allies in opposing the measure. The law has given Canada, Mexico, and the member states of the E.U., in unison or separately, a unique opportunity to show autonomy in defiance of the world's only remaining superpower. At the same time, the Helms-Burton Act has prompted some foreign governments to reevaluate their own relations with Cuba. While continuing to oppose Helms-Burton, they have sought ways of inducing Cuba to reform and respect human rights. In countries with "special" relations with Cuba, such as Spain, the law and its attendant controversies have served to rekindle internal confrontations.

The law has also allowed Cuba to blame its increasingly poor economic situation on the U.S. embargo, thereby deflecting criticism of its economic policies. And while the law has proven to be ineffective politically and economically, in the U.S. domestic arena it has served to strengthen the political power of its main backers. Helms-Burton constituted a guarantee to the hard-core sector of the Cuban exile community that U.S. policy toward Cuba would not change because it codified the requirements for an eventual softening of the embargo. These include development of a concrete process of democratization in Cuba, and a replacement of the current political leadership. Finally, the controversial legal profile of Helms-Burton has attracted the attention not only of foreign interests but also of U.S. legal scholars on issues as sensitive as extraterritoriality, violation of international law, and the citizenship protections afforded by the U.S. courts. Helms-Burton may be a case study for generations of law students to come.

Most efforts at finding redeeming value in Helms-Burton are reduced to the self-serving praise of its main advocates in Congress. While hard-liners in the Cuban-American exile community have favored the law, some moderates warn that it could actually prolong Castro's rule. Overall, most observers are sorrowful, concerned, and angry. Many focus on the violation of international law. In the United States, opinions are couched in harsh words: "nonsense," "a bad law," "a bad mistake," "a source of embarrassment," "a dangerous precedent," "blatant illegality," "a direct attack on neighbors," and "one of the worst mistakes of the U.S." (this last from former president Jimmy Carter). Witty and sarcastic comments characterize the law as "a godsend to Castro," "a full employment for lawyers act," "a loose canon," "an out-of-control King Kong," "the Bacardí bill," "the Cuban-American Millionaire Protection Act," and "a dictatorship-enabling act." Normally mild U.S. jurists call Helms-Burton "irrationality at its maximum" and "a monstrosity." In other countries, incensed government officials and observers have called the law and its consequences "blackmail," "armed robbery," "a declaration of economic war," "a diplomatic ambush," "sledge-hammer diplomacy," "an act of brigandage," and "bad faith." Stressing the principal motivations, Senator Helms, the main figure behind the law, called it "the Adiós, Fidel" act. All these characterizations will be dealt with in context in subsequent chapters.

Only time will determine the effect of the tentative and ambiguous agreements of 1997 and 1998 between the European Union and Washington, and how influential Canada and Mexico will be in pressuring the United States to compromise. Time will also be necessary to assess the impact of the death of Mas Canosa. In both cases, the course of the pre-transition process that has begun in Cuba will constitute a major factor. This event is, however, outside our immediate reach. We can only guess about the actions and reactions of the Cuban regime and the announced continuation of policy according to the White House, the U.S. Congress, and the Department of State. The same can be said about the potential for change within the Cuban exile community, which is experiencing a period of significant adjustment.

What is certain (although still open to interpretation) is the background of the law and its evolution through Congress and the White House. The scholarly legal and political analysis of Helms-Burton, as well as the foreign reverberations of the law, will probably remain part of the legacy of this intriguing episode in U.S. domestic policy and foreign relations. The dimensions of the law and the conflicts they created are likely to become the subjects of future study and analysis. With this idea in mind the following pages are offered.

Background

On April 11, 1997, the European Commission, represented by its vice president and United Kingdom (U.K.) commissioner Leon Brittan, who was charged with foreign trade and relations with North America, and the government of the United States, represented by Undersecretary of State for Foreign Trade Stuart Eisenstat, agreed on a compromise that temporarily and partially neutralized the Helms-Burton Law, just a year after it went into effect. With the eventual implementation of portions of the agreement (which depended on very problematic congressional approval in part), this accommodation represented the suspension of one of the most serious disagreements between Washington and Brussels since the end of the Cold War. On May 18, 1998, both parties signed an expanded Understanding that included mutual concessions. It was hoped that the agreements signed by the United States and the E.U. would be enlarged and reciprocated by a parallel compromise crafted with the U.S. partners in NAFTA, Mexico and Canada. In this fashion, a potential commercial war originating in U.S. domestic politics would have been aborted. All parties recognized the possible consequences of their fixed positions.

In retrospect it appears that the principal authors and advocates of Helms-Burton gave little consideration to the likely international repercussions of the legislation. For them, parochial objectives were paramount. And when President Clinton signed the bill, he was concerned with securing votes in Florida and New Jersey in the 1996 presidential campaign. However, U.S. commercial partners in Europe and the Americas quickly perceived that their legitimate interests were threatened. The law was seen as a serious violation of international conventions, basically centering around the issue of extraterritoriality. In a world ruled by free trade, a legal instrument that sought to curtail the free flow of goods and investments seemed certain to invite strong opposition. A trade war was in the making, with the United States on one side and the European Union, Canada, and Mexico on the other, and no obvious resolution was in sight.

The potential for significant damage to the U.S. economy finally began to be recognized by the advocates of Helms-Burton. The specific concern was the undermining of the newly created World Trade Organization. In the case of Mexican and Canadian interests, the issue was their investment in NAFTA. All parties finally resorted to compromise, but the tentative truce reached between the United States and the European Union has been challenged in the U.S. Congress, and probably will continue to be as long as Castro remains in power. This will compel the U.S. trading partners to maintain their promise of retaliation. However, at the end all parties will be forced again to come to the table and negotiate an agreement.

An Overview of the Development of Helms-Burton

Any analysis of the origin and consequences of the Helms-Burton Law has to take into account three distinct and complementary dimensions. The first is the narrow issue of U.S.-Cuba relations; the second is a broader and more diffuse picture of strategic thinking in U.S. economic and political centers; and third is the historical background related to the Monroe Doctrine. In one of the earliest and most explicit identifications between the letter of H-B and the spirit of the Monroe Doctrine, Jorge Domínguez stated: "The Helms-Burton Act is quite faithful to the themes of the Monroe Doctrine and the Roosevelt Corollary. It claims for the United States the unilateral right to decide a wide array of domestic policies and arrangements in a nominally sovereign post-Castro Cuba.... The Helms-Burton Act rediscovers the ideological brio of imperialism. At the end of the twentieth century, as in centuries past, the United States is demanding the right to set the framework for the political and economic system it would tolerate inside Cuba."[1]

To begin with the U.S.-Cuban relationship, it is obvious that the objective of the LIBERTAD Act has been fundamentally political. It has aimed at discouraging foreign investment in Cuba through the threat of lawsuits and the imposition of restrictions on U.S. travel for executives of foreign companies that "traffick" in "stolen" Cuban properties. More fundamentally, it seeks to deepen the economic deterioration in Cuba in order to accelerate the fall of the current regime.

These goals reflect the growing influence and importance of Cuban exiles in the United States. Their influence is evident in domestic politics particularly in metropolitan Miami, but it also extends throughout Florida and into Cuban-American and Hispanic enclaves outside the state. Their political influence has been felt in congressional and presidential elections and, as we have seen, in the design of foreign policy.

In an essay that seems destined to have as much impact as his classic *The Clash of Civilizations,* Samuel Huntington offers a perspective for this recent linkage between Cuban-American politics and the overall U.S. foreign policy. In "The Erosion of American National Interests" he points out that "the institutions and capabilities created to serve a grand national purpose in the Cold War are now being subordinated and redirected to serve narrow subnational, transnational, and even nonnational purposes."[2] He warns that American foreign policy is becoming a policy of "particularism increasingly devoted to the promotion abroad of highly specific commercial and ethnic interests." As "products of the Cold War, Cuban-Americans ardently support U.S. anti-Castro policies."[3] However, foreign critics point out that the Helms-Burton Law may be a reflection of the U.S. will to control the future restructuring of global trade and investment as is currently administered through intergovernmental networks such as the new World Trade Organization.

The legislative foundation of the law resides in the Cuban Democracy Act (CDA) of 1992, the so-called Torricelli law, and other previous legal instruments to enforce the embargo. Its development begins with its introduction as a bill in Congress, and includes its congressional approval, its endorsement by President Clinton, and his subsequent and provisional suspension (for renewable periods of six months) of the controversial Title III. This part of the law authorizes legal action against individuals or companies maintaining commercial relations or use of any type with respect to properties confiscated from U.S. citizens or companies (including Cubans who later became U.S. nationals) that were seized without appropriate compensation following the Cuban Revolution.

The repercussions of the law have thus far been more evident in the political arena and in international diplomacy than in trade and investment networks, although its impact in these two sectors is by no means negligible. Curiously, in addition to discouraging foreign investment in Cuba, the controversies provoked by the law have supplied justification to U.S. sectors opposed to free trade, especially in regard to Mexico, Canada, and the member states of the European Union. Not coincidentally, these are the countries most affected by the law and thus the most vocal in their opposition to it. Foreign observers very closely monitored the initiative undertaken by the U.S. government.

This scenario began to take shape at the beginning of the 1990s, when two complementary developments occurred. The first was the end of the Cold War and the search by the United States for its role in the new world order. The second was the perception in some U.S. circles and in the Cuban exile community that the new political climate, far from facilitating the end of the Castro dictatorship, could transform Cuba into a low-priority item in the political and strategic agendas. Cuba no longer posed a risk to U.S. security, as numerous analyses offered by the Pentagon and the U.S. intelligence community made abundantly clear.

This perception was confirmed by the fact that European and Latin American interests were eager to improve commercial and investment relations with Cuba. At the same time, U.S. companies that had maintained indirect links with Cuba were anxious to develop these in the short or medium term. The views of the hard-liners were reinforced by their counterparts in the Cuban exile community, who feared that the end of the dictatorship would only come by inertia and the internal evolution of Cuban society. In this new scenario, the perception was that new foreign interests would compete with the United States in a future Cuba. In order to maintain a sense of tension, some influential Cuban exile groups resorted to convincing U.S. Republicans that it would be beneficial for them to remain loyal to a cause that was part of their past agenda. The stubbornness of the Cuban government in resisting even modest political change, while permitting moderate economic reform, gave the exile community and its allies in Washington sufficient ammunition to continue to attempt to bring about the end of the Cuban dictatorship.

The Role of Exile Politics

This effective political strategy was the result of much more than simple mastery of the U.S. lobbying system. Cuban exiles had managed to capture leading positions in local governments (as mayors of Miami and other municipalities) and in the Florida state legislature. They also obtained appointments at the second and third tiers in the presidential cabinet and entered the heart of the U.S. political system by having Cuban-Americans elected to Congress for the first time in history. Lincoln Díaz-Balart and Ileana Ros-Lehtinen (both from Florida), as well as Robert Menéndez (New Jersey), joined the growing ranks of Hispanics on Capitol Hill.

Díaz-Balart and Ros-Lehtinen contrast with their Hispanic colleagues in two significant ways. They are the first members of Congress to have been born in Cuba, and they are conservative Republicans. They espouse liberal measures concerning immigration, and they endorse the rights of Central Americans as much as they fight for Cubans. However, they frequently clash with other Hispanic members of Congress (who are overwhelmingly Democrats) over the sensitive issue of Cuba. The role played by these two key Republican members in the backing of the Helms-Burton legislation is expected in the context of bipartisan politics. Significantly different (and even more influential) is Menéndez, whose advocacy has not received the deserved attention from observers, despite the centrality of Title II, which he is credited with writing. This topic will be analyzed in the following chapter.

The alliance between the Republican Party and the Cuban-American exile community deserves consideration. Initially it seems surprising because most Cuban-Americans have benefitted from measures developed by Democrats, from welfare programs to the actions taken in the 1960s to guarantee them safe exile in the United States. However, the wrath many feel against Democrats stems from the perception that Presidents Kennedy and Johnson ceded Cuba to the Soviets and Castro and that they failed in attempts to return the island to a form of liberal democracy. Three pivotal events remain imprinted in the minds of the Cuban-American leadership. First was the fiasco of the Bay of Pigs invasion. It was followed by the compromise made with the Soviets to end the missile crisis, by which the United States promised not to invade Cuba. Finally, an invasion attempt organized by exiles was scuttled by Johnson in 1964, when he reported to the British government a plan to launch an operation from the Bahamas. The fact that Republicans did not take any aggressive steps to end the Castro regime is immaterial; Democrats were perceived as closet socialists and the Republicans as staunch anticommunists. As we will see later, when the realities of the post–Cold War era became evident, party lines lessened in importance. The need to obtain crucial backing in Congress required Cuban-Americans to lobby both Republicans and Democrats, as the cases of Menéndez and Torricelli would show. Still, the heart and the votes of a majority of the Cuban-American community sided with the Republicans.

Legal Development and Political Context

The evolving political attitude of the United States toward Cuba culminates in the Helms-Burton Law.[4] The law also constitutes a reflection and an extension of the overall U.S. policy toward Latin America, the perception of its leadership on the political capabilities of Latin Americans, a renewed declaration of the hegemony of the United States, and a warning to the rest of the world that the spirit of the Monroe Doctrine is still alive. As subsequent chapters will show, each one of the parties affected took note of the dimension that specifically pertained to them. European states realized that, as in 1823, they were not welcome in the "backyard" of the United States. Spain was reminded of the defeat of 1898. Canada, Mexico, and the rest of the Latin American states were reminded of the corollaries to Monroe and the limitations of the inter-American system. To Cuba it appeared that the Platt Amendment imposed by the United States in 1902 was still in effect.

As its own juridical chronology shows,[5] all U.S. legal actions have been responses to the inexorable inclination of the Cuban government toward the Soviet political and economic orbit. In her thorough study of the U.S. embargo, Donna Rich Kaplowitz opens a chapter on the origins of the U.S. measures with an assessment that is shared by many scholars: "It is unclear which nation—Cuba or the United States—started the spiral of antagonism that ultimately led to one of the most restrictive and longest lasting embargoes in modern history."[6] No one can really say for sure if the United States "pushed" Cuba into the arms of the Soviet Union, or whether Castro and his followers were sincere Marxist-Leninists from the beginning. While some experts consider the spark that ignited the U.S. reaction against Cuba to be the nationalization of agriculture, others believe that Castro had earlier global ambitions. The centerpiece of his policies was the "liberation" of Latin America and the backing of other revolutionaries, with Castro himself becoming a Third World leader.[7]

In any event, it all perhaps began with the Cuban Land Reform Law of May 17, 1959, which provoked frictions with U.S. property owners. Tensions increased with the visit of the Soviet foreign minister to Cuba in February 1960, a visit resulting in agreements to exchange sugar and oil. In addition, Cuba received loans and considerable technological aid from the USSR. In response, President Eisenhower progressively reduced the amount of sugar (once 70 percent of the island's exports) that the United States had been importing from Cuba. On July 6, 1960, the American Sugar Bill completely eliminated the quota. Then U.S. and British oil companies refused to refine Soviet crude. In retaliation, between June 29 and July 1, 1960, Cuba began to nationalize all American and British properties. In October, the United States imposed an economic embargo limited to U.S. goods (other than food and medicines). The U.S. government's response to Cuban actions culminated with the breaking of diplomatic relations on January 3, 1961. On April 16, 1961, Castro declared Cuba a socialist state. The following day, the Bay of Pigs operation exploded, resulting in the defeat and imprisonment of a Cuban exile force backed by the United States.

On January 22, 1962, the government of Cuba was suspended from the Organization of American States (OAS). On February 3, 1962, President John F. Kennedy used two laws, the Trading with the Enemy Act (passed in 1917 in the context of World War I) and the Foreign Assistance Act of 1961, to establish a total embargo on U.S. trade with Cuba in Presidential Proclamation 3447. On March 19, 1962, food rationing began in Cuba. The most serious crisis followed the placement of Soviet nuclear missiles in Cuba, resulting in the blockade declared by Kennedy. On July 8, 1963, the Treasury Department announced the Cuban Assets Control Regulations Act, by which U.S. citizens were forbidden to engage in any commercial or financial relations with Cuba, except for activities undertaken through foreign subsidiaries of U.S. companies. Upon the discovery of Cuban-sponsored political and guerrilla activities throughout Latin America, diplomatic relations between all the Latin American states (with the exception of Mexico) and Cuba were terminated in 1964.[8] In March 1968 the Cuban government nationalized most of the private businesses. In July 1972 Cuba became a member of the Council of Mutual Economic Assistance (CMEA or COMECON), the Soviet economic bloc.

Many Latin American governments began to reestablish diplomatic relations with Havana in the aftermath of an OAS meeting of foreign ministers held in 1975, where a majority voted to lift the multilateral sanctions. It was declared that each member state should decide whether it wished to resume diplomatic and trade relations with Cuba. The United States voted with the majority to lift the sanction, though it did not rescind its own embargo or reestablish relations. However, secret discussions took place with a view to engagement. This and other developments generated an appearance of normalcy.

However, Cuba's entry into the Angolan civil war in the fall of 1975 ended those negotiations.[9] In spite of these difficulties, travel restrictions for Americans to visit Cuba were lifted by President Carter in 1977 and Interest Sections (one step below the ambassadorial level) were established in Havana and Washington, D.C. The Mariel boatlift of 1980 (when more than 100,000 Cubans left the island and arrived in Florida) provoked a new deterioration in U.S.-Cuban relations. With the change of the U.S. administration, President Reagan imposed travel restrictions in 1982. The Republican administrations of Presidents Reagan and Bush were inclined to exert pressure on U.S. companies to suspend their indirect links with Cuba. The imposition of obstacles to the sending of donations and goods by Cuban exiles to their relatives in the island was also under consideration. However, the banning of trade links between U.S. subsidiaries and Cuba did not occur until the passing of the Cuban Democracy Act of 1992 (the Torricelli law)—ironically, when the Cold War was over.

As a prelude to later change, Cuba began to foster economic reforms and foreign investment. In 1982 Havana approved a law to regulate the activities of business consortia,[10] as well as allow the long-term lease of properties. Labor regulations were modified in 1990 to facilitate the establishment of tourism-related enterprises. The end of aid and trade that accompanied the December 1991 collapse of the Soviet Union brought a substantial blow to the economy. In response to this crisis, in 1992 articles 14, 15, and 18 of the Cuban constitution were adapted to soften the prevailing Marxist-Leninist intransigence against private enterprise. Accordingly, a series of measures that are the basis of capitalist markets were taken, with the result being a modest opening to new economic activities.

In August 1993, the National Bank of Cuba announced Law No. 140, by which penalties imposed on Cuban citizens for having foreign currency were terminated. Since then, Cubans may not only legally trade in dollars but also buy products once only available to foreign citizens. In September 1993, Law 141 and Resolution No. 1 established the regulations for self-employment in at least 117 work activities. In the same month Law 142 allowed the establishment of cooperatives. In a major restructuring of the bureaucracy, in April 1994 fifteen ministries were combined with other government agencies. In August 1994, Law 73 established a novel tax system. Law 191 was issued in September 1994 to allow the trading of certain agricultural products in the free market. In October 1994, Law 192 made similar provisions in the industrial and crafts sectors. In June 1995, Resolution No. 4 of the Ministry of Labor allowed the opening of private enterprises for the preparation and sale of food and drinks (among them the *paladares*, or private restaurants established in homes). In July 1995, university graduates were allowed to engage in work different from their training, under Resolution No. 10 of the Ministry of Labor. Finally in September 1995, Law No. 77 was issued to regulate foreign investment, in place of Law No. 50 of 1992. The same month, Cuban citizens were authorized to have savings accounts in domestic or convertible funds.

Trends in Foreign Investment in Cuba

According to the Cuban government these measures brought noticeable changes, but the results were slow to arrive and actual investments were comparatively modest.[11] Cuba was not one of the favored destinations for foreign investment among the developing countries, or even in the Caribbean and Latin American markets. For example, foreign direct investment (FDI) in Cuba between 1993 and 1996, when Helms-Burton was approved, equaled the one received by the tiny island nation of Dominica (*not* the Dominican Republic, which received $160 million in 1996 in comparison to only $12 million invested in Cuba). European Union investments in Cuba were only 0.2 percent of the total European investment in Latin America (see table 1).[12]

Nothwithstanding these numbers, foreign business activity in Cuba grew. At the end of 1993 about 140 joint ventures were operating in Cuba, with Spanish investors accounting for the single largest share (30 of these enterprises had Spanish capital). According to Cuban sources that are confirmed by Spain's Argentaria (a government banking conglomerate), at the end of 1994, 185 joint ventures were registered. At the end of 1995, a total of 212 were counted. Spain was again in the lead with 47 partnerships, followed by Canada with 26 and Italy with 17.[13]

In more recent estimates, the total of foreign investment topped U.S. $2 billion. However, other indicators suggest that only about half of this investment is effective (delivered). Other sources estimate that about U.S. $5

Table 1. European Union direct investment flows to Cuba, 1990–96 (U.S.$ million)

	1990	1991	1992	1993	1994	1995	1996	1990–96
Cuba	1	10	7	3	14	5	17	57
Latin America	1,801	2,144	1,918	1,838	5,170	5,858	7,099	25,828
Cuba as % of L.A.	0.1	0.5	0.4	0.2	0.3	0.1	0.2	0.2

Source: IRELA, *Direct Investment in Latin America*; Christian Freres, "The Role of the European Union."

billion represents the investment that is announced, with another U.S. $700 million allocated for commitments and actual investment. In a December 1997 compilation, the U.S.-Cuba Trade and Economic Council announced U.S. $5.5 billion as the figure for "announced" investments and U.S. $1.2 for "committed" or "delivered" investments.[14] Subsequent predictions included $620 million for investments made in 1998 and $700 million for estimated operations in 1999 (table 2).[15]

Table 2. Foreign investment in Cuba (in U.S.$ million)

Country	Announced	Committed/delivered
Australia	500	n.d.
Austria	0.5	0.1
Brazil	150	20
Canada	1,807	600
Chile	69	30
China	10	5
Dominican Republic	5	1
France	100	50
Germany	10	2
Greece	2	0.5
Honduras	7	1
Israel	22	7
Italy	397	387
Jamaica	2	1
Japan	2	0.5
Mexico	1,806	450
The Netherlands	300	40
Panama	2	0.5
Portugal	15	10
Russian Federation	25	2
South Africa	400	5
Spain	350	100.3
Sweden	10	1
United Kingdom	75	50
Uruguay	0.5	0.3
Venezuela	50	3
Total	6,119	1,767

Source: U.S.-Cuba Trade and Economic Council.

It is important to maintain some skepticism regarding the true source of some of these investments. Mexico (about $250 million), Spain ($125–150 million), Canada ($100 million), and Italy ($85 million) are consistently listed as leading investors in Cuba. But the inclusion of Australia, South Africa, and, above all, the Netherlands Antilles on lists of important investors raises questions about their real origin. In data provided by the Cuban government in 1995, 31 of the 212 joint ventures registered their origin as "paraísos fiscales" (tax havens).[16] An additional reason for caution is the hesitation of many agencies and companies to reveal the actual level of their investments in Cuba, for fear of providing the U.S. government with justification for implementing Title IV of Helms-Burton, or a basis for litigation under an activated Title III.[17]

From Expropriations to Investment

For more than thirty years, the United States did not seem to pay much attention to the properties that were taken as a result of the nationalization process decreed by the Cuban Revolution. Washington and Havana never came to terms in negotiating a settlement. While the United States insisted on full compensation, the Cuban authorities responded that they should also be reimbursed for the damage caused by the U.S. embargo. The figure consistently quoted by the Cuban government is $60 billion.[18] While other nations quietly negotiated modest lump-sum settlements for lost property, the claims of the former U.S. owners remained in a legal limbo. Among the reasons why the U.S. business establishment temporarily gave up the fight was an unprecedented modification of U.S. tax laws. As attorney Robert Helander points out, "normally losses to personal property caused by confiscation by a foreign country are not considered, for tax purposes, to be casualty or theft losses."[19] But during the most serious period of confrontation with Cuba, U.S. law was changed to allow deduction of the fair market value of a loss if the claimant was a U.S. citizen or a company owned by U.S. citizens at the time of the Cuban Revolution. The law was changed again in 1971 to include losses of investment property "against ordinary income without limitations."[20] While U.S. taxpayers paid the bill for Castro's expropriations, Cubans who became U.S. nationals after the revolution could not benefit from this coverage, a disparity that was to be redressed by the Helms-Burton Law. Meanwhile, however, some U.S. companies were generously compensated in tax benefits.

The lack of a well-defined compensation process in the Cuban case became an anomaly in the U.S. experience. The period of decolonization that followed World War II forced the United States and other developed countries to come to terms with the reality of nationalization and expropriation, and to develop processes for recovering at least part of their losses. As other developed countries did, the U.S. government negotiated collective compensations. In 1949 Congress passed the International Claims Settlement Act and created the International Claims Commission, which transferred its functions to the Foreign Claims Settlement Commission (FCSC) in 1954. In 1964 Title V was added to the existing law, and became known as the "Cuban Claims Act." U.S. losses in Cuba were initially calculated at about $1 billion, but only about $60 million were available for compensation in the form of frozen Cuban assets. For this reason a process of adjudication was established, with the result that 8,816 claims were registered for about $1.8 billion in all.

The Foreign Claims Settlement Commission ruled that a simple annual interest of 6 percent should accrue to the loss amount, making the total value of U.S. claims as high as U.S. $5.5 billion in 1994. According to the FCSC (see table 3), among the major U.S. properties that were expropriated were the following, valued in 1970 dollars: Cuban Electric Company ($268 million), International Telephone and Telegraph ($131 million), North American Sugar ($109 million), Moa Bay Mining ($88 million), United Fruit Sugar ($85 million), West Indies Sugar ($85 million), American Sugar ($81 million), Standard Oil ($72 million), Bangor Punta Company ($63 million), and Texaco ($50 million). Never satisfied, and with a huge interest penalty accumulating, the unsettled claims for compensation would constitute a substantial problem for any future government in Cuba. Significantly, the claim by ITT, ranking in second place on the list, became controversial when the Italian telecommunications company Società Telefònica e Telegràfica (STET) bought a substantial interest in the Cuban phone network previously owned by ITT.

Meanwhile, the former U.S. owners managed to recover part of their losses at the expense of U.S. taxpayers. It is estimated that most of the large corporations whose properties were taken by the Cuban Revolution received some or a substantial compensation (depending on the case) through this indirect tax write-off mechanism. However, the U.S. law on expropriations and the tax regulations did not compensate companies with less than 50 percent U.S. ownership, or those Cuban-Americans who were not U.S. citizens at the time of the expropriations. Conservative estimates calculate that properties belonging to these groups are worth at least ten times more than the original certified claims. More accurate calculations have valued the claims of former Cuban citizens as high as U.S. $6.9 billion in 1957 dollars, or about U.S. $20 billion in 1993.[21]

Table 3. Certified claims (U.S.$ millions)

Company	Certified claims
American Brands	10.6
Amstar	81.0
Atlantic Richfield	10.2
B.F. Goodrich	2.2
Boise Cascade	279.3
Borden	97.4
Bristol-Myers Squibb	1.7
Chase Manhattan Bank	7.5
Citicorp	6.2
Coca-Cola Company	27.5
Colgate-Palmolive	14.5
Continental Group (now Continental Can)	8.9
DuPont	3.0
Esmark	6.0
Firestone Tire & Rubber	8.3
First National Bank of Boston	5.9
Freeport Minerals	33.0
Ford Motor	0.2
F.W. Woolworth	9.2
General Dynamics	10.4
General Electric	5.9
General Motors	7.7
Goodyear Tire & Rubber	5.1
International Harvester	8.3
International Paper	1.1
ITT	130.7
King Ranch	1.7
Libby, McNeil & Libby	5.7
Lone Star Industries	24.9
Moa Bay Mining (now Freeport MacMoran)	88.3
Navistar	8.3
Owens Illinois	8.1
Pepsico	0.2
Pepsi Cola Metro Bottling	1.6
Procter & Gamble	5.0
Reynolds Metals	3.4
Sears Roebuck & Company	3.7
Sherwin Williams	3.4
Bristol-Myers Squibb	1.7
Standard Brands	1.4
Standard Oil (now Exxon)	71.6
Sterling Drug	1.3
Texaco	50.1
Texaco (Latin America)	5.1
United Brands	85.1
U.S. Rubber (now Uniroyal)	9.5
Warner-Lambert	1.6
Willson International	0.2

Source: U.S.-Cuba Trade and Economic Council.

While equity arguments might have justified compensating these companies and individuals, the existing law was strict. Robert Helander, a corporate law attorney, asked about the advantages for nonclaimants in being included in the pool.[22] The hard-liners backing the embargo might find it useful to form a coalition with the certified claimants, who could not pursue any other avenue for compensation than the usual settlement through a lump sum to be paid by the Cuban government to the U.S. Treasury and then distributed to the claimants. But this procedure was never executed because the two governments never agreed on the details. Advocates of new approaches then began to urge both groups of claimants ("certified" claimants, who were mostly U.S. citizens and corporations, and "uncertified" claimants, generally Cuban-Americans) to press for measures that would allow them to be paid sums closer to the real value of their losses.

Helander was well aware that if the U.S. government decided to open the claims process to the originally noncertified owners, the companies and individuals on the original claimants' list might sue on the basis of discrimination. Actually, this has not happened because Title III of the Helms-Burton Law has been suspended every six months since the law went into effect. Further, the loose coalition was weakened when some of the most powerful corporate claimaints initiated a lobbying campaign against Helms-Burton. When the Torricelli law was passed, the apparent discrimination between the two groups remained intact. This little-discussed episode will be analyzed later in the text.

Commerce and Tourism

Cuban trade showed a steady shift from its former overwhelming dependency on the Soviet bloc to an unstoppable linkage with the market economies. While in the 1980s Cuba had conducted only 7 percent of its trade with Europe and about 6 percent with Latin America and Canada, in the mid-1990s these partners accounted for 90 percent of Cuba's total commerce. By the early 1990s, Canada, Japan, Spain, The Netherlands, Italy, France, Germany, Portugal, and the U.K. had become the most important destinations for Cuban products. By the mid-1990s, Russia still purchased 15 percent of Cuban exports, while Canada (9 percent), China (8 percent), Egypt (6 percent), and Spain (6 percent) were the next most important buyers. Spain (17 percent), Mexico (10 percent), France (8 percent), China (8 percent), Venezuela (7 percent), Italy (4 percent), and Canada (3 percent) were the most important sources of Cuban imports. In total, Europe at the end of the 1990s accounted for about a third of all Cuba's trade activity.

Once disdained as one of the darkest sides of capitalism, tourism was again courted by the Cuban government, showing a steady increase from

300,000 visitors in 1990 to over 700,000 in 1995. Gross income from this source increased five times from 1990 to 1995, from 200 million pesos to about 1 billion.[23] Canada, Italy, Spain, and Germany contributed the greatest number of tourists.[24] Twenty-one joint enterprises investing over $667 million helped provide tourist services. In 1997, according to Cuban government sources, income from 1,171,000 tourists grossed U.S. $850 million. Italy, Canada, and Spain again were the main countries of origin. By the end of 1998 the number of visitors reached 1,400,000 and spending passed the $1 billion mark, matching Cuban government projections. Projects to add eighteen hundred rooms to the existing twenty-five hundred in hotel joint ventures were planned in 1998. Officials estimated that these projects would generate over four thousand new jobs. Cuba became in 1998 the fifth most popular Caribbean tourist destination.[25]

The Renewal of the U.S. Embargo

The Empire Strikes Back

One might expect that the normalization of U.S. international relations following the collapse of the Soviet Union would favor new commercial exchanges with countries, including Cuba, that were once polarized by the superpowers' confrontation. However, against predictions that it would collapse with the loss of Soviet support, the Castro regime survived the "special period,"[26] making the renewal of an economic relationship problematic for the United States. Instead, in the words of Jorge Domínguez, "U.S.-Cuban relations went from Cold War to a colder war."[27]

The first measure to crystallize the new relationship was the Cuban Democracy Act, signed on October 23, 1992, by President George Bush during his second presidential campaign. Originally sponsored by Congressman Robert Torricelli (D-New Jersey), the bill was also endorsed by Democratic presidential candidate Bill Clinton, who was actively courting Hispanic (and especially Cuban-American) voters' support. The new measure threatened sanctions against U.S. companies that maintained dealings with Cuba through foreign subsidiaries. The law also prohibited the use of U.S. harbors by ships that had previously docked in Cuban ports. Notwithstanding these harsh provisions, the law gave the executive branch the option of "calibrated responses" (that is, a selective lifting of sanctions) to reward positive actions by Cuba.

The new phase in U.S. Cuban policy began with the perception that a new threat to U.S. interests had taken the place of the Soviet-allied Cuban

Revolution. In the past, Washington had demanded the termination of Cuba's support of Latin American revolutionaries and of its ties with the Soviet Union as a condition for normalization. With the 1970s détente, Cuba appeared less threatening, and domestic opinion favored a rapprochement, with the result that the precondition of ending Cuba's link with the Soviet Union disappeared from the agenda. However, Castro's actions in Africa and the Mariel boatlift created the justification for President Ronald Reagan's hard-line policy.

At the same time that the end of communism shifted U.S. policy priorities toward the promotion of democracy worldwide, conservative Cuban-Americans began to gain influence in selected political spheres. Cuba's action in downing the Brothers to the Rescue planes, coupled with the growing power of the Cuban-American National Foundation, helped shift the political balance so that international priorities became less influential than domestic considerations in shaping U.S. policy toward Cuba.

Scholars, theorists, and practitioners of foreign policy have tried to explain the political shift that led to Helms-Burton. One of the most readable analyses was offered by William LeoGrande, adapting Robert D. Putman's metaphor of international bargaining as a two-level game.[28] In the case of Cuba, U.S. leaders have been negotiating at two levels, international and domestic, each level enjoying preferred status at one time or another. For the first part of the confrontation, international concerns, mainly Cuba's intimate relations with the Soviet Union, controlled the decisions of the United States. At the same time, U.S. presidents were pressured by domestic opponents who accused them of being soft. Expropriations and the missile crisis influenced American public opinion, so that a majority supported the embargo.

LeoGrande notes that 1960 public opinion polls showed that over 80 percent of the people had a negative opinion of the Castro regime, and only 2 percent had a favorable opinion. A year later, 63 percent supported the trade embargo; in 1971, 61 percent still supported it. However, the ranks of opposition increased to 21 percent, a prelude to 1973, when 53 percent favored normalization. In the mid-1970s, the pressure for normalization increased in Congress. While Republicans welcomed Cuba's activities in Africa and Central America as justification for a hard-line position, the Mariel incident contributed to negative public opinion toward Cuba.

Jorge Domínguez has offered one of the most concise and complete explanations for the continuation of the U.S.-Cuban feud in the 1990s. First, he asserts, "The U.S. government was angry that Cuba's political regime did not crumble. The U.S. hostility toward the Cuban government heightened as the Cold War came to an end and precisely when Cuba ceased to pose a security threat to most interests. Neither realism nor neorealism can explain this *temper tantrum* [my italics] toward Cuba, or why U.S.-Cuban relations went from Cold War to a colder war."[29] Domínguez then turns to ideological and historical explanations, and in this context he perceives Helms-Burton as a coherent continuation of the imperialist traditions inaugurated by the Monroe Doctrine. Finally, he stresses the influence exerted by domestic politics, especially the electoral context of the United States, as one of the "mobilizing" factors.

Mark Falcoff discusses a poll taken in 1988 showing that only 9 percent of Americans had a "somewhat favorable" opinion about Castro and only 1 percent were favorable, while 37 percent were "somewhat unfavorable," and a full 44 percent very unfavorable.[30] What is most interesting in this sample is that it differentiated between elite respondents and those from the general public. The contrast shows that 31 percent of elite respondents were either somewhat or very favorable to Cuba, 35 percent considered Castro to be good for Cuba, and an impressive 65 percent did not perceive Cuba as a security problem for the United States, in contrast with the 26 percent of the general public who did. While a slight majority of the general public favored Cuban-U.S. diplomatic relations, 94 percent of the opinion leaders endorsed such links. Moreover, 90 percent of elites favored negotiations on key problems. A more recent poll (1995) analyzed by Falcoff shows an increase in the gap between the perception of the general public (not much affected by the end of the Cold War) and the opinion leaders. Of the latter, only 19 percent would favor military intervention in Cuba if a popular uprising should happen, in contrast with 44 percent of the general public. However one interprets these findings (and Mark Falcoff offers a rather negative assessment of the elite's prescriptions on Cuba), the record shows that American politicians are aware of the general public's perceptions of the Cuban "problem," and they act accordingly.

What about the Cuban-American perception? In one of the most credible and carefully conducted polls of the Cuban exile community of Miami, opinions tend to support the reasons of the proponents of the embargo. While 51 percent would support dialogue with the Cuban government, 75 percent consider H-B a good way to bring change to Cuba. In an apparent contradiction, while only 25 percent feel that the embargo has worked well, 78 percent support its continuation, 70 percent support punishment for foreign companies dealing with Cuba, and 79 percent favor suing companies that are dealing with seized properties. Significantly, 70 percent admit that the local candidate's position on Cuba is important for their vote.

However, the poll did not make a distinction between the different titles of the law, and it did not seek specific responses to Title II.[31] However, some notes of caution are in order. First is the fact that answering that one has knowledge of Helms-Burton does not mean that the respondent has actually read it, much less fully comprehended it. Second, even in the elite circles, a sample of interviews reveals that most highly educated and sophisticated Cuban-Americans do not understand the differences between titles II, III, and IV of the law. When fully aware of the implications of Title II, a majority of Miami Cuban-Americans who endorse the embargo in principle, indicate that the provisions of Title II are a mistake. Further, informal discussions, conversations, and interviews conducted over several years reveal that the same persons who in public statements indicate that the embargo has accomplished its goals, admit in private that it has helped Castro. As described by Lisandro Pérez, the reality is that the policy crafted by a political and economic minority has won wide public approval, while the majority, especially the younger generations, have elected to remain silent or simply endorse the official policy. Demographic change has not translated into ideological transformation.[32]

From the point of view of the protagonists of failed attempts at reform of the U.S. policy toward Cuba, the post-Soviet era did not mean the disappearance of security threats from Cuba. However, they are now of a different nature. Defined by Richard Nuccio, President Clinton's main adviser on Cuban policy during his first term, "the fundamental national security threat facing the U.S. from Cuba is a societal collapse that leads to widespread violence. This scenario is the most likely to produce either significant outflows of refugees, or active involvement of U.S. forces and of Cuban Americans in Cuba. U.S. policy should, therefore, attempt to promote a transition in Cuba, but in a way likely to maximize a peaceful outcome."[33]

These concerns were also evident in the Presidential Review Directive (PRD) 21 for the Latin American and Caribbean region, conducted in the first year of the Clinton administration. It lists as U.S. interests in the region the promotion of democracy, protection of human rights, expansion of free markets, combating narco-trafficking, control of illegal immigration, and protection of the natural environment. Communism was not on the list of concerns.[34] In consequence, the U.S. administration sought ways to reduce the threat of violence and to tackle serious problems such as the wave of Cuban rafters arriving on Florida shores in the summer of 1994. Use of the mechanism in the Torricelli law known as Track II was recommended to create more direct links with the still weak civil society in Cuba and encourage private initiative and democratic openings.[35]

In any event, partially due to the fact that the new incentives for reform offered to the Cuban government were not properly used or were rejected by Havana, the fundamental and better known objectives of the Torricelli law remained in place. The law's limitations on trade with Cuba became a cause of irritation for U.S. allies and trading partners.

Profile of the Torricelli Law

The Cuban Democracy Act is not a long document. While it is precise in stating its justification and objectives, it also makes generous use of political language. In its first part (Findings), the law is extremely blunt and personalistic: "The government of Fidel Castro has demonstrated consistent disregard for internationally accepted standards of human rights and for democratic values"; "the Cuban people have demonstrated their yearning for freedom"; "the Castro government maintains a military-dominated economy"; "there is no sign that the Castro regime is prepared to make any significant concessions to democracy."

Given these considerations, the document goes on to say, it should be the policy of the United States "to seek a peaceful transition to democracy" in Cuba, and the president "should encourage the governments of countries that conduct trade with Cuba to restrict their trade and credit relations." Further, in the event of noncompliance, "the government of such a country shall not be eligible for assistance under the Foreign Assistance Act." Transactions between U.S. firms and Cuba were explicitly banned in section 1706(a), and a new weapon to discourage third countries' trade with Cuba was added: "a vessel which enters a port or place in Cuba to engage in the trade of goods or services may not, within 180 days after departure from such port of place in Cuba, load or unload any freight at any place in the United States." The Torricelli Act was a novelty in the sense that it codified the foreign policy of the United States toward Cuba. Stripping the executive of its prerogative to conduct foreign relations with flexibility and according to the national interests of the case involved, the CDA spelled out the conditions for lifting the trade limitations. Once enacted, the provisions of the law can only be rescinded by the president if Cuba "has held free and fair elections conducted under internationally recognized observers"; "has permitted opposition parties"; "is showing respect for the basic civil liberties"; "is moving toward establishing a free market economic system"; and "has committed itself to constitutional change."

The Perception of the Embargo and the Laws to Reinforce It

The U.S. embargo against Cuba soon became the subject of studies and commentaries published outside of the customary academic journals and books. Numerous essays appearing in opinion-oriented periodicals focused on the legality, appropriateness, and effectiveness of the embargo.[36] What is most significant, however, is that critical commentaries did not appear only in the liberal or left-leaning publications that traditionally opposed U.S. policy on Cuba. Critical studies also emerged in peer-reviewed journals published by the centrist or conservative law schools of prestigious universities (Emory, Vanderbilt, Duke, and Fordham, among others), as well as the New York Bar Association. These articles typically include at least two main features. First is their critical assessment of the continuing legality of the embargo, given the end of the Cold War. Second, the commentaries speak of the right of any sovereign nation to choose its trading partners and to secure its borders as it sees fit.

The political nature of the U.S. embargo against Cuba, its update through the new laws passed by Congress (especially the Torricelli and Helms-Burton laws), and the use of the forum of the General Assembly of the United Nations to condemn the embargo have complicated the whole issue without minimally resolving the international law dimension of the imposition of the U.S. embargo on Cuba. Reviewing a volume addressing U.S. economic sanctions against Cuba, one expert summarizes this issue: "The discourse about unilateral economic measures, with its range of terms including embargo, boycott, sanctions, coercion and aggression, reflects the broad variety of perspectives on the status of such measures under international law. Given that decisions with respect to unilateral sanctions are taken in an insulated environment, principally characterized by domestic demands and constraints, it is perhaps unsurprising that the criteria for assessing the legality of unilateral economic measures according to international law remains unsettled."[37]

In what is perhaps the only professional article to offer partial support for the U.S. policy, the Committee on Inter-American Affairs of the New York Bar Association noted that embargoes such as the one imposed by the United States on Cuba cannot be considered to violate the tradition of international law.[38] In fact, historical evidence shows their widespread use: "the use of economic sanctions by countries around the world indicates that, as a general matter, and as an instrument of foreign or diplomatic policy, the Cuban embargo cannot be said to violate the customary law principle of non-intervention." In other words, embargoes may be unethical, irritating, inconvenient, and harassing, but the fact that they are a historical reality makes them a part of custom, and therefore not contrary to *customary* international law. Although the New York Bar Association acknowledged the tradition of embargoes as commonplace, the rest of the article was very critical.

Regarding the prospects for judicial opinions on the Torricelli law's provisions, the report states that the CDA satisfies the Supreme Court's standard "for the proper exercise of extraterritorial jurisdiction" of an act of Congress, but a court still might conclude that that fails to meet "the conditions of reasonableness." On the status of the foreign subsidiaries, the legal experts were of the opinion that "the factors arguing against U.S. regulation of the activities of foreign subsidiaries of U.S. companies would outweigh the factors favoring such regulation" and, moreover, that "the claim that links of ownership and control in the corporate context are 'analogous' to links of nationality—is incorrect as a matter of international law. . . . The notions of 'control' or corporate affiliation as tests of corporate nationality have not met with wide acceptance and cannot be considered consistent with international law." The New York Bar also noted that "the Cuba embargo may be inconsistent with the General Agreement on Tariffs and Trade (GATT) [because] Cuba is no longer a security threat." The report warned that the "OAS charter may be interpreted as prohibiting sanctions as intrusive as those contained in the U.S. embargo." While "the UN charter does not prohibit economic sanctions such as those involved in the U.S. embargo of Cuba . . . a number of UN General Assembly resolutions have condemned the use of economic measures."

Report Card on the Embargo

Individual scholars have been very critical of the embargo. Some elect a legalistic point of view, saying it "violates the standards set forth by the American Law Institute in the *Restatement (Third) of Foreign Relations*, the UN Charter and the GATT," and that "the motivating force of the embargo is to foster political change within Cuba."[39] The shifting U.S. rationale for the embargo has also come under criticism. In the most complete general study of the embargo, Donna Rich Kaplowitz summarizes the U.S. objectives, from the overthrow of the Cuban regime to simple internal reforms. The U.S has justified the embargo as a retaliation for nationalization, a tool of the policy of containment, a mechanism to break the Cuban-Soviet ties, and as simple symbolism, a reminder to the world that the Monroe Doctrine is alive.[40]

Extraterritoriality and National Sovereignty

A constant in the legal commentaries on the embargo and the implementation of the Torricelli law has been the issue of extraterritoriality. Legal scholars critical of U.S. policies argue that "states are subject to follow both UN standards as well as customary law norms" and that "the concept of the prohibition against extraterritorial application of laws exists as a well-recognized international law norm . . . an outgrowth of the sovereignty principle which recognizes autonomy as an accepted international precept."[41] None of the recognized exceptions to these principles apply to the Cuban embargo: unlawful acts, acts that have consequences within the state territory, and the nationality principle. The OAS charter prohibits extending the sovereign rule to influence or control the internal affairs of another state.[42] The U.S. courts' "rule of reasonableness" to resolve the extraterritorial conflict seem to fail in the Cuban case.

An Old Weapon: The Trading with the Enemy Act

On the validity of one of the cornerstones of the U.S. legislation against Cuba, the Trading with the Enemy Act (TWEA) of 1917, legal scholars consider that the "the source of the embargo is no longer applicable."[43] They argue that new international circumstances nullify its legal force: "In light of the new world order, the embargo, established from and based on the President's TWEA powers, is illegal. The TWEA only allows the President to take steps to protect national security. When no national security interests are at stake, sanctions pursuant to that Act are outside the scope of Congress delegation and are therefore illegal."[44]

International Law

Once it is accepted that abnormal circumstances (such as a national security threat) do not exist, a state is obliged to submit itself to the rule of law. Therefore, an "analysis of the existing structure of international legal principles leads to the conclusion that the U.S. policy is unjustifiable under international law," and consequently "the embargo violates basic tenets of international law." As a result, the attempt to codify the embargo (the CDA) "has violated public international law" because it "infringes upon a State's exercise of national sovereignty" and because it "ignores instances when U.S. prescriptive jurisdiction is unreasonable and, thus, limited by public international law."[45]

Domestic Origin and Consequences

Representative Charles B. Rangel once pointed out that "the [Torricelli] bill is not just a legislative initiative, but it is more a political statement . . . not being concerned so much about the future of the people living in Cuba as it is an appeal to the Cuban Americans in Dade County."[46] Scholars stress this point in their analysis, characterizing the CDA as the product of an election year battle between the Democratic and Republican parties for important Cuban-American votes in Florida. . . . To lure Cuban-American voters from their traditional Republican stance, then-Governor Clinton surprised Republican leaders by endorsing the CDA. . . . President Bush reluctantly endorsed the bill soon after, despite strong reservations about the provisions affecting foreign subsidiaries. . . . In order to counter the negative appearance left by his hesitation to support the bill, President Bush quickly issued an executive order prohibiting ships that traded with Cuba from docking at American ports.[47]

Observing the immediate consequences of the embargo and the CDA, scholars warned that "until the embargo is lifted, U.S. entrepreneurs can only watch their foreign competitors control markets which could otherwise be theirs."[48] Another scholar has concluded that "the value of stopping trade between foreign subsidiaries of U.S. corporations, even if possible, is not worth the international distraction it creates."[49]

The International Impact

Addressing the main objective of the embargo, opposition voices in Congress warned early on that "the Communist nations that have fallen have done so internally. It has [sic] not done so as a result of the United States providing sanctions against them."[50] Scholars have pointed out that the embargo "has not isolated or destabilized the Castro government, but only hurt U.S. business interests" and that the "CDA alienated allied nations" and "weakened U.S. businesses competitiveness." In addition it "brought international attention and condemnation of U.S. attempts to control other sovereigns' public policies."[51]

Simultaneously, the U.S. academic and political establishments witnessed international reaction to the law. Kim Campbell, attorney general of Canada and later its prime minister, labeled the CDA an "unacceptable intrusion of U.S. law into Canada [that] could adversely affect significant Canadian interests in relation to international trade of commerce. For that reason, Canadian companies will carry out business under the laws and regulations of Canada, not those of a foreign country."[52] In fact, the Canadian government issued an order under the Foreign Extraterritorial Measures Act to block compliance by Canadian-based firms.[53]

As a pioneer in the European arena, Great Britain also acted to circumvent the CDA. The British government invoked the existing Protection of Trading Interests Act to prohibit British companies from complying with the CDA.[54] In Latin America a group of legislators from Argentina, Chile,

Bolivia, and Uruguay wrote a critical letter to the Speaker of the House.[55] Confirming the fears of many observers about the benefits that the U.S. policy would give the Castro government, the reaction in Cuba was clear. Ricardo Alarcón considered that, "for the first time, the U.S. had been placed on the defensive."[56]

Think Tanks and Policy Groups

In the four years between the passage of the Torricelli law and the approval of Helms-Burton, a flurry of reports on Cuba appeared in the hope of influencing U.S. policy. These were concerned in part with evidence that foreign interests were taking advantage of the apparent opening of the Cuban economy. Conservative and middle-of-the-road think tanks that in the past were occupied with security matters in the context of the Cold War took note of the new circumstances of Cuba.

Among these was the Atlantic Council, an organization normally concerned with NATO-related matters. In *A Road Map for Restructuring Future U.S. Relations with Cuba,* a report in its Policy Paper Series, the Working Group concluded that "restoring normal relations will require immediate lifting of the trade embargo and other economic sanctions." The report's authors summarized the realities of U.S.-Cuba relations under the Cuban Democracy Act:

> While the president of the United States could establish diplomatic ties unilaterally, he cannot independently lift the trade embargo . . . unless he can certify to Congress that the Cuban government has met those conditions. . . . Under current U.S. law, trade with Cuba cannot be fully resumed until Cuba introduces substantial political and economic reforms, including the holding of free and fair elections supervised by international observers. The Cuban Democracy Act provides for sanctions to be progressively lifted—in the CDA's terms—"in carefully calibrated ways in response to positive developments in Cuba," but it also specifies that sanctions will be maintained so long as the Cuban government continues to refuse to move toward democratization and a greater respect for human rights.

"Once the president is able to certify to Congress that Cuba has met the conditions of the Cuban Democracy Act, Sec. 1708," the report continued, "he can lift the trade, transportation and travel sanctions imposed by section 1706. Congress should then pass legislation repealing any additional sanctions."[57]

2

Getting Their Act Together

Content and Initial Perception

The Platt Amendment has left Cuba with little or no
independence. . . . It is entirely in our hands and I do not
believe that a single European government would consider it
other than what it is, a virtual dependency of the United States.
General Leonard Wood, former commander
of U.S. forces in Cuba, and governor, 1902

For the purposes of this Act . . . a transition government in Cuba is a
government that does not include Fidel Castro or Raúl Castro.
Cuban Liberty and Democratic Solidarity Act of 1996 (Helms-Burton Law)

All we are saying to these countries is, obey our law.
Senator Jesse Helms, CNN, March 12, 1996

Hogwash. It's a little bit painful to witness the hypocrisy of
these countries. After all, the United States of America has
rescued every one of them from tyranny at one time or another.
Senator Jesse Helms, July 9, 1996

The Prelude

A Turn of the Screw

For some influential opponents of the Castro regime, the U.S. embargo and its codification through the Cuban Democracy Act was not enough. The Torricelli act was a weapon with a limited and indirect impact. It had no political teeth, so to speak, most significantly in the international arena. And despite some investors' worries about the uncertainty of the new Cuban market, the fact was that "since the end of the Cold War the most important news about European and Canadian relations with Cuba has appeared on the business page, rather than in political columns."[1] Militant Cuban-Americans saw this development as a threat to their interests, one that the Torricelli law was ineffective in forestalling. They needed further developments, or "mobilizing incidents" as Jorge Domínguez put it, to enable additional measures against Cuba.[2] The first of these developments was a political realignment in the U.S. Congress. It was followed by a serious, tragic episode involving private planes piloted by Cuban exiles.

Potential new investors in Cuba had more than the island's political uncertainties and the machinations of the U.S. Congress to worry about. In certain Cuban exile sectors, dreams abounded that, in the event of a sudden change in Havana, they would be called upon to control the economic and political destiny of Cuba. Jorge Mas Canosa, leader of the influential Cuban-American National Foundation (CANF), considered himself to be a potential presidential candidate in a post-Castro Cuba.[3]

Late in 1994, Mas Canosa sent an unprecedented letter to the embassies of several governments representing companies that still maintained operations in Cuba. Besides referring to investment on the island as an act of "collaborationism," Mas warned that these companies were "taking a serious risk" and that "any investment made during the present regime would be subject to accounting in a post-Castro government."[4]

Important changes in the leadership of the U.S. Congress would help the exiles' cause. In the congressional elections of 1994, the Democrats lost their majority in Congress. In the process, Senator Jesse Helms (R-North Carolina) became the new chair of the Senate Foreign Relations Committee. Soon after, in February 1995, Helms announced that "the spirit of the Torricelli law" would be strengthened with the passage of the new "Cuba Liberty and Democratic Solidarity Act." Under the Helms legislation, companies that operated in the United States while trading with former U.S. properties confiscated by Cuba could become liable for legal action.[5]

In the House, a companion bill was introduced by Representative Dan Burton on February 14 and referred to the committees and subcommittees of the House for review. The Committee on International Relations approved the bill by a vote of 28 to 9 on July 11, 1995. Simultaneously, critics voiced warnings about the negative consequences of the bill. Harvard Professor Jorge Domínguez, one of the most respected academic specialists on Cuba, branded the bill "a godsend" to Castro, a *disparate* (foolish, silly, nonsensical idea), and a "bad mistake." Speaking at a Capitol Hill forum sponsored by the group Inter-American Dialogue, Domínguez articulated what was to become the standard liberal critique of the legislation: that the bill "would allow Castro to justify and sustain the kinds of policies he has followed in the past."[6] Participating in the annual meeting of the Association for the Study of the Cuban Economy (ASCE), Ernesto F. Betancourt, a former director of Radio Martí, justified most of the U.S. measures on

Cuba, but had this thought about Helms-Burton: "The legislation has the potential to encourage the end of Castro's regime. But, in its present form, it could help to prolong his rule."[7]

The bill was approved by the House on September 21, 1995, by a vote of 294 to 130.[8] Received with initial caution in the Senate, the bill was first considered there on September 27, 1995. Senator Robert Dole (R-Kansas), the Senate majority leader, and Senator Phil Gramm (R-Texas) were running for the Republican presidential nomination, and they took the opportunity of the Helms-Burton debate to display a hard-line attitude toward Castro. However, strong opposition from some senators and lobbying from the White House made its approval unlikely.[9] Then Senator Helms introduced the bill with only Titles I and II included. This detail raised doubts and added much debate about the real intention of the bill, because the text then ended in combining both aims—the conditioning of the embargo imposed on a future Cuban government (Title II) and the penalties against foreign investors (Titles III and IV).[10] After much discussion and a series of amendments, the bill (still reduced to titles I and II) was approved by a vote of 74 to 24 on October 19, 1995. A House-Senate conference committee was composed to reconcile the differences between the House and Senate versions of the bill. However, the committee did not meet until February 28, 1996, and the text did not make substantial progress until a crisis propelled the bill to its final stage.

The spark came with the tragic shooting down of two Cessna airplanes belonging to the Cuban exile organization Hermanos al Rescate (Brothers to the Rescue) by the Cuban Air Force on February 24, 1996. As the novelist Gabriel García Márquez might put it, the incident could be called the "chronicle of a death foretold" if one considers the chain of events leading to the incident. Despite clear warnings by Cuban officials, U.S. authorities apparently made no move to stop a series of flights by the exiles' planes over Cuban territory. These flights originated from U.S. territory, and during some of them leaflets were distributed over the skies of Havana. Serious as Cuba's downing of the planes was, the episode could have become the pretext for a more dangerous confrontation. President Clinton received a recommendation from his advisers for armed retaliation against the Cuban Air Force, the first of its kind since the 1962 missile crisis.[11]

Days before the incident, Representative Bill Richardson had embarked on the latest of several visits to persuade Castro to open up his regime. Castro was apparently convinced that Richardson had the full authority of the White House, and had forwarded the Cuban warnings to the highest levels. Thus, when the flights did not cease, Castro made the decision to attack. Cuba's warning was apparently not well understood by the State Department officers who debriefed former U.S. ambassador to El Salvador Robert White, who was also in Havana meeting with the Cuban military just before the shooting incident.[12]

After the tragic incident, there was public outcry in Miami and shock in most of the nation. Recognizing the weight of public opinion against Cuba, President Clinton, in a letter to Senate Republican leader Robert Dole, recommended the approval of the Helms-Burton legislation "as a strong message that the United States would not tolerate more losses of American lives." Following the president's decision, negotiations resumed to resolve the bill's most controversial provisions.[13] On March 1 the House-Senate Conference filed its report and on March 5 the Senate agreed to the conference report by a vote of 74 to 22. The following day, the House approved the measure by a vote of 336 to 86. It was presented to the president on March 11, and on March 12 Clinton signed the bill, which became Public Law No. 104-114.[14] However, possibly bending to advisers who warned him about Helms-Burton's possible consequences, the president partially neutralized the law by delaying the enforcement of Title III, using a loophole conveniently inserted in the text of the law.[15]

Initial Reactions and Prelude to Confrontation

The new law provoked at least three kinds of reactions. Its supporters exulted in triumph. Its critics looked forward to the day when the law's full consequences would become apparent. And foreign governments and international organizations expressed the beginnings of what would become a more cohesive opposition all over the Americas and in Europe.

Just before the law was signed by President Clinton, Canadian and Caribbean leaders, who were meeting in Grenada on March 4–5, issued a statement objecting to the bill. According to the officials of the Caribbean Community and Common Market (CARICOM), the bill was a violation of international law and an obstacle to trade liberalization. When the bill was signed, Canada asked for formal consultation under the NAFTA rules, which took place on April 26, with a second round on May 28. On April 16, Canada, the European Union, Mexico, and Japan expressed opposition to Helms-Burton at the WTO. On May 3, the European Union requested a consultation with the WTO, which took place on June 4.

On the domestic scene, Paul Coverdell, the Republican rapporteur on the bill in the Senate, was among those elated with the bill's passage. He argued that business dealings with Cuba were not normal commercial transactions but involved "a brutal assassin, an evil force in our hemisphere." Republican Senator Phil Gramm expressed support for "getting rid of Castro this century." Senator Helms promised to get the bill passed "before blood gets dry in Castro's hands." The heightened rhetoric continued as he equated foreign governments who traded with Cuba with World War II "collaborationists," and referred to Canada as doing what France thought it could do with Hitler. Representative Dan Burton asserted that "anybody who trades with confiscated property is an accomplice or a thief." House Majority Leader Newt Gingrich said that "no one in the world can expect the embargo to be lifted without democracy in Cuba." Gingrich also equated the new measure to the decision of the United States to intervene in Cuba in 1898: "The same we did with Spain, we have to liberate Cuba from Castro." Cuban-American National Foundation officials welcomed the approval of the law as a clear message for Castro.

Some domestic voices were more cautious or clearly opposed to Helms-Burton. While "all of us want to see Castro packing," said Democrat Senator Christopher Dodd, he warned that the law would cause friction between the United States and its trading partners, and he wondered what would happen when a visa was denied to Canadians and Israelis. Democrat Jeff Bingaman spoke of "the hypnotic ability that Castro and his enemies in South Florida maintain to generate the stupidity of U.S. officials." Overall, Democrats argued that the bill was approved in the heated context of the shooting down of the planes, but in the long term it would block the president from making changes in the U.S. policy toward Cuba, and it would produce a wave of lawsuits. Florida Representative Sam Gibbons remembered that thirty-five years earlier he voted for the same "crazy laws." Recognizing his error, he predicted that the new law would "damage more the U.S. than Castro." As a representative sample of the sentiment of moderate, nationalistic, or pro-Castro Cuban-Americans, Fidel Castro's one-time comrade in the revolutionary struggle, Eloy Gutiérrez Menoyo, now in exile after many years of imprisonment, opposed the law as *injerencista* (meddlesome). In his opinion, H-B would not "bring the downfall of the Castro government ... it would, however, impede [any] kind of peaceful change."[16]

Anonymous U.S. officials who opposed the measures suggested that the Cuban affairs office should be closed, since there was no longer a U.S. policy toward the island. Considering the new law's stringent conditions for the normalization of U.S.-Cuban relations, another source said the policy change could only come by virtue of "two bullets." State Department officers expressed annoyance that the law virtually eliminated the role of the executive in designing foreign policy toward Cuba. This concession of constitutional power was confirmed by Díaz-Balart. Some in the academic community stressed that the message for Cuba was that no reward would come from the United States for an improvement in human rights policies or economic reforms.[17]

Officials in the Castro government and representatives of several Cuban organizations expressed strong public indignation over Helms-Burton. Significantly, however, some Cubans had difficulty hiding their elation; they welcomed the U.S. measure as a weapon in an international war of public opinion. Foreign Minister Roberto Robaina took the lead, saying, "the world perhaps understands us better today because the U.S. is trying to enforce against the world what they have enforced against Cuba for more than 30 years."[18] In Mexico City a few days later, Robaina added that his country remained "open to foreign investment" but now offered a new advantage: "there is no U.S. competition."[19] During the course of a press conference held on March 19, Robaina released one of several official declarations of the Cuban government. The text argues that the law's intent is "to punish Cuba for its effort to decide, in a free, sovereign, and independent manner, it own political, economic, and social organization." It adds, "the intention to starve the Cuban people into submission will fail."[20] The National Union of Cuban Lawyers felt that there was no better judgment against Helms-Burton than "the four successive resolutions of the UN General Assembly, condemning the U.S. "economic, commercial and financial blockade against Cuba."[21]

The Law

Codification of a Policy

To a legal expert reading Helms-Burton, it would seem that one of the intentions of the law is the refining of legal and constitutional standards in the field of U.S. international relations. On the basis of the precedent of the Torricelli law, the Helms-Burton text is striking for its unusually blunt language, its specificity of targets, and its focus on a political objective. This perception is strongest with respect to Title II of the act.

The law's main provisions can be summarized in a few points. First, it prohibits loans, credits, or financing by U.S. citizens or residents for transactions involving confiscated property. Second, it forces the United States to vote against the admission of Cuba to international financial institutions, such as the International Monetary Fund (IMF) and the World Bank, until democracy exists in Cuba. Third, U.S. citizens are allowed to sue in the U.S. court system anybody who "traffics" in U.S. property nationalized by Cuba; Helms-Burton extends this right to people who were not U.S. citizens at the time of the expropriation. Finally, the law blocks entry to the United

States by foreign citizens (corporate officers, families, shareholders, and others) involved in "trafficking" with confiscated property.

In constitutional terms, the most significant provision of the law is that it expands on a feature of the Torricelli law: it further codifies the existing regulations on the foreign-policy relationship between the United States and Cuba. Helms-Burton gives Congress, and not the president, control over future changes. Speaking at a March 1998 conference, President Clinton's Cuba adviser, Richard Nuccio, sought to explain how the president came to sign the bill:

> At the Cabinet level meeting to review recommendations to the President on Helms-Burton most Cabinet officers, including Attorney General Janet Reno, Defense Secretary William Perry, and Joint Chiefs Chairman Shalikashvili, were shocked to learn that Helms-Burton codified the U.S. economic embargo. The attorney general's first reaction was to suggest a review of the bill's constitutionality. However, all objections to signing the bill were overruled first by George Stephanoupoulis and Leon Panetta, then by National Security Adviser Tony Lake. At the time Helms-Burton was signed there was some debate within the Administration about how restrictive the legislation was. Some held that the Executive Branch retained its ability to promulgate regulations and, hence, change Cuba policy without prior approval, others that Helms-Burton was an intolerable, even unconstitutional, intrusion on the President's ability to conduct foreign policy. Those who recommended that he sign did not understand the full implications of Helms-Burton.[22]

Nuccio added that when President Clinton was ready to sign the document in the Oval Office, he remarked that the law would cause him much trouble with the Europeans. To this, National Security Adviser Tony Lake answered that "it was o.k." and that the problem would be fixed later on, "after winning the presidential election."[23] U.S. Cuba policy had effectively become a domestic issue, and it is useful to consider whether the same outcome might have been permitted with respect to other sensitive international relationships. In the words of William LeoGrande, "it seems highly unlikely that Clinton would have accepted such a Congressionally imposed straightjacket on policy toward the Middle East, Russia, China, or Japan, where Washington had substantial international interests at stake."[24]

Nevertheless, the bill was signed and the process of its creation is now history. Popular culture has an expression to describe a virtually impossible change: "It will take an act of Congress." That is exactly the case for

Helms-Burton: It will take *another* act of Congress to redress the limitations imposed by the law.

The Setting: Cuba's Economy and Politics

As the introduction to the House-Senate Conference Report states, it was the intention of the legislators "to seek international sanctions against the Castro government in Cuba, to plan for support of a transitional government leading to a democratically elected government in Cuba." Helms-Burton is basically divided into an introduction and four titles.

Parts of the "Findings" section of the introduction set the tone and justification for the law. First the legislators offer a description and a very negative historical interpretation of the current Cuban economic situation, placing blame on the Castro leadership. The language is personalistic, echoing the declarations of hard-liners in the Cuban exile community. Fidel Castro's name frequently appears in the Helms-Burton law, which also comments on the character of the Cuban leadership. Because of its "totalitarian nature," the Cuban regime is blamed for the absence of any substantive political reforms, the repression of the Cuban people, and violations of fundamental human rights (par. 3, 4). Moreover, the law defends previous U.S. policy, stating that the "consistent policy of the United States towards Cuba since the beginning of the Castro regime, carried out by both Democratic and Republican administrations, has sought to keep faith with the people of Cuba, and has been effective in sanctioning the totalitarian Castro regime" (par. 8). In sum, the law justifies the continuation of the embargo and its corollary measures on the same grounds that justified the imposition of the Platt Amendment: that the Cuban leaders are not suited to govern the country effectively and according to the standards of the United States.

The Charges against Cuba

The accusations against the Cuban government in its domestic and world behavior are detailed: involvement in the illegal international narcotics trade (par. 13), harboring U.S. fugitives from justice (par. 13), threatening international peace and security by engaging in acts of armed subversion and terrorism, as well as training and supplying groups dedicated to international violence (par. 14), torture in various forms (including psychological), as well as execution, exile, confiscation, political imprisonment, and other forms of terror and repression (par. 15) as means of retaining power. In addition, the text mixes polemics with political assessments. On one hand, the law decries that Castro has defined democratic pluralism as "pluralistic garbage" (par. 16), and on the other hand it states that innocent

Cubans are held hostage solely because their relatives have escaped the country (par. 17). Among other violations of international conventions, Congress charges that the Cuban government surrounds embassies in its capital with armed forces "to thwart the right of its citizens to seek asylum and systematically denies that right to the Cuban people, punishing them by imprisonment for seeking to leave the country and killing them for attempting to do so" (par. 18). Moreover, the legislators seem incensed by the fact that the Castro government "continues to utilize blackmail (par. 19), such as the immigration crisis with which it threatened the United States in the summer of 1994, and other unacceptable and illegal forms of conduct to influence the actions of sovereign states in the Western Hemisphere."

The text also comments on instances when the Cuban government has not acted according to international norms. For example, the United Nations Commission on Human Rights "has repeatedly reported on the unacceptable human rights situation (par. 20) in Cuba and has taken the extraordinary step of appointing a Special Rapporteur," but the Cuban government "has consistently refused access to the Special Rapporteur" (par. 21) and expressed its decision not to "implement so much as one comma" of the resolutions appointing the rapporteur. In sum, the law states that the United Nations has determined that "massive and systematic violations of human rights" may constitute a "threat to peace" (par. 24). In sum, and in consideration of these findings, Helms-Burton concludes that the Cuban government "has posed and continues to pose a national security threat to the United States."

The Goals of the Law

Following this introduction, a series of objectives are outlined in section 3 ("Purposes"). First, the authors of the law wished to show that they were assisting the Cuban people "in regaining their freedom and prosperity, as well as in joining the community of democratic countries that are flourishing in the Western Hemisphere" (sec. 3, par. 1). Thus it is their intention to: "strengthen international sanctions (par. 2) against the Castro government"; "to provide for the continued national security of the United States in the face of continuing threats from the Castro government of terrorism, theft of property from United States nationals," (par. 3) and "the political manipulation by the Castro government of the desire of Cubans to escape that results in mass migration to the United States"; "to encourage the holding of free and fair democratic elections"; and "to provide a policy framework for United States support to the Cuban people in response to the formation of a transition government or a democratically elected government in Cuba" (par. 5). Finally, the law should "protect United States nationals against confiscatory takings and the wrongful trafficking in property confiscated by the Castro regime" (par. 6).

Words and Explanations

In order to provide the necessary interpretation for the mix of everyday language, political comments, and legal terminology, the legislators found it advisable to offer a sort of detailed glossary in section 4 ("Definitions"). Some of the most salient entries for the purposes of our study are the following:

> (A) By "confiscated" (par. 4) the law means the nationalization, expropriation, or other seizure by the Cuban Government of ownership or control of property, on or after January 1, 1959—
> (i) without the property having been returned or adequate and effective compensation provided; or
> (ii) without the claim to the property having been settled pursuant to an international claims settlement agreement or other mutually accepted settlement procedure; and
> (B) the repudiation by the Cuban Government of, the default by the Cuban Government on, or the failure of the Cuban Government to pay, on or after January 1, 1959—
> (i) a debt of any enterprise which has been nationalized, expropriated, or otherwise taken by the Cuban Government;
> (ii) a debt which is a charge on property nationalized, expropriated, or otherwise taken by the Cuban Government; or
> (iii) a debt which was incurred by the Cuban Government in satisfaction or settlement of a confiscated property claim.

Then the law inserts one of the most rigorous conditions for the modification of U.S. policy. In order for the president or Congress to adopt a more open policy toward Cuba, they would have to show that it had a "democratically elected government." Specifically, this meant "a government determined by the President to have met the requirements of section 206." That section's requirements are precise and written in language that is full of personalistic references, and their intent is unmistakable: the current Cuban leadership would have to leave their posts.

The Meaning of "Trafficking"

Legal scholars and political observers alike took note of the blunt term "trafficking" in a text emanating from Congress. Congressional sources that inspired the use of this term admit that they used it deliberately as a way to equate the conduct of the Castro regime with the activities of the drug cartels. For the authors of Helms-Burton, a person "traffics" . . . [if] knowingly and intentionally (par. 13, i) sells, transfers, distributes, dispenses, brokers, manages, or otherwise disposes of confiscated property, or purchases, leases, receives, possesses, obtains control of, manages, uses, or otherwise acquires or holds an interest in confiscated property, (ii) engages in a commercial activity using or otherwise benefitting from confiscated property, or (iii) causes, directs, participates in, or profits from, trafficking . . . by another person, or otherwise engages in trafficking . . . through another person, without the authorization of any United States national who holds a claim to the property.

Perhaps seeking to reduce the effects of such a sweeping interpretation, the law makes a small number of exceptions. For example, it states that the term "traffics" does not include "the delivery of international telecommunication signals to Cuba." Also exempted are properties necessary for lawful travel to Cuba, meaning ships and aircraft. Most interestingly, the law also does not include the uses of property by a person "who is both a citizen of Cuba and a resident of Cuba." In other words, it apparently sends a message to honest owners of houses or apartments. However, the text is adamant about officials of "the Cuban Government or the ruling political party in Cuba": they will have to vacate their current lodgings.

Continuing and Deepening the Embargo

The legislators also felt it necessary to clarify what was meant by "embargo." The term is interpreted as including "all restrictions on trade or transactions with, and travel to or from, Cuba, and all restrictions on transactions in property in which Cuba or nationals of Cuba have an interest," as prescribed by the Foreign Assistance Act of 1961, the Trading with the Enemy Act of 1917, the Cuban Democracy Act of 1992, and any other applicable measures such as the Food Security Act of 1985.

Despite these past measures, the legislators judged, the past policy had failed to obtain the desired results. Therefore, specific additional mechanisms were needed to reinforce the existing embargo. A portion of the law ("Strengthening International Sanctions against the Castro Government," Sec. 101, Statement of Policy) expands on these issues. The text then deals with what the legislators consider a continuation of Cuba's Cold War dependency on Soviet technology and strategic capabilities in two sensitive areas: nuclear facilities and intelligence gathering.

Section 102 (Enforcement of the Economic Embargo of Cuba) seeks to make individual or state commercial or political relations with Cuba more difficult and seeks to impose similar restrictions on other countries. For example, by the expanded enforcement of the Trading with the Enemy Act, a fine "not to exceed $50,000 may be imposed by the Secretary of the Treasury on any person who violates any license, order, rule, or regulation issued in compliance with the provisions of this Act." Travel to the United States by Cuban officials will be made more difficult by denying visas to Cuban nationals "considered by the Secretary of State to be officers or employees of the Cuban Government or of the Communist Party of Cuba."

Sections 103 and 104 are dedicated to further limiting any financing related to the contested properties. Section 103 ("Prohibition against Indirect Financing of Cuba") prohibits "loans, credit, or other financing" by a "United States national, a permanent resident alien, or a United States agency to any person for the purpose of financing transactions involving any confiscated property." In turn, international agencies that offer economic assistance to the Cuban government will face a budgetary problem. Section 104 mandates a series of measures, among them a reduction in U.S. payments, if any international financial institution approves a loan or other assistance to the Cuban government.

As a mechanism to reinforce the isolation of Cuba in the Western Hemisphere, section 105 states that as long as Castro is in power, Cuba is permanently suspended from the OAS.

Section 106 deals with the "assistance by the independent states of the former Soviet Union for the Cuban Government" in sensitive areas such as the nuclear and intelligence facilities still in operation on Cuban soil. Section 107 regulates broadcasting to Cuba, mainly the continuation of Radio Martí (a part of the Voice of America) and other means of sending information to Cuba via the airwaves.

Record Keeping and Information Gathering

Then the text of Helms-Burton becomes a detailed mandate for the compilation of a mix of academic research, intelligence gathering, and general data collecting. Section 108 concerns reporting on commercial activity "with, and assistance to, Cuba from other foreign countries." Congress mandated the collection of vast amounts of information, on a scale that may be well beyond the resources of the agencies charged with information gathering. Secretary of State Madeleine Albright summarized the problem as it affects the State Department: "For the past decade, we have been cutting foreign policy positions, closing diplomatic posts, and shutting U.S. Agency for International Development (USAID) and U.S. Information Agency (USIA) missions. We lack the funds to provide full security for our people overseas."[25] Members of Congress who slashed the funding for State Department operations evidently failed to consider the burden imposed by information gathering, leaving U.S. foreign service officers to choose between security functions and record-keeping on "traffickers."

Another portion of the text (sec. 108–11) seeks to ban the import into the United States of any product originating in Cuba, even if only in small part. For that purpose the law mandates that the White House file detailed reports on agreements of trade and assistance programs between other foreign nations and Cuba, with a special attention given to military products or those with potential military use. Section 112 regulates the eventual "reinstitution of family remittances and travel to Cuba." The conditions include that the Cuban government "permit the unfettered operation of small businesses." As a sign of the lack of enforcement of this mandate and responding to the wishes of the Cuban exile community, the fact is that 100,000 Cuban exiles travel each year to Cuba. Moreover, a figure estimated to be as high as $500 million constitutes what the Cuban exile community in the United States sends annually to families in the island. As a consequence, hard currency contributed by family reunions and remittances is funneled to the small private economy, such as family restaurants (*paladares*).

Finally, section 113 deals with "Expulsion of criminals from Cuba," and section 114 regulates the eventual establishment of "News bureaus in Cuba." In spite of Helms-Burton's conditions and others imposed by the Cuban government, some U.S. media networks have established permanent offices in Havana, including the Cable News Network (CNN) and later the Associated Press.

A Blueprint for a New Nation

Changing Cuba

The Helms-Burton Act was not created by any single legislator. Although it may be the product of a small group of drafters, it is the result of a long give-and-take procedure, of a series of amendments, corrections, and insertions. The final document incorporates not only an impressive contrast of objectives but also of styles. While some sections of Title III seem to be framed in the logic and language of legal minds, Title II is strikingly candid in language and purpose. It is not an outline of measures to impede foreign investment in Cuba (as Title IV is) or to establish compensation for "trafficking" with expropriated properties (as Title III mandates). Instead, Title II is a clear plea for a new Cuba.[26] It is, in fact, a separate law, a significant detail that has been lost in analyses of the overall consequences of the act.

Originally, Title II was a separate document, the brainchild of an influential new member of Congress, Representative Robert Menéndez (D-New Jersey). In the 103d Congress, he had drafted legislation titled "Support for a Free and Democratic Cuba Act," which was never reported out of the House Foreign Affairs Committee. The Republicans' strong showing in the 1994 elections produced a more favorable environment. Menéndez caught the attention of the Cuban-American National Foundation, the leaders of which were showing uneasiness about the role played by moderate circles of the exile community.[27]

Title II conveys a clear message: that the lifting of U.S. sanctions on foreign companies will not come without a high price. The cost was to be political, and the party that was destined to be most damaged was not a foreign company, nor even the Cuban government, but the Cuban nation, an issue that was lost in the international controversy between trading partners. Although this book deals primarily with the international consequences of Helms-Burton, some consideration should be paid to this extremely important issue simply because it is at the root of the perennial problem between the United States and Cuba. Title II is an open book about the ideology of the United States regarding not only Cuba, but the whole of Latin America and perhaps the rest of world.

Significantly, given the conditions imposed by Title II, the parties affected by Titles III and IV wondered about the real aims of the whole document in policy terms. Some foreign observers shared the interpretation of the Cuban government: the ultimate goal of the document was to dictate what kind of government Cuba could have. While economic matters might be open to negotiation, political fundamentals were not.

While Titles III and IV became an irritant for foreign investors, they were gladly welcomed by a majority of Cuban-American exiles (especially those who were granted the opportunity to sue "traffickers" and recover part of the value of their confiscated properties). Title II struck the conscience of the Cuban people, both on the island and in the exile community. While the most vocal sector of the Cuban-American community praised the Helms-Burton Act, a significant number of exiles shared with the Cuban government a sense of apprehension and injury to the national pride. Many Cuban-Americans admitted in private that the Helms-Burton law gave more benefit than harm to the Castro regime, and they considered the spirit and the content of Title II a humiliation. In essence, Cubans were told that the United States had imposed standards on them about how they should govern themselves if they were ever to see the embargo lifted. Revolutionaries, counterrevolutionaries, moderates, and any Cuban with a sense of history saw the obvious: the Platt Amendment had been reborn.[28]

Paradoxically, from the U.S. point of view, this part of Helms-Burton was consistent not only with U.S. policy toward Cuba but also with its traditional approach to Latin America as a whole, a point that was not lost on perceptive scholars. In discussing Title II, Jorge Domínguez points to the Monroe Doctrine as an explanation for the U.S. attitude toward the Castro regime: "The Helms-Burton Act captures well this ideological tradition in U.S. foreign policy."[29]

In *Beneath the United States: A History of the U.S. Policy toward Latin America,* Lars Schoultz argues convincingly that the actions of the United States are not irrational and compulsive but instead are consistent with a historical pattern pursued by the U.S. political elite. Schoultz concludes that three interests have shaped United States policy toward Latin America: "the need to protect U.S. security, the desire to accommodate the demands of U.S. domestic politics, and the drive to promote U.S. economic development."[30] Most observers of U.S.–Latin American relations would agree with this assessment and also endorse his view that periodically the United States has shifted its priorities from fear of communism to dismay at human rights violations, from Big Stick and Dollar Diplomacy to Good Neighborliness, from promoting free trade to concerns over drug trafficking and immigration. A mix of policies has coexisted, held together by the three central interests.

What is most novel in Schoultz's study is his systematic use of primary sources, reports buried in dozens of archives, as well as classic statements and writings of key U.S. leaders, well known to the public, in order to explain U.S. actions regarding Latin America. The United States' central concerns for security, domestic politics, and economic expansion are governed, says Schoultz, by the "underlying beliefs that U.S. officials hold about Latin Americans and, specifically, their belief that Latin Americans are an inferior people."[31] Monroe, John Quincy Adams, McKinley, Theodore Roosevelt, Wilson, Franklin Roosevelt, Kennedy, Reagan, and Bush are some of the presidents who assumed that the United States has a duty to teach Latin Americans how to govern themselves through "real, stable, honest governments." U.S. leaders have sought to fulfill this duty with a vision "that blends self-interest with what the Victorian British called their White Man's Burden and the French their *mission civilisatrice.*"[32]

Ironically, Schoultz shows that most U.S. policy makers had never traveled to Latin America and did not understand its history and culture. Further, opinion polls show that their negative perception of Latin America is shared by a broad spectrum of the U.S. public. Public officials, once charged with implementing a new chapter of U.S. policy toward Latin America, simply adapt a basic set of beliefs to fit the new circumstances.[33] When U.S.

property rights are violated (as in the confiscations executed by the Castro regime), compensation is a logical demand. When security is a major concern, Latin American political "inferiority" is the threat to be addressed (as during the crisis of U.S.-Cuban relations during the Cold War). When domestic politics dominate the scene, something like Helms-Burton comes to the rescue. When foreign citizens and companies disregard the U.S. embargo toward Cuba, and threaten to compete in trade and investment, a reborn Monroe Doctrine is propelled into action in the form of Titles III and IV of Helms-Burton.

Regarding Cuba's governance, Schoultz shows that the words of General Leonard Wood, before he left as governor of Cuba in 1902, are still in effect: "There is, of course, little or no independence left to Cuba under the Platt Amendment." Orville Platt, the senator who planted this provision in the new Cuban constitution, had said, "The United States will always, under the so-called Platt Amendment, be in a position to straighten out things if they get seriously bad."[34] Title II of Helms-Burton suggests that, in the U.S. view, things are still so bad that Cubans need the United States to show them how to "behave decently," as Teddy Roosevelt said in 1904.

Broad Strokes of the New Platt

Title II states its purpose is to promote and assist in the creation of a free and independent Cuba. Section 201 outlines several components of a "policy toward a transition government and a democratically elected government in Cuba":

(1) To support the self-determination of the Cuban people.
(2) To recognize that the self-determination of the Cuban people is a sovereign and national right of the citizens of Cuba which must be exercised free of interference by the government of any other country.
(3) To encourage the Cuban people to empower themselves with a government which reflects the self-determination of the Cuban people.
(4) To recognize the potential for a difficult transition from the current regime in Cuba that may result from the initiatives taken by the Cuban people for self-determination in response to the intransigence of the Castro regime in not allowing any substantive political or economic reforms, and to be prepared to provide the Cuban people with humanitarian, developmental, and other economic assistance.

Section 202 instructs the president to provide economic assistance to Cuba when it is determined that a transition government or a democratically elected government is in place in Cuba. The necessary steps include seeking to obtain the agreement of other countries and of international financial institutions and multilateral organizations to provide assistance to a transition government. Moreover, Congress instructs the White House to send appropriate signals to the Cuban people and also to inform the legislators of its performance of the prescribed measures.

Congress mandated that White House staff should be specifically charged with these tasks. Section 203 instructs the president to designate "a coordinating official who shall be responsible for implementing the strategy for distributing assistance" and "a United States–Cuba council to ensure coordination between the United States Government and the private sector." The figure of the "coordinating official" is one of the most troubling requirements of the document. Some see this official as a reborn viceroy or a sort of high commissioner, a representative of a former colonial power in a country that still maintains intimate links to the old empire. The impressive authority bestowed on the "coordinator" makes the position a sort of governorship, like the one in place before the 1902 Constitution.

Ricardo Alarcón, Cuba's former minister of foreign affairs and now president of the National Assembly, lost no time in denouncing the project: "This gentleman will be responsible for implementing the strategy the United States will follow for the poor country finally destroyed through hunger, misery, disease—the total blockade."[35] While Alarcón did not mention annexation directly, some observers of Title II perceived the spirit of the U.S. legislators as being very close to the ideology of the *anexionistas*. Both in the United States and in Cuba, they saw that, in the minds of some U.S. political leaders, the final remedy for Cuba's ills should be the conversion of the island into one more state of the union. Or its status might resemble that of the Commonwealth of Puerto Rico, a prospect likely to enrage most Cubans, both those living in Cuba and those in the Cuban-American exile community.

What Is a Transition Government?

As one key condition for suspending the embargo and therefore the effects of the law, Congress prescribed that Cuba should be ruled by a "transition government." In political science, the term "transition" is usually applied to the evolution from an authoritarian or totalitarian government to a certain degree of political opening, with the end result expected to be a regime resembling a liberal democracy. However, some recent historical examples have fallen short of this hopeful vision. Possibly in order to avoid misinterpretations regarding the transition expected in Cuba, Congress directed the president to determine whether Cuba's transition government was in fact consistent with the requirements of the law, which are minute and detailed.

Ricardo Alarcón argues that under the terms of Helms-Burton "there would be no Cuban government and no Republic of Cuba. There would be a U.S. council designed by the U.S. President that would look after the Cuban economy."[36] To the historian of U.S.–Latin American relations, this scenario sounded familiar. It was what Cuban moderates in exile have feared and opposed for years, while enduring the scorn of the hard-liners.

In fact, however, it is not fully clear what steps the United States would take in the event of a change in the Cuban government. Would it then suspend all actions? Would the projected lawsuits be blocked? Would all dreams of restitution vanish? The law only says that the president should end the embargo if the Cuban people meet the law's stated requirements for a "democratically elected government" and comply with its demands regarding property. That may mean that Helms-Burton's Title III would still be operational, a veritable nightmare for the new government.

The Fine Print

The text then enters one of the most controversial parts of the law's requirements. Its authors were evidently unaware of how their seemingly good, democratic intentions would be read by those familiar with the long history of U.S. intervention in the political affairs of Cuba. In section 205, Congress decrees that a transition government is one that, in general terms, "has legalized all political activity." It insists that all political prisoners should be released. An added condition implies lack of trust: the new Cuban regime will allow for investigations of Cuban prisons by appropriate international human rights organizations. The U.S. lawmakers then become more specific about what institutions they will not tolerate. The new Cuban authorities have to "dissolve the present Department of State Security in the Cuban Ministry of the Interior, including the Committees for the Defense of the Revolution and the Rapid Response Brigades." With respect to electoral procedures, the law reminds the new Cuban authorities that they will need to make "public commitments to organizing free and fair elections for a new government to be held in a timely manner within a period not to exceed 18 months after the transition government assumes power." Just in case the new government is tempted to experiment with halfway measures, Congress insists that the elections should be open, involving the participation of multiple independent political parties. Further, all political participants will "have full access to the media on an equal basis."

Again expressing reservations about the Cuban capacity for self-governance, the U.S. Congress mandates the voting procedure "to be conducted under the supervision of internationally recognized observers, such as the Organization of American States and the United Nations." When Congress adds that the new regime must show that it has "ceased any interference with Radio Martí or Televisión Martí broadcasts," one may reasonably wonder what need there would be for such media in a free and democratic Cuba. Finally, the law mandates that the new government will make "progress in establishing an independent judiciary." Evidently it is too much to expect a perfect judicial system; one just "making progress" may be the best Cubans are capable of. In general the new system should show respect for "internationally recognized human rights and basic freedoms as set forth in the Universal Declaration of Human Rights, to which Cuba is a signatory nation."

Perhaps more important than what the document says is what it omits. In a text so inclined to detail, it is surprising that the topic of social restructuring is absent. Social policies receive only minor attention, by way of a provision calling for "the establishment of independent trade unions as set forth in conventions 87 and 98 of the International Labor Organization, and allowing the establishment of independent social, economic, and political associations." The rest of the social system is left to the discretion of the new Cuban leadership; there is no mention of salvaging some of the social, health, and educational accomplishments of the revolution. It is open to speculation whether the legislators recognized that Cuba would probably need the cushion offered by social-democratic policies and welfare state mechanisms that are typically the target of neoliberal policies.

The Changing of the Guard

The final touch of this section is actually the personalistic centerpiece of Title II (if not the general philosophy of the law) that makes clear what (rather, *who*) the U.S. Congress would not accept in a transitional or democratically elected government. In contrast with the usual circuitous declarations from governments, which are diplomatically worded and generally avoid personalistic references, Helms-Burton is forthright. Under whichever procedure the Cuban people choose to elect a new government, the expectation is that it *will not include Fidel Castro*. This requirement seems logical in view of the centrality of the Cuban leader as a factotum of the gains and as well as the damage brought by the revolution. But the legislators wanted to condition the transitional period further. Thus, the text adds another unacceptable name: that of Raúl Castro. For readers inclined to statistical analysis, the name of Castro occurs no less than thirty-two times in the total text of the law, a fact that probably gave enormous satisfaction to the Cuban leader.

However, these demands conflict with the recommendations and wishes of Cuban dissident nongovernmental organizations and moderate circles within the Cuban exile community. Pressed by circumstances and wishing to contribute to a peaceful transition, they have accepted the necessity for the transition process to be monitored, if not controlled, by the current Cuban leadership.[37] Since the law does not mention other proscribed names, one wonders what would happen if a transition government were to include other family members of Fidel Castro. Observers interested in historical comparisons might point out that if the logic of the U.S. Congress had been applied to the post-Franco period in Spain, then Juan Carlos de Borbón would have been an unacceptable figure to preside over the transition process because he was named as successor by the dictator, much in the manner that Fidel named his brother Raúl. The same logic could be applied to the case of Adolfo Suárez, who held important positions during the last stages of the Franco regime and was named premier by King Juan Carlos to lead the effective democratization of the political system. Nevertheless, the conditions imposed by Congress were mild compared with the original requirements that sought to ban *anybody* appointed by the Castro government, which effectively disqualified the bulk of Cuba's adult population.

Helms-Burton's emphasis on banning the current leader is consistent with expectations that quick and simple solutions, such as elections and free trade, will produce the desired changes in Cuba. This is the same logic popularly expressed by bumper stickers often seen in Miami in the late 1980s and early 1990s (some cars still have them): "No Castro, No Problem." However, a Cuban intellectual writing under the nom de plume of Julián Sorel warns that "Castro is no accident but the substance and summary of the history of Cuba . . . the remedy is more complex and delicate than what optimists suppose."[38]

With the Helms-Burton Act partially suspended, and thus not being tested in the courts, there is no way to know what kind of constitutional conflict it may represent, nor what violations of international law. Parties prosecuted under Titles III and IV may be able to point to the violation of international standards in Title II in order to obtain favorable judgments. The damage inflicted by Title II is not only political but legal.

Redressing Wrongs

Another highly unusual provision in Helms-Burton is the prescriptive language used in section 205(b)(1)(B): "permitting the reinstatement of citizenship to Cuban-born persons returning to Cuba." Different governments have different ways of recognizing the rights of former citizens to recover their original citizenship. Some seek to bestow citizenship upon the descendants of citizens by a generous application of the jus sanguinis tradition, under which the citizenship of the child is determined by the citizenship of the parent, as is done in Spain and Italy. But what is unusual is the imposition of citizenship procedures by a foreign law. Cuban officials were prompt to exploit this issue for domestic political purposes. Ricardo Alarcón, in a broadcast interview, reminded his audience that "never before [has] a legislature anywhere in the world dared to make laws regarding the citizenship of another."[39] What H-B and Alarcón failed to note is that, according to Cuban law, unless the Cuban state specifically deprives a person of Cuban birth of citizenship, said person retains his or her original citizenship, even if that person becomes a naturalized citizen of another state. The problem for Cuban-Americans has been that the United States will not recognize U.S.-Cuban dual citizenship, not that Cuba will not.

The U.S. law demands not only a post-Castro "right to private property" but also that a new Cuban leadership take "appropriate steps to return to United States citizens (and entities which are 50 percent or more beneficially owned by United States citizens) property taken by the Cuban Government from such citizens and entities on or after January 1, 1959, or to provide equitable compensation to such citizens and entities for such property." Commenting on this issue, Alarcón challenged the populistic claims of the law and expressed concern for the millions of Cubans who since the triumph of the revolution have acquired ownership of residences that were previously rented to them and were subsequently confiscated.[40] "They will take this over my dead body," said one Cuban woman. In a process that is common in Cuba, she inherited her house from her parents, who, after renting it for years, had purchased the house through the urban reform laws in the 1960s, when the former owners left the country. Cuban law provided for the former owners of expropriated property to receive monthly payments, a life annuity. But by leaving the country, they lost that right.[41]

The questionable process of expropriation may make the Helms-Burton requirement of returning properties to their former owners seem just and fair. However, the act in its closing clarifications exempts houses used as primary residences from becoming the subject of lawsuits under Title III. The text specifies that the law does not apply to "transactions and uses of property by a person who is both a citizen of Cuba and a resident of Cuba," unless this person is also "an official of the Cuban Government or the ruling political party in Cuba." This exemption contradicts the mandate of Title II, however, which insists that *all* properties must be returned to their former owners as a precondition for the ending the U.S. embargo. In other words, Cuban-Americans may not sue the current users of their former properties except in certain limited circumstances, but the same properties should be returned to the original owners in order to "certify" the new Cuban government as democratic and free-market oriented.

The burden on any new Cuban government regarding contested properties may be monumental. Unless it is prepared for a massive redistribution of properties from the current occupiers to the former owners, with considerable social disruption if not outright mass conflict, there is no reason to expect that this condition will ever be met. No Cuban government is ever likely to have the resources necessary to compensate the former owners of the expropriated properties equitably. If the intention of the U.S. legislators was to send a populist message to their domestic supporters, they were successful. However, the delivery of the promised compensation is an impossibility, even considering that a portion of the estimated aid package for rebuilding the Cuban economy could be diverted into compensation for properties taken in the early 1960s. As Cuban-American economists established before the enactment of the law, the burden is so monumental that simple common sense should have removed this condition from the text.[42]

In an impressive study of the confiscations issue, Rolando Castañeda and Plinio Montalván, participating in the annual conference of the Association for the Study of the Cuban Economy, addressed various proprosals to return confiscated properties to the former owners. They reasoned that "since the government of Cuba does not have (and will not soon have) the means to compensate promptly, adequately and fairly, restitution is the best (only) workable alternative." However, they add that "fortunately, most Cuban expatriate groups have recognized that restitution of dwellings or residential property is not advisable." They comment that "the discussion can then be restricted to non-residential property." The authors point out, however, that the return of nonresidential property would not contribute greatly to developing the Cuban nation because a substantial portion of the best nonresidential property would have to be returned to non-Cubans, a move that would effectively return the Cuban economy to the situation of the 1950s. On the approved list of claims, U.S. companies are shown in 1958 to have owned 90 percent of Cuba's electrical industry, 100 percent of the telephone system, most of the mining industry, and between 1.5 and 2 million acres of Cuba's best land. The authors wisely conclude that returning these properties "would be tantamount to insisting that nationalistic feelings in Cuba due to foreign ownership of the country's principal assets never had a basis in fact."[43] While they argue that "all non-residential property in Cuba belongs to the state," other experts conclude that the "present possessors are owners of the property they possess" according to the tradition of usucapion (that is, ownership based on lengthy occupancy in good faith).[44] However, this opinion is contested by wide sectors of the exile community. While usucapion may be reasonably applied to residential property, many argue that nonresidential property that was expropriated without compensation should be subject to negotiation between the new Cuban government and the former owners, all parties taking into account the financial limitations of the new regime. A final requirement written into Helms-Burton may at first seem reasonable. The text demands that the new government show that it "has extradited or otherwise rendered to the United States all persons sought by the United States Department of Justice for crimes committed in the United States" (sec. 205[b][3]). The law does not impose a similar requirement on the U.S government, however, for crimes allegedly committed against Cuba by people residing in the United States, either before or during the transition process.

Considering Helms-Burton's overbearing and unprecedented controls on Cuba's future political institutions and its international obligations, usually mild and objective scholars felt compelled to react. Jorge Domínguez offered this commentary on Title II:

> Even if one were to agree that TV Martí should be seen and heard in Cuba, that those who lost their citizenship should regain it, that market economies works best, that Fidel and Raúl Castro's services are not needed in a future Cuban government, and that property should be returned or compensated, all these desiderata go well beyond any internationally recognized criteria for the determination of democratic or transitional democratizing governments under the charters of the United Nations or the Organization of American States. Mandating them in U.S. legislation as defining characteristics of a democratic or transitional government makes a mockery of the pledge to respect Cuban sovereignty.[45]

Punishing Foreign Investment

In Pursuit of "Traffickers"

While the first two titles of Helms-Burton may seem designed primarily for Cuban consumption, both in the U.S. exile community and in the Cuban republic, Titles III and IV have attracted the attention of observers around the world. As we have seen, Title III is dedicated to the "protection of property rights of United States nationals." Section 301 outlines its "Findings." Here the legislators expressed themselves in strong, personalistic language: "Since Fidel Castro seized power in Cuba in 1959 he has trampled on the fundamental rights of the Cuban people; and through his personal despotism, he has confiscated the property of millions of his own citizens, thousands of United States nationals; and thousands more Cubans who claimed asylum in the United States as refugees because of persecution and later became naturalized citizens of the United States." Such declarations may better belong in Titles I or II, but the fact that the final act is the product of two projects accounts for the repetitious rhetoric. It is a further indication that Title II is addressed to Cubans and Title III to foreign investors, who apparently need to be reminded of the wrongs committed by Fidel Castro.

Further, Congress argues that these wrongs are not confined to the past. Rather, the Cuban government continues to compound them by "offering foreign investors the opportunity to purchase an equity interest in, manage, or enter into joint ventures using property and assets some of which were confiscated from United States nationals." This would make the Cuban government and the investors co-conspirators in a sort of illegal activity, because "trafficking" in confiscated property provides badly needed financial benefit, including hard currency, oil, and productive investment and expertise, to the current Cuban government and thus undermines the foreign policy of the United States.

How, then, can the former property owners and the U.S. government remedy this situation? The problem is that, according to the authors of Helms-Burton, the prevailing system for compensation through international procedures "as currently structured, lacks fully effective remedies for the wrongful confiscation of property and for unjust enrichment from the use of wrongfully confiscated property." Thus, any government wishing to protect its own interests or those of its citizens, when their rights have been violated outside the national border, must take proper recourse. In the opinion of the U.S. Congress, "International law recognizes that a nation has the ability to provide for rules of law with respect to conduct outside its territory that has or is intended to have substantial effect within its territory." This is the central justification for executing a clear case of extraterritoriality. In any event, the true novelty of the Helms-Burton law is not in its lofty declarations but in the explicit punitive measures that it intends to implement in order to discourage the "trafficking" with expropriated property in Cuba.

Section 302 is dedicated to the "liability for trafficking in confiscated property claimed by United States nationals." It is striking that, on one hand, the text is so detailed and personalistic while, on the other hand, it omits a full definition for who is a U.S. national, at least for purposes of this section of the law. Tucked into the parts on how to file a claim is this statement: "A United States national, other than a United States national bringing an action under this section on a claim certified under Title V of the International Claims Settlement Act of 1949, may not bring an action on a claim under this section before the end of the 2-year period beginning on the date of the enactment of this Act."

For a casual reader, the meaning of this convoluted provision is likely to be unclear. Any Cuban-American with an attorney knows what it means, however: the U.S. nationals in question "may not bring an action . . . under this section" simply because they were not U.S. citizens in 1959. In other words, they are mostly Cuban-Americans; otherwise, their claims would have been certified. Now, by virtue of the Helms-Burton Law, they had recourse to the U.S. courts. This detail has become the focus of legal controversies over Helms-Burton. The law, in effect, makes no distinction between Cuban citizens who became U.S. citizens after migrating to the United States and the original U.S. citizens (or companies) whose properties were confiscated by the Cuban regime after the Cuban Revolution. By extending the protection of U.S. law to current U.S. citizens for actions that took place *before* they became U.S. nationals, Congress may be demonstrating an unusual generosity. Nonetheless, Congress did impose a kind of "handicap" on Cuban-Americans when it mandated a two-year waiting period.

A cynical interpretation is that the delay allowed the certified claimants (those who were U.S. citizens in 1959) a first shot at recovering their losses; then, after the waiting period, the Cuban-Americans could do so. This provision may invite litigation charging discrimination. In any event, scholars were ready from the start to claim that this provision on behalf of claimants who were not U.S. citizens at the time of the expropriations is a violation of international conventions. The domestic background for this intriguing anomaly reveals another protagonist in the creation of Helms-Burton.

The Bacardí Connection

Helms-Burton has been called by cynics the "Bacardí law," the "Bacardí Claims Act,"[46] and the "Bacardí Rum Protection Act,"[47] in reference to the company's sizeable assets in Cuba that were expropriated by the revolution. Another critic has termed H-B "the Cuban-American Millionaire Protection Act,"[48] reflecting the fact that heirs of the former owners of this company and other Cuban-Americans of considerable wealth lobbied for the bill.

While this is true in essence, however, the global picture is more complex. First of all, it would be inaccurate to equate the size of companies (American or Cuban in origin) and the degree of wealth expropriated with the energy employed in lobbying for the bill. It is also inaccurate to identify *all* large American companies with expropriated property (and therefore included in the original claims list) with those opposed to the H-B expansion of the citizenship requirements. The reality is that *some* American companies initially included in the U.S.-certified list of claims were in favor of the development of the law. This is the case of Gary Jarmin, chairman of the U.S.-Cuba Foundation. Initially a supporter of the bill, Jarmin concluded that H-B was not in the best interests of his company and subsequently became one of its strongest opponents. He is cited as the author of the expression "Bacardí Run Protection Act" and retained attorneys to lead the new strategy.

Most of the large American companies as well as many individuals hoping to press claims for restitution were not pleased by the *widening* of the potential pool of claimants to confiscated Cuban assets, because this would diminish their chances of recovering substantial sums by litigation. Most companies included as claimants in the 1960s preferred that the list not expand, so their prospects for compensation would be protected. An association called the Joint Corporate Committee on Cuban Claims, based in Stanford, Connecticut, and composed of more than half of the companies with certified claims (among them Coca-Cola, ITT, Borden, United Brands, Texaco, and Exxon), opposed the Helms-Burton bill for that reason. Some companies, which had changed their investment and property priorities since the early 1960s, were more interested in compensation for the expropriations, while others preferred to keep their rights of restitution intact once Cuba became an open market and a democratic state.[49] David Wallace, chairman of Lone Star, expressed special opposition to Title III on the basis that the bill would "clog U.S. courts and denigrate certified claims."[50]

Helms-Burton originated in part in Miami. In 1993, during meetings of the Cuban-American Bar Association, some members expressed dissatisfaction with the limitations of the Torricelli law. The issue arose of adapting a new Florida statute that granted the victims of theft the right (in addition to criminal proceedings) to sue in civil courts the buyers of stolen property for damages and restitution. Cuban-American lawyers suggested the same could be done in response to the expropriation of properties by the Castro government, particularly targeting foreign companies that were making use of confiscated assets. The local forum was expanded to panels organized by the American Bar Association, and finally the idea was presented coinciding in a timely manner with preparations for the 1994 Summit of the Americas in Miami, hosted by President Clinton and attended by all the Western Hemisphere heads of state except Fidel Castro.

The original idea was developed by Cuban-American lawyers who belonged to the Cuban-American National Foundation. They shared it with CANF chairman Jorge Mas Canosa, who adopted the concept as one of the top priorities of the organization. At the same time, the idea was shared with U.S. legislators, including Senator Helms, who enthusiastically endorsed it. Thus it happened that a coherent U.S. view of Latin America, expressed in a continuation of the Monroe Doctrine and the Platt Amendment, had found common ground with the economic elite of the Cuban-American community. One sector of the Cuban exiles (led by CANF) wanted to exploit the political dimensions of the U.S.-Cuba historical controversy. The second centered its energies on the issue of property: it aimed to obtain the support of the former owners in expectation of restitution or compensation. The stigma of the law as *plattista* (Platt-like) was thus balanced by the objective of the return of the properties. The text of Helms-Burton reflects the complex marriage of these three objectives, and presumably the same factor explains some of the law's internal contradictions.

Bacardí's name did not appear on the original list of certified claimants because at the time of the expropriations it was a Cuban firm (Compañía Ron Bacardí, S.A.), a majority of whose shareholders were Cuban citizens. Once they left Cuba, under international law they were not entitled to compensation other than that provided (or imposed) by the Cuban government on national companies. Subsequently, the enterprise was financially rebuilt and incorporated through a set of five companies (Bacardí-Martini of North America, Latin America, Asia Pacific, Europe, and Bacardí International), all under the umbrella of a holding incorporated in Bermuda (although they were subsequently entitled to U.S. tax write-offs).[51]

Bacardí-Martini of North America, as a U.S. company, has taken the lead in efforts at dealing with potential claims against the Cuban government; the multinational nature of the Bacardí holding apparently is not an obstacle for qualifying under the provisions of Title III. Bacardí did not qualify for a place on the U.S.-sponsored claims list originally prepared in the 1960s, but its attorneys consider that it does today under Title III, thanks to the expansion of the concept of nationality. The provisions of the law may have benefited most of the individual stockholders, as former Cuban citizens who are now U.S. citizens.

The company's involvement in sanctions legislation was not limited to the activities of some of its directors and legal advisers in influential exile organizations. Bacardí's interest in Helms-Burton is also related to two different rum products, the original Bacardí rum and another brand of rum, Havana Club, property of another company, which came under the control of the revolutionary government and was subsequently marketed by the

Corporación Cuba Ron.[52] When Cuban authorities crafted an alliance with France's Pernod-Ricard, the move alarmed Bacardí's corporate officers on two grounds. First, Bacardí saw its market share being threatened by the Cuban-French partnership. Some connoisseurs allege, for example, that Bacardí's quality is inferior to the original Cuban products (Havana Club and the original Bacardí). Additionally, in some countries a product that can be marketed as authentically Cuban has more appeal than an international-ized drink. Whatever the reasons, Bacardí's world sales had in fact dropped from 22.9 million cases in 1990 to 20 million in 1993. In 1995 the loss of sales was estimated as high as $25 million; this was largely attributed by the company to the economic problems of Mexico, a major market with an important distributor base. In any event, Title III would allow legal action against Pernod-Ricard, a company dealing with expropriated properties.

A second aspect of the confrontation between Bacardí and Pernod-Ricard arose from the fact that the Cuban government had registered the Havana Club trademark in the United States back in 1976. (The U.S.-imposed embargo, interestingly, allows the registration of Cuban trademarks in the United States, but not the importation of the products.) Then Bacardí began the initial marketing of its own Havana Club product in the United States. How was this possible, given the Cuban-French joint venture? Because the former owners of Havana Club, the heirs of the Arachabala family, had sold their rights in the company to Bacardí. In a bold move, in December 1996 the Cuban-French holding sued Bacardí and its distributors for infringement of trademark.[53] A New York federal court halted the Cuban legal action. The court decision did not consider to whom the original company and product belonged, but it advised both parties to refrain from using the word "original" and ordered Bacardí not to market the new made-in-the-U.S. product while they awaited a final court ruling. For Bacardí's attorneys this development was positive because they hoped that if they were successful in keeping Pernod's Havana Club out of the important U.S. territory, the French company would reconsider its investment, in the process slowing the erosion of international market share of Bacardí's products.[54]

The issue was resolved in October 1998, in the unlikely form of an attachment to the U.S. federal budget bill. Section 211 of the bill, a measure sponsored by Senators Connie Mack and Bob Graham of Florida and approved by Congress, allowed for the rejection of the protection in the United States of registered brands of companies that were expropriated by the Cuban government, a clear reference to the Bacardí claim. The fears of the Cuban government and its French partners, as well as the hopes of

Bacardí officials, were confirmed on April 14, 1999, when the New York court ruled in favor of Bacardí, thus allowing the company to make and market Havana Club rum in the United States.[55]

The Bacardí case is further complicated by the fact that the Cuban government has continued to authorize the registration of U.S. trademarks in Cuba. Enraged by the U.S. decision to let Bacardí produce Havana Club in the United States, Fidel Castro has threatened to produce clone imitations of well-known U.S. brands (soft drinks and sports equipment included), for consumption in Cuba with the potential for spillover into other markets. The possible damage to the image and integrity of these brands is immense.[56]

The battle over the right to make transnational variances of certain products may represent an alternative strategy to the uncertain provisions for restitution allowed by Helms-Burton. The compensation process prescribed by Title III (even if enacted) is arduous, and the monetary amount involved may never be known because of the suspension of this title. The law prescribes that, after a three-month period, the "traffickers" in properties confiscated by the Cuban government on or after January 1, 1959, could be liable to "any United States national who owns the claim to such property" for the following: "money damages in an amount equal to the sum of the amount which is the greater of the amount, if any, certified to the claimant by the Foreign Claims Settlement Commission under the International Claims Settlement Act of 1949, plus interest." This is a cumbersome, unpredictable process that may never satisfy the expectations of the former owners. Thus it is not surprising that some have elected other strategies.

It is not clear how the Bacardí company regards the avenues opened by Helms-Burton, given that Title III has not been implemented. While Bacardí is on record as one of the most active backers of the Helms-Burton legislation, in actuality the company has not been eager to enter the complicated arena of court procedures against "traffickers" in order to receive a compensation that would be worth far less than its ultimate aim: to return to the Cuban market. The company would also like to avoid the damage to public relations that would likely accompany any legal action. Winning battles with the current Cuban government and protecting the company's world market, however, are still very much part of the picture.

The Activation and Suspension of Title III

The time frame of the law included a schedule for activitation: August 1, 1996. However, a peculiar novelty of the final text of the law was that it would allow the president to activate a waiver of Title III, the most controversial part concerning foreign countries, but under certain (vague but difficult) conditions. According to Richard Nuccio, Congress wanted "to restrict the President's ability to exercise his waiver by insisting that it not merely meet the test of being 'in the national interest,' but also that 'it expedite a transition to democracy in Cuba'."[57] The language of the waiver was intended to make its implementation unusual and difficult, but that has been ignored by the White House. Commentators will forever speculate about why the legislators left a door open for the suspension of crucial aspects of the law, why they simultaneously passed a controversial measure and at the same time inserted an easy-to-use clause allowing the president to suspend it. One possible explanation is that legal advisors recommended the loophole in order to defuse the expected conflict with other nations over H-B's potential violation of international law. As subsequent chapters (especially chapter 5) will discuss, the presidential use of the clause can also be interpreted as an extra effort to win European support for the U.S. strategy of promoting a peaceful, democratic transition in Cuba.[58] Another interpretation is simply that the suspension clause was a compromise between Congress and the White House to keep the president's options open. Both parties, in this fashion, looked like winners.

In any case, what remains is the reality of the law—the president may suspend Title III for a period of not more than six months if he "determines and reports in writing to the appropriate congressional committees at least 15 days before such effective date that the suspension is necessary to the national interests of the United States and will expedite a transition to democracy in Cuba." This clause has been so effective that President Clinton has used it every semester since, with the result that its suspension has ceased to be news. In January 1999, the announcement of the renewal of the freezing measure was buried in stories about impeachment proceedings.[59]

Barring Foreign "Traffickers" from Entering the United States

For foreign companies, the second greatest irritant in Helms-Burton is Title IV, which deals with the "exclusion of certain aliens." Section 401 targets those who "have confiscated property of United States nationals or who traffic in such property." It stipulates that a visa will be denied to any foreigner who the secretary of state determines has "confiscated, or has directed or overseen the confiscation of, property a claim to which is owned by a United States national; or converts or has converted for personal gain confiscated property, a claim to which is owned by a United States national; traffics in confiscated property, a claim to which is owned by a United States national." The measure also bars "a corporate officer, principal, or shareholder with a controlling interest of an entity which has been involved in the confiscation of property or trafficking in confiscated property, a claim to which is owned by a United States national." Moreover, the punishment may be extended to "a spouse, minor child, or agent of a person excludable."

The Day After: Conclusion

International and Domestic Reaction

As is to be expected, many foreign governments, including traditional U.S. allies in the European Union, protested that the law is an "extraterritorial application of United States law" that "violates the sovereign prerogatives of foreign governments to regulate the commerce of their citizens with Cuba," and imposes a secondary boycott, potentially violating many provisions of international trade agreements administered by the World Trade Organization.[60] Complaining that the United States has no right to use its economic power to force other countries to comply with American foreign policy, the European Union filed complaints with the World Trade Organization (WTO). Moreover, European countries and Canada have enacted their own laws that would retaliate against American companies that won judgments in American courts under Helms-Burton provisions. Canada and Mexico, in particular, flatly rejected the Helms-Burton law as a means for achieving democracy in Cuba.

Following the enactment of the bill, important U.S. leaders spoke against its implementation. Senator Christopher Dodd (D-Connecticut), a steady critic of Republican-led U.S. policies toward Cuba, distinguished himself in warning against the consequences of the Helm-Burton Act. He considered the legislation "a direct attack on the citizens of some of our closest neighbors." He branded it a mistake "to deny entry into the United States of any individual in any way associated with questionable Cuban properties" because it was a "clear violation of our GATT and NAFTA commitments in this area." Addressing the most important issue, he lamented "the codification into law of all existing sanctions and regulations against Cuba. This completely ties the hands of this president and future presidents to respond flexibly to change in Cuba when it counts."[61] Former president Jimmy Carter stated: "It is one of the worst mistakes my country has ever made [because it means] obstruction to the democratization of Cuba [and] makes Castro look like a David."[62] Former New York Governor Mario M. Cuomo commented that the "U.S. should end the embargo against Cuba immediately."[63] In moderate circles of the Cuban-American exile community, observers feared that the measure would prove to be counterproductive. Summarizing this opinion, José Ignacio Rasco, president of the Christian Democratic Party in exile, declared that "the law has converted Castro into an international hero, [making him] a David facing Goliath, a distraction from the true Cuban problem, a problem between the government and the Cuban people, not between Washington and Havana."[64]

Political Commentaries and Recommendations

The complexity of Helms-Burton results from its diverse mix of objectives, including sanctions, compensation, sovereignty, and nation-building. Each of these provisions was crafted to please different constituencies and backers, and the result is what in the political jargon of Spain is called *pasteleo* (wishy-washy backroom deals), an unkind term for legislative compromise.

In the international sphere, the law lost important potential support for an issue on which a certain consensus might have existed: democracy and human rights. By mixing these laudable goals with provisions regarding "trafficking" and reparations, as well as efforts to dictate the nature of any new Cuban government, Helms-Burton failed to win foreign support or even the active endorsement of centrists in U.S. political circles. Instead, in fact, it has attracted the wrath of knowledgeable observers. Wayne Smith, for example, a U.S. diplomat who served twice in Cuba, has been one of the most vocal critics of Washington's policy.[65] Others have ventured sharp criticisms as well. A summary of the arguments offered by two articles published in London will serve to illustrate what are widely shared sentiments.

In one, Stephen Lisio warned that the United States was "testing the limits of international law," adding "it remains to be seen how far the United States is willing to jeopardize its diplomatic relations." For him the Helms-Burton Law is not simply a coercive measure affecting trade but may be rightly interpreted as a more serious aggression: "The conflict inherent in Helms-Burton lies in the issue of the sovereignty of U.S. allies in the conduct not simply of economic policy, but of foreign policy as well." He considers that "the tightened embargo is less likely to force Cuban dictator Fidel Castro from power and more likely to entangle the United States in a series of retaliatory exchanges with its allies in both bilateral and multilateral fora . . . the U.S. attempt to dictate the economic and foreign policies of its allies is misguided." Regarding the law's intent to foster democratization in Cuba, the author remarks: "the tightening of the embargo is inconsistent with the U.S. interest of promoting peaceful transition to democracy in Cuba." Moreover, "the most critical shortcoming of Helms-Burton is that it does not constitute an effective tool with which to promote democracy [and the] embargo may be more counterproductive to the cause of democracy." In sum, the law "goes beyond the point of diminishing returns by compromising the very U.S. interest it purports to achieve: the peaceful transition in Cuba." The main problem is the widening of the gap between the Cuban process and the U.S. goals, because the new measures "could ultimately weaken the U.S. influence over a situation in which it has, for the past 36 years, exercised minimal control." The law seems not to take notice of the international political changes in recent years, because it "is inconsistent with post–Cold War U.S. policy of reconciliation with its former communist adversaries."[66]

For his part, William LeoGrande considered that the economic impact of Helms-Burton on Cuba was "likely to be much more circumscribed." At the same time, reflecting on the codification of U.S. policy, he believed that the law destroyed "Clinton's policy of 'calibrated response' developed after the Cuban refugee crisis by eliminating the president's ability to respond positively to anything except the fall of the Castro government." In view of the law's challenges to U.S. allies, "convincing Europe and Latin America to cooperate will take formidable diplomatic skills." The basic problem is that Clinton had got off on precisely "the wrong foot by using the threat of Helms-Burton to try to coerce the allies into conformity with U.S. policy." However, he did create an opportunity for foreign initiative: "perhaps the Europeans and Latin Americans, less burdened by the ideological baggage of the Cold War and the vocal exile community, will have better luck bringing Cuba in from the Cold." He ended up with a blunt assessment: "They can't do any worse."[67]

3

Lawyers Meet the Law

U.S. Voices Critical of Helms-Burton

Anybody who trades with confiscated property is an accomplice or a thief.
Representative Dan Burton, 1995

If a nation shows that it knows how to act with reasonable efficiency and decency . . . it need fear no interference from the United States. Chronic wrongdoing, or an impotence which results in a general loosening of the ties of civilized society, may in America, or elsewhere, ultimately require intervention by some civilized nation, and in the Western Hemisphere the adherence of the United States to the Monroe Doctrine may force the United States, however reluctantly, in flagrant cases of such wrongdoing or impotence, to the exercise of an international police power.
Roosevelt Corollary, 1904

The Legal Resistance

Some critics initially characterized the Helms-Burton Law as a "full employment for lawyers act." But if the anticipated rush to litigation has been forestalled by President Clinton's repeated suspension of its provisions, the preparation of the bill did produce noticeable activity in law firms in the expectation of court suits and countersuits.[1] The law has also provided an opportunity for students and legal scholars to study one of the most peculiar creations of the U.S. Congress: Its impact has been visible in the realm of scholarly and professional publications.[2]

Early Warnings

In the months following the enactment of the law, the pages of the legal periodicals anticipated what the scholarly journals would later generate. The *New York Law Journal* and the *Los Angeles Daily Journal*, among other publications, offered representative points of view on Helms-Burton, with an emphasis on critical assessment.[3] While some commentators were adamant in defending the conditions imposed on Cuba and others were cautious,[4] most writers were negative. They unleashed an early warning about the international reactions.[5]

Setting the tone of most of his colleagues, Anthony Solís called Helms-Burton simply a "bad law" and a "dangerous precedent" that would "undermine the confidence in the international legal order."[6] Luisette Gierbolini, perhaps one of the most forthright critics of the law and its possible consequences, titled her article "Inconsistency with International Law and Irrationality at Their Maximum."[7] Legal scholars Theodor Meron and Detlev F. Vagts bluntly concluded a short note in the *American Journal of International Law*: "We urge that, in the interest of keeping the United States in compliance with international law and avoiding unnecessary tensions with our closest allies in Europe and the Americas, President Clinton again exercise the authority to suspend the provisions of the Act."[8] These experts were not alone.

Juridical Dissection

The various legal analyses express similar criticisms, the most important of which concern the potential violations of international treaties and law, the implications derived from U.S. domestic and constitutional law, and the consequences for judicial procedure.

On the Cuban expropriations, the main topics center first on the Cuban properties that were taken by the revolutionary government and the lack of monetary compensation. As a result of this, claimants have expected appropriate restitution to be a final result of the embargo. The second issue related to the expropriations is the process for identifying claimants and the issue of what should be the citizenship status of the former owners in order to bring suit in U.S. courts. Third, scholarly attention has been given to the nature of foreign investment and the interpretation of the term "trafficking."

With respect to domestic consequences, issues of concern are, first, the constitutionality of the law regarding trade and travel. Second, and more importantly, commentators raise the question of the codification of U.S. foreign policy with respect to Cuba. Experts also warn about the implications of Helms-Burton for international relations. The fundamental issues concern the extraterritorial nature of the law and the alleged violation of international treaties and agreements signed by the United States. As will be discussed later in this chapter, the violation of the state doctrine, the sidetracking of the "estoppel" concept in interpreting the citizenship of claimants, and the application of extraterritoriality constitute a basis for claiming that the Helms-Burton law violates international law. While the state doctrine guarantees that jurisdictional borders are properly respected as far as citizenship goes, the estoppel concept in fact inserts a correction when a violation of long-established legal tradition has been detected.

On Property and Citizenship

"Trafficking" with "Stolen" Property

The jurists who endorse the Helms-Burton Law have based their arguments largely on the evidence that compensation claims for properties nationalized in revolutionary processes normally have low prospects of ever being satisfied. This problem is not confined solely to the case of Cuba. Distinguishing himself as one of a small number of backers of the law, Bacardí's attorney Brice Clagett has denounced the general lack of enforcement of existing compensation procedures. Due to "notorious weakness and ineffectiveness of international enforcement mechanisms" and "because the jurisdiction of international tribunals is consensual, it is only rarely that a confiscation case can be brought in such a forum," notes Clagett. Hence, "espousal of claims by the victims' government can take generations to bear any fruit."[9] A likely complication in this case is that both the U.S. and Cuban governments can be said to share some responsibility for the impasse over the expropriations issue. The United States never agreed to the initial vague and limited conditions offered by Cuba and the Castro government in turn has been adamant in presenting counterclaims relating to the monetary damage inflicted by the U.S. embargo on the Cuban economy.

In any event, with the Helms-Burton opening to claims potentially presented by Cuban-Americans, scholars have pointed out two main aspects directly emanating from the explicitly stated (punitive and compensatory) monetary objectives of the law. The first is that, in principle, the potential object of contention is huge: "all properties on the island with which the government of Cuba is involved in some way are subject to suit."[10] With virtually no private property of any real value, any attempt to deal with any portion of the Cuban economy is subject to legal procedures involving the Cuban government. The second item is the fact that the law rests, in Lowenfeld's opinion, "too much on expropriated property."[11] As the discussion in this chapter has shown, the political and economic climate in a Cuba in transition would demand special attention from the U.S. government with a different set of priorities: "I cannot imagine that the United States would wait until all the property issues were sorted out before offering assistance of all kinds." His other concern is the fact that these properties can be traced back at least two generations, and successory rights are also subject to interpretation under two different legal systems.[12]

When they elected to use the loaded term "trafficking," with its connotations of "unethical," "criminal," and "illegal," legislators clearly meant to describe what in normal circumstances are routine commercial transactions. The word has not only irritated foreign interests, it has also alarmed legal commentators. Andreas Lowenfeld notes that "trafficking" is "a word heretofore applied in legislation almost exclusively to dealing in narcotics."[13] The problem is that almost any commercial activity in Cuba can in principle be considered "trafficking" and could be affected by the implementation of Helms-Burton, a fact that has foreign lawyers alarmed.[14]

As Lowenfeld pointedly denounced, the application of the guidelines developed and observed by the U.S. legal community is not acceptable in this case. The authors of Helms-Burton included this crucial statement in the findings: "International law recognizes that a nation has the ability to provide for rules of law with respect to conduct outside its territory that has or is intended to have substantial effect within its territory" (section 301[9]). This is an almost direct quote from the guidelines of the *Restatement (Third) of Foreign Relations Law of the United States*. Developed by the American Law Institute, the restatement is "meant to serve as an impartial recitation of international law," and "it represents the opinion of that institute as to the rules that an impartial tribunal would apply if charged with deciding a controversy in accordance with international law."[15]

The application of this specific guideline in this case is, in the words of Lowenfeld, "fundamentally flawed" because it misses one added condition: "Even when one of the bases for jurisdiction is present, a state may not exercise jurisdiction to prescribe law with respect to a person or activity having connections with another state when the exercise of such jurisdiction is unreasonable" (section 402[1]). The key point is that effect of the damage was caused *by the government of Cuba*, not by the "persons over whom jurisdiction is sought to be exercised." In other words, critics point out that the United States is punishing foreign companies out of frustration because it is unable to obtain any results derivating from the long embargo imposed on Cuba. Therefore, to impose U.S. policies in such a case is considered as "unreasonable by any standard."[16]

Regarding the amount of compensation that can be expected for the expropriated properties, there is a real possibility that the monetary expectations may be considered unreasonable by legal standards and thus undermine the success of the legal process. As one scholar put it, investors may find that "the choice is between an ice cream [resuming business in Cuba] and a root canal treatment [expensive court suits and loss of business in the United States]." It is for this reason that "the proponents are fairly confident that persons who contemplate investing in Cuba will change their minds."[17] That this is in fact one of the unstated motives of the law is an opinion shared by proponents and critics alike.

Even backers of the law recognize that its measures are punitive rather than compensatory in nature. However, "even assuming that it could be proven that the damages are not truly compensatory and that the act reaches persons only tangentially involved in the targeted trafficking," attorneys who justify the law predict that the remedy conferred would not "approach the level necessary to be disproportionate for due process purposes."[18]

In any event, Brice Clagett argues that the controversial Title III does "no injustice to the 'traffickers' because they are fully aware that they are dealing in 'tainted' property . . . dealing in stolen goods . . . and therefore they are taking a risk."[19] Clagett also observes that "international human rights law recognizes that, at least in certain circumstances, a state violates international law when it confiscates the property not only of aliens but of its own citizens." One of the reasons for Title III, he claims, is the "premise that international law in all cases forbids a state to confiscate the property of its nationals without just compensation." The endorsers of Helms-Burton even blame the home states of companies dealing with expropriated properties in Cuba because "confiscation" is a violation of international law.[20]

Citizenship: An Expanded Concept

Perhaps the most controversial aspect of Helms-Burton, and at the same time its most fascinating legal issue, relates to the fact that the pool of potential plaintiffs has been significantly widened. The law opened a Pandora's box with respect to a potential new definition of effective citizenship. It allows Cubans who have become U.S. nationals recourse to the U.S. courts in order to redress damages that occurred *before* they obtained U.S. citizenship. From the beginning, some Cuban-American scholars expressed considerable concern for this provision. For example, as the bill was being discussed in Congress, Ernesto Betancourt, a former director of Radio Martí, spoke at a conference of Cuban economists in exile:

Castro has been holding sessions throughout the island to raise fear among people that their house and land may be subject to reclamation from those Cubans who have become American citizens after their properties were seized. Without denying the legitimate desire of former owners to regain the holdings, not only for economic reasons but in many cases for sentimental reasons involving childhood and family memories, the question that should be put to them is: if your offering to renounce your claim could encourage the end of the Castro regime, would you insist in getting it back? Perhaps Cubans have changed a lot, but the history of the last decades shows that the much maligned Cuban-American and exile community has been capable of reacting with generosity and willingness to forgive whenever faced with crisis.[21]

Robert Freer, a lawyer and a general counsel for the U.S.-Cuba Business Council, a participant in the same conference, presented a detailed and persuasive defense of most of the points of the law. Nevertheless, he was adamant regarding extension of the privileges of nationality: "The U.S. has both a responsibility to initiate advances in international law on the one hand [and] to be careful not to 'break the crockery' on the other."[22] Freer acknowledged that the U.S. legal tradition supports the notion that "if a man steals from another and a third party knowingly and intentionally takes advantage of that theft to receive or beneficially use the fruits of the theft, that person would be as guilty of that theft as the original perpetrator."[23] However, while stating that Helms-Burton filled a vacuum in international law, Freer was not so sure about its possible consequences:

[B]y allowing individuals who were not citizens of the U.S. at the time their loss occurred to take advantage of this privilege, it deviates from the norm. Those who favor this extension suggest that the action created is not a remedy for the "theft" that occurred when they weren't citizens years ago, but rather for the "trafficking" that is occurring now when they are citizens and entitled to equal access to our courts.[24]

Echoing the Cuban-American sentiment, Freer continued, "I am sympathetic to this plea, but . . . I question as a matter of policy whether it is worth the potential disadvantage to all of us, including Cuban-Americans, in our world-wide trading arrangements, should this notion of a remedy for post-confiscation nationals gain wider acceptance."[25]

Robert Muse, an attorney vocal in opposing Helms-Burton, had earlier warned that similar "constitutional arguments will be advanced by other national-origin groups."[26] In fact, U.S. law offers no such retroactive privilege to former citizens of other countries or regions (for example, Palestinians, Eastern Europeans, Vietnamese). The precedent established by Helms-Burton is an open invitation to lawsuits charging discrimination based on ethnic or national origin. On a more concrete level, Muse points out, the original 5,911 certified claimants "will see their claims diluted to meaninglessness by virtue of thousands of Cuban American judgments entered against Cuba in the U.S. federal courts."[27]

The potential for numerous and lengthy court proceedings has been high because Title III permits all individuals or companies with expropriated properties worth at least U.S.$50,000 in 1960 (about $150,000 today) to become plaintiffs. To some observers this figure, set by Congress, is purposely high, and suggests the influence of some important wealthy former owners in the law's passage. Some have noted that the number of claims is likely to rise further if the law considers the fair value of the confiscated properties with interest added. Altogether, approximately 400,000 Cuban-Americans may be entitled to bring lawsuits.[28] In contrast, only about 300 U.S. companies or individuals could benefit from this law, because, of the 5,911 originally registered U.S. claimants, only a few could meet the figure.[29] Some attorneys argue that a class-action suit may be a way to press these claims,[30] although the cost of litigation would likely be a significant impediment for individual plaintiffs. It is estimated that an effective legal action would cost each claimant between $20,000 and $25,000.[31]

Facing a U-Turn: The Principle of Estoppel

Jurists of all kinds of training recognize that "the nationality of claims principle is a rule of customary international law."[32] This universally accepted principle implies that a state has jurisdiction over its own citizens and therefore extends its legal protection over them for actions inflicted on them while they were citizens of that state, not before they became citizens. However, because the legislators who drafted Helms-Burton seemed to wish to obtain as much sympathy as possible, they added, in a retroactive fashion, another dimension to the already loaded problem of the political objective of the law (the end of the Cuban regime). In the words of Robert Muse, "in order to achieve a foreign policy objective," Helms-Burton has "violated the nationality of claims principle of public international law."[33] It extended the protection of U.S. law to current U.S. citizens for actions that took place before they became citizens.

In fact, in terms of recent history Helms-Burton is an aberration. After the passage of the International Claims Settlement Act of 1949, the claims commission has never been required by Congress to violate international law by considering the claims of non-nationals at the time of the expropriation of property.[34] Until now, Robert Muse notes, "Congress and the Executive Branch have been in consistent accord in rejecting the inclusion of claims of anyone other than U.S. nationals at the time of loss."[35] What both the White House and Congress may not have understood is that by adhering to this policy, they were setting legal precedents that would render legally void any future actions in contradiction of those principles. This is because of the legal principle of estoppel, applicable both in international and domestic law.

Thus, while the United States may claim that it is not legally bound by international agreements on grounds of national security, or because it feels compelled to redress the injustice of expropriations, a well-established legal principle works against this logic. The United States is—to use the legal terms—estopped from adding Cuban-Americans who were not U.S. citizens at the time of the expropriations onto the list of those qualified to file suit under an activated Title III. Why is this? Because this action would contradict the estoppel principle.

Estoppel applies when a person acts as though certain facts exist upon which another person takes action. The first person cannot later deny these facts. The estoppel derives originally from municipal law and it is also known as "preclusion" in civil law. Applied to international law, estoppel is a restraint upon a state that in the past has declared and carried out actions in conformity with a given position, and then seeks to take action contrary to these precedents. Because international law can only succeed and be respected if it is based on good faith, contradictory behavior is considered a violation. Members of the international community cannot easily accept that a well-established doctrine exercised by a state is suddenly and unilaterally considered void. Such a situation can only create confusion and the loss of mutual good faith. A party can invoke estoppel "when induced to undertake legally relevant action or abstain from it by relying in good faith upon clear and unambiguous representation by another State."[36] The International Court of Justice has insisted on that need: "The primary foundation of this principle is the good faith that must prevail in international relations, in as much as inconsistency of conduct or opinions on the part of a state to the prejudice of another is incompatible with good faith."[37] The doctrine dictates that a "representing party is barred ('Estopped' or precluded) from adopting successfully different subsequent statements on the same issue,"[38] as Judge Spenser said in one classic case (*Temple of Preah Vihear*): "The principle operates to prevent a State contesting before the Court a situation contrary to a clear and unequivocal representation previously made by it to another state."[39] In the recent past, in cases not involving Cuban-Americans, the United States has opposed the expansion of protection of claims to persons who were not citizens at the time of their loss. All branches of the U.S. government are on record in complying with this rule. The president, Congress, and the courts were "undeviating in their adherence to the nationality of claims principle of international law."[40] Thus, while the sudden inclusion of Cuban-Americans in the pool of potential plaintiffs is a pleasant surprise for them, it is also "nothing less that an act of bad faith on the part of the U.S. in its relations with other nations and it is, as matter of international law, estopped from lending support to such claims."[41]

Lawyers also apply the estoppel concept to challenge claims that the expropriations violated international human rights law. The recent U.S. legal tradition in this field rests on the guidelines of the American Law Institute known as *Restatement (Third) of the Foreign Relations Law of the United States* of 1984. The list of acts that justify a change in an established legal pattern are the following: genocide, slavery, murder, disappearance, torture, prolonged arbitrary detention, systematic racial discrimination, and gross violations of internationally recognized human rights. Opponents to Helms-Burton claim that the list does not include "deprivations of property."[42]

In any event, the debate can be maintained for as long as the contenders find new grounds for their arguments, either on the basis of national security, ethics, or violations of human rights. Innocently one may ask: "What is wrong with Congress bestowing a U.S. federal lawsuit right on individuals and companies who, it must be emphasized, were Cuban citizens that had properties in Cuba taken by the government of Cuba pursuant to the laws of Cuba?" Muse answers his own question: "The short answer is that international law forbids it."[43] He continues, "The principle of international law that eligibility for compensation requires American nationality at the time of loss is so widely understood and universally accepted that citation of authority is scarcely necessary."[44] In contrast to the Helms-Burton authors, Muse is precise: "May the United States provide support to the claims of non-nationals? The answer is unequivocal: NO."[45]

Brice Clagett defends the "expanded citizenship" bestowed on Cuban-Americans, claiming that the former Cuban citizens are now U.S. nationals and therefore "to the extent they are citizens, the prejudice to them has a substantial effect on the United States."[46] This logic seems to be an interpretation of the concept of "espousal." Derived from the notion of "espouse," it implies a similar meaning to marrying or adopting someone, as in sharing privileges with or extending protection to someone who originally was not entitled to them. However, critics of Helms-Burton point out that in order to be legally acceptable, the concept of espousal needs to meet certain requirements: U.S. nationality of the claimant, continuous ownership, wrongful act caused by damage to or loss of property, reasonable proof of the value of the loss, exhaustion of all local remedies, and negation of anticipated defenses. This is obviously a set of conditions that Cuban-Americans cannot easily meet.[47]

Some backers of the legislation are confident that the law is fair and that it would stand in court. They are even concerned that Cuban-Americans may file suit against the two-year waiting period required for entering their cases in court. Some lawyers may be tempted to claim that the Helms-Burton Law discriminates against Cuban-Americans for making them wait a longer period than other former owners who were citizens at the time of the expropriations. In any event, Álvarez-Mena and Crane consider that Cuban-Americans "will have a difficult time proving that the two-year waiting period is based on ethnicity."[48]

While defenders of the law do not dwell on this issue, others believe that widening the concept of citizenship served to increase the constituency supporting the Helms-Burton legislation. Indeed, it appears that the bill needed all the Cuban-American help that it could amass. Briefing the U.S. Senate, attorney Ignacio Sánchez stated: "inclusion of Cuban-Americans is imperative to accomplish the foreign policy goals."[49] Ironically, an additional effect of the law either was sought by the legislators or it was a welcome by-product. In any case, the widening of the pool has not only increased the potential number of claimants, it also "invites more Cubans to become citizens."[50] And while backers of the law may be satisfied with the prospect, a spectacular increase of legal suits could clog the court system, resulting in considerable delays in reaching judgments. Paradoxically, this would undermine the swift resolution of claims sought by Clagett. In sum, when more Cuban refugees become citizens, and more are induced to sue, their chances of receiving compensation are reduced. However, we should not lose sight of the real aim of the law. This was to discourage foreign investments in Cuba in order to produce an economic deterioration that would accelerate the end of the Castro regime. This would guarantee the implementation of the rules of Title II for a new Cuban political system that would permit the full suspension of the embargo.

On Codes and States

Tampering with the Constitution

The constitutionality of Helms-Burton remains to be tested in court, and until that happens the matter is only a topic for speculation. Critics hope that someday a high court will declare the law unconstitutional; supporters deny that its constitutionality is in serious question. They accept that the law may be controversial, but argue that it does not substantially depart from numerous federal precedents.[51] The reality, in any event, is that the law as it exists today is only valid at a political level, and has exerted only limited influence through its economic consequences. Title III remains suspended and Title IV has been invoked just a few times for purposes of denying visas, so that until a court acts or until the president (perhaps a Republican) decides not to bar its implementation the law is a ghost.

As happened with respect to previous legislation concerning the embargo against Cuba, critics have targeted the limitations imposed on U.S. citizens. Helms-Burton, they charge, "perverts immigration and travel laws."[53] Specifically, they allege that Section 102 violates the Constitution's Fifth Amendment, which guarantees freedom of travel to all U.S. citizens.

A related issue, also controversial, is the law's threat to deny U.S. entry visas to individuals and their families who are employed by companies that "traffick in" expropriated properties. It is widely accepted that any state has the right to regulate its borders in the way it deems fit. While governments are exercising their sovereignty when they impose requirements for legal immigration and tourist visits, at least two issues may lead to challenges to the law's constitutionality. The first is the connection between the denial of visas and the international commitments of the United States. For example, Canada and the United States were already bound by pre-NAFTA free-trade commitments. The denial of visas to Canadian executives may violate this treaty, which is constitutionally binding. In turn, American interests whose constitutional rights have been violated by being denied access to Canadian resources may have valid grounds for legal action against the U.S. government.

Then there is the fact that the visa provisions are part of a legal text that, as a whole, may violate international law. In other words, a simple administrative restriction that in normal circumstances may be not only legal but reasonable (the denial of visas for various reasons) may in the context of Helms-Burton be a violation. Thus, the visa provision may be ruled unconstitutional because it is part of a statute that violates international law, which is legally binding on the U.S. government.[53]

However, critics may have even better grounds for claiming the unconstitutionality of the law when studying the most basic aspects of the text and its most explicit objectives.

Codifying the Embargo

Its backers and opponents agree on at least one thing—that Helms-Burton is unique, a "codification of U.S. foreign policy."[54] Moreover, the Helms-Burton Law has imposed a foreign policy goal on the U.S. court system. Critics alleged that this is a violation of the separation-of-powers doctrine and an unprecedented restriction upon the right of the president to conduct foreign policy. Additionally, the law elevates a transitory foreign policy objective to the status of federal law. It forces the president to seek the consent of Congress to modify the requirements of the embargo, and makes its abrogation conditional upon the establishment of democracy in Cuba, the political disappearance of Castro himself, and the rebirth of a market economy.

Even though the president can suspend the implementation of Title III for six months at a time, the political character of the law renders it easily manipulable. For example, even when a political change takes place in Cuba, the law's requirements may not be met if the ensuing reforms are slow and gradual, or if the details are not to the liking of the backers of the law. Lowenfeld states: "freezing the details of a program of economic denial as of a given date is unwise. I do not go so far as to say it is unconstitutional, but it does impair the ability of the President to conduct foreign relations."[55] He further warns that the Helms-Burton Law "hampers the discretion of the executive branch" and "it purports to micromanage a transition whose contours no one can predict."[56]

Other scholars signal that this is a case of "growing domestication of American foreign policy." Perhaps this is a sign that "foreign affairs may no longer be different" from other policy areas, John Yoo observes, but the real danger is the "injection of adversarial legalism into the foreign policy decision-making process."[57] Specialists predict that "with the continued passage of increasingly bold extraterritorial legislation, the judiciary will be less and less able to maintain a passive role in foreign affairs."[58] As a consequence, the dilemma is "whether turning the federal courts into weapons of foreign policy ultimately is in the nation's interests."[59]

Some experts are unequivocal on this issue. According to Lowenfeld, "Congress wants to use the courts as instruments in furthering its own foreign policy objectives . . . [and] this is an unhealthy development."[60] Solís concurred : "executing foreign policy via U.S. courts is both an abuse of the judicial process and an unwise precedent."[61]

On the other side of the debate, Álvarez-Mena and Crane, who are among the minority of lawyers who justify the law's weakening of presidential power, argue that "the separation of federal powers, as they relate to foreign affairs, is by no means a well-settled question." In their view, and "unlike the War Powers Act . . . Helms-Burton deals only with areas in which Congress and the President share concurrent power." Álvarez and Crane prefer to believe that the president is empowered to conduct foreign affairs, but "he does not hold exclusive power to formulate foreign policy." The difference is subtle: "The President has power to administer, but not necessarily to formulate, foreign policy." Following the logic of Helms-Burton, then, "directing the President to pursue particular policy objectives pursuant to the United States' existing treaties seems to be an entirely reasonable exercise of congressional power." This is justified because "the Supreme Court has yet to draw many of the boundary lines between Presidential and Congressional powers in foreign affairs, and because the Constitution itself is relatively silent on these issues." However, a confrontation between the executive and the legislative powers, something that has not yet happened, is unpredictable. Álvarez and Crane think that it is "impossible to state for certain that Helms-Burton would survive a challenge of the sort raised by the State Department."[62]

Still, what jurists and political commentators have focused on is the extraordinary precedent in U.S. domestic law of the president handing a major foreign-policy decision to Congress. In contrast, the Torricelli law, at least, provided for "carefully calibrated responses" in lifting the embargo. The Helms-Burton Law, if fully implemented, does not offer this flexibility.

Detecting the Real Purpose of Helms-Burton

Focusing on the possible violation of U.S. law, the scholarly consensus is, with a few exceptions,[63] very critical of the constitutionality of the Helms-Burton Law. This criticism is based on the political objectives of the law taking precedence over juridical and commercial concerns. Some of the most concrete criticisms are blunt and direct.

For most, Helms-Burton is a "foreign policy exercise disguised as jurisprudence."[64] Solís characterizes it as "little more than foreign policy adorned with the legal equivalent to the emperor's clothes."[65] Critics can find little to praise in the bill: "Perhaps all this could be forgiven if the Helms-Burton Act could really bring about liberty and democracy in Cuba [but] I see no reason to believe that it will do so."[66]

It is clear to all that the aim of Helms-Burton is, as Lowenfeld puts it, to "deter nationals of third countries from doing business with and investing in Cuba."[67] The principal objective is not, despite its being touted for political purposes, "to compensate investors hurt by the Cuban revolution, but to affect the behavior of persons in third countries."[68] British attorney Nick Mallett advises prospective clients that the point is to "create a psychological perception that to do business with Cuba will subject a non-U.S. business person to claims in the U.S. and denial of a U.S. entry visa."[69] But some commentators consider this as a positive measure. Saturnino Lucio remarks that the "U.S. appears to have drawn a 'line in the sand' against Cuba and has now explicitly required foreign persons to essentially choose between the United States and Cuba," with the hope that "these foreign persons will prefer to maintain their ties to the United States and consequently foreign investment in Cuba will cease or substantially decline."[70] In any event, from a European point of view, the objective of discouraging investment is, according to Altozano, already accomplished, "just by publishing the law."[71] However, American scholars predict failure as far as the ultimate stated goal is concerned—the fall of the Castro regime. As Lowe puts it, "The lesson apparently inferred from this is that if 36 years of sanctions have proved ineffective to change the Castro regime, we must have more. The wisdom of that policy is not self-evident."[72]

A Thorny Issue: Extraterritoriality

Both critics and supporters of Helms-Burton acknowledge that, in effect, it extends the reach of U.S. courts to cover actions that take place beyond the American borders. Extraterritoriality has been a battle word ever since the passing of the Torricelli law. That Helms-Burton seeks to enforce conformity with U.S. law outside of normal U.S. jurisdictions is so obvious that it has not been contested by the law's supporters, who have also been unapologetic about this dimension of the law. But for Lowenfeld, as for most experts, this is an obvious case of a "classical secondary boycott,"[73] which is contrary to international law because it seeks unreasonably to force conduct that takes place outside of the state willing to exercise its jurisdiction. The aims of the Helms-Burton Law are clear: "it seeks to impose American policy judgments on nationals of friendly foreign states in a manner that is both unlawful and unwise."[74] International observers perceive the same problem. In the words of Vaughn Lowe, "the United States is usurping the rights of foreign States when it legislates for conduct of foreign persons in foreign countries."[75]

Any legislation that seeks its own implementation across national borders is bound to conflict with the issue of state doctrine. As Solís notes, the doctrine "precludes U.S. courts from inquiring into the validity of public acts that a recognized sovereign power has committed within its own territory."[76] A hundred years ago the U.S. Supreme Court inaugurated its long tradition of adherence to this doctrine with the milestone case *Underhill v. Hernández.*[77] The court's ruling concluded: "Every sovereign state is bound to respect the independence of every other sovereign state, and the courts of one country will not sit in judgment on acts of the government of another done within its own territory." David de Falco concludes that Helms-Burton "violates international law because it does not have a legally accepted basis on which it may apply extraterritorially to acts by foreign nationals on foreign soil."[78]

A basic principle of international law is that if a state acts illegally according to international law, the injured parties cannot initially place the matter before international tribunals, but must first file claims in the state where the damage was done. If this procedure fails to obtain satisfactory results, plaintiffs may then ask their own state to file a complaint against the violator at the international level.[79] Helms-Burton is a shortcut for an established grievance procedure that has never been implemented in the case of Cuba.

In the landmark case of *Banco Nacional de Cuba v. Sabbatino,*[80] the U.S. Supreme Court declined to apply the state doctrine to cases that may violate international law. For this reason, Congress passed the Hickenlooper Amendment to the Foreign Assistance Act of 1961, which permits courts to deny the application of the state doctrine if U.S. properties were taken in apparent violation of international law. Backers of Helms-Burton were understandably eager to use this proviso in their favor. Just in case, Congress was also seeking further guarantees to ensure the implementation of the measure.

The Helms-Burton legislators attempted to protect themselves by declaring that the courts would not be able to apply the state doctrine and would be obliged to decline action if suits were filed based on it. As Lowe observes, Congress "does not trust the executive branch, and it does not trust the judicial branch."[81] Susan Long adds, "Title III still presents constitutional problems since it expressly requires U.S. courts to disregard the Act of State Doctrine. Such a provision runs in the face of the U.S. Constitution's framework regarding separation of powers and the power of the Executive and Legislative branch to have a final say regarding foreign affairs."[82]

Backers of Helms-Burton respond to critics that the extraterritoriality provisions are justified by the U.S. legal tradition of the restatement. Section 402 of the *Restatement (Third) of Foreign Relations Law of the United States* indicates that some extraterritoriality is permissible. Legislators and scholars who favor Helms-Burton claim that the expropriations and other actions of the Cuban government have had a detrimental impact on the territory of the United States. For this reason the application of extraterritoriality may be reasonable. Critics reply that while the Cuban government caused the injury, the punishment is directed at foreign corporations. Meanwhile, the Castro government, the real culprit, is not legally affected.[83]

Lawyers defending Helms-Burton admit that "Congress intended Helms-Burton to apply extraterritorially" because its aim is to prosecute anyone who "trafficks" in confiscated property. They claim that "the Supreme Court has never suggested that the Constitution imposes any limit upon extraterritorial statutes," even though the Ninth Circuit has declared some limits. However, "in the vast majority of cases there will be some slight link to the United States so as to satisfy even the dictates of the Ninth Circuit."[84]

Regarding the effects of Cuban actions on the United States, Clagett argues,

Because of the proximity of Cuba to the United States and the history of relations between the two countries, Cuba's persistence in suppressing democracy, violating human rights and refusing to satisfy international law claims against it has substantial impact on the United States in a variety of ways, including the recurring crisis caused by the flight of refugees. The United States has legitimate interests in [seeking to bring] these problems to an end. It has reasonably concluded that discouraging foreign investment in tainted Cuban property is an appropriate and proportionate means toward that goal.[85]

Agreements and Conventions: Violation of International Law

In a statement summarizing the judgments of expert observers, Meron and Vagts comment, "While there are divisions among American international lawyers as to whether they [Helms-Burton and Congress] violate international law, there seems to be general agreement—which we share—among foreign governments and publicists that they do."[86] The risk of violating international law was so obvious that high-ranking U.S. officials warned about it from the start. During the first term of the Clinton administration, as the president resisted endorsing the bill, the Secretary of State recommended that he veto it.

Foreign experts have pointed out Helms-Burton's potential violations of Article 2.1 of the United Nations charter and Resolution 2625 (XXV) of the General Assembly, regarding principles of international law.[87] The Helms-Burton Law may also be in conflict with the decision of the International Court of Justice via its judgment of June 27, 1986, related to the confrontation between the United States and Nicaragua.[88]

The International Monetary Fund (IMF) and the World Bank (WB), the twin institutions created at Bretton Woods, are also affected, because the Helms-Burton Law provides that if any financial institution approves a loan or other assistance to Cuba, the U.S. government is ordered to withhold payment of a corresponding amount. This is a violation of articles 8 and 9 of the IMF and articles 6 and 10 of WB regulations.[89] Articles 2 and 11 of the Inter-American Development Bank (IDB) regulations are violated on the same grounds. Helms-Burton also runs counter to the juridical and trade principles of the NAFTA agreement, especially Articles 1105 and 1603 and possibly 309.

Finally, the operations of the General Agreement on Tariffs and Trade (GATT) and the World Trade Organization (WTO) are affected by the U.S.

decision. Article 11 of GATT would permit various challenges on the basis of curtailing commerce. Moreover, Washington's announced use of Helms-Burton in defense of national security threatens GATT protections of the multilateral trading system. Experts argue that "Helms-Burton uses ambiguous language to discourage foreign business relationships with Cuba." Therefore, potential GATT challenges to the law would include "denial of most-favored nation treatment under Article I and denial of national treatment under Article III. Finally, even if the United States maintains that Cuba is a national security threat, Helms-Burton does not counter this threat in a proportional way."[90]

Supporters of Helms-Burton respond to these concerns by arguing that "the U.S. did not relinquish its sovereignty when it signed international agreements, such as NAFTA and GATT."[91] U.S. government officials in their limited public discussions justified Helms-Burton's provisions on the basis of the expropriations undertaken by Cuba almost four decades ago. David Kaye, representing the State Department, defended the law by saying, "it still remains to be shown that international law contains any principle or rule that would deny the United States the right to create such a domestic civil remedy." For Washington, there are still "good reasons" to justify Helms-Burton: "mass nationalization of property of foreign nationals, carried out in a discriminatory manner, without the provision of an effective domestic remedy to obtain compensation and without the willingness to provide compensation in a negotiated settlement."[92]

A Price to Pay: Consequences

The Political Cost

As we have seen, the Helms-Burton Law has attracted the attention not only of political analysts but also of legal experts. Significantly, both groups concur in their emphasis on the political consequences of the law.

Vaughn Lowe is clear in summarizing the issue: "Problems will continue as long as States persist in using businesses as tools of an over-reaching foreign policy, and do so in a manner which displays a cavalier indifference to the constraints of the rules of international law."[93] Lawyers forced to become foreign-policy analysts are blunt in anticipating trouble. Robert Muse rhetorically asks, "If the United States elects to violate the nationality provision of international claims law today, can it tomorrow condemn with any moral authority a nation which chooses to violate, with respect to U.S. citizens, the full compensation standard of that same body of law?"[94] He believes that "the U.S. and its citizens, both corporate and individual, have a great stake in the effective international rule of law," and that "to be effective, this law must be adhered to by all nations of the world—it is neither right nor ultimately wise for the U.S. to do otherwise. The price, in the end, will prove too great for everyone."[95]

The application of Title IV is problematic, and has the potential to present the State Department with insurmountable difficulties in enforcement. To compile data about the details of foreign companies investing in Cuba and their links with U.S. firms is a very cumbersome task. Given limited human resources and reduced budgets, it is not clear how the State Department can obtain information about every foreign company that is reluctant to have it disseminated. Then there is the sensitive matter of warning letters regarding the denial of visas, a mission that many diplomats would prefer not to undertake. Overall, the law is considered a "source of embarrassment to the U.S. State Department . . . an expression of a parochial policy of the U.S. towards Cuba."[96]

Other commentators agree that the law will likely produce negative repercussions for the United States, given that the "exclusion of foreign nationals on this basis could damage diplomatic relations, interfere with foreign policy objectives, and negatively impact both international business commitments and domestic industries."[97] The image of the United States suffers as well: "when U.S. power is brought to bear to enforce a law whose legality among the international community is at least suspect, if not firmly rejected, the legitimacy of both U.S. power and international law are threatened."[98] In sum, the law breeds "resentment toward the U.S."[99]

Experts question the time and energy that the Helms-Burton process has consumed. They ask about the "hours spent dealing with the extraterritorial aspects" and insist that "it is undesirable to rest the implementation of foreign policy upon the accidents of private litigation, and to impose the cost of that policy upon random individual and corporate defendants."[100] The result has been that alternatives to solve the basic problems have been derailed. Lowe denounces that "the determination of the authors of Helms-Burton to enact watertight legislation has deflected attention away from more pragmatic solutions."[101]

On a more practical level, given the priorities of today's global economy, experts counsel "against taking bold unilateral actions in foreign and trade policy matters at a time when nations are moving toward more interdependent trade arrangements and relying on bilateral and multilateral trade cooperation rather than unilateral mechanisms such as quotas and tariffs."[102] Ultimately, the United States is the loser. Speaking at the Hastings symposium, Dodge points out that the "violation of international law norms have been aggressively challenged by other nations and this, in turn, has pressured the U.S. towards compliance with international law by suspending the right of action under Title III."[103] Finally, on the apparently pragmatic solution reached by the administration, Quickendon is particularly unkind: "what good is Title III if political concerns require it to exist in a state of indefinite suspension?"[104] She points out that this "dual position," where the United States defends the law and then suspends it, "only serves to discredit the legislation."[105] In fact, President Clinton has suspended it four times.

Lawyers Counsel on Foreign Policy

The political nature of Helms-Burton has induced the legal community not only to assess the law's juridical status but also to venture policy recommendations of the kind that normally emanate from think tanks. A few commentators seem to agree with the course taken by Congress because they see the law as the "most effective way of discouraging" foreign investment in Cuba.[106]

The majority of experts, however, do not share this view. Some are more blunt than others, but most share a cluster of negative perceptions of Helms-Burton, and they make similar recommendations to correct its flaws. The basic problem, according to the majority of legal experts, is that the means chosen by the United States to discourage investors have the effect of infringing international norms. With considerable humor, Robert Muse pointed out that allowing such penalties for confiscations is like permitting drivers who find parking spaces filled by pedestrians to run them over.[107] In order to redress this anomaly, these experts argue, the Helms-Burton Law either should be repealed or should be modified.

A number of analysts believe that the United States needs to become more flexible and pragmatic in its aims toward Cuba. They suggest that Washington might form a cooperative arrangement with other nations regarding investment in Cuba as well as to seek ways of facilitating a peaceful transition. An examination of some of their commentaries will provide further insight into their arguments.

Luisette Gierbolini, for example, considers that Helms-Burton may backfire because "it has provided the Castro regime with support from Cubans on the island who otherwise may have risen against the regime." In her view, "Helms-Burton confirms the rhetoric of the U.S. as an imperialistic, evil neighbor." The terms of the law are "unrealistic," and "they have been drafted by Washington bureaucrats and lobbyists who failed to consider the reality of international relations and who disregarded the importance of consistent U.S. trade policies." As such, "the Act must at least be modified and, at best, repealed. If Helms-Burton is not found to be a violation of international law, nothing will stop Congress from passing similar laws in the future. Other countries could follow U.S. steps."[108]

According to Robert Muse, the law, consequently, "must be amended to remedy that violation. If the U.S. persists in a continuing breach of international law it will undermine the global rule of law to the detriment of the citizens of this country." He takes this logic one step further: "How after all, can the U.S. demand compliance with international law by other nations when it is in violation of that very system of law? The short and obvious answer is that it cannot."[109] The isolation of the United States is obvious: "Statutes that expressly flout international law, however, may set a dangerous international precedent. In general, countries do not wish to be perceived as outside the international legal system."[110]

The voices of reason then concentrate on the urgent need to change course. Solís thinks that the "best interest of the U.S. is to amend the Act in order to maintain foreign policy consistent with, at the very least, the international legal principles that it recognizes and to show respect for the international agreements and bilateral relationships from which it greatly benefits."[111] Quickendon advises that "Congress should consider severing Titles III and IV." However, because the U.S. government will lose face if it does not somehow enforce Title III, "Clinton should consider its permanent suspension."[112] Other commentators leave a door open to positive alternatives: "Flexibility will permit the executive to raise potential violations of international law as justifications for avoiding implementation of certain statutory provisions."[113]

For other commentators, the right course is a more cohesive and coordinated policy to ameliorate the friction caused by foreign investment in Cuba and to foster the ultimate political aim, Cuba's political transition. For example, instead of implementing isolated measures, the United States must try to reconcile its goals with other views: "to retain dignity, the U.S. must successfully obtain concrete measures from both the European and Canadian allies to work with Cuba in the promotion of democracy."[114] As another commentator had earlier said, instead of wasting resources on measures that will be difficult to implement, what is needed is a diplomatic dialogue.[115] At the core of the controversy is the innate nature of coercive moves: "Because U.S. sanction laws often are the source of international condemnation and legal challenges, Congress may avoid the legal problems associated with laws such as the Helms-Burton Act by enacting a comprehensive international sanction law."[116] It is therefore mandatory to "repeal Helms-Burton and formulate Cuban policy principles that reflect sound international legal concepts."[117] Specifically, there is a need to "replace the current litany with more general principles."[118]

Fairey bases his arguments on the fact that "the globalization of commerce has resulted in a closer relationship between international and domestic legal systems." For this reason, in the United States, "lawmakers must understand the consequences of enacting legislation that impinges on international legal obligations." In his view, "the Helms-Burton Act provides a good example of a foreign policy sanction law that may have its purpose undermined by the judiciary's interpretive rules." One important problem is that "the Act appears to have no purpose without extraterritorial application, but it is textually ambiguous," and therefore is open to judicial interpretation. Fairey considers that "although violation of international law comes at a cost, Congress has the domestic authority to decide to pay that price in exchange for what it determines to be important national priorities." In turn, "absent clear congressional intent, however, courts may undermine those priorities. The courts may not have an interpretive role in applying the Helms-Burton Act, because certain provisions never may become effective." As a consequence, "courts increasingly will face the problems the Act raises." Fairey sums up: "Congress has the legal authority to avoid the problems, Congress has the legal responsibility to adhere to the international obligations it created."[119]

What the United States needs is a more pragmatic approach to defuse the situation created by the long-standing confrontation with Cuba: the expropriations, the embargo, and the recent legislative measures. Rupinder Hans reminds us that "LIBERTAD has been called the dictatorship-enabling act, because it strengthens Castro's only remaining asset, his capacity to blame the United States for Cuba's problems."[120] Other observers believe that "by joining the rest of the world in limited trade with Cuba, the United States will remove the smoke screen that Castro is presently using to keep the truth from the Cuban people."[121] Rupinder Hans recommends that "the embargo should be replaced by a policy of reconciliation with Cuba, which stands a far better chance of initiating meaningful political change, and also, allows American businesses a chance to invest in a growing economy. In the long run, cooperation rather than conflict is more likely to achieve change."[122] According to David Fidler, what is needed is compromise and cooperation:

[T]he U.S. and its liberal allies use economic interdependence with a vengeance against Castro's struggling regime. This strategy would not condition expanded trade and investment on democratic reforms in Cuba; it advocates for opening the floodgates of capitalism on Castro's rickety regime . . . recasting liberal realism and liberal internationalism in this way would pit the Marxist dinosaur Castro against the high powered, fast-moving forces of global capitalism. Castro would have difficulty controlling the consequences of such a liberal strategy . . . the next convergence has to come on the roles of international organizations and international law . . . [and] using multilateral fora to negotiate an agreement among liberal States that addresses the controversy in international law exposed by the Helms-Burton dispute over third-state nationals knowingly profitting from illegally expropriated property. . . . Finally, an ethical convergence has to be created . . . [and] negotiations between the U.S. and Cuba on a lump-sum settlement for victimized property owners will have to be undertaken as their relations normalize.[123]

Solís offers unsolicited advice to foreign interests in their confrontation with the United States: "if Europeans obey the Helms-Burton law, a dangerous precedent could be set . . . [they] would be committing utter folly if they neglected to oppose the Helms-Burton Act . . . [the] EU would find a great deal more of its foreign and trade policies being written in Washington rather than in Europe."[124]

Conclusion

Even if it fails to accomplish its political goals and its validity in court is never tested, the Helms-Burton Act has obtained two positive results with respect to its legal dimensions. As we have seen, Helms-Burton has become a case study to be analyzed in law schools in the future. As well, the new historical circumstances of the post–Cold War order have renewed interest in the enforcement of international law.

In his exhaustive legal analysis of the Helms-Burton Act, especially Title III, Robert Muse wonders about two attitudes he found in Congress regarding international law. First was a simplistic attitude implying that "there is no such thing as international law."[125] Regarding Helms-Burton's potential violation of international law, some legislators also seemed in essence to say: "So what if it violates international law." The real problem in these two complementary attitudes is that by violating international law, "the U.S. loses the moral authority to demand compliance with the same system of law by other countries. . . . The U.S. has an enormous interest in the preservation and extension of the international rule of law, if for no other reason than because the scale of its citizens' global activities makes it the chief beneficiary of that rule of law." In sum, the benefit bestowed by Helms-Burton, as Muse sees it, is that it has forced attention toward the "question of what organizing principle ought finally to determine relations between nations in the aftermath of the Cold War." The conclusion is that "no policy objective in international relations can be legitimate and therefore permitted if it contravenes public international law. . . . The alternative to an international rule-of-law governed world is a world unilateral adventurism that will prove productive, in the end, of little else but insecurity and conflict."[126]

If a sort of expert-witness testimony could influence the permanent suspension of Helms-Burton, history might well credit the U.S. legal-academic community for the demise of the law. It remains to be seen, should a case be brought to court under the terms of Helms-Burton, whether scholarly opinion can influence the outcome of the judicial decisions. Meanwhile, in popular terms, the "jury" has reached its decision and the verdict is "guilty."

With this view, it is time to inspect what the rest of the world has said about Helms-Burton, how different governments and organizations have felt its impact, and finally how they have coped with its effects.

4

The World's Response
Protest in the Americas

If you want to have an isolationist policy, that's your business.
But don't tell us what to do. That's our business.
Jean Chrétien, prime minister of Canada, 1997

[Helms-Burton is a] colonial reabsorption of the Republic of Cuba,
a continuation of the application of the "manifest destiny,"
and the Platt Amendment, and of intervening
in the internal affairs of Cuba.
Law No. 80, Reaffirmation of Cuban Dignity and Sovereignty, December 24,
1996, presented by Ricardo Alarcón, president of the National Assembly

The Europeans, Latin Americans and Canadians
are trading with Castro to make a buck.
Caleb McCarry, staff member of the House
International Relations Committee, March 13, 1998

In addition to failing to produce the fall of the Castro regime, the Helms-Burton Law has become a source of confrontation between friendly commercial partners and political allies. This has occurred precisely when the end of the Cold War should have eliminated the perception that alignment with the United States meant taking policy dictates from Washington. Just when the temptation of the "non-aligned" position seems to make the least sense, the law has given some nations a reason for keeping a distance from the United States.

As expected, each stage of the development of the law was met by an immediate reaction on the part of Cuba. But a number of U.S. trading partners have also reacted strongly to Helms-Burton. This chapter takes up the responses within the hemisphere, focusing first on those of the U.S. partners in NAFTA and then of the countries in the rest of the hemisphere.

Reverberations in Canada

Canadian Uneasiness

Three facts have coalesced to make Canada the first and most vocal opponent of Helms-Burton, as well as one of the countries most visibly targeted for the law's retaliatory measures. First is Canada's geographical proximity and close economic relationship to the United States. Years before the existence of NAFTA, Canada and the United States had formalized their social and economic relationship with a free-trade accord. Second, and in spite of the long-standing confrontation between Washington and Havana, Canada has been for decades one of the most active traders with Cuba. While in the 1980s Canada had a favorable trade balance, as the 1990s progressed figures show a benefit for Cuban exports, ending with an equilibrium (see figure 1). Third, Canada is today Cuba's largest investment partner, surpassed only by Italy in the field of tourism. Some of Canada's investors are especially visible and provocative, such as those engaged in mining on expropriated lands.

For these reasons, it was clear that the new U.S. measures to curtail foreign trade and investment with Cuba would have an important effect on U.S.-Canada relations. Because of Canada's dependency on the overpowering U.S. economy, leaders in Ottawa have frequently found it advisable to display a degree of economic autonomy and political independence. Similar to its vote-grabbing attractions for U.S. politicians, Helms-Burton has given Canadian politicians a populist and "progressive" cause to embrace for voters.

John Kirk, a leading expert on Canadian-Cuban links, summarizes the relationship between the two nations over the last four decades. A period of misperception and poor communication followed the Cuban Revolution; these problems are less in evidence today. Eventually diplomatic pragmatism and recognition became the norm. Canada's traditional deference toward Washington governed Canadian-Cuban interactions during the term of Prime Minister Mulroney (1984–93). Finally, recent years have been characterized by Canada's determination to coexist with Cuba and to seek a mutually advantageous bilateral relationship.[1]

Thus, when U.S. policies toward Cuba threatened Canadian dealings with Havana, Canada felt compelled to make its position clear. The Ottawa government in general "believes that nearly four decades of the U.S. approach to Cuba constituted a major failure in U.S. foreign policy." Canadians in general "have spoken out in defense of Canadian policy because they are furious at the Helms-Burton law which they see as discriminatory and harmful."[2]

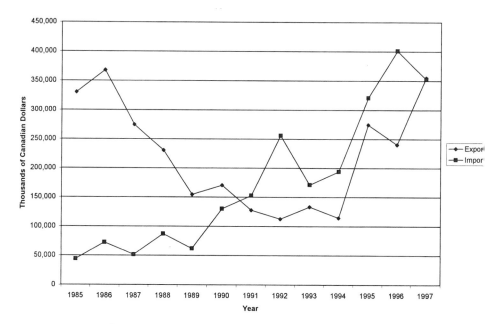

Fig. 1. Canadian-Cuban merchandise trade: Exports to and imports from Cuba, 1985–97

Canadians do not see their relationship with Cuba as "special," in the sense that the U.S.-U.K. and Spain–Latin America relationships are special. Instead, business people emphasize that they prefer a "normal" relationship with Cuba, similar to what they have in Mexico or Chile. Kirk notes that "there is nothing earth-shattering in that approach, nothing radical or particularly innovative."[3] What Canada is seeking in its relationship with Cuba and also with the United States is "a level playing field . . . to be able to trade with Havana in the same way that Great Britain or Japan can."[4]

Canada considers the potential internationalization of the U.S.-Cuban conflict, via the Torricelli and Helms-Burton laws, to be "wrong, immoral, and impractical."[5] Canada believes that the best way to influence Cuban behavior is through a policy of constructive engagement. Nevertheless, the fact remains that commercial ties between Canada and Cuba are not without problems. It is on the record that official trade credits did not increase when other countries (France or Spain) were increasing theirs. Government literature advises potential Canadian investors that political and commercial risks in Cuba are high.[6] Further, Canada "does not ignore the negative aspects of Cuba, the abuses of human rights."[7] But the main difference with U.S. policy remains the same: Canada would like to bring change in Cuba "through engagement and dialogue rather than isolation."[8]

With the signing of the Helms-Burton law, Canada was compelled to reinforce its policy of cooperation with the rest of the Americas and to reaffirm its commitment to friendly commercial ties with Havana. In view of the legal measures enacted by the U.S. government, Canada had basically four options, besides complying with the limitations imposed by the United States.[9] The first weapon was a combination of blunt diplomatic protests and lobbying in the U.S. tradition to influence President Clinton to use the Helms-Burton waiver at the next opportunity.[10] The second and third mechanisms were to file complaints with NAFTA and the WTO. The latter cannot be legally activated simultaneously with the first. Canada's protests could be added to the procedure implemented by the European Union when it calls for the constitution of a panel (to be discussed in chapter 5). The final approach was to try to retaliate with "mirror" actions for the damage caused by Helms-Burton. To date, however, Canada has used the first tactic (diplomatic protests and lobbying) and has maintained the options of actions in NAFTA and the WTO as threats. Most effectively, Canada has resorted to the fourth option as a protection for its investments, in the form of the expansion of previous legislation.

Soon after the approval of Helms-Burton, Canada's Minister of Foreign Affairs Lloyd Axworthy, in a declaration made in Washington on March 27, 1996, summarized his government's attitude: "The issue is whether it is appropriate for any country unilaterally to take measures intended to force other countries to agree with its foreign policy." Participating in a conference on Helms-Burton held in Spain, John Kneale, a representative of the Canadian embassy in Madrid, stated that Canada shares "the same goals as the United States" and that the Canadian "aim is a peaceful transition in Cuba to a genuinely representative government." However, the problem remains that Canada differs from the United States "on how to reach these objectives. . . . We have chosen the path of engagement and dialogue; the U.S. has picked isolation. . . . Helms-Burton is the wrong tool to fix this problem. . . . The U.S. Congress is trying to impose U.S. foreign policy on other countries" in a manner that violates NAFTA.[11]

Diplomatic and Legal Motions

In an unprecedented visit to Havana in February 1997, Axworthy sealed a broad cooperation agreement with the Cuban government that includes protection for investors and a commitment of support for economic reforms. Neither the State Department nor the *New York Times* were pleased by the Canadian initiative, which they considered to be too lenient on Cuba.[12]

The Canadian government's most specific legal response to Helms-Burton was the expansion of previous protective legislation in the form of a new measure: "Amend Provisions under the Foreign Extra-Territorial Measures Act (FEMA) of 1985 (passed in 1984), Expanded and Updated as Foreign Extraterritorial Measures (United Act) Order (1992), order 15 January 1996." The main elements of this measure include:

* permitting the attorney general to block attempts by foreign claimants under Helms-Burton to enforce judgments in Canada;

* giving Canadian companies recourse in Canadian courts if awards are made against them in U.S. courts (by providing a right to claim damages in Canada for an equivalent amount against the U.S. claimant); and

* increasing penalties under FEMA to discourage compliance with objectionable foreign laws (while the previous penalties included a $10,000 fine or five years imprisonment, the maximum fine was increased to Can$1 million).

Subsequently, the House of Commons introduced an amendment to FEMA to counteract Helms-Burton Title III, and the Senate adopted it on January 1, 1996. The most important changes are the expansion of the objective which now covers Canadian-Cuban trade in Cuba; the second is the fact that the Canadian measure is a "clawback" provision, and the third is that the punitive results are again increased, to a maximum of Can. $1.5 million.

The same day Clinton signed the Helms-Burton Law, Canada initiated the NAFTA Chapter 20 dispute-resolution procedure by requesting formal consultations.[13] However, the specific procedure to follow this through has not been implemented.[14]

Serious and Tongue-in-Cheek Confrontation

One isolated case of apparent Canadian impotence concerns the U.S. actions against Sherritt International. This Canadian company is using facilities in Moa Bay, in eastern Cuba, that were previously owned by Freeport-MacMoran Company of New Orleans, with an investment of more than $500 million, and used for nickel-extraction operations. It is estimated that Sherritt's assets in Cuba are worth about U.S.$275 million, but the company has no sales connections or assets in the United States. Canada was not able to prevent the U.S. denial of visas for its executives, and could only file notes of protest when the U.S. Department of State sent warning letters to Ian Delaney, president of Sherritt, and eight other officers.[15] The Canadian government also initiated an investigation into the decision made by Wal-Mart to withdraw from its stores Canadian pajamas made in Cuba.[16]

In a move that succeeded in poking fun at U.S. policy, the Canadian Parliament considered a bill presented by Peter Godfrey and Peter Milliken, seeking legal recourse for Canadian descendants of the British colonizers whose properties were confiscated by the American revolutionaries of 1776.[17] News of the bill was picked up by the U.S. media and reverberated throughout the country. The popular CBS program *60 Minutes* interviewed its proponents on prime time,[18] to the amusement of the U.S. public, many of whom had never heard of the Helms-Burton Law, and to the embarrassment of U.S. officials.

In spite of the fact that the U.S. government has actually paid millions in land claims settlements to Native American tribes (thus nullifying private claims that might be made), historic similarities occurred to other commentators. Attorney Robert Muse compared the Helms-Burton demand to a lawsuit brought by the Native Americans whose lands were taken by the United States, a line of thought that surfaced frequently in the op-ed pages of *Miami Herald*. For example, it was argued: "Let them [Helms and Burton] propose legislation that would require any individual or company profiting today from the U.S. government illegal seizure of Native American property to compensate the victims or their descendants."[19]

U.S. State Department spokesman Nicholas Burns responded to the Godfrey and Milliken bill with a corresponding sense of humor: "Should the bill become law, I'm sure we'll give it the same warm welcome that Canada gave Helms-Burton."[20] On the other hand, U.S. Congresswoman Ileana Ros-Lehtinen argued that the colonizers who suffered confiscations had been compensated by the 1783 Treaty of Paris and other agreements, including the Jay Treaty of 1795.[21] It is historical fact, however, that the U.S. government promised compensation to the British colonizers, but it was never paid.

Other forms of protest were suggested by non-government organizations. A pro-Cuba boycott against Florida tourism was announced in Canada, with no more noticeable effects than press attention.[22] Canadian Anglicans called for a similar measure.[23]

Canada had included a measure aimed at "combatting secondary embargoes"—a direct reference to the U.S. legislation—in the text of a Joint Political Declaration on Canada-E.U. Relations signed on December 17, 1996. However, coordination with the European Union has not always been trouble-free. When Brussels decided to announce a compromise with the United States to avert the scheduled confrontation at the WTO, Canada's position was initially unknown, and it preferred to keep its options open.[24]

Speaking at the Hastings symposium, former Canadian prime minister Kim Campbell summarized the views of the most active Helms-Burton opponents in Canada: "I can tell you here and now—Canada is against the Helms-Burton Act and hopes to see it repealed. . . . We think this is bad law—and bad policy—which violates international law and agreement in numerous ways. The irony is that many in this country in politics, government, media and business agree with us. Rarely does an American action galvanize such universal opprobrium among its closest friends, neighbors and trading partners."[25]

Conclusion

Canada's position in the context of the Helms-Burton controversy is unique. On one hand, Canada is the closest U.S. neighbor among the industrialized states, a member of the G-7, a group of the seven richest nations in the world. On the other hand, although Ottawa's inter-American relationships have grown very substantially in the last decades, Canada cannot wait for other Latin American and Caribbean countries to forge a cohesive response to U.S. measures that are damaging to Canadian interests. At the same time, while Canada is one of the closest political and commercial partners of the European Union member states, the agreements made between the E.U. and the United States are not necessarily applicable to Canada's relations with the rest of the world. That is why when the E.U. and the United States crafted their May 1998 truce, the situation became awkward for Ottawa. While unguarded observers may have ventured that the agreement unofficially covered Canada and Mexico (and other Latin American partners), Canadian government officials felt compelled to clarify Ottawa's position: "We are in no rush to go to Washington and say: 'Please sir, will you give us the same thing?'"[26]

The other side of the coin is that Canada, despite its investments, tourism, and close diplomatic relations, does not want to be seen as endorsing Castro's policies and a Cuban political system that is contrary to Canadian attitudes regarding democracy and human rights. For this reason Ottawa has insisted that the conflict over Helms-Burton does not fall under its Cuban policy, but that it is a matter of U.S.-Canadian relations. While Mexico has seen in recent years a decrease in its economic relations with Cuba, Canada has maintained and actually increased its previous levels of trade, investment, and tourism.[27] And while both U.S. neighbors have suffered a loss in the exchange rate, the fact that vacationing in the United States has become more expensive for Canadian tourists may make Cuba a favorite destination for Canada's tourists and retirees.[28]

The View from Mexico

A Neighbor in Transition

South of the border, Mexico has recently suffered a decline in the considerable autonomy it enjoyed during the Cold War. In those years Mexican leaders were able both to maintain a leftist foreign policy and preserve the political monopoly of the ruling PRI party. Mexico's close relations with Cuba constituted for some time an exception in the overall picture of Latin American compliance with U.S. demands for isolation. As late as the Salinas de Gortari administration, Mexico's special links with Havana caused frequent friction with Washington.[29] While economics has replaced ideology since that time, Mexico's commercial relation with Cuba remains important for both parties. Cuba is one of the most important clients for Mexican goods. The trade balance between the two countries shows an impressive surplus for Mexico, from which Cuba receives such key products as oil (see table 4).

Recently, Mexico had to employ all available legal mechanisms to counteract (at least for public consumption) the image of submission to the United States that accompanied NAFTA. On April 19, 1996, the president of the Foreign Relations Committee of the Mexican Senate called Helms-Burton an "armed robbery." Serious conflict threatened over Mexico's U.S.$350 million in commercial relations with Cuba. On May 8 the secretary of foreign relations promised the business community that a blocking statute would be adopted. On May 13, the European Union and Mexico made statements regarding the coordination of their actions. On May 16, Mexico and Canada agreed on joint measures in the Inter-Parliamentary meeting, and in the context of NAFTA. The same day, the president of the Foreign Relations Committee of the Mexican Senate announced that Mexico would prepare a law to counteract Helms-Burton. On May 25, Mexico and France organized diplomatic consultations. The following day

Table 4. Mexican-Cuban bilateral trade, 1994–97 (U.S.$ thousands)

	1994	1995	1996	1997
Mexican exports	173,742	355,096	318,227	290,120
Mexican exports (minus oil)	144,853	279,671	278,418	n.d
Mexican imports	11,716	6,224	22,850	34,223
Trade balance for Mexico	162,026	348,872	295,327	255,897

Sources: Kirk et al., "Canada, Mexico and Helms-Burton." Data from Bancomext (Mexican Bank for Foreign Trade).

Mexico announced that it was joining Canada, France, Spain, and the United Kingdom in a coordinated action.

As a result of the formal consultation that took place among NAFTA members on May 28, 1996, Mexico and Canada declared that the Helms-Burton law "violated International Law" and might not meet "obligations derived from the NAFTA legislation."[30] For its part, the Mexican Congress passed a resolution that included the following assertions:

The Helms-Burton law is a "violation of Mexican sovereignty."

- It punishes "countries that do not share U.S. foreign policy toward Cuba," a situation that is "contrary to the tradition of Mexican foreign policy based on the principles of non-intervention and self-determination."

- The law is contrary to "international law in its extraterritorial intent."

- Mexico reaffirms its "solidarity with the Cuban people," and instructs the Mexican government to carry out "joint actions with other countries."[31]

- In addition, Mexico asked for the convening of the NAFTA Commission when the details of Title IV of the Helms-Burton law were published in the Federal Register,[32] in view of the fact that they represented a threat against companies trading with third countries.[33]

Regarding articles 2006(3) and 1105 of the NAFTA Treaty, Mexico has reminded the United States that Helms-Burton should not affect transactions protected by this international agreement and that the United States should not enact travel restrictions.[34] The Mexican position was summarized as follows:

- Mexico has rejected U.S. sanctions on Cuba and has condemned the blockade, on the ground that International Law prohibits such coercive measures.

- Mexico opposes the law because it punishes Mexican citizens and interests for having financial and commercial operations in Cuba.

- Measures intended to isolate Cuba did not contribute to produce changes in Cuba's domestic and foreign policies, the evolution of which belongs exclusively to the Cuban people.[35]

On May 28 the president of the Confederación Patronal de la República Mexicana (Employers Confederation of the Mexican Republic, COPARMEX) charged that the United States was using the law "to displace other countries for when Castro leaves." The Consejo Nacional de Comercio

Exterior (National Council on External Commerce, CONACEX) stated that Helms-Burton would cause a loss of U.S.$40 million a year in trade links with Cuba. On May 29 the secretary of trade said that Mexico was preparing a response with Canada using the provisions of NAFTA. The following day the Domos Company announced that it would continue its operations in Cuba, but Cementos Mexicanos (CEMEX) said that it would leave. The president of CONACEX called for action, and the Permanent Commission of the Mexican Congress confirmed that it would pass the blocking law. Representatives of the private sector noted that some twenty-five to thirty companies could be affected, and they proposed several specific actions. The secretary of trade announced in Venezuela that Mexico was ready to raise the issue in other forums. The Commission of Political Parties represented in the Mexican Congress issued a statement of solidarity with Cuba and against the Helms-Burton law, while the right-wing Partido de Acción Nacional (Party of National Action, PAN) called for support in the Latin American Parliament (PARLATINO). On June 1, the Secretaría de Comercio y Fomento Internacional (Secretariat for Business and International Development, SECOFI) said that Mexican companies could file claims against Helms-Burton in NAFTA. Actions began in the OAS and the Rio Group, while on June 6 some Mexican hotel enterprises announced that they would not leave Cuba.

The Mexican "Clawback"

On October 23, 1996, the official Mexican Register published the Law for the Protection of Trade and Investment, a blocking measure directed at Helms-Burton. Its most important items are the following:

· It forbids acts derived from the extraterritorial effects of foreign laws. Among such effects are the "imposition of an economic blockade," "the claiming of payments for expropriations occurring in the country where the blockade takes place," and "restrictions on entering the country issuing the law."

· The law forbids supplying information requested by foreign courts.

· It requires citizens and companies to inform the Mexican government regarding damages and notifications about the above-mentioned cases.

· It authorizes Mexican courts not to recognize judgments or other decisions made by foreign courts on related matters, and to recognize that individuals or companies prosecuted and compelled to pay for damages as a result of foreign legislation will be allowed to sue in Mexican courts for the payment of a similar compensation.[36]

In spite of its earlier assertions, CEMEX bowed to U.S. pressure and told Washington that it was going to withdraw from Cuba. CEMEX had already suspended its activities as a precautionary measure. Simultaneously, on July 4, ING-Barings announced that it would finance the next Cuban sugar crop because of the Helms-Burton Act.[37]

Mexico solicited the opinion of the International Court of Justice, and urged the UN General Assembly to consider a resolution on the extraterritorial application of laws. However, on balance, it seems that the recent Mexican response to Helms-Burton can be summed up as strong in words but mild in action. Overall, it is a fair to say that "Mexico has taken a more conciliatory attitude to the Act than Canada. Mexico seems determined to go through all the NAFTA hoops before it starts to take reprisals. Canada, on the other hand, has already prepared its retaliatory legislation. It is only using the NAFTA mechanism as a backup."[38] When isolated actions regarding immigration visas come to the public's attention, they make the lack of concrete Mexican countermeasures to Helms-Burton more evident: the United States has indeed taken *some* retaliatory measures against *some* Mexican firms.

On a lighter side, the Helms-Burton controversy inspired an advertising campaign on Mexican television for cellular phones. A character in one commercial was identified as "Burton Helms." Because the advertisement was contracted by TELMEX, the government-owned telephone company, it can be considered an official Mexican protest against the law during the administration of Salinas de Gortari. (Subsequently, the company was privatized, sold at a lower price than the real market value.)[39] In the same light vein, a possible Mexican countermeasure for the denial of visas to business people could be the case of U.S. nude dancers working in Mexico City who were denied work permits, with the legal justification that they are not included in the high-technology categories protected by the NAFTA agreements.[40]

Reaction in the Rest of the Americas

The Inter-American System

In the OAS system, Mexico joined in a resolution opposing the Helms-Burton Law in a session that took place in Panama on June 3, 1996. A joint declaration of the ministers of foreign relations of the Rio Group, then meeting in Bolivia, was considered, with an instruction to the Inter-American Juridical Committee to present an Opinion to the OAS Council on the validity of the law. The most important items in this opinion are the following:

- The Helms-Burton law does not conform to international law (a) because the national courts of a given state (in this case the United States) are not a competent forum for the resolution of claims between different states; (b) because the United States does not have the right to assume claims of persons who were not U.S. citizens at the time of the events; (c) because it does not have the right to attribute responsibility to nationals of third countries for claims against another state or for the use of expropriated goods situated within the expropriating state; and (d) because it does not have any right to impose a compensation superior to the amount of damages.

- According to international law, extraterritoriality is permitted only in the event that actions have a direct, substantial, and predictable effect on the territory of the state dictating such law.

- The events do not conform to international law practices regarding the "trafficking" of confiscated property.[41]

Cuban officials were delighted with the negative decision of the OAS Juridical Committee concerning Helms-Burton. The Cuban government noted that this was the first time that the OAS, an organization that "no one can say is manipulated by Cuba, speaks out against a U.S. position against the island."[42] In the rest of the Americas, the law reinforced the belief held by many leaders critical of Castro that the maintenance of commercial links is the most appropriate way to induce a political opening in the island. This is especially apparent now that ideological infiltration and guerrilla activity have disappeared from Havana's strategic agenda.

Very early on, the Central American governments had expressed opposition to Helms-Burton. In June 1997, Cuban Foreign Minister Roberto Robaina visited all the Central American presidents and gave them a personal letter from Fidel Castro explaining his views. In advance of a regional summit to be held in Panama the following month, all Central American leaders reiterated their displeasure with the U.S. law. At the same time, they confirmed their endorsement for Cuba to be the site of the 1999 Ibero-American summit, a project that the United States had been allegedly discouraging. However, as will be discussed in the concluding chapters, this apparent Central American unanimity regarding the appropriateness of the site for the 1999 Ibero-American gathering began to show signs of strain when Nicaragua's president, Arnoldo Alemán, announced his intention not to attend (in protest of Fidel Castro's policies against internal dissidents).

Fernando Naranjo, foreign minister of Costa Rica, confirmed the Central American condemnation of Helms-Burton and any attempt to enforce it. Panama's Ricardo Alberto Arias stated that his country would reject any measure that inhibits free commercial exchange, and asserted that Helms-Burton violates international agreements. President Alemán asserted that no country can impose its laws extraterritorially. Víctor Lagos, vice minister of foreign affairs of El Salvador, also condemned the Helms-Burton Act. Eduardo Stein, minister of foreign relations of Guatemala, reiterated his government's rejection of the U.S. embargo.[43]

Almost simultaneously, representatives of the Asociación Latinoamericana de Integración (ALADI) held a special session that, by a unanimous vote, "condemned Helms-Burton, as a menace for the process of hemispheric integration." According to ALADI, the U.S. law is "against the objectives and principles of Latin American integration and places at risk the purpose of establishing a Free Trade Area of the Americas."[44]

After the approval of the Helms-Burton Law, the Secretariat of Sistema Económico de América Latina (SELA) Council reiterated its opinion on the U.S. embargo policy, originally stated during the Twenty-first Ordinary Session of July 13, 1995, and expressed in its Decision No. 360, inserted in the UN General Assembly Resolution No. 50/10 of November 2, 1995. In this document, the SELA Council branded the "economic, commercial, and financial blockade" as "illegal" and demanded its suspension. When Helms-Burton was approved, the Council's report expressed concern on two main points: the extraterritorial nature of the measure and the retroactivity of some of its provisions. It also indicated that the law violates the charter of the OAS (articles 18 and 19), the Charter of Economic Rights and Obligations of the United Nations, and Resolution 2625 of the General Assembly on principles of international law, norms of customary international law as detailed by the International Court of Justice, the NAFTA treaty, GATT (articles 1 and 2), and several other rules, as stated by the Juridical Committee of the OAS.[45]

The heads of government of the Rio Group (assembled for their tenth meeting at Cochabamba, Bolivia, on September 3 and 4, 1996) issued an explicit declaration of opposition to "the extraterritorial effects of national laws." While omitting to criticize Cuba (as had been done in the past), the Rio Group proclaimed: "We reject every attempt to impose unilateral sanctions having extraterritorial effects, because it violates the law that rules the coexistence between states and ignores the basic principle of respect for sovereignty, in addition to violating international law." The Rio Group reaffirmed its strong rejection of the Helms-Burton law and, to this effect, pointed out "the significance of the unanimous opinion issued by the Organization of American States Inter-American Juridical Committee, in the sense that the grounds and eventual application of the law do not conform to international law."[46]

Tremors in the Caribbean

The Helms-Burton conflict has proved a source of friction between Puerto Rican–American members of Congress and their Cuban-American counterparts. Meanwhile, politics on the island replicate in microcosm the chasm between liberals and hard-liners on the mainland. The embargo against Cuba has attracted the attention of the independentist circles of Puerto Rico, with Rubén Berrios leading the demands to lift it.[47] Cuban-Americans residing in Puerto Rico have expressed their opposition to investment in Cuba.[48]

Respectfully siding with the United States on other issues (such as the Grenada operation and lobbying for free-trade advantages), the countries of the Caribbean Basin have expressed criticism of the U.S. attitude toward Cuba in a variety of ways, from espousing the membership of Cuba in the founding of the Organization of Caribbean States to pursuing closer diplomatic links. Although the Caribbean nations were critical in principle of the Helms-Burton legislation, its impact was not noticeable in their modest economies as far as investment is concerned. As H. Michael Erisman has outlined in a review essay, Cuba's relations with its Caribbean neighbors have evolved drastically from the revolutionary activities of the 1960s. Since the early 1970s emphasis has been placed on the normalization of diplomatic relations, a trend that has been reinforced in the 1990s in the economic field. The result of this normalization has been Cuba's closer links with CARICOM and participation in the founding of the Association of Caribbean States (ACS),[49] and most recently the support of the Caribbean nations for Cuba's observer status in the African-Caribbean-Pacific (ACP) group. The general trend has been one of "progression from pariah to partner."[50] The United States has cautiously observed Cuba's rapprochement with its neighbors, even as it moved away from its own Cold War strategies for avoiding "another Cuba." In specific cases (the Dominican Republic, Grenada), the threat was stopped by military means. In the new era, NAFTA and an expansion of the concept of the Caribbean Basin Initiative have been used as an incentive for the Caribbean nations not to get too close to Havana. Nevertheless, relations have been maintained at a cordial level.

The most vocal reactions in the Caribbean came in response to a sort of by-product of the Helms-Burton model that was proposed by Congresswoman Ileana Ros-Lehtinen. It was a reaction to the start of talks between Cuba and CARICOM regarding Havana's eventual membership in the regional integration organization. Ros-Lehtinen announced that she would introduce a bill in the U.S. Congress penalizing the fifteen-nation community with the loss of financial assistance and blocking any plans for a free-trade pact.[51] Reactions in the region were predictably hostile.

"An open challenge to the governments' sovereignty," a declaration of "economic war," and an example of "cold, simple, sledge-hammer diplomacy" were some of the charges coming from the Caribbean media and public officials.[52] "A diplomatic ambush," said an editorial.[53] "An outrageous act of brigandage," said a writer in Jamaica's *Sunday Herald*.[54] Cartoons in the most vicious anti-Yankee tradition were revived: Uncle Sam was seen washing his feet in a bowl titled "Caribbean basin."[55] CARICOM ambassadors sent a blistering letter to Ros-Lehtinen: "The CARICOM countries' relations with Cuba are based on our firm belief in the principle of non-interference in the internal affairs of sovereign states."[56] Jamaica's *Daily Gleaner,* usually friendly to the United States, said that "No one should challenge Jamaica's right to foster ties with Cuba." Barbados's *Nation* pointed out that "one policy is reserved for a big nuclear power like China, while a different one is being practiced with the apparently small and easily intimidated countries of the Caribbean." Trinidad's *Express* lamented that "Caribbean governments appear to be between the proverbial rock and hard place. The continued attempt to increase the portfolio of U.S. investment means that it will come at a price." An editorial reminded that the Caribbean nations "are not trust territories of the U.S. We are fully independent. When will Americans understand this and learn to live with it?"[57] Predictably, Cuba's *Granma* called the U.S. move a "blackmail."[58] The result was that the Caribbean countries pursued their agenda, and the U.S. legislative project languished. The Caribbean nations stepped up their links with Cuba, including high-profile trips to Havana by such leaders as Jamaica's prime minister.

Elsewhere: Chile

The controversy over Helms-Burton has placed some Latin American governments in a sensitive position. For example, its vocal protests over Helms-Burton do not make Mexico appear grateful for the development of NAFTA and the rescue of its economy with huge financial packages. Chile was placed in an awkward position when it was introduced as a possible fourth partner of NAFTA, in the premature announcement by President Clinton at the Summit of the Americas held in Miami at the end of 1995. This possibility has deterred Chilean officials from protesting the U.S. measure.

While scholarly analyses of Helms-Burton have been rare in Latin America, an exception is an article by the Chilean diplomat María Soledad Torres, in which she expressed her country's concerns over the law's restrictions of trade and violations of international norms. She invoked the "prohibition against interference" inserted in the UN Charter (2.1), arguing that "the U.S. must accept the law of the state in which the property is located" and respect the "principle of sovereignty of a state over its properties (Lex Rei Sitae) and the persons in its territory."[59] Like other knowledgeable observers, Torres recognizes that "while control over the entry, departure, and visitation of foreigners in a state territory belongs to the jurisdiction of that state, in this case what is questionable is its foundation in a piece of legislation that violates international law." Like other observers, Torres finds that the law was passed for political purposes, and that the "objective of the law has been accomplished just by its promulgation; it has expanded its intimidatory effect, tightening juridical insecurity derived from the retroactive application of previous legal sanctions."[60] Regrettably, she finds that in Cuba the law has produced more benefits than harm. She also points to an overlooked aspect of Helms-Burton, one that weakens the ethical justifications of the law: "Some companies have been founded in the U.S. under the Cuban Claims Program, and they have transferred the claims, transforming the implementation of this title into a business."[61]

Perceptions in Cuba

With its revolutionary policies and its opening to foreign investment, Cuba was also a protagonist in the Helms-Burton controversies. Cuban leaders welcomed this renewed example of harassment and proceeded to a policy of "circling the wagons." First, H-B provided an explanation for Cuba's economic difficulties. At the same time, a series of hard-line measures targeted institutions and individuals considered to be excessively liberal or outright counter-revolutionary.[62] Perhaps one of the most evident links between the signing of the bill into law and the reaction of the Cuban government was the dismantling of the Centro de Estudios sobre América (CEA), regarded by many foreign scholars as one of the most important and objective research centers in Cuba. Maurizio Giuliano explains how the CEA staff became the first domestic victims of H-B, an outcome opposite to what some backers of the law had publicly stated as a goal of the legislation—to encourage the formation of a moderate opposition in Cuba.[63]

The Cuban government stressed that the law (especially Title II) was an affront to national sovereignty and pride, and had the potential to affect the national economy and Cuba's political future. At the same time, Fidel

Castro embarked on a campaign to align Cuba with various foreign governments and investors as fellow victims of the U.S. embargo, which until then had apparently only affected Cuba. This section summarizes the political declarations and other official measures undertaken by Cuba from the signing of the act until the end of 1996. Discussion of the economic impact of Helms-Burton on Cuba appears in chapter 7.

As three decades of political discourse would have foretold, a continuous public-relations campaign was carried out by the Cuban government. Helms-Burton was equated to a long history of similar measures, from the Torricelli law back to the infamous Platt Amendment. For Cuba's foreign affairs minister, all were the same policy under different names.[64] *Granma* called the law the culmination of "disrespect for the independence of a nation," raised fears that in the event of the defeat of the revolution, a "most brutal and savage reaction would be in power,"[65] and took note of the world-wide opposition to H-B and the difficulties of the U.S. government with its allies.[66]

In the first May Day rally after the law's passage, Cuban leaders confirmed that the nation would adhere to communism despite the U.S. actions.[67] A statement issued by the Communist Party in July 1996 is typical of official statements from that period. It charges that "with the approval of the Helms-Burton Act, the U.S. has taken a further step in its policy of aggression and harassment of Cuba." Second, it argues that "the objective of the law is to make the rest of the world observe the blockade imposed upon Cuba for more than 35 years and to apply it in a total way." Finally, the Cuban observers recognize that U.S. foreign policy has been codified in the law and predict that "the blockade would not be lifted after the destruction of the revolution and its institutions."[68]

Then the document takes up the central bone of contention: the expropriations. First, Cuba denounces that "the U.S. did not accept the terms provided by the law to compensate U.S. owners and enterprises." The statement points to the U.S. Supreme Court decision in *Banco Nacional de Cuba v. Sabbatino*, which states that "the U.S. courts can only decide the legitimacy of acts carried out by the sovereign state in its own [i.e., U.S.] territory." Then, very significantly, the Cuban communist leadership hints at a future compromise to solve the expropriations problem: "Theoretically some day it may be possible to find a solution, a way to compensate a given number of U.S. citizens and enterprises that were American at the time of the land reform and when the nationalization law was passed in Cuba." However, they stress that "this is a problem that exists only between Cuba and the United States—mutually satisfactory solutions were found with all other countries affected by these laws." In other words, Cuba will deal with the United States on properties taken from persons or entities having U.S. citizenship at that time, but not from those who were originally Cuban citizens.

The statement ends with expressions of anger against the United States for including in Helms-Burton explicit recognition of "opposition groups" and for mandating the U.S. funding to support them: "It is outrageous that legal sanction is given to open, public support to the opposition in another country . . . [to] a program of annexation and violation of the sovereign rights of the Cuban state." In sum, the law "violates the very basis of international law, the principle of independence of states." Finally, Cuba makes it clear that it will not change course (besides the "opening and restructuring process of our economy"): "In spite of the threats and the new measures taken to subdue us, Cuba will not turn back from the road it has taken." Moreover, confirming the prediction made by numerous foreign observers, the new U.S. measures have given Cuba additional determination: "Fearlessness in the face of an arrogant and hostile neighbor has allowed us to survive up to now."

When on July 6, 1996, President Clinton announced the implementation of the law and simultaneously delayed legal action until the following February, Cuban sources sarcastically characterized his actions as making "a circle square or . . . a square round" or, in the popular Cuban saying of Spanish origin used by Roberto Robaina, as being "on good terms with both God and the devil." Addressing the U.S. trading partners, Robaina pointed out that "the supreme empire has granted the world a respite not to violate its sovereignty for a period of six months."[69] Rafael Dausá, foreign affairs deputy director for North America, called the decision "political blackmail."[70]

In view of the approval of several blocking statutes legislated by Canada, the United Kingdom, and the European Union, it was expected that Cuba would not remain silent. In retaliation to the U.S. law, the Cuban Legislature passed its own blocking statute, Law No. 80, titled Reaffirmation of Cuban Dignity and Sovereignty, on December 24, 1996. The law is consistent with the official discourse of the Cuban authorities. The goal of Helms-Burton is said to be the "colonial reabsorption of the Republic of Cuba." The law is a continuation of "manifest destiny" and the Platt Amendment, and a general history of U.S. intervention in Cuba's internal affairs. In consequence, article 1 declares the Helms-Burton Law "illegal and inapplicable," and announces that claims based on it will be declared as void, and any person using the U.S. regulation will be excluded from future negotiations regarding the contested properties. In order to offer protection to investors, the Cuban regulation authorizes the government to formulate appropriate measures. Moreover, article 8 of the text defines as illegal any type of "collaboration" with the U.S. law, including the "diffusion, dissemination, or help to distribute information that may favor the application of the law."[71]

Damage at the United Nations

Whatever the economic or legal consequences of Helms-Burton may turn out to be, in the United Nations the outcome is already obvious: the United States has lost a public relations war.[72] Year after year throughout the 1990s, as resolutions were presented calling for an end to the embargo of Cuba, all the U.S. allies but one gradually but inexorably changed their positions, and an ambiguous attitude shifted to a voting pattern explicitly opposing coercive measures against Cuba. When the issue was first put to a test in 1992, 59 countries voted to condemn the United States, while 71 abstained and only 3 voted against (the United States, Israel, and Romania). In 1993, 88 voted for the resolution, 4 against, and 57 abstained. Albania, Israel, and Paraguay sided with the United States, while Romania chose to abstain. In 1994, abstentions fell to 48, while 101 nations voted against the embargo; the United States was left with Israel as its lonely partner in voting against the resolution. In 1995, while celebrating the fiftieth anniversary of the organization and applauding a speech by Fidel Castro, 117 countries voted to lift the embargo. This time the United States picked up an unexpected ally: Uzbekistan. Only 38 abstained. Even some adamant backers of the United States and critics of Castro, such as Argentina, changed sides.[73] After the approval of the Helms-Burton law and despite the controversy caused by the downing of the Brothers to the Rescue planes, the voting in 1996 confirmed and deepened the isolation of the United States.[74]

Cuban Foreign Affairs Minister Roberto Robaina addressed the UN General Assembly on September 3, 1996. Using the occasion to chastise the United States for not paying its dues to the organization, Robaina reminded his audience that Helms-Burton ("the most sophisticated monstrosity") was "conceived as an additional effort to defeat" the Cuban people "through starvation and extreme poverty." He then linked the embargo with the new law, which "assaults many countries and forces them to feel in their own sovereign hearts something Cubans have been facing for a long time." Calling for collective opposition, Robaina called the U.S. policy "an out of control King Kong who has escaped from his cage, who is destroying and crushing everything around him, without any guidance."[75] Carlos Lage, executive secretary of the Council of Ministers, spoke to the General

Assembly just before the UN body was ready to vote on the U.S. embargo and reiterated the Cuban claims.[76] The UN delegates renewed their condemnation of the embargo: With only 3 votes against and 25 abstentions (down from 38 in 1995), 137 countries sided with Cuba (up from 117 in 1995).

A year later, on November 5, 1997, Ricardo Alarcón, president of the Cuban National Assembly, made the customary address to the United National General Assembly. After reviewing the general trend of condemnation of the U.S. embargo in that world body, Alarcón attacked Helms-Burton as a measure "out of the Stone Age." Denouncing the fact that Cuba was not part of the negotiations on Helms-Burton, the Cuban official reminded his audience that "the U.S. blockade against Cuba was not contrived to defend the interests of the former U.S. owners. . . . Far from favoring them, it has harmed them. . . . The new Law directly turns them into victims of those who allegedly represented their interests."[77]

In 1997 only 17 nations abstained and 143 countries demanded the end of the embargo. These included all 15 members of the European Union, and key U.S. allies such as Argentina, Brazil, Canada, Australia, and New Zealand, which had abstained in the past. Again, the United States, Israel, and Uzbekistan were the only countries voting against the resolution.[78]

In 1998 Uzbekistan joined the nations abstaining on an end to the embargo, leaving Israel as the only country siding with the United States. Abstentions were reduced to El Salvador, Estonia, Georgia, Latvia, Lithuania, Macedonia, Morocco, Nepal, Nicaragua, Republic of Korea, Senegal, and Uzbekistan. Absent were Albania, Kuwait, Marshall Islands, Micronesia, Oman and Palau, while Bosnia-Herzegovina, Iraq, Kampuchea, Liberia, Republic of Congo, São Tomé and Príncipe, Somalia, and Yugoslavia were ineligible to vote for lack of payment of dues or other reasons.

Table 5. UN vote on resolution against the U.S. embargo on Cuba

Year	In favor	Against	Abstentions
1992	59	3	71
1993	88	4	57
1994	101	2	48
1995	117	3	38
1996	137	3	25
1997	143	3	17
1998	157	2	12

Source: UN data.

Conclusion

In summary, Canada and many Latin American countries exerted pressure on Castro even as they condemned the Helms-Burton Law in different forums, such as the Organization of American States and the Ibero-American summits. However, from the point of view of Western Hemisphere neighbors, Helms-Burton has not had any appreciable success in accomplishing its fundamental objective, the end of the Castro regime. On the contrary, it seems to have provided a new incentive to the Cuban dictatorship to persist in its hard-line political stance. Moreover, it caused a declining support for the United States in the United Nations.

5

The Washington-Havana Feud
as Seen from Brussels

Perceptions and Reactions of the European Union

*The European Union condemns the repeated violations of
human rights in Cuba, in particular in the political field.
The E.U. believes that the U.S. trade embargo against Cuba is
primarily a matter that has to be resolved bilaterally.*
European Union, Explanation of Vote,
United Nations General Assembly (New York, October 26, 1994)

*The U.S. has enacted laws that purport to regulate activities
of persons under the jurisdiction of the member states of the European
Union; this extra-territorial application violates international law
and has adverse effects on the interest of the European Union.*
European Council Regulation, November 1996

*If Cuba wishes to receive a favorable treatment through a cooperation
agreement, it must show progress in the democratic process.*
European Council Common Position, 1996

Numerous countries and organizations have expressed their opposition to
Helms-Burton, even as they focus on different issues and arguments. The
legacy of the legislation will include numerous protests from U.S. think
tanks and the legal establishment. Governments in the Americas, as well as
organizations in the hemisphere, have expended an extraordinary amount
of energy on Helms-Burton. European governments have been impressively
united in opposing the law, although the response of some, such as the
United Kingdom and Spain, is influenced by their special relationships with
the United States and Cuba respectively. The European Union has been at
the forefront of the European response to Helms-Burton. To date it has
provided the most effective answer to the U.S. law, and it has been able to

coordinate a compromise with the United States that succeeded in averting a trade war of serious consequences.

Ironically, what originally was a U.S.-Cuban conflict that had escalated into an international confrontation has now given way to an isolated compromise from Washington regarding the Cuban revolutionary process. Ironically, while the Monroe Doctrine was prompted by the insertion of Russia into the American continent, the Helms-Burton corollary was developed when the Soviet Union disappeared and Cuba lost its most important backer and the cause of its conflict with the United States. In the following pages, collective and individual responses to the Helms-Burton Law will be analyzed.

Europe Deals with Cuba

Conflict and Cooperation

The Helms-Burton Law caused noticeable damage to trans-Atlantic relations at an inopportune time—that is, when any trade disagreement might provoke a serious confrontation in the restructuring of economic blocs. Europeans have reluctantly come to accept U.S. leadership in difficult scenarios such as the Persian Gulf War and the pacification of the former Yugoslavia. France has shown a new willingness to reinsert itself into the European security network, especially in the context of NATO. A consensus has been reached regarding economic and military cooperation with Russia. A North Atlantic free-trade agreement may become a reality simply because of the similarities between the United States and the European economies. In contrast, the dispute over Cuba is an anomaly that nobody (with the exception of the Helms-Burton backers, it would seem) desires.

The problem is that, as Scherle R. Schwenninger wrote in *The Nation,* "when Washington declares war on what it considers to be the world's worst outlaws—Cuba, Iran, Iraq and Libya—America's allies in Europe and North America find themselves increasingly caught in the crossfire." Adding to the injury of not being consulted with, European allies find insult in "the way the U.S. tries to impose its policy on them . . . with legislation that has an extraterritorial reach [and] violates international law." The result is "evidence that the U.S. acts in bad faith in its trade diplomacy."[1]

Certainly, there are other economic and policy differences between the United States and Europe, as Francesc Granell, a director in the E.U. Commission, has noted.[2] There are problems in the agricultural sector, disagreements over the import of U.S. products into Europe, and arguments regarding the quality of certain American products destined for human consumption. In trade policy, the E.U. and the United States have had problems over the naming of the WTO head, the conditions under which developing countries can qualify for international aid, and trade preferences enjoyed by the African-Caribbean-Pacific (ACP) countries, under the guidelines of the Lomé Convention. In the area of economic and social policy, Europe and the United States do not share the same enthusiasms for the survival of the welfare state or the expansion of neoliberal measures. Major differences also remain in the field of environment, as illustrated by the fiasco of the Earth summits. The E.U. and the United States also disagree on UN reform and the expansion of NATO. Their most recent economic clash was over the merger of Boeing and McDonnell Douglas. In fact, the U.S.-Cuban confrontation is often overshadowed by issues for which the economic stakes are higher.

"It is ironic that in the midst of volatile economic times, the two strongest and least affected economic powers seem to be nearing a trade war," commented E.U. Ambassador Hugo Paemen during the December 1998 summit held in Washington, D.C.[3] The dispute Paemen was referring to was not about Cuba but over bananas. The United States was threatening to impose 100 percent tariffs on luxury products from Europe in retaliation for the preference given by the E.U. to Caribbean banana growers.[4] The relative importance of Cuba is revealed in the fact that the United States and the E.U. compromised on their impending WTO confrontation over Helms-Burton, but the issue of bananas remained to be settled in that organization.

Cuba's Trade Tilts toward Europe

Simultaneously with the economic reforms it undertook at the end of the Cold War, Cuba began to pursue normalized relations with Western European states (or, to be more precise, with the members of the European Union).

The history of relations between revolutionary Cuba and what was called Western Europe in the Cold War period provides clues to the disagreements between the United States and European states in the 1990s. Although in the 1960s and 1970s there was nothing to compare with the E.U.'s incipient Common Foreign and Security Policy, the European states dealt with Cuba in similar ways. Each one, according its own interests, maintained a link despite pressure and warnings from Washington. West Germany's moderate linkage contrasted with the close relationship between the communist German Democratic Republic (GDR) and Cuba. Britain (under both Conservative and Labor governments) and Gaullist France provided Cuba with industrial products that helped keep the economy afloat. In monetary terms, the figures for Western European–Cuban trade were modest, in comparison to Cuba's dependency with the Soviet bloc.

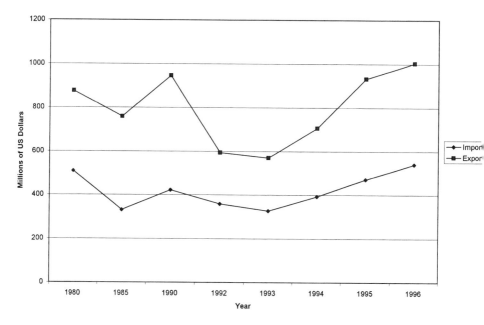

Fig. 2. European Union trade with Cuba, 1980–96

Nevertheless, Alistair Hennessy, in his pioneer volume on Cuba-European relations, argues that "without European links the [Cuban] Revolution might well have floundered."[5]

As recently as 1989 Cuba's trade with today's European Union states was only 6 percent of the total trade between Havana and the rest of the world. Just five years later, in 1994, 38 percent of Cuba's imports and 29 percent of its exports were with the European market (see figure 2). More than half of all joint ventures established in Cuba now have European investments. Foreign aid funds have also been coming from Europe, from 6 million European currency units (ECUs) in 1993 to a high of 15 million in 1995.

London's Bridge to Havana

As early as 1992 (that is, before the Torricelli and Helms-Burton bills), the United Kingdom became the first European state to take defensive action against the U.S. embargo, in the form of the "Protection of Trading Interests (United States Cuban Assets Regulations)."[6] Similar to the Canadian protective measures, this British regulation ordered that no person should comply with any requirement of the U.S.-Cuban assets regulations.

A fitting indicator of general British reaction to Helms-Burton might be the commentaries appearing in a widely read London weekly, *The Econo-*

mist, hardly known for a blatant anti-U.S. attitude. A brief sampling from headlines and selective quotes will suffice to represent the British mood. "Dealing with Mr. Castro: America Can Lift the Trade Embargo without Losing Face" read one editorial headline.[7] Following the incident with the downed planes, the weekly wrote about "Cuba the Outlaw (and America's Stupid Response)."[8] In a piece titled "Biter Bitten," the British commentators ventured: "The difficulty that President Clinton was warned he would face from his foreign allies if he signed the Helms-Burton law has arrived."[9] Another piece characterized Helms-Burton as an example of "how to lose friends and annoy people," and warned that "Bill Clinton's fudge in Cuban trade will get him nowhere."[10] In "Total War: Effects of D'Amato and Helms-Burton Laws Worry E.U.," *The Economist* indicated the problem was the "willingness of President Clinton to pander to ambition in an election year."[11]

The blocking regulation and the comments critical of the United States culminated in a consistent British opposition to the U.S. demands that can be traced to the beginning of the Cuban Revolution. London maintained cordial and profitable relations with Cuba while the U.K. proceeded to decolonize the Caribbean islands.[12] Sensitive British actions, such as the selling of Sea Furies military airplanes to Cuba and the transportation of Soviet crude oil, caused some tension with the United States. Brief friction between Havana and London over Cuba's support for the Argentina invasion of the Malvinas/Falkland Islands did not become a major obstacle. At the end of the 1980s, Cuba occupied sixth place among Latin American states as a destination for British products. In the early 1990s, U.K.-Cuban trade was the fifth highest in E.U.-Cuba transactions, but in recent years it has fallen further behind the commercial links with other E.U. states. While Leyland buses were the emblematic product of a past era, today Rothschild, Fidelity, and British Borneo Petroleum are listed among the many British companies with interests in Cuba.

Right after the enactment of the Helms-Burton Law, the U.K. made its attitude known. Traveling in Latin America, Nicholas Bonsor, minister for Commonwealth and Western Hemisphere affairs, stated that the law is unacceptable because it tries to control the actions of citizens outside the jurisdiction of the United States. Bonsor indicated that the U.K. would press for its elimination, in part because it has accomplished the opposite of what the United States intends, since it helps Castro "feel like a fortress."[13]

From de Gaulle to Mitterrand

French leaders of all parties have expressed displeasure with Helms-Burton, a position that is consistent with France's long-time independence from the

United States in policy matters. The activities of Fidel Castro's armies in Africa and Cuban support for Algerian independence raised the concerns of French authorities, but with the passing of time this isolated source of confrontation gave way to very cordial relations.

With the end of the Cold War, France became Cuba's second highest E.U. trading partner. An impressive 22.3 percent of European exports to Cuba were French, while 18.8 percent of all Cuban imports originated in France. The benefits for France also show in the fact that while in the 1980s only a maximum of 1.5 percent of the total French trade was with Havana, in recent years this figure has increased to 4 percent. Economics, culture, and politics go hand in hand. French cultural activities are today well established in Cuba. This reflects a long Cuban fascination for French culture and products, as well as the attraction of the Cuban Revolution for the leftist French circles in the 1960s.[14]

The excellent French-Cuban relationship received an impressive boost under the government of President François Mitterrand. Foreign Minister Claude Cheysson crafted France's ambitiously independent policy in the Caribbean and Central America, an approach he later duplicated as E.U. commissioner in charge of North-South relations. It is not surprising that Mitterrand called the Helms-Burton Law "stupid" and gave Castro a warm state reception when he visited Paris for a function of the United Nations Educational, Scientific, and Cultural Organization (UNESCO). Although Mitterrand's successor, the conservative president Jacques Chirac, adopted a more cautious policy toward Cuba and bestowed an award on Cuban dissident leader Elizardo Sánchez, France has reaffirmed its independence vis-à-vis the United States.

When the E.U. and the United States signed the compromise agreement that allowed them to avoid a scheduled confrontation in the WTO, this decision did not seem to inhibit the bilateral activities of France. The French government crafted a commercial agreement with Cuba to protect investors. It was signed in April 1997 by Franck Borotra, French minister of industry, and Ibrahim Ferradaz, Cuban minister for foreign investment and international cooperation.[15] This was interpreted as "a new European challenge to the Helms-Burton" law, and the result was displeasure in Washington. The U.S. government commented that it was expecting "equal activism" from the French government aimed at "the protection of human rights in Cuba." The French government responded by reviewing a recent history of similar investment agreements between Cuba and other foreign states. In fact, no fewer than eighteen countries already had similar arrangements; Germany, the U.K., Italy, and Spain were the European states that had already preceded France. The French minister then took the opportunity to issue a critical assessment of "extraterritorial measures," such as Helms-Burton, that seek to curtail foreign investment in Cuba.[16]

Among the many French companies with substantial interests in Cuba are Alcatel, Pernod, Pierre Cardin, and Rhone-Poulenc. A group of French enterprises led by the public gas and electricity conglomerate EFDF-GDT has financed the lighting for the Havana waterfront, centering on the Morro Castle, the jewel of colonial architecture.[17] Another important French company with investment in Cuba is the oil conglomerate Total. It is the source of a major disagreement between the United States and France that has the potential of seriously damaging global commercial networks. However, the main reason for the confrontation is not investment in Cuba but in Iran. Total has signed an agreement for oil exporation in Iran. The French government has elected to link the extraterritoriality of the Helms-Burton Act and the Iran-Libya Sanctions Act (ILSA) of 1996. This law—also known as the "D'Amato Law" for its main backer, former New York senator Alfonse D'Amato—aims at objectives similar to those H-B seeks, discouraging investment in Libya and Iran. France also threatened to veto the planned transatlantic free-trade arrangement. At the same time, Paris has put pressure on the European Commission to make the suspension of both laws mandatory for opening discussions of the Multilateral Agreement on Investment (MAI).[18] Incidentally, France's opposition to the free-trade pact is not solely about the Helms-Burton controversy but also expresses the displeasure of the French government for the European Commission's decision to discuss a delicate matter (high-level economic and political deals) that Paris considers the exclusive prerogative of the European Council, the EU's body composed of the heads of state and government, where each government has veto power.[19]

Bonn's Caution

The attitude of the Federal Republic of Germany toward Cuba, before the collapse of the Berlin wall, was reticent and cautious because of its close relations with the communist German Democratic Republic.[20] The GDR controlled more than 5 percent of total Cuban trade, only surpassed in volume by the Soviet Union. For this reason, Cuba and West Germany did not have diplomatic relations between 1963 and 1975. Bonn maintained a respectful wait-and-see attitude. When the Cold War ended, and with the country reunited, German policy toward Cuba reveals a sort of double track. On one hand, Germany has become one of the main trading partners of Cuba by virtue of Germany's industrial power and strong presence in Latin America. German business people have been cautious, but an Investment Promotion and Guarantee Agreement signed in 1996 has helped to promote new activities. Today, German companies operating in Cuba include Mercedes-Benz, BASF, Bayer, LTU, and Lufthansa. German tourists in Cuba rank among the top spenders. German hotel investment is only surpassed by Spain.

On the other hand, the German government has implemented a policy of restraint concerning human rights and prospects for democratization. Germany's requirements for granting Cuba a cooperation agreement have been criticized by Cuban observers as a double standard. While expectations concerning democratization and human rights are inserted into the conditions for development aid to Latin America (with a special focus on Cuba), they are absent in comparable documents outlining Germany's relations with Asian countries. While Cuba appreciates Germany's opposition to Helms-Burton and Bonn's consistent voting pattern regarding the embargo at the United Nations, Germany's conditions for aid are attributed to U.S. influence.[21]

Italian Boldness and Contradictions: The Case of STET

Italians are the leaders in tourism in Cuba, and commercial links between the two countries have been very strong.[22] The fashionable Benetton stores are an ideal target for legal suits under Helms-Burton, because of their visibility in tourist zones. Italian investment has also shown a certain degree of autonomy when compared to the rest of European involvement in Cuba. For example, at one time the Italian cruise industry (along with its U.S. and Norwegian counterparts, the most important in the world) had a keen interest in expanding the traditional Caribbean circuits by including Cuban ports of call. Infrastructure projects were planned for Havana piers, but these were subsequently put on hold.[23] This contradictory signal of an apparent compromise (or of a backing off) matches the characteristics of one recent episode of serious confrontation (and subsequent compromise) between the United States and a foreign company over the guidelines of Helms-Burton. It derives from the opposition of the former U.S owner of the Cuban telephone system for the planned transfer of the operation to an Italian company.

While commercial and investment arrangements depend on the continuous implementation of the compromise crafted by the European Union and the U.S. government, the prospect for a confrontation in the WTO remains a perturbing possibility, with unpredictable consequences for new ventures.[24] This is the reason that some companies have elected to follow a safer route, just in case. One example is the deal crafted between ITT and the

Italian company STET (since mid-1997, Telecom), apparently under pressure from the U.S. State Department. Taking over about 30 percent of the shares of the Cuban telephone system that the Mexican company Domos had elected to abandon, the Italian company agreed to pay ITT (the former operator of the Cuban telephone network) an undisclosed amount, rumored to be about $300 million,[25] although the figure was also placed at only $30 million.[26] The U.S. State Department issued statements praising the negotiation.[27] The Cuban-American National Foundation also expressed satisfaction, but raised concerns over the continuing business link with Cuba.[28] However, the STET decision raised eyebrows in diplomatic, business, and political circles in Europe, and was seen as a sign that the Italian company had elected to protect its investments in the United States by paying the price demanded by Washington. This constituted a dangerous precedent in view of the explicit policy announced by the European Commission, but the executive body of the E.U. elected not to take any action, claiming that STET's move was not a violation of the regulations.[29]

Ironically, what may be viewed as a victory for the backers of Helms-Burton has caused other side effects. First, the original political principles of the law have become mixed with the issue of compensation for former U.S. properties. Second, its concerns for principles, human rights, and democracy have receded in importance. The deal between ITT and STET reveals a contradiction in U.S. policy. By paying a sum of money, a previously labeled "trafficker" may now be a legal partner of the Marxist, totalitarian, human-rights violator, Fidel Castro. The transformation is not based on principle but money. The U.S. position is therefore weakened by this pragmatic policy.[30] It raises the worst stereotype of the United States in world perceptions.

This pragmatic policy has also expanded the opposition to Helms-Burton in other countries, especially in Spain, where the socialist opposition is eager to use any opportunity to confront the conservative government and denounce unethical U.S. moves. Critics now also include wide sectors of the Cuban exile community, who are understandably incensed that the sin of collaborating with Castro can be redeemed at an affordable price. Finally, the STET negotiation is seen as a dangerous precedent for similar cases that are affected by the D'Amato Law. As mentioned, the French company Total has signed an agreement for oil exploration in Iran, a decision contested by the United States.[31]

Another issue has contributed to the confusion over restitution, while undermining the hopes of Cuban-Americans for compensation through the Helms-Burton Act. Whatever the exact figure that the Italian conglomerate agreed to pay ITT for a share of the Cuban telephone system, the important point is that all the compensation will be enjoyed solely by ITT.[32] This is despite the fact that the original property was distributed into common and preferred stock, and ITT owned only 65.6 percent of the common stock. In other words, most of the outstanding stock was owned by other shareholders, and most of them were Cuban.[33] However, when the U.S. Foreign Claims Settlement Commission determined in 1970 who the claimants of expropriated properties were and how much they were entitled to, the result was that ITT and the U.S. owners were entitled to U.S.$130 million. The commission, understandably, could not award any claim to non-U.S. citizens at the time of the expropriations. Now the Italian company has followed the U.S. law and agreed to pay compensation to a minority of the stockholders of the Cuban telephone company. The majority, because they were not U.S. citizens in 1960, will not receive anything. And, so long as Title III of the Helms-Burton Law is suspended, they cannot bring suit in U.S. courts against anyone "trafficking" with the original property. There is an obvious parallel with the Bacardí case, whose major owners, excluded (as a non-U.S. company) from the original list of claimants, were expecting, by virtue of an activated Title III, to sue "traffickers" for compensation.

The STET-ITT deal became the first case to confirm some warnings made in Congress. Instead of deepening the embargo, the Helms-Burton Law may actually have encouraged more foreign investment in Cuba. Some claimants of expropriated property may find it more advantageous to take a portion of the profits of the current operation than to litigate against the "traffickers." What the law has accomplished is to create a loophole to violate the permanent U.S. embargo. Potential foreign investors may find this system, conditioned to profits, safer than venturing into Cuba on their own.[34]

From the Vatican to Jerusalem

Although they cannot be considered European in the narrow sense, two additional viewpoints should be included in this review. In a shock to the United States, the Vatican released its criticism of Helms-Burton just before Castro's epoch-making visit to the Pope on the occasion of his attendance at a Food and Agriculture Organization (FAO) meeting held in Rome. Siding with the Cuban Catholic Church leadership, and acting as a spokesman, Cardinal Roger Etchegaray called the embargo and Helms-Burton measures "unacceptable" because they affect poor countries, and he characterized H-B's extraterritorial application as juridically "questionable."[35]

The historic visit of Pope John Paul II to Cuba in January 1998 revealed once more that the leadership of the Catholic Church thought that a policy of engagement was preferable to isolation. The consequences of the historic visit for the restructuring of the U.S. embargo and the evolution of the

Cuban regime are still to be seen, but the immediate impact was notable. The papal visit produced the first serious disagreements within the Cuban exile community and made a change in U.S. policy toward Cuba more urgent than ever. Pope John Paul's policy of engagement forced other European actors, such as Spain, and Latin American countries such as Argentina, to reconsider their own attitudes toward the Castro regime.

The second non-European response to be considered is that of Israel. Even though Israel was one of only two countries siding with the United States when the UN condemned the American embargo against Cuba, Israeli businesses participated in building the first corporate office complex in Cuba. Monte Barreto, a joint venture composed of Israel's BM, Spain's Lares, and Cuba's Cubalse, built a complex on seventeen acres in Miramar. BM received a warning letter from the State Department.[36] Israel's isolation during the UN voting on the embargo is officially justified by the Tel Aviv government not as a sign of loyalty to the United States, but as a protest against Cuba for past injuries. This animosity can be traced back to the 1973 Middle East war, when the Cuban army fought along with Syria in the Golan Heights. Israel considers this a gratuitous, hostile act, one not to be forgotten. In addition, Israel is worried that any trend toward the lifting of embargoes would lead to aggression by Iran and Iraq.[37]

Perception and Reaction in Brussels

Early Warnings

Reflecting the attitudes of member states beginning with the the Torricelli law and culminating with Helms-Burton, the main European Union institutions have issued official declarations extremely critical of the policies of the United States.[38] Concurrently, it must be stressed, the E.U. has systematically denounced violations of human rights in Cuba.[39] Typical of the official E.U. attitude toward the U.S. embargo is the following 1994 statement by Ambassador Gerhard Henze, Germany's representative to the General Assembly of the United Nations, acting as president of the E.U. members:

- Because of its choices in economics and politics, the Cuban government is largely responsible for the deterioration of the situation in the country.
- The European Union condemns the repeated violations of human rights in Cuba, in particular in the political field.
- We have opposed U.S. legislative initiatives, including the CDA [Torricelli law], designed to further tighten the unilateral trade embargo against Cuba by the extraterritorial application of U.S. jurisdic-

tion. We believe that such measures violate the general principles of international law and sovereignty of independent states.

• The E.U. believes that the U.S. trade embargo against Cuba is primarily a matter that has to be resolved bilaterally.[40]

This even-handed approach has been consistent over the years. It has governed the dual policy of opposing the U.S. unilateral measures while determining in part what the E.U. would offer Cuba in the way of humanitarian aid, commercial preferences, and comprehensive cooperation agreements. In this regard, Cuba has been and still is the exception in the Western Hemisphere. The political and human rights profile of the Castro regime is the main obstacle to the implementation of a global package. However, the European Commission hoped that a two-track approach (trade and investment with Cuba, coupled with pressure on behalf of human rights) would obtain better results than the big-stick policy of the United States. However, unforeseen events disrupted the process toward an agreement.

The Derailment of the Cooperation Agreement

The shooting down of the Brothers to the Rescue planes and the subsequent approval of the Helms-Burton Law interrupted the progress toward a cooperation agreement between Brussels and Havana. These two crucial events also formed the background for subsequent measures taken by the European Union: the approval of a blocking statute to oppose Helms-Burton, and the drafting of a Common Position on Cuba, containing conditions for future agreements.

However, the abrupt ending of negotiations for the cooperation aid agreement was the outcome of an arduous path that was doomed to failure. That process began following a June 1995 recommendation of the European Commission, with a visit by delegates from France, Spain, and Italy to Havana on November 6–10, 1995, for exploratory conversations. The European Council meeting in Madrid on December 15, 1995, requested that the Commission draft a cooperation agreement during the following semester. For this purpose, Manuel Marín, the senior Spanish commissioner and the vice president of the European Commission visited Havana on February 8–10, 1996, where he met with Fidel Castro and other Cuban leaders. Just days after, however, the Cuban Air Force MiGs shattered all prospects for an agreement.

But even without the crisis provoked by this incident, the possibilities for an E.U.-Cuba accord on the conditions posed by Brussels were slim, considering the fragility of Cuba's domestic politics at the time. Reform of Cuba's penal code and recognition of the internal political opposition were basic requirements for the signing of the cooperation package, and these measures were a serious obstacle for Cuba.[41] Castro considered the requirements a humiliation and elected to take advantage of the situation, claiming to be the target of harassment and an international conspiracy.

The lack of understanding between the E.U. and Cuba is still the subject of debate. According to one interpretation, the disdain expressed by Castro toward all the offers and suggestions from Brussels exhausted the patience of E.U. officials. Manuel Marín, the seasoned E.U. commissioner and vice president, demonstrated that he tried until the minute his plane took off from Havana airport. He finally "threw in the towel." Another interpretation is that, in reality, Marín had set the bar too high on purpose.[42] Knowing that the Cuban leader would be increasingly more reluctant and that he would show ever more resistance to change, the European conditions were placed at a higher level.[43] The imminent change of government in Madrid, as a result of the March 1996 elections, was as coincidental as the change of leadership in Paris, in both cases from a socialist government to a conservative one. According to confidential sources in the E.U., there is speculation in diplomatic circles that the Spanish socialists, anticipating that they would lose the March 1996 elections, wanted to close the Cuban account with a bold move with slim prospects of success. In this interpretation, if they could obtain concessions from Castro, they would reap the benefits; in the event of failure, the new Spanish government would suffer the consequences.

In more strategic terms, the pact failed because it was interpreted as a coalition effort involving the United States, something that Castro was not ready to allow.[44] Although the meeting of the minds between Brussels and Washington at that time was impressive, and frequent consultations between U.S.-Cuban policy protagonists and Spanish, Italian, and French negotiators were carefully undertaken, a pact between Europe and the United States on Cuba was an open secret. The Cuban government suspected that some sort of cooperation was in the offing. Finally, on a personal level, the bold move failed because of a lack of calculation on the part of Manuel Marín, notwithstanding the usually impressive skills of the young but experienced vice president of the European Commission. It is hard to believe that the attempt to win an agreement with Castro was executed without close consultation with the rest of the Commission as well as influential sectors in Spain, especially in Marín's own political party, the PSOE. In any event, according to sources in the European Commission, the experience left an indelible mark in the mind of Manuel Marín, who decided to maintain a distance from direct negotiations with Cuba. With the "Latin American track" of a cooperation agreement closed to Cuba, the alternative route of the ACP Lomé Convention was left open. This possibility (a "back door," in one cynical view) was to be energetically explored by the Cuban government.

The record of the PSOE's attempts to influence the Cuban regime does not end with the above negotiations. Other attempts to break the Cuban impasse include the frequent travels and meetings coordinated by Xavier Rubert de Ventós, a socialist European Parliament member who shuttled from Brussels to Miami and Havana, trying to serve as a bridge between all Cuban factions. This triangular diplomacy involved the cooperation of some Latin American figures, including writers Gabriel García Márquez and Carlos Fuentes.

From a Cuban perspective, what was called the "stagnation" in the relationship with the E.U. was caused by a combination of factors. In an extended article published in the *Revista de Estudios Europeos*, Cuban researcher Eduardo Perera Gómez, while recognizing that the E.U. was displeased with the lack of Cuban compliance with European expectations, placed most of the blame on other factors. First is the subordination of the E.U.'s foreign policy to the constraints imposed by the member states, with the result that final decisions reflect the wishes not only of the most important countries but also those emanating from states that held key positions at that time, for example, the rotating six-month presidency. It is also important simply to be part of the "troika," which is composed of the representatives of the country presently holding the presidency, the previous president, and the country to have the office for the next six months. Second is the "preference for strategic considerations always to be referred to the framework of the Atlantic Alliance," a reference to the influence of the United States. Predicting a pattern of compromises between Washington and Brussels to avoid confrontation over Helms-Burton, Perera reasoned that "Cuba is not important enough for the Union to confront the U.S. politically by signing a cooperation agreement, particularly when it is demanding the WTO to condemn [Helms-Burton]." Finally, the failure of the agreement was caused by the "alignment of the conservative government [of Spain] led by the PP [Partido Popular] not only with Washington's official Cuban policy but also with the policy promoted by most of the reactionary forces within the Cuban exile community in Florida."[45]

Once the rapprochement failed, the second hard-line response from Brussels would come as a supplement to the E.U. criticism of Helms-Burton. While the planned blocking statute was the first initiative in the E.U. activities, a critical Common Position on Cuba would also have a place in the annals of the European Union's developing foreign policy, because it was the first to be taken on a Latin American country.[46] The spirit and the letter of the Common Position have been maintained to date, with the expected protests of the Cuban government. The renewal of this policy took place during the Council of Ministers meeting held in Brussels on December 9, 1997,[47] and it was confirmed after the signing of the May 1998 truce between the United States and the E.U.

The Road to Compromise

Meanwhile, evidence of an under-the-table compromise between the E.U. and the United States surfaced in the media. Months before the announcement of the freezing of the aid agreement, Alberto Sotillo, the Brussels correspondent of the conservative Madrid newspaper *ABC*, had revealed in a lead story that the United States was asking the E.U. for a "gesture" in order to delay the execution of the Helms-Burton law. Washington needed this move regarding the Cuban regime to allow Clinton to concentrate on the electoral campaign and, therefore, to help him suspend the application of the Helms-Burton law. Among the conditions of this "gesture," it was mentioned that investments should benefit the whole of Cuban society and that companies should not be forced to deal directly and exclusively with the Cuban government.[48] The intermediaries in this "negotiation" might have been members of a delegation of Euro-parliamentarians who visited Washington, among them some members of the Spanish Partido Popular who had direct knowledge of the Cuban problems and, more broadly, European–Latin American relations, including Carlos Robles Piquer, Guillermo Galeote, José Ignacio Salafranca, and Gerardo Fernández Albor. Even though it may not have been exactly what was expected, the suspension of negotiations for the cooperation-and-aid agreement between Brussels and Havana certainly seemed to fit the bill as the awaited "gesture."

Some other ambiguous decisions were taken within the course of the European Union deliberations, all dictated by the constraints of the forums within which the Spanish government and the leaders of the party in power had to act. For example, the Organization for Economic Cooperation and Development (OECD) had avoided issuing a condemnation of the United States for its retaliation against Cuba and China during its May 1996 meeting, while discouraging measures against the agreements emanating from the World Trade Organization.[49]

The Blocking Statute and the Understanding

Under the threat of the law, the European Union decided to denounce Helms-Burton in the World Trade Organization, asserting that action could not wait until after the U.S. elections. During the second half of 1996, the U.S. government made a considerable effort to convince the European Union to find an elegant face-saving solution. However, the European governments had their hands tied by a new measure adopted by the Council of Ministers (also known as the Council of the European Union) in November. They could not afford to appear to be negotiating under the threat of retaliation. The European Parliament and the European Commission had already issued sufficient signs of protest.[50] It was now the turn of the Council of Ministers to take action to counter the U.S. law.

The Council's regulation against the application of the law was published on November 22, 1996.[51] It is significant that the mechanism chosen was the highest in the ranking of E.U. legislation. When regulations are issued by the European Commission, they are mostly administrative and technical in detail. Regulations given by the Council are concerned with broader, more important and controversial matters. Regulations are binding on all member states and do not need to be translated or interpreted into national law. This specific regulation contains protective measures blocking the extraterritorial effects of the Helms-Burton Law.

First, the European Council outlined its reasons for opposing Helms-Burton: One of the objectives of the European Union is to contribute to "the harmonious development of world trade and to the progressive abolition of restrictions on international trade." Moreover, the E.U. "endeavors to achieve to the greatest extent possible the objective of free movement of capital between Member States and third countries, including the removal of any restrictions on direct investment—including investment in real estate—the provision of financial services, or the admission of securities to capital markets." In accordance with these goals, the European Council regulation's main objectives were stated as follows:

- The U.S. has enacted laws [the Torricelli and Helms-Burton Laws][52] that purport to regulate activities of persons under the jurisdiction of the member states of the European Union; this extraterritorial application violates international law and has adverse effects on the interests of the European Union.

- Therefore, the regulation provides protection against the extraterritorial application of these laws and obligates the persons and interests affected to inform the Commission.

- No judgment of a court outside the European Union regarding the effects of these U.S. laws will be recognized and no person shall comply with any requirement or prohibition derived from them.

• Any person affected shall be entitled to recover any damages caused by the application of these laws.

With the measures taken by the European institutions, especially the Commission and the Council of Ministers, the European Union aimed to concentrate on removing what it perceived were the most adverse effects of Title III and Title IV of the Helms-Burton Law. More than anything else, the blocking statute supplies protection against the extraterritorial application of the U.S. laws.

Jürgen Huber, a member of the Legal Service of the Council of the E.U., explains that Article 6 represents the cornerstone of the whole regulation. It contains the so-called "claw-back clause which enables . . . recover[ing] any damages, including legal costs [caused] . . . by the application of the Helms-Burton Act." The regulation provides, however, that the sanctions must be effective, proportional, and dissuasive. The Council also adopted a Joint Action, by which each member state shall take the measures it deems necessary.[53] Huber notes that the European Commission did not suggest any Joint Action, and this apparent oversight raised legal problems within the Council. The main issues facing the Council concerned whether the Community (the first pillar) was competent to adopt the proposed measures, apparently belonging to the second pillar (Common Security and Foreign Policy). If yes, what scope could the regulation have under Community law?

The Council was confronted with a choice between several options. The first option would have been to restrict the scope of the regulation to issues of commercial policy, which is an exclusive E.C. competence. In other words, the E.U. should stick to trade issues. As a second option, the E.U. might not limit its actions to merely commercial ventures, but include other objectives. In fact, it was clear that the measures proposed went far beyond the common commercial policy. Measures taken under Article 113 of the E.C. Treaty must deal specifically with international trade. The proposed measures did not. So, Huber reasons, "rather than limit its actions to the objectives covered by the exclusive EC competence under the common commercial policy, the Council added the objective of Article 73c, concerning the free movement of capital." The dilemma is "that assessing whether action is necessary is partly a legal and partly a political matter," making it necessary to find the borderline between the regulation and the Joint Action.[54] The consequences of the decision are that the "member states have to take measures themselves by legislating in order to implement the Joint Action and to determine the sanctions to be imposed in the event of a breach of the provisions of the regulation." Anticipating what many observers are still asking, Huber noted that it may be "too early to assess how provisions on authorizations for compliance will operate, how many persons will ask for such authorization, and how many authorizations will be granted."[55] At the same time that the E.C. Regulation was announced, a similar verbal message was received by Stuart Eisenstat. The surprised U.S. envoy was traveling in Europe as a special representative of President Clinton in consultations with European leaders. The U.S. representative, who was earlier in his career the U.S. ambassador to the E.U., fully comprehended another interesting detail in the text and spirit of the E.U. Regulation that makes some suspect it of being part of a "conspiracy." A close comparative analysis of Canadian, Mexican, and European anti-Helms measures reveals a pattern of striking and unsurprising similarities. It looks as if the drafters of the corresponding legislatures and agencies were in close contact. While the E.U. officials may claim to have approved the most comprehensive of the blocking statutes, the British certainly were first, even before the enactment of Helms-Burton.

Showdown at the World Trade Organization

When European demands failed to produce a policy change in Washington, a decisive legal initiative against the United States was scheduled for debate in February 1997 within the framework of the new WTO, successor of the GATT.[56] The European Union had warned that the temporary suspension of Title III was not sufficient. The rest of Helms-Burton was still considered a violation of the principles of commercial exchange guaranteed by the WTO. As a first action, the organization agreed to form a panel charged with producing an opinion within six months.

The United States countered that the Helms-Burton Law did not concern the WTO, since the limitations it imposed on trade with Cuba were a matter of national security. Ironically, this amounted to an explicit admission that the law has a *political* objective, as its most ardent advocates had made abundantly clear all along. Congresswoman Ileana Ros-Lehtinen, upon returning from a trip to Europe in January 1997 (where she had been explaining her point of view to various European governments), insisted that the Helms-Burton Law was simply a mechanism to guarantee the U.S. full control of its borders by facilitating the withdrawal of visas from the executives of companies dealing in confiscated properties in Cuba. She also insisted that the law did not forbid all investments in Cuba, only those involving confiscated properties.[57]

The exchange between Europe and the United States had other dimensions. The E.U. left the sensitive issue of Cuba untouched and seemed not to be concerned with the political and social evolution (or lack of it) of the Cuban regime.

Cuba Loses a Second Round: The "Common Position"

On December 2, 1996, the powerful Council of Ministers of Economy and Finance (also known as ECOFIN) approved a Common Position on Cuba. Its objective was "to encourage a process of transition to pluralist democracy and respect of human rights and fundamental freedoms."[58] Normally, such an action would be buried among the hundreds of documents approved by the European institutions. This was a novelty, however, for different reasons. First, it was about Cuba, the country that was the center of the Helms-Burton controversy. Second, the measure came just after the European Union issued the Regulation and the Joint Action opposing the U.S. law. Third, it was also the first to be applied to a Latin American country, specifically the only one that still does not enjoy a cooperation agreement with Brussels. Finally, it was the first of such actions under the newly inaugurated Common Foreign and Security Policy (CFSP, better known as PESC in French and other languages). However, any observer of the E.U.'s relations with Cuba recognized that the Common Position did not contain any startling new initiatives. Instead, it reconfirmed a well-established policy. Because such measures are binding on all E.U. member states, the European Union had, like the United States, also effectively codified its foreign policy toward Cuba. However, in contrast with the U.S. policy, the E.U. made it clear that it wanted to continue the dialogue with Cuba.[59] On November 14, 1996, Spain had presented the initial draft of the proposal, which was examined by the Political Committee of the E.U. Council on November 25. Some members considered the wording too close to the U.S. thesis and demands. While the U.K. sided with Spain, most of the influential members (Germany, Belgium, France, Italy, and the Netherlands) asked for changes. The final document included the following main points:

- The E.U. encourages a peaceful transition in Cuba to a pluralist democracy. The E.U. prefers this to come about through the initiative of the Cuban government, not by coercion from outside.
- If Cuba wishes to receive favorable treatment though a cooperation agreement, evidence of progress in the democratic process must be shown in periodic reports submitted by the Commission to the Council. The reports should specifically show evidence of respect for human rights, the release of political prisoners, reform of the criminal code, and an end to the harassment of dissidents.

- The E.U. wishes to maintain dialogue not only with the Cuban government but with all sectors of Cuban society.
- The E.U. recognizes the progress Cuba has made in economic reforms and is willing to offer economic cooperation through the member states.
- Finally, humanitarian aid will continue through appropriate NGOs.

Understandably, this set of conditions was not well received by the Cuban regime. Reflecting the official attitude, Eduardo Perera Gómez pointed out that the E.U. had not required comparable conditions in similar cases, such as in its agreements with Morocco, Israel, and Guatemala, and noted that the E.U. was "implementing a custom union agreement with Turkey and [had] signed four cooperation agreements with China, accused of human rights violations."[60] For these reasons, the Cuban government rejected that its political conduct should be dictated by the E.U. report. Moreover, Spain became the object of Cuban retaliation when Havana withdrew the *placet* (diplomatic approval) for the new ambassador, an action that unleashed a serious diplomatic crisis between the two countries just months before the commemoration of the 1898 independence war.

Also understandably, the Common Position was extremely well received by the State Department.[61] As a reward for the European gesture, a more concrete and positive U.S. response was expected from the White House.

Despite the friction over the Common Position, and in compliance with its terms, the European Union has continued its humanitarian aid to Cuba through programs administered by the European Community Humanitarian Office (ECHO). Since 1993, the E.U. has granted U.S.$64 million to assist with damage caused by storms and flooding, and for diverse medical programs. Funds are distributed through European NGOs. For its part, Cuba has welcomed the euro, the European common currency, to be mandated in foreign trade operations of the country as announced by the president of Central Bank of Cuba, Francisco Soberón. Cuban authorities favor the new European currency "because it threatens to reduce the power of the dollar, and that is good for the world and it is good for Cuba."[62] Among the financial reasons, Soberón listed the end of the international system's dependency on the U.S. dollar, and the fact that more than 50 percent of Cuba's tourism is of European origin and 44 percent of Cuba's trade is with the European Union.

Clinton's Suspension of Title III

In an effort to defuse tensions and as an apparent counter-gesture to the European concessions contained in the Common Position on Cuba, on January 3, 1997, President Clinton suspended, for the second time, the controversial Title III of the law, with its provisions that angered and alienated U.S. allies. Clinton explained, "I took this step so that we could have time to develop a more common approach with our allies and trading partners to promote democracy, human rights and fundamental freedoms in Cuba. We and our allies agree on the vital need for a transition to democracy on the island, but differences over how to achieve that aim have often overshadowed the goal itself. That is why I decided to make maximum use of Title III to increase pressure on the Castro regime by working with our allies—not against them—to accelerate change in Cuba."

Clinton added, "These and other steps have sent a clarion message of hope to the Cuban people. They underscore that it is Castro who is isolated, not those who welcome the democratic tide of history. They demonstrate the international community's resolve to end the dictatorship so the people of Cuba can enjoy the freedom and prosperity they deserve."[63]

President Clinton's initiative, coupled with renewed talks emphasizing support for a democratic transition in Cuba, defused tensions with the European Union and somewhat enhanced the perceptions of the United States in the international arena. Welcoming the move, the U.S. media commented that the change shifted the blame from the United States, "as an international bully and embargo tightener to Castro, as a democracy and human rights laggard."[64]

The Making of a Truce

The Understanding

An important roadblock remained in U.S.-European relations, however. Monday, April 12, 1997, was the deadline for the European Union to formalize its first complaint about Helms-Burton in the WTO, which had agreed to an E.U. request to set up a panel to settle the dispute. The main obstacle was that the United States had claimed exemption under national security provisions and threatened to boycott or ignore the WTO proceedings, insisting that Helms-Burton was not fundamentally a trade issue. Europe continued its pressure. Observers pointed out that the U.S. claim of exemption would severely embarrass the WTO and hurt the enforcement powers of the fledgling trade organization. They recalled that the United States had used the exemption argument twenty-three times since the inception of GATT in 1995 to force open the markets of other countries. After fifty hours of negotiation, the United States and Europe reached an agreement to avert the transatlantic trade dispute, at least until the following October 15 (a six-month truce). Under the accord, the White House committed itself to pressure the U.S. Congress to moderate portions of the law that penalize foreign companies for investing in Cuba (Title III), and remove the section that would deny visas to executives of corporations having investments in expropriated property (Title IV). In return, Europe agreed to take action against firms dealing in property confiscated by Havana and other regimes. More importantly, the E.U. would drop its WTO complaint against the United States.[65]

The Sunset of the Helms-Burton Law: Act One

Shortly after the first anniversary of the Helms-Burton Law, pressure for a compromise had built up considerably. News of the E.U.-U.S. talks had leaked to the press in the preceding weeks.[66] Initial commentaries reported that the United States was offering some readjustment in the Helms-Burton Law in exchange for the withdrawal of the European Union's appeal to the WTO and its commitment to "discourage" investment in properties confiscated by the Cuban regime. President Clinton announced that the general U.S. policy toward Cuba would not change.[67]

This compromise was crafted in the aftermath of an escalation of verbal declarations and retaliatory actions between Spain and Cuba. The dispute involved problems with a Spanish tourist in Havana and restrictions on Spanish diplomatic functions. At the same time, a Spanish businessman was charged in a Miami court for violating the U.S. embargo by sending merchandise to Cuba through third countries.[68]

The United States and the E.U. also maintained an ambiguous dialogue in another setting. During the yearly meeting of the UN Human Rights Commission, held in Geneva, the member states of the European Union, while voting in a solid bloc to express concern for the situation in Cuba, also revealed an apparent ambivalence. First they passed a resolution opposing the U.S. economic sanctions.[69] Then they endorsed U.S. claims against Cuba for human rights violations. This apparent contradiction was the result of different factors, including the controversy generated by the inclusion of a Cuban national in the Nicaraguan delegation. Out of 53 members, 19 voted for, 24 abstained (as opposed to 28 the year before), and 10 voted against (5 more than in 1996). After making a statement of protest against the Helms-Burton Law, all E.U. member states (and other European partners) voted in favor of the U.S.-inspired measure.[70] However, one must question the meaning of such unanimity and whether the actions by the fifteen members of the E.U. were really the product of international solidarity to end communism and Castro's regime in Cuba, or just a concession to the United States to avoid a trade clash.

In this increasingly heated context, the sudden and unsurprising news of the agreement between the European Union and the United States was announced. The combination of the series of collateral events and the final compromise seem to confirm that the numerous incidents were not sufficiently grave to warrant a confrontation between the two most powerful economic powers on earth that could undermine the nascent World Trade Organization.

Other arguments were also persuasive. E.U. commissioner Leon Brittan was well aware that President Clinton could not obtain a total dismantling of the Helms-Burton Law through a Congress still dominated by the Republican Party. The White House and the State Department, on the other hand, recognized that the demand presented by the E.U. at the WTO would inflict collateral damage to all free-trade agreements being negotiated by the United States in a climate made increasingly difficult by protectionist sectors.[71]

Details and Reactions

The text of U.S.-E.U. agreement included the following major points:

- Both sides confirm their commitment to continue their efforts to promote democracy in Cuba. On the E.U. side, these efforts are set out in the Common Position.

- The U.S. reiterates its presumption of continued suspension of Title III during the remainder of the President's term so long as the E.U. and other allies continue their stepped up efforts to promote democracy in Cuba.

- The E.U. and the U.S. agree to step up their efforts to develop agreed disciplines and principles for the strengthening of investment protection, bilaterally and in the context of the Multilateral Agreement on Investment (MAI). . . . These disciplines should inhibit and deter the future acquisition of investments from any State which has expropriated or nationalized such investments in contraversion of international law.

- The U.S. will begin to consult with Congress with the view to obtaining an amendment providing the President with the authority to waive

Title IV of the Act. In the meantime, the United States notes the President's continuing obligation to enforce Title IV.

· In light of all the above, the E.U. agrees to the suspension of the proceedings of the WTO panel. The E.U. reserves all rights to resume the panel procedure, or begin new proceedings, if action is taken against E.U. companies.[72]

Based on that agreement, both parties pledged to cooperate to bring democracy to Cuba, and both claimed to have obtained benefits. Brittan considered that, in exchange for withdrawing the E.U. claim in the WTO, he had obtained concessions. The agreement includes the protection of other investments in other regions (such as Libya and Iran). The pact limits its scope to future investments and does not affect present contracts, and it neutralizes this type of extraterritorial aim in future laws.[73] Stuart Eisenstat congratulated himself for having prevented irreparable damage to the WTO by creating "a first and true opportunity for developing a multilateral discipline that will ban investment in confiscated properties."[74]

When the deal was made public, the main backers of the law rushed to claim victory. The Cuban-American National Foundation, through spokesman José Cárdenas, invoked a familiar expression to characterize the agreement: "The other side has blinked."[75] The confrontation around the Helms-Burton Law was thus equated to the 1962 missile crisis, which presented the risk of obliterating the planet. While Cárdenas's assessment of the European reaction may be correct, the reality is that both sides blinked, and both elected to back down.

Reactions to the agreement also revealed cracks in the coalition that created the Helms-Burton law. While the office of Senator Helms considered the agreement positive, Representative Burton and Cuban-American Representatives Ros-Lehtinen and Díaz-Balart denounced it as a "surrender"[76] and an attempt to confuse Congress. European observers soon detected a solid front of domestic opposition to the overtures by President Clinton.[77]

Canada and Mexico, the other leading critics of Helms-Burton, did not officially join the U.S.-E.U. agreement. Canada never expressed an interest in adopting the deal, and, as we have seen, it rejected the expanded truce of 1998. Mexico has remained somewhat troubled by the pact. Foreign Secretary José Ángel Gurría suggested that the E.U. had sacrificed principle to pragmatism: "It seems to be a non-aggression pact in which the Americans will not cause problems for European companies and Europe will moderate its actions against the law."[78]

Conclusions

Given the continuing suspension of Title III and the understanding that Title IV would be constrained by the Washington bureaucracy, the outcome of the actions and reactions between Brussels and Washington can be considered generally positive. Considering the potential for irreparable damage to commerce, most of the leaders involved showed a degree of reason and statesmanship. But this is not the end of the story. The peculiarities of the relationship between Spain and Cuba and the stormy link between the United States and Cuba required consideration and resisted fitting the overall pattern of standard interpretations. These two special relationships, plus the unpredictable future of the Cuban regime, warn us that the next steps are far from certain. The next two chapters develop these considerations. Chapter 6 focuses on the Spanish-Cuban ramifications of Helms-Burton, and chapter 7 considers the lasting consequences of the original conflict between the United States and Cuba.

6

The Ever Faithful Island

Spain's Relations with Havana under U.S. Policy

"If you move a piece, I will move mine."
José María Aznar, Prime Minister of Spain, November 1996

"The destiny of nations cannot be played on a chess-board."
Fidel Castro, November 1996

"The same we did with Spain, we have to liberate Cuba from Castro."
Newt Gingrich, Speaker of the House of Representatives, 1997

When Spaniards (especially of the older generations) comment on the value of any loss, they sigh, "Más se perdió en Cuba" (that's nothing compared to what we lost in Cuba). In 1997 the phrase had a new ring. The expansion of the U.S. embargo exposed the historical patterns of Spanish-Cuban relations and generated internal contradictions in Spain's domestic politics. Within the context of the 1898 centennial commemoration, the role (*injerencia*, some voices say in Spanish, "meddling") of the United States in what was basically a bilateral relationship became more obvious, causing Spain to question whether U.S. policy toward Cuba is consistent with Spain's own perceptions and interests. At the same time, the process of regional integration and globalization has radically altered the contemporary isolation of Spain in the world arena, giving it new opportunities and obligations as a member of the European Union. Among its other effects, the Helms-Burton law has provided a new occasion for observing the trilateral relationship formed by the United States, Europe, and Latin America, including the unique ties between Spain and Cuba, both distant from and close to the United States.

Introductory Reflections

The link between Spain and Cuba is not an ordinary relationship between two ordinary states, as both history and some significant recent events make clear.

Contradictions and Confrontations

To begin with, Spain's General Francisco Franco, an authoritarian, anti-communist dictator allied by a military treaty with the United States, maintained close political and economic relations with the Cuban Marxist dictator Fidel Castro. Franco never caved in to the U.S. embargo against Cuba. Iberia Airlines was for decades Cuba's only air link to the West, and Spain became for many Cubans of Spanish extraction a temporary refuge en route to permanent exile in Miami. Some believe, in fact, that relations between Madrid and Havana were carried out with the covert support of the United States and the Vatican, for different and complementary reasons. Washington wished to use the Spanish Embassy as a source of information, while the Catholic leadership was reluctant to lose its traditional base in Cuba.[1]

On a personal level, Castro rarely professed any admiration for Franco, although he acknowledged Franco's independent stance vis-à-vis the Americans. In his in-depth study of the relationship between Franco's Spain and Castro's Cuba, George Lambie states that "apparently the two leaders shared an empathy which transcended politics."[2] He adds that in 1985 Castro acknowledged Cuba's debt to Franco. "Don't touch Cuba" was Franco's terse instruction to his ministers. Castro, in turn, recognized the gesture of the Spanish *caudillo:* "the *gallego* acted very well, *caramba.*"[3] U.S. ambassador Robert White recalled meeting with Fidel Castro in 1984. Reacting to an unkind comment that White had made about Franco, the Cuban leader responded "firmly and with conviction": "You can criticize the old *gallego* but it was he who kept us alive during the most difficult days of the U.S. embargo. I must admit to a certain admiration for the old fox. Like all *gallegos,* he is stubborn and opinionated but he never let ideology get in the way of Spanish-Cuban relations."[4] While Franco never issued special endorsements for Castro, diplomatic sources reveal that he had a fascination for a trio of well-known revolutionaries of his day: Mao Zedong, Ho Chi Minh, and Fidel Castro.[5] The three shared a mastery for guerrilla warfare, a Spanish invention in the war against Napoleon.

Democracy was reborn in Spain with the end of the Franco regime, and expectations regarding political pluralism became a condition for full diplomatic relations between Spain and other governments. For this reason, and despite the apparently friendly relations between Spanish socialists and Castro, by the end of 1998 Cuba remained the only Latin American country that King Juan Carlos of Spain had never visited. Some pragmatism is nevertheless evident in Spain's diplomatic protocols. Communist China and a number of authoritarian Arab states have enjoyed the same respectful treatment accorded the liberal democracies. But in Latin America, with the exceptions of Argentina and Uruguay, the King never visited a country where full democracy was not enjoyed.

While the rest of Latin America has professed a traditionally respectful attitude toward the *madre patria,* Castro's relations with Spain have been more contentious. As the quincentennial of Spain's 1492 discovery of the Americas was approaching, Castro characterized the date as *infausto y nefasto* (unfortunate and ill fated). He was not punished for this, however. To the contrary, he is regularly invited to the annual Ibero-American summits, where he has become a media star, especially when he attended the opening of the 1992 Barcelona Olympics and the World's Fair of Seville, and traveled through Galicia, his father's birthplace. Nonetheless, Castro's other two visits to Spain (one to Madrid and another to the Canary Islands) were technically brief stopovers, and his dream of a formal state visit will probably never take place. In November 1998 the Cuban leader extended his visit to the Ibero-American summit held in Oporto, Portugal, and accepted an invitation to visit the Spanish region of Extremadura, ending his trip in Madrid, where he had a brief interview with Spanish premier José María Aznar.

Spain is the only European country to have had two (socialist) senators expelled from Havana's airport by Cuban police, led by Cuban generals, as they attempted to visit the island. Castro may be the only world leader to call the socialist president of the Spanish Chamber of Deputies a *tipejo fascistoide* (a fascist crook). Not only was Castro not rebuffed for this, he later received a commemorative medal from the president of the Spanish Senate. But this was not a one-sided war of insults: one of Franco's ambassadors called Castro a liar on live television and to his face. Understandably, the diplomat was expelled, but when he arrived in Madrid General Franco censured him. Once *Granma* characterized Spain's foreign minister as a "colonial corporal," the Cuban minister of foreign relations accused his Spanish counterpart of blackmail. In a more recent diplomatic dust-up, Josep Coderch, Spain's ambassadorial nominee, was rejected by Castro in retaliation for Spanish conservative premier José María Aznar's hardening of policy toward Cuba. For good measure Castro called Aznar a *caballerito* (literally, a "little gentleman"), a remark expressing class resentment, disdain, and derisive paternalism—not to mention generational differences.

Change and Continuity

Notwithstanding these diplomatic contretemps, Spain has maintained very cordial economic relations with Castro's Cuba since the triumph of the Cuban Revolution, both during and after the Franco regime. Spain carried on the largest volume of trade with Cuba, and in the last decade has also given Cuba one of the largest amounts of development aid of any state in the Americas. All this may be explained by the fact that in the past Cuba was known as "the ever faithful isle." Apparently, faithfulness works both ways since, following independence, Cuba received one of the highest numbers of Spanish immigrants in Latin America. Spaniards never felt they were living in a foreign country; Cuban Spanish never coined pejorative epithets for Spaniards. Cuba became so Spanish, in fact, that in the 1930s a law was passed to limit employers to hiring no more than 50 percent foreigners (that is, Spaniards). Thousands of Spaniards avoided this restriction by becoming Cuban citizens; when the Cuban Revolution exploded, many returned to Spain, claiming original citizenship through the *jus sanguinis* tradition.

One central thought has to dominate any attempt to gauge the effect of America's Cuba policy on relations between Madrid and Havana. The relationship between Spain and the former colony is indeed very special, if not peculiar. Anyone ignoring this fact is likely to misinterpret the actions of either party. Moreover, this sensitive, friendly, and stormy relationship is usually prone to being manipulated and distorted when it becomes part of a triangular relation, particularly when the third party is the United States. While the twentieth century in European terms began with World War I, in the Americas its beginning is marked by the interposition of the United States into what was basically a family quarrel in Cuba. In fact, Cuban fighters for independence were ready to defeat the Spanish administrators when President McKinley pressed for the U.S. intervention after the *Maine* affair. Popular history has enshrined this confrontation as "the Spanish-American War." The fact that this crucial historical event is known in Cuba as "the War for Independence" and in Spain as "the Disaster" is evidence of the need for closer consideration of the events of 1898, their background, and lasting consequences.

The war not only granted a limited independence to Cuba, it also propelled the U.S. to its status as a world power. The "disaster" sank Spain into soul-searching, and the most positive result was the rich literary production of the Generation of '98. Members of Spain's defeated military, who believed they had been betrayed by the politicians and the weak monarchy, were reborn as *regeneracionistas,* Some of them became the most visible *africanistas* in an adventure in Morocco, where they sought to erase their shame over Cuba by building a substitute empire. Francisco Franco, the youngest general in Europe, was one of these, and his *regeneracionista* policy was so strict that the toppling of the Second Spanish Republic (1931–36) was the first act of the tragedy known as the Spanish Civil War (1936–39). It all began somehow with the sinking of the *Maine*.

The abrupt end of its colonial status by virtue of the U.S. intervention made Cuba an unfinished nation. The following period of U.S. administration and the imposition of restrictions such as the Platt Amendment produced a scar that was ready to be reopened by political circumstances. Historians have pointed out that the roots of the Castro Revolution can be traced to Cuban resentment against the United States in 1898. The humiliation inflicted on Spain by having to sign a treaty of surrender with the United States has become part of the contemporary Spanish political psyche. A hundred years later, a steady political, social, and economic relationship between Spain and Cuba has again suffered the insertion of the United States. The spirits of William McKinley and Teddy Roosevelt are revived in the persons of Jesse Helms and Dan Burton.

When U.S.-Cuban relations deteriorated following the shooting-down of the Brothers to the Rescue planes in February 1996 and the subsequent passage of the Helms-Burton Law (both events coinciding with a change of government in Madrid), Spain's relations with Cuba suffered important repercussions. For the first time in a century, Spain not only had a contentious relationship with the United States (over Helms-Burton), but also with Cuba (over political differences).

A Family Relationship

One factor in this new dynamic was that approval of the Helms-Burton Law coincided with the change of government in Spain following the March 1996 parliamentary elections. The conservatism of the winning party, led by the new Prime Minister José María Aznar, led observers to expect a more critical attitude toward Castro. However, the issue was more complex.

A Curious Internal Affair

In the international arena, Spain, especially during the PSOE administration (1982–1996), was blamed for the development of Helms-Burton, by virtue of its strong trade and investment links with Havana, which can be traced back to the Unión de Centro Democrático (UCD) governments (1976–1982) and even to the Franco era. For a long time, the topic of Cuba had the potential to become one of the few points of disagreement between Madrid and Washington—before and after the Spanish political transition, during and after the end of the Cold War. Moreover, Cuba was the source of an ongoing dispute between the Spanish government and the opposition (before and after the March 1996 election).[6] The importance of Cuba became fully apparent when U.S. Undersecretary of State for Latin American Affairs Alexander Watson was interviewed (some would say "interrogated") by the foreign-affairs committee of the Spanish Congress. Responding to the passionate interest expressed by the Spanish deputies (especially the Socialists), Watson asked a critical question: "Is Cuba a domestic question for Spain?" The resulting stream of declarations and press columns made it very clear that, indeed, Cuba is an internal affair for Spain, a very special one.[7]

It is well to recall here that the seemingly neutral term "internal matter" has a recent historical connotation. Most of today's Spanish deputies were already working in government when, on February 23, 1981, a colonel in the Guardia Civil named Antonio Tejero stormed the legislative palace and threatened Spanish democracy at gunpoint. When Alexander Haig, then U.S. secretary of state, was informed of the incident, he responded that it was "an internal matter" for Spain. The protests coming from the Spanish political class are still ringing in the air, and the expression has become part of the political vocabulary for a sort of biblical washing of hands as an easy response to a difficult task.[8]

In any event, the Socialists were seen (inaccurately) as antagonists of the United States by the Cuban exile community and the conservative political circles of Spain. On the other hand, the Partido Popular was perceived (simplistically) to be taking its cues from Washington in the eyes of the rank and file of the PSOE and Izquierda Unida (United Left). Reinforcing this perception were the frequent endorsements and expressions of gratitude coming from the Cuban exile community in Miami and the U.S. Department of State for the Spanish policy toward Castro.[9]

In reality, these perceptions were not entirely accurate. First, relations between the PSOE and Cuba were not as rosy as the Spanish conservatives and the exiled Cuban community portrayed them. As we have noted, there were frequent confrontations in the Madrid-Havana relationship. They include the skillful operation led by PSOE's premier Felipe González to maintain Spain as a member of NATO (a decision publicly questioned by Castro) by virtue of the referendum held in 1986, the crisis produced by the invasion of the Spanish Embassy in 1990 by Cubans seeking asylum, Castro's negative remarks about the 1992 quincentennial commemorations, and his personal insults directed against high Spanish officials. The PSOE administration, especially when the politically unaffiliated Francisco Fernández Ordóñez (*un cabo colonial,* a "colonial officer") was in control of foreign affairs in the cabinet of Felipe González, was very careful not to let

Cuba interfere with its relations with President Reagan and, especially, President Bush.

Incidentally, Spain has not been the sole Cuban ally to come under Castro's criticism. Mexico, for a long time the closest of Cuba's international backers, was publicly criticized at the end of 1998 for its part in the development of NAFTA and for forming close economic ties with the United States. A brief diplomatic tension resulted when the Cuban leader made additional comments regarding the dubious cultural level of Mexican schoolchildren, who, in his view, knew Mickey Mouse better than the heroes of Mexican independence.

Cuba in the Eyes of Spain and the United States

It is interesting to compare the role of Cuba in the domestic politics of Spain and the United States. In the United States, a hard stance toward Cuba during and after the Cold War era was likely to be rewarded by voters in certain locales (Miami, New Jersey). But members of Congress who represent voters outside these Cuban-dominated enclaves also find that a strong anti-Castro position is well received by the generations that consider the "loss" of Cuba a historical affront. In addition, this antagonism represents a commodity to be traded in the daily dealings of Congress, and it is also a valuable asset for fund-raising purposes. Overall, however, Cuba is not a vital issue in U.S. politics. To be hard on Cuba helps not to lose votes in certain congressional districts, but it does not help significantly to win elections. Cuba is, in summary, a peculiar internal matter in selected localities. Elsewhere in the United States, Cuba is little more than a footnote, if that much. This assessment may sound like a contradiction when one considers the polls taken over the decades regarding the negative perceptions of Cuba in the eyes of the U.S. people (see chapter 2). However, the polls only report the answers to specific questions; they do not reflect fundamental preoccupations, and Cuba is not one of them.

In Spain the issue of Cuba is also complex, and its political manipulation has its roots both in history and contemporary politics. Ironically, anti-U.S. attitudes can be detected in conservative and traditional Spanish circles, as well as at the other extreme of the political spectrum. The first group may attribute their antagonism to historical and cultural issues, including the perception that the United States is a Protestant-dominated nation. Another reason has to do with the humiliation of Spain in 1898. More recently, the anti-U.S. attitude can be attributed to the debasing of the Spanish military in the 1950s and 1960s, when they were granted surplus military equipment in exchange for an agreement allowing U.S. military bases on Spanish soil. This agreement effectively converted Spain into a target for Soviet nuclear missiles. Spanish leftists and intellectuals also found cause to resent the United States, believing that the survival of the Franco regime was attributable solely to the support of the United States.

As memories of the "loss" of Cuba faded within Spanish military circles as a source of resentment against the United States, the Castro regime became a central issue for conservative Spanish parties seeking to influence Spain's Socialist government. Once in power, the most vocal sectors of the Partido Popular insisted upon converting the Cuban issue into an integral part of the party's domestic program. While the Socialists perceived that a friendly attitude toward Cuba and a cautious distance from the United States would be rewarded at the ballot box, the *populares* perceived that their supporters demanded a hard line against Castro. The parties' positions were also dictated by ethical considerations and old-fashioned ideology: conservatives are supposed to stand up against Marxism, and socialists are inclined to act as progressives. An additional factor has been the continued fascination with the Cuban Revolution on the part of a sizable number of Spanish intellectuals, as expressed in the recent wave of books and novels published by travelers and other observers in the context of the 1898 commemoration and the visit of the Pope to Cuba. A book by the influential writer Manuel Vázquez Montalbán, *Y Dios entró en La Habana,* exemplifies this trend.[10]

United against Helms-Burton We Stand

The usual conservative-leftist scheme does not quite work on the Cuba issue. Manuel Fraga Iribarne, former minister of information and tourism under General Franco and now president of the autonomous region of Galicia, and Christian Democrats José Antonio Ardanza, president of the Basque Country, and Josep Antoni Durán Lleida, the Catalan leader of Unió Democràtica (the Christian Democratic party allied to Catalan president Jordi Pujol's Convergència Democrática), have visited Cuba and have expressed critical views about the U.S. policy toward Castro and the attempts to isolate his regime. While Fraga (who lived in Cuba as a child of Galician immigrants) suffered the rage of Spanish ultraconservatives for his friendly overtures to Castro, the visit of the Basque leader produced the expected controversies.[11]

With the above exceptions, the battle lines customarily dividing left and right were drawn differently in response to Helms-Burton. This politically motivated law created a unified response that was unique in the Madrid political scene. All the main political parties were for the first time in agreement on one topic. Taking into account that not even the constitution or Spain's membership in the European Union and NATO are free of contention, and the fact (proudly recognized by all) that no two Spaniards are likely to agree on anything, the universal opposition to Helms-Burton is remarkable. It has to be considered a signal achievement of U.S. foreign policy.

Once in power, the PP—naturally more inclined toward free enterprise—was firmly aligned with the PSOE and Izquierda Unida in opposition to the Helms-Burton legislation. Spain also sided with other European countries in opposing the new U.S. law. Some European partners had already begun to design countermeasures. The United Kingdom, for example, had approved protective mechanisms for its investments, including the Protection of Trading Interests Act of 1992. It would have been surprising that a government that campaigned for privatization and the preeminence of free enterprise would burn the bridges that the previous government had extended toward Cuba in the form of private and public investments that, after all, had generated jobs.

From the left and right, countermeasures were set in motion. The fact that the Socialists were in some ways outpaced by the conservatives was a novelty. Guillermo Gortázar, a PP member of parliament who had distinguished himself by criticizing the Socialist posture toward Cuba, rushed to propose a package of measures to protect Spanish investment in the island—not as a guarantee against action by the Cuban government, but as a precaution against Helms-Burton. Among these measures were regulations on confidentiality of investments in Cuba, in order to withhold this information from U.S. agencies and thus avoid subsequent retaliations. These measures could have notable consequences for scholars and other observers in calculations of the volume of investments. The figures are usually very opaque regarding not only the exact amount but also the actual origin of investments and the use of third countries and, especially, financial havens. Supplementing the collective mechanisms of the European Union, the policy known as Obligatory Diplomatic Protection was designed to convert the Spanish administration into a co-defendant in embargo-related U.S. lawsuits. Finally, some European-wide countermeasures were contemplated, including the denial of visas to potential litigants against European interests. Such individuals would be prevented from entering European Union territories, as well as barred from future investment in the E.U.[12] Yet once the European Union approved its own collective measures, the Spanish government did not enact its own special mechanisms until early 1998, when the cabinet approved a bill similar to the blocking measures produced by Canada and the U.K.[13]

Expanding the Playing Field

The bilateral relationship between Spain and Cuba began to expand in the setting of the annual Ibero-American summits inaugurated in 1991 in Guadalajara, Mexico. The new Spanish government had begun to play along two fronts—Europe and Ibero-America—and this time elected to use the forum shared with its closer linguistic and historical partners.

The Globalization of a Bilateral Relationship

The November 1996 summit was held in Santiago and Viña del Mar, Chile, and partly because the central issue was "governability," Castro's presence again attracted world attention. He also became a focal point when the Spanish premier managed to insert in the Declaration of Viña del Mar a detailed definition of democracy as a requirement for permanent membership. Even though Castro co-signed the declaration, there has been no move to have Cuba expelled for not complying with the democratic conditions, as occurred when Cuba lost its membership in the OAS. However, Ibero-American declarations may exert an indirect influence on Cuba, similar to the effect of the Helsinki Agreement on Eastern European regimes formerly controlled by the Soviet Union.

Curiously, unanimity against the Helms-Burton Law coincided with the pressure exerted privately by some Latin American dignitaries on Castro to initiate a political opening, in addition to the public demands made by the Spanish premier, José María Aznar. The conflict began with a series of public declarations by Aznar and Fernando Villalonga, Spain's undersecretary of state for Ibero-American cooperation. Explicit Spanish statements indicated that Aznar's policies would in essence continue the PSOE's line, with few exceptions—but one exception was Cuba. Irritated by Madrid's new attitude, Cuba's foreign minister, Roberto Robaina, sent a verbal note (a written diplomatic communication) to his Spanish counterpart complaining about the commentaries issued by Spain on Cuba's human rights situation. These critical remarks were to be enclosed in the proposed conclusions of the summit, a fact that the Cubans disliked. Villalonga retaliated by asking Robaina for explanations. The result was the creation of a poor atmosphere that cast a shadow over the meeting.[14]

Once in Chile, Aznar adopted a line independent from his colleagues, saying, "If they don't want to move [on Cuba], it's their problem."[15] Meanwhile, the King of Spain tried to soften the hard-line approach of his premier in informal conversations with Castro. Nevertheless, the Spanish officials made explicit that the renewal of bilateral cooperation agreements required real political reform, not only of "division of political functions, but of division of powers."

As luck would have it, the customary lottery seated Aznar and Castro together for lunch. When President Ernesto Zedillo of Mexico offered some comments about his electoral experiences, Aznar asked the Cuban leader, "What about your elections?" Castro answered that he held an election every year. Then President Carlos Menem of Argentina ventured ironically that it would be odd if the Cuban leader were to lose running unopposed. "Against whom would you rig the elections. You alone?"[16] After this lunch-time friction, Aznar continued the theme in a press conference, using language that was not the most diplomatic. He said that he advised Castro, "Si mueves pieza, yo moveré la mía" (If you move your piece [democracy], I'll move mine [aid]). Days later Aznar confirmed to the press that Castro wanted "to continue being dictator."[17] The leaders then exchanged their corresponding ties, a detail widely discussed by the press and the officials attending the event, among other reasons because Castro had just barely begun to use ties instead of his normal olive military shirt. He had inaugurated his new fashion in his visit to the FAO meeting in Rome (allegedly under the guidance of one of the leading men's fashion tailors), and apparently Aznar made a pleasant remark about it. The Cuban leader suggested an exchange. Afterward, Aznar added that Castro got the better deal because the Spanish tie was more expensive. To this day we do not know if Castro was more irritated by the chess-like offer, the political suggestions by Zedillo and Menem, or the comments on his ties. The fact is that when Castro returned to Cuba, he insultingly referred to Aznar as a *caballerito* at a meeting of the Cuban Assembly of Popular Power.[18] He followed that salvo with the ritualistic admonition that "the dignity of Cuba cannot be played on a chess board."

As a consequence of this exchange, a new expression, *mover pieza* (to make a move), has entered the political vocabulary of Spain. Two examples will suffice. The first appeared in *El País,* in a headline referring to the series of meetings between the Pope and Castro: "El Papa mueve pieza" (The Pope makes a move).[19] Francisco Safont, a business reporter, titled one of his stories "¿Mueve pieza Cuba?" (Does Cuba make a move?).[20] His closing comment was representative: "Today Spain is the first trading partner of Cuba among the European Union member states. However, in order to be able to maintain this leadership, the current political relations between the two countries will have to improve. Isn't it time to make a move?"

To date, observers cannot fully explain why the Spanish premier decided to pressure Cuba with public statements that proved so counterproductive.

One reason for his bold and risky comments was the insistence of the foreign-policy advisers of the PP. The remarks provoked the dismay of most seasoned diplomats, however, and the ridicule of Foreign Affairs Minister Abel Matutes, who was sidelined by Undersecretary of State Fernando Villalonga, an appointment imposed by Aznar.[21] The deterioration of Spanish-Cuban relations surprised the U.S. State Department staff, who had sought the cooperation of the previous Socialist administration and especially the personal involvement of Aznar's predecessor, Felipe González, in reading the Cuban situation.

Other sources for the fiasco include the alleged funding and campaign logistical support for Aznar's party provided by CANF leader Jorge Mas Canosa, including traveling in his private jets in trips throughout Latin America and between there and Miami. An added part of the explanation was Aznar's lack of experience in foreign affairs and his need to distance himself from the standard policy of the PSOE. The issue of Cuba provided this opportunity.[22]

Almost simultaneously with Aznar's proposal, Spain presented to the Council of Ministers of the European Union a new cooperation-aid plan for Cuba entirely conditioned on the implementation of political reforms. This initiative was not received with equal enthusiasm by all European partners. While some found it acceptable, others saw it as a subservient nod to the United States. For some U.S. State Department and White House observers, the new Spanish policy was an oddity, mainly because it was never the subject of an official lobby, especiallly in the Clinton administration. Nevertheless, the main principles were approved by the Political Committee on November 15, under the Irish presidency.

What ensued as a direct consequence was one of the most serious incidents between Spain and Cuba in recent years. The ostensible cause was a press interview granted by the new Spanish ambassador to Cuba, Josep Coderch, in which he expressed hope that a gradual political change in Cuba would coincide with his tenure in Havana. Fidel Castro expressed offense at the ambassador's remarks and withdrew the Cuban acceptance to Coderch. The real reason behind the withdrawal was Spain's sponsorship of the new measures approved by the Political Committee of the European Union.[23] Castro was also visibly annoyed by the establishment in Madrid of a Cuban-Spanish Foundation, a sort of branch of the Cuban-American National Foundation, with the full participation of the PP leadership. (The evolution of the foundation has not been smooth, and two of its most important founding members, CANF's leader Jorge Mas Canosa and writer Carlos Alberto Montaner, resigned.)[24]

In view of the frictions between Spain and Cuba, it is not surprising that the rejection of the Spanish ambassador was not to be the last diplomatic incident. In March 1997 the detention of a Spanish tourist in Havana prompted Spain's foreign minister, Abel Matutes, to declare that the Spanish government would not recommend that Spaniards visit Cuba. Roberto Robaina, Cuban minister of foreign affairs, responded by calling Matutes a "meddler," a "liar," and a "blackmailer."[25]

When the Spanish leadership brought the issue of Cuba before the forum of the European Union, the Socialist opposition saw it as another example of the *desespañolización* (de-Hispanization) of Spain's relationship with Cuba. For the PSOE, the relationship (whether contentious or amicable) between Madrid and Havana is better understood as a kind of family affair, and sensitive issues are best handled bilaterally. In the PSOE's view, once these issues are placed within the global context of the European Union, they run the risk of being diluted. Proposals that seem excessively radical to Nordic or British representatives often emerge considerably moderated. A degree of anti-Americanism contributes to this attitude, in that certain institutions of the E.U., especially the Parliament and Commission, are perceived as excessively pro–United States. In the view of the PP, however, contentious exchanges between Cuba and Spain are more likely to be resolved in a manner beneficial for Madrid within the Brussels context. Spain's European partners would logically side with Madrid over issues that do not threaten their own economies or strategic interests. What is good for Spain may be good for the rest of Europe, seems to be the logic. But for the PSOE, converting the bilateral relationship into a portion of the pooled sovereignty means a loss of independence and the loss of direct, person-to-person negotiations.

Ironically, Spain suffered the most damage in a conflict that originally involved only Washington and Havana. Spain lost one of its shrewdest observers in the diplomatic field, a handicap that followed on the heels of the inopportune resignation, at the end of 1994, of Spanish ambassador José Antonio San Gil, due to never-clarified disagreements with the Socialist government. San Gil's shortened term was also followed by the barely year-long tenure of his successor, Eudald Mirapeix, who was seen as too lenient toward Cuba by the new Conservative Spanish government.

The only prior recorded rejection of a Spanish diplomat in Cuba was the case of Pablo de Lojendio, who was expelled from the island on January 28, 1960, after he confronted Castro on live television and proceeded to call him a liar for accusing the Spanish diplomatic mission of connivance with the Cuban opposition.[26] In the 1997 annual congressional debate known as "the State of the Nation," the PSOE leader Felipe González had only one major criticism for the foreign policy of José María Aznar: Spain was the only E.U. member state without an ambassador in Havana.[27]

Impact on Economic Relations

Spanish investors in Cuba feared lack of protection when the financial guarantees and other investment incentives (frequently tied up to the purchase of Spanish goods) were withdrawn by Madrid. As a result, there was risk of a significant slowdown in the commercial flow between the two countries. Meanwhile, European countries not publicly involved in the controversies with Castro could very well fill the space left by Spanish interests. On the other hand, the European Union institutions were in the same position as before the incidents. There was no aid agreement with Cuba, and the requirements for a future one remained the same. Cuban authorities rushed to announce that the disputes with Spain should not influence future dealings with Brussels or other European capitals.

The approval of the H-B law and the change of the Spanish government produced a degree of uneasiness in the business community. Some investment projects from other countries were put on hold. The Spanish government announced the suspension of plans to build eight hotels that would be managed by a consortium formed by the Cuban government agency Gran Caribe and the Spanish public company Paradores de España, with an investment of $16 million.[28] Occidental Hoteles, an enterprise that manages a hotel in Miami, announced that it was withdrawing from a project, in conjunction with the Cuban company Gaviota, to build a resort in Varadero.[29] Some companies announced they were leaving Cuba as a result of the uncertainty caused by the U.S. measures and the collapse of the European Union's cooperation-aid proposal,[30] but it is difficult to place a dollar value on these losses.

Other business signals were, in contrast, very positive. Spanish-Cuban trade, for example, has continued at historical levels. The trade surplus enjoyed by Cuba in 1975, the year Franco died, has shifted to an unstoppable advantage for Spanish products. During the 1980s the ratio was between 2:1 and 3:1 for Spanish exports. In the 1990s Cuba has imported four times more Spanish goods than Spain has bought from Cuba. In 1995 Spain became Cuba's second most important trading partner (in contrast to its sixth place in 1994).[31] Spanish exports experienced a 14 percent increase in 1995,[32] 40 percent during the first half of 1996,[33] and 30 percent for the total of 1996, topping 17,000 million pesetas ($113 million) for the first quarter of 1997, a figure similar to the one recorded for the same period in 1996.[34] Thus, trade figures do not seem to have been noticeably affected by the Helms-Burton Law or the political friction between Spain and Cuba.[35]

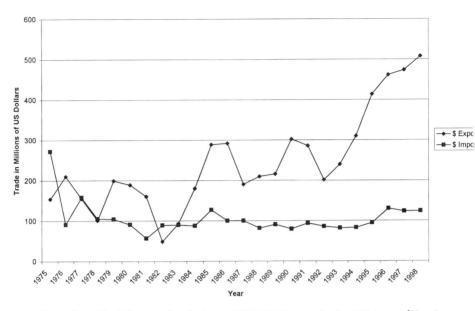

Fig. 3. Spanish-Cuban trade relations, 1975–98. *Source:* Spain, Ministry of Foreign Affairs and Ministry of Commerce.

In 1998 Spain became the most important commercial partner of Cuba. Global figures between the two countries topped $600 million (see figure 3). Spanish investment in Cuba for 1996 reached $11.4 million, tripling the figures of 1995.[36] Spanish tourism investment reached $1 million in 1996, and the trend continued in 1997 and 1998.

In contrast, and as a sign of the critical new policy of the Spanish government, a line of credit for exports to Cuba was cancelled.[37] However, in typical roller-coaster fashion, it was later announced that 40 million pesetas (about U.S.$250,000) were available in aid,[38] along with an overall program of development cooperation that included an additional 100 million pesetas (about $660,000) in commercial loans and 11 million pesetas ($733,000) for humanitarian aid and scholarships.[39] In spite of the tense relations in 1997, the 1998 cooperation plan (including loans and other measures) showed about $10 million reserved for Cuba. Cuba now leads the list of countries in debt to Spain, the amount topping more than $500 million in unpaid loans.[40] In February 1999, the debt was recognized to be as high as $1 billion, including official long-term loans, as a result of a very poor performance of payment of loans, mostly connected to aid packages.[41] That is the reason why aid figures sometimes appear to be inconsistent, depending on whether loan plans are included or only direct donations.

Conclusions

These figures reveal the disproportion between the attention Spain has given to Latin America generally, and the narrower terrain occupied by Cuba, and the real trade and investment value of the Latin American subcontinent within Spain's global strategy. Latin America and Cuba are important to Madrid for reasons not limited to trade and commerce.

The Nature of Spain's Relations with Cuba

When the Cuban-Spanish relationship in this century is studied in the broader context of Spain's relations with Latin America, some general characteristics are evident. Spain's foreign policy toward Latin America since the defeat of 1898 is seen as one of *obligación* (duty), for historical, cultural, and linguistic reasons. Since the end of the Spanish Civil War, it has been labeled first as one of *sustitución* (substitution), to fill the space left by more complex scenarios which were too complicated for Spain's for political or economic reasons. Then it became a policy of *presión* (pressure) to be used by the new democratic governments of the UCD and then by the PSOE in both the inter-American context and in the European Community negotiations, before and after Spain's accession. When its friendly political relations with Castro were questioned, the PSOE justified the policy as a renewed *obligación*. Profitable trade and investment relations could then be termed a policy of *negoción* (fast business),[42] to use a neologism that would rhyme with the rest of the labels.

In informal presentations made in Spanish, I have used the Spanish word *follón* (roughly translated as "a hell of a row") to characterize the tensions that followed Aznar's pressuring of Castro at the Ibero-American summit. This Spanish expression was actually used by high officers of the Ministry of Foreign Affairs when they met with Minister Abel Matutes in Montevideo, where he finally rejoined the Spanish entourage. In disbelief over the fiasco caused by Aznar's remarks to Castro, the officers asked Matutes for an explanation: "What is that *follón*?" Still in the dark himself about Aznar's plans, the Minister of Foreign Affairs responded, "Let me find out [déjame que me entere]."[43]

All the variations on the above labels can be summarized as reflecting a policy of *frustración* (frustration), as Socialists and Conservatives have shared the same sense of impotence in the face of the Cuban government's resistance to change. When the Aznar government moderated its cool policy toward Castro and embraced the engagement strategy espoused by the Socialists, the PSOE leadership took the opportunity to question Aznar about the contrast between his new position and the harsh criticism he had directed to the Felipe González government in the midst of the 1996 electoral campaign. New candidate Josep Borrell sarcastically asked Aznar why Spanish investment was considered "immoral" during the PSOE administration because it allegedly lengthened the Castro government, but later it was acceptable that the Spanish minister of industry would lead more than a hundred executives on a business trip to Havana. Borrell did not question the move toward a normalization of relations but rather the motivations for the drastic shift in policy. Although it is virtually impossible to prove, the reasons may have to do with contacts made between Aznar and the CANF leadership during his successful candidacy for Spanish premier.[44] When, in 1998, the Spanish government reverted to its hard-line policy toward Cuba, emissaries of the Partido Popular on several occasions rushed to Miami to meet with CANF members and clarify the new approach. In late December 1998, the Spanish consulate was the target of protests, and Cuba threatened to boycott Spanish products. The former editor of the conservative Havana newspaper *Diario de la Marina* protested the new Spanish policy by returning an important decoration awarded to him by the king of Spain.

The sudden change of policy adopted by the new Spanish government in March 1998 toward a rapprochement with Castro and the apparent honeymoon that followed between both governments has not been lost on observers. Representative of a line of thought that can be described as center-left, Antonio Elorza, a University of Madrid professor, expressed perplexity regarding the role played by Spain through a shift from the attitude of Aznar as "a delegate of Mas Canosa in Europe, [and] a lone ranger confronting Castro," to a policy of reserving a space for the "spokesmen of the Castro dictatorship" and the "legitimating sympathizers."[45] In his view, Spain had gone from one extreme to the other. From a critical attitude toward Castro, Aznar changed to a too close relationship.

In any case, the link between Spain and Cuba will always have a special character. History and culture, perceptions and images are part of the explanation for actions that seem on the face of it illogical and energy consuming. This is a dimension that both Brussels and Washington need to understand when dealing with the triangular relationship generated by the Helms-Burton Law.

A Balance Sheet for All

Curiously, all the parties involved with Helms-Burton could claim partial or total success. The European Union saved face by explicitly opposing the law and approving the Common Position on Cuba. The Spanish government has shown firmness toward the law while appearing as a major advocate of the Common Position. Castro could demonstrate that he did not collapse under pressure, nor did he accept overtures such as the offer made by President Clinton in January 1997 of a huge aid and reconstruction package that would have required the current Cuban political leadership to step down. Naturally, in Cuba the offer was received with disdain expressed in the retort "Cuba is not for sale."[46]

The Cuban exile community and various sectors of U.S. public opinion expressed both enthusiasm and skepticism about the proposed aid package, known as "Support for a Democratic Transition in Cuba."[47] In a way, it can be said that it tried to revive the basic hopeful spirit of the Torricelli law in its strategy of "calibrated response." Observers were reminded of the parallel with other attempts to redress Cuban history, such as the attempt to "buy" Cuba from Spain[48] or the offer made by President William McKinley in 1901.[49] The document enticed the Cuban military to lead the transition process, promised aid through NGOs, promoted the development of private enterprise, planned compensation to Cuban exiles for the expropriations with the offer of shares in the privatized industries, and promised to sponsor the reentry of Cuba to the OAS.[50] The figures in the package included aid from international organizations and the already impressive sum of money regularly remitted to their families in Cuba by U.S.-based exiles (more than $500 million a year). That amounts to about 50 percent of the $8 billion promised for an eight-year period that would begin once the initial reforms were under way. Although the Cuban government can claim that the threat of Helms-Burton has hindered its obtaining loans for the sugar harvest, the collapse of the regime is not in sight.[51]

Meanwhile, the U.S. government has maintained the threat of Title III, which officially has been only temporarily suspended. Even when one considers that the Cuban government has hardened its internal policies (as confirmed by the adoption of measures designed to harass dissidents in 1997), the Spanish Socialists may also claim some success. They can argue that more satisfactory results could have been obtained with their "carrot" policies of inducements to Castro. In contrast, no benefits have yet been obtained by the "stick" brandished by the government of Aznar nor the more diplomatic approach of the European Union through its Common Position.[52]

Further Tensions and Uncertainties

A new incident occurred in the aftermath of the escalation of tensions outlined above. In this already tense scenario, Francisco Javier Ferreiro, a Spanish businessman, was arrested in Miami for transporting U.S. merchandise to Cuba by way of third countries, in violation of the U.S. embargo. This incident provoked declarations by both the Spanish Embassy in Washing-

ton and the Foreign Ministry in Madrid, stating that while Spain still opposed the Helms-Burton Law, the alleged crimes of the Spanish businessman were covered by the previous (1960s) laws.[53] This mild response provoked protest by the Spanish opposition, this time led by former Spanish
Prime Minister Felipe González.[54] Subsequently, on the occasion of an official visit by Spanish Prime Minister Aznar to Washington, the Ferreiro case
was taken up with Secretary of State Madeleine Albright.[55] However, in
October 1997, Ferreiro admitted violating the U.S. law and received a mild
jail sentence, while his partner and accuser was acquitted.[56] He was released
in July 1998.[57]

During the summer of 1997 another perturbing development in the U.S.-
Cuban relationship had as its epicenter some of the most emblematic Spanish investments in Cuba. One by one, the most important hotels in Havana
were hit by bombs. Some of these hotels belong to, or are managed by,
Spanish firms. In the context of Helms-Burton, it is important to recall that,
while Spain may be one of the leading investors in Cuba, Spanish interests
do not seem to be directly connected with expropriated U.S. land or buildings. However, most of the Spanish investment is visible because it is based
on hotels catering to tourism. Although it seems that the bombs have not
been a deterrent for Spanish tourism in Cuba, they created a disturbance in
Spanish political and economic circles. Cuban tourism minister Eduardo
Rodríguez de la Vega recognized that the bombs had a small impact in the
number of tourists arriving in Cuba in September 1997, from an increase of
19 percent in the same period in 1996 to an 18.1 percent increase in 1997.[58]
Whether the bombs were planted by Cuban exiles or by internal dissidents,
the message was the same: tourism was the target, and Spain was the most
important trading partner with Castro.

A Tentative Closing

By the end of 1997, Spanish-Cuban relations displayed contradictory signs.
While trade not only did not decrease but experienced a rise, and tourism
was threatened but still maintained its previous levels, political relations
were in a suspended state. The appointment of a new Spanish ambassador
was in limbo.[59] The pressures exerted by the Aznar government had had no
noticeable effects in the evolution of the Castro regime. The Spanish expectation of Cuban "gestures," such as approval for the opening of a Spanish
cultural center in Havana, had not been met by the Cuban government.[60]
However, a subtle change in the Spanish attitude led to a more practical
policy of engagement with Cuba, very similar to the one practiced by the
preceding Socialist government. A series of significant events, concentrated
in the period between late 1997 and the first months of 1998, deserve care-

ful consideration. Some of these occurred prior to the visit of Pope John Paul II to Cuba, while some of the most important decisions made by the Spanish government seem to be attributable to the papal visit.

With respect to cooperation aid, Spain decided to include Cuba on its list of priorities for 1998, together with Guatemala and Colombia. Although the aid intended for Cuba was still subject to the conditions of the Common Position adopted by the E.U., the sum of 1 billion pesetas (about U.S.$6.6 million) is about the same as in 1997.[61] Spain's persistence in strengthening cultural links on the eve of the 1898 commemoration paid off, and the Cultural Center was finally opened in Havana. The first lecture was delivered by Joaquín Ruiz Jiménez, a former minister of Franco and a father figure of the Spanish political transition.[62] Just a few days earlier, the Cuban exile writer Guillermo Cabrera Infante was awarded the prestigious Cervantes Prize.[63] The Spanish television network TVE opened a permanent bureau in Havana, a privilege previously enjoyed only by CNN.[64] Another milestone was the naming of a military attaché at the Spanish embassy in Havana, the only one of its kind from the countries of NATO and the E.U. bloc.[65] On the negative side, unconfirmed reports about Basque terrorists living in Cuba, while receiving support from the Castro government for their actions against the Spanish government, clouded the confusing bilateral relationship.[66] At the same time, Spanish diplomatic staff (including the military attaché) endured residency status and housing limitations imposed by the Cuban authorities alleging parity and reciprocity. Havana imposed in this way limitations similar to those placed by the Spanish government in Madrid.

The papal visit to Cuba caught the Spanish government flat-footed. Months later, when Foreign Affairs Minister Abel Matutes claimed credit for facilitating this event, the PSOE leadership reminded him that the Spanish conservative government had tried, in fact, to influence scuttling the visit. As a reward for his efforts to this end, the consul general in Miami (who acted as an intermediary between the presidential candidate Aznar and the CANF's leader Jorge Mas Canosa) was appointed ambassador to the Vatican.[67] During the commemoration of the Spanish-American War, Spain did not have a fully accredited ambassador in Havana, while King Juan Carlos I would have to skip Cuba during his visits to the former Spanish colonies lost as a result of the war. Allegedly, pressure from the U.S. ambassador in Madrid had made this epochal royal visit a continuing question.[68] Observers feared the worst for the papal visit, in view of the unkind remarks against Spanish colonization of Cuba that Castro expressed upon the arrival of John Paul II in Havana. Raúl Castro's project of building a monument in Santiago de Cuba dedicated to the "genocide" of Cuban patriots added to the uncertainty.

However, a dual announcement seemed to signal a truce. Fidel Castro declared on Cuban television that he had not intended any affront to the Spaniards, many of whom had fought alongside the Cuban patriots.[69] As the media offered lively speculation, Foreign Affairs Minister Matutes announced that the appointment of a Spanish ambassador was imminent, while a visit for King Juan Carlos I to Cuba was being considered for 1998.[70] Madrid apparently made a drastic shift in its policy toward Cuba, moving toward the attitude of engagement espoused by the Socialist administration. A delegation of Spanish Partido Popular (PP) members of the European Parliament visited Havana and held high-level talks on the topic of improved Spanish aid programs and a package sponsored by Brussels.[71] In a belated move already discussed, the Spanish cabinet approved a bill (in effect, a blocking statute consistent with the U.K. and Canadian measures) opposing the application of the Helms-Burton Act, as prescribed by the regulation passed by the European Union in the fall of 1996. The bill would prohibit persons and companies from complying with the demands of the U.S. legislation regarding investments in Iran, Libya, and Cuba.[72]

In sum, in foreign policy terms, the government of José María Aznar can claim credit for winning an important role in the institutions of the European Union. The Spanish government has also enjoyed the praise of the United States—and paid the corresponding price of abuse by the opposition. However, Aznar had lost ground in one important area. With no ambassador in Havana and limited diplomatic relations, he was no closer to achieving his objectives with respect to Cuba: there was no reform of the system, and the political transition in Cuba was as cloudy as before. Madrid and Washington then shared the same frustration. This probably explains the subtle change of policy in early 1998 and the apparent implementation of a strategy of "calibrated" offers to Havana.

It is interesting to note that the public confrontation between Spain and Cuba in 1996–97 contrasted with the extraordinary degree of diplomatic restraint shown by Washington and the European Union, who sought to avoid irreparable damage to trade relations (the WTO, especially). All this was happening as the 1998 celebrations were approaching. With no changes in the confrontational attitude, some may have said, as in 1898, that "más se perdió en Cuba."[73] The visit of the Pope to Cuba and some degree of common sense made the difference. However, as we will see in the concluding chapter, the hardening of Cuba's legal measures against dissidents caused Spain to reassert its cautious wait-and-see policy toward the Castro regime.

7

Disproportionate Influence Still
Creates Outsized Problems

*H-B has played a role in unifying the Cuban people, has unified the
international community, has increased our adrenaline flow, and has
allowed the Cuban people to confirm that the success of the U.S. policy
toward Cuba would mean hunger and misery for our people.*
Carlos Lage, Cuba's minister of economy, September 21, 1996

Let the world open up to Cuba.
Pope John Paul II, Havana, January 1998

They have turned the planet into a giant casino.
Fidel Castro, January 1, 1999

On May 18, 1998, at the end of a transatlantic summit held in London, the
European Union and the United States announced that they had reached a
compromise that would suspend the provisions of the controversial Helms-
Burton and D'Amato acts with respect to investments in Cuba, Libya, and
Iran.[1] The agreement has to be read as a confirmation and an extension of
the 1997 accord crafted by Brussels and the White House. The U.S. administration hailed the new agreement, which as recently as early 1997 had
been considered a "mission impossible."[2] Officers of the U.S. Permanent
Representation to the European Union in Brussels admitted that their main
task had been to convince the Europeans that the State Department and the
White House were their allies and the real "enemy" was the U.S. Congress,
an account confirmed in my interviews with representatives of the E.U.
member states and officers of the European Commission.[3]

For the purposes of this book, the 1998 agreement marks a major milestone and dictates a pause in our analysis. For this reason, the following
pages review the events that contributed to this compromise, assess the
consequences of the law, and offer some tentative explanations for the persistence of the U.S.-Cuban confrontation.

A New (and Final?) Truce

The May 1998 understanding reaffirmed the 1997 promise by the E.U. not to pursue retaliatory measures against the United States in the setting of the WTO and also to discourage investment in certain questionable properties. Surprisingly, the E.U. accepted the U.S. contention that some of the Cuban expropriations might have violated international law. The White House, in exchange, promised to pressure the U.S. Congress to further neutralize the Helms-Burton legislation. The United States and the European Union agreed to establish a Registry of Claims and to work jointly in the context of the Multilateral Agreement on Investment (MAI). The United States agreed to respect the current status of foreign investment in Cuba and not to make pre-May 1998 expropriations the target of lawsuits, as prescribed by Title III of the Helms-Burton Law. Future expropriations and subsequent investment in such properties would be mutually scrutinized, however.

In a controversial move, the E.U. agreed to discourage post-1998 investments in questionable properties by denying the customary diplomatic protection, insurance, commercial and tax incentives, and other supports. Investment in properties illegally expropriated after May 18, 1998, would be prohibited. In sum, the agreement confirmed the course taken more than a year earlier when, as we have seen, both parties sought a compromise to avoid a serious confrontation with unpredictable consequences. However, the new agreement was not free of problems. It was reluctantly accepted by some of the E.U. member states,[4] various commentators,[5] and U.S. sources.[6] Understandably, Cuba opposed the arrangement.[7] Moreover, its implementation was still dependent upon hard-to-obtain congressional cooperation,[8] as well as the development of policies regarding sensitive European interests in Libya and Iran.[9] Significantly, a year later the United States softened its policy sanctions toward Iran, Libya, and Sudan while maintaining its hardline approach to Cuba, Iraq, and North Korea.

The combined problems of a lack of time to obtain a compromise to be inserted into the summit declaration and the need for language that would please all parties to the negotiations generated a very confusing document. Hailed as an exercise in "creative conflict management" by E.U. insiders,[10] it was labeled as an example of *pasteleo* (result of backroom deals) or, worse, *chapuza* (shoddy work) in the colorful political jargon of Spain. Alarmed as conflicting interpretations began to emerge, E.U. Commission officers rushed to alert delegates abroad to be ready to clarify several points.

First, the E.U. position stressed the "political" nature of the agreement and disclaimed any legally binding status, explicitly stating that the understanding could not be implemented until evidence of a waiver on Title IV was in hand. Second, the E.U. declared that it was not obliged to follow the U.S. position on the questionable legality of the Cuban expropriations, with the clarification that investment in Cuba was still possible, and that the denial of official support was at the discretion of individual E.U. governments. Third, guidelines pointed out that any prohibition of investment in Cuba would only apply to expropriations that took place after May 18, 1998, the date of the agreement, but not to any of the controversial expropriations that took place prior to that time. Finally, the E.U. Commission advised its diplomatic representatives to extend due consideration to the U.S. Congress, in anticipation of a complete waiver of actions specified under Titles III and IV. Only under these circumstances would the understanding take effect.[11]

European governments immediately denied that the understanding was legally binding. Belgium argued that article 73C of the Maastricht Treaty prohibits limitations on capital movement and investment. The French representatives insisted that the "ball is in the U.S. court," and that the E.U. simply had to wait for the U.S. legal modifications and waivers.[12] The understanding became the subject of a debate in the Spanish Congress between the minister of foreign affairs and a large majority of the political opposition. Legal commentators pointed out the apparent contradiction between the new political understanding and the strict legality of the previous measures taken by the European Union, especially the protective regulation and the joint action of November 1996.[13] On the political level, critics stressed that the new understanding violated the spirit of the regulation because it recognizes the political aim of the Helms-Burton Law.[14] These observers also questioned the authority of the sole E.U. negotiator, E.U. Commission Vice President Leon Brittan, to sign agreements that exceed the jurisdiction of the European Commission and pertain to foreign policy and security matters that are still the prerogative of the member states.[15]

The Spanish deputies were particularly irritated by the fact that the Spanish government remained silent on these controversial items. Most especially, they complained about what they saw as a loss of sovereignty and what they considered the incorporation of the requirements of Helms-Burton into a politically binding agreement. Disagreeing with the Spanish government's claim that current and future investments in Cuba were better protected than before the understanding, Congressman Ignasi Guardans described the prospect of Spanish investment in Cuba as more risky than "opening a hotel in Rwanda."[16] This member of parliament is the spokesman for the center-right Catalan party, which has insured the survival of the Spanish government with its congressional backing since the election of 1996. Once again Helms-Burton had become a force in the internal politics of Spain and confirmed that political alignments are not inflexible when Cuba is the subject under consideration. As an illustration of the positive aspects of the Understanding, Matutes referred to the reaction of the backers of the D'Amato act. They claimed that the U.S. negotiators had caved in to the pressure of the European Union. Another anomaly of this peculiar congressional hearing was the presentation by a university professor of a commissioned legal study justifying the U.S.-E.U. understanding. This report has remained incomprehensibly classified.

Critical British voices were also heard immediately upon the conclusion of the agreement. Representatives of the consulting firm Cuba Business, based in London, reacted negatively to the understanding at a special hearing held by the Committee on External Relations of the European Parliament. Correcting and expanding the interpretations of opposition to the understanding as expressed by Senator Helms, the Cuba Business report pointed out that the aims of the agreement are "to negotiate a rewriting of international law under the principles developed in the Helms-Burton Act" and stated that "if wiser heads within Europe do not prevail, the understanding will prove yet another step towards Europe's acceptance of Helms' political agenda." They claimed that Europe has been forced to be committed to a "U.S.-designed project of redefining the ground rules for international business. . . . Little by little Europe has ceded ground to Washington."[17]

Finally, attention should be paid to a customary pattern in U.S.-Cuba relations, as aptly described by Richard Nuccio in a paper ("Cuba: A U.S. Perspective") presented to a Brookings Institution conference in March 1998. When conditions seem to signal a lessening of tensions, the radical wings within the U.S. and Cuban polities seem to work in unison to derail a process that would deprive them of their roles.[18] This is the same "coalition" that Jorge Domínguez has described, formed by hard-liners in the United States and Cuba who "have become each other's best allies." An example of this occurred when Cuban-American lobbies pressed for the passage of Helms-Burton, and the Cuban government responded with "standing orders to shoot, and to crack down on Concilio Cubano." U.S. threats under H-B have also been mirrored by the Cuban government's "propensity for political repression and intolerance of even slightly different ideas," such as in 1999, when harsher laws were passed.[19]

In a June 1998 letter addressed to Secretary of State Madeleine Albright, Senators Helms and Gilman expressed their disagreement with the understanding on the basis of its "weak" sanctions, the limited scope of the "prohibition" of investment in Cuba, and the fact that the E.U. blocking statutes were still active. The senators demanded that all 5,911 U.S. claims be included in the agreement, and they complained that the properties of Cuban-Americans might be excluded, although this matter is the subject of contradictory interpretations. (While the understanding does not explicitly mention the claims of the Cuban-Americans, the door for their inclusion in the new registry might be open.) Finally, the senators rejected the European conditions of a permanent waiver of Title III and insisted on the continuous implementation of Title IV.[20] This pattern of mutual rejection would be confirmed in January 1999, when the White House announced mild liberalizing measures.

On the other side of the battlefield, the Cuban government expressed its own concerns about the E.U.-U.S. understanding. Just after it was announced, Fidel Castro lambasted the agreement at the WTO in Geneva, calling it a "shrewd maneuver . . . to internationalize the principles of the infamous Helms-Burton act under the umbrella of a multilateral agreement."[21] Castro made similar comments in Havana while receiving members of the European Parliament. Ricardo Alarcón, president of the Cuban Assembly, minimized the concessions made by the United States.[22] Furthermore, in a speech given at the European Parliament, Cuban Foreign Affairs Minister Roberto Robaina demanded the elimination, not the modification, of the Helms-Burton Law, objected to the "negotiation of Cuban sovereignty," warned the E.U. about the "dangerous" precedent posed by the understanding, and outlined its contradiction with the previous regulation and other E.U. measures.[23]

Considered together, these responses indicate that the potential for further confrontation has increased, especially given the involved parties' previous contentious relations over Cuban trade issues.

A Mid-Term Review

The second anniversary on March 12, 1998, of President Clinton's signing of the Helms-Burton Bill into law was a bittersweet occasion for the law's backers.[24] Congresswoman Ros-Lehtinen commented that nobody was happy with the situation.[25] The road to a compromise, crafted by once seemingly irreconcilable parties, appeared to be in the making. However, historical obstacles and long-standing patterns of obstruction also appeared to block any move toward a normalization of relations between the United States and Cuba.

The momentum for change generated by the papal visit seemed to be an energy that numerous actors wanted to use.[26] The Vatican itself elected to take the lead, engaging its experienced diplomats in receiving U.S. and Cuban representatives and sending senior cardinals to pursue further conversations in Havana,[27] despite the strong objections of hard-liners in the

U.S. Congress to any kind of rapprochement with Cuba.[28] The hard-liners warned of new sanctions against Cuba[29] as well as measures against countries dealing with Cuba;[30] they chastised liberal sectors[31] and made accusations at the OAS against Cuba for violating human rights.[32]

The White House unveiled new liberalizing measures that would allow direct humanitarian flights to and from Cuba,[33] shipments of medicine and food, and cash remittances.[34] Meanwhile Secretary Albright announced that a new era of relations with Cuba would begin, anticipating the scene in post-Castro years.[35] The announcement was well received in the U.S. press[36] and by political observers of U.S.-Cuban relations.[37] For its part, the Pentagon announced a report finding that Cuba posed no security threat to the United States,[38] even though the State Department still keeps Cuba on its list of "terrorist countries."[39] The Pentagon's assessment was quickly contested by sectors of the Cuban exile community and members of Congress, however.[40] The Pentagon decided to delay the release of the announced report to Congress on the grounds that the text needed revision in accordance with the latest official policy of the U.S. government.[41] This corrective action took place in the context of renewed pressure from the embargo's backers in the U.S. Congress. They were assisted by House Majority Leader Newt Gingrich, who accused the White House and the Pentagon of "politicizing" the report, an accusation that was made on both sides.[42]

The announcement of the liberalizing measures reinforced the divisions within the exile community and made more apparent the leadership vacuum following the death of Mas Canosa.[43] Some Cuban-Americans expressed a sincere desire for change,[44] while others resisted any loosening of the embargo on the grounds that Cuba was seeking to substitute Western aid for the Soviet subsidies[45] and because any relaxation in the U.S. Cuban policy would be seen as the wrong message.[46]

Until this point in the story, there was little of substance that was new, although prospects for improved relations had significantly increased, thanks to the intervention of the Vatican. However, the forces that usually coalesce when a compromise is in the works between Cuba and the United States reappeared in full strength. When Fidel Castro made a spontaneous positive remark, his foreign minister, Roberto Robaina, lambasted the intermediation of the Catholic Church[47] as an intrusion by the United States in the Vatican-Cuban relationship, and he announced his refusal to have talks with what he branded as the "hysterical mafia of Miami."[48] For him, humanitarian aid was an insult while the embargo was in effect. Therefore, the lifting of the U.S. embargo should be the precondition.[49] Even more surprisingly, Cuban Cardinal Jaime Ortega declared in Havana that the announced humanitarian aid was an "offensive charity," and he blasted the embargo as "immoral."[50] Nevertheless, it was becoming clear that the controversy was losing steam. Paradoxically, the increase in the volume of noise was actually evidence of a compromise in the making, as the parties who perceived they were losing ground vented their frustration.

In Spain the situation had become more confused regarding the projected visit to Cuba by King Juan Carlos and the naming of the new Spanish ambassador. The PSOE leader Joaquín Almunia continued the pressure on these two issues, coinciding with Castro's views.[51] In contrast, the office of Prime Minister José María Aznar seemed to be at odds with the Ministry of Foreign Affairs[52] and a delegation of members of the Partido Popular in the European Parliament.[53] While Spain insisted that the new Spanish envoy should have complete freedom to contact dissidents in Cuba,[54] the Cuban government stressed that the visit of the King and the naming of a new Spanish ambassador were two different matters.[55]

Although many seasoned observers expected a long delay before these issues were resolved, the Spanish government abruptly announced the appointment of Eduardo Junco as its new ambassador in Cuba.[56] Usually well-informed sources described the move as a "thawing" in Spanish-Cuban relations.[57] Moreover, it was revealed that the agreement had been reached during a personal telephone call between Castro and Aznar. The project of the royal visit to Cuba for the 1998 centennial was then revived. The announcement was received by the Spanish opposition as "long overdue"[58] and by the Spanish press as "common sense."[59] The same day, José María Robles Fraga, a PP member of the Spanish Congress and an influential foreign policy adviser of Aznar, met in Miami with Cuban-American National Foundation leaders to explain that the new decision did not mean a change in Spain's policy toward Cuba.

Nevertheless, the honeymoon between the hard-liners in the Cuban exile community and the Spanish government was over, a casualty of the new pragmatic policy espoused by Aznar. This change was welcomed by Castro, who anticipated that the Spanish conservatives would hold power for an additional term. Castro's fascination for the PSOE had also seemed to lessen in view of the confusing composition of the new party leadership once headed by Felipe González.[60] A bold and more democratic system of internal primary elections had been implemented, and it had resulted in the defeat of some old-timers and the rise of new political stars. Such was the case of former minister Josep Borrell, who then replaced the new secretary-general of the PSOE, Joaquín Almunia, as candidate-elect for the next congressional elections to be held in late 1999 or 2000. However, Borrell, facing a tough campaign, resigned in May 1999. This confusion in the PSOE leadership probably confirmed Castro's intuition that his best bet was to continue courting good relations with the Spanish conservatives.

During this period Canada reaffirmed its wishes for closer relations with Cuba and promoted the return of Cuba to the OAS.[61] In a controversial move, Gilbert Parent, speaker of the House of Commons, got the media's attention when he warmly received visitors from the Cuban Assembly, justifying his action with the comment that in some provinces of Canada only one party is represented in the legislature.[62] Simultaneously, and adding to this Canadian contradiction, Ottawa denied visas to five of the nineteen political prisoners that it had agreed to accept as part of a deal with the Castro government.[63] In the rest of the hemisphere, the government of Argentina was compelled to correct the reports that a trip by President Menem to Cuba was imminent.[64]

Meanwhile, in the United Nations, Cuba was again the subject of concern over human rights violations, and it was reprimanded for refusing to allow the visit of special rapporteur Carl J. Groth.[65] In a surprise for the United States, however, a 1998 proposal to appoint a human rights monitor failed by a vote of 16–19, with 18 abstentions among the 53 voting members. While all the European Union member states sided with the United States, all the Latin American nations except El Salvador and Argentina abstained.[66] A cycle of diplomatic overtures leading toward normalization had begun partly as a result of the papal visit of January 1998. However, as a consequence of the hard-line law decreed by Cuba in early 1999, the result of the annual UN inquiry taken in April 1999 was against Cuba by one vote. This was heralded by the Cuban exile community as a major accomplishment and credited to the leadership of Poland and the Czech Republic.[67] All European Union member states (and hopefuls) voted against Cuba; Mexico, Peru, and Venezuela sided with Havana, while Colombia, El Salvador, and Guatemala abstained.

Whatever the outcome of the new actions announced by the United States and the related initiatives by the Vatican and other involved parties, it is startling to consider the reasons put forth by the various parties for supporting or opposing the embargo. During the Cold War, it was clear to many foreign observers that U.S. actions in the international sphere were explained with pragmatic and sometimes cynical arguments informed by a central foreign-policy objective: to contain the spread of Marxism and the threat of world domination by the Soviet Union. Violations of human rights by U.S. allies and proxies were justified with this central objective in mind. It was, in a sense, a continuation of Franklin Roosevelt's alleged remark about the Nicaraguan dictator Anastasio Somoza: at least he was "our SOB." The same justification was used for the so-called Kirkpatrick doctrine; authoritarian governments were seen as redeemable, while totalitarian regimes were not. At the same time, it was acceptable to trade and make compromises with Communist China because of its sheer size and nuclear capability. Defenders of human rights in Europe did not accept this pragmatic explanation.

With the Cold War in the past, roles paradoxically seemed to reverse. The United States now presents itself as defending the Cuban embargo on grounds of morality and respect for human rights, while the Europeans, Latin Americans, and Canadians are trading with Castro "to make a buck."[68] This simplistic characterization is basically incorrect, but it has the potential to be believed by numerous observers, especially in Cuba. This may make the post-transition period more difficult and the role that the Europeans and other U.S. partners in the Americas play more trying.

The Aftermath: When the Dust Settled

Consolation Prizes

Depending on the perspective of the different observers, the interests of the various protagonists, and the degree of their advocacy, the legacy of the Helms-Burton Law will be seen as either positive or negative. As in wars and earthquakes, however, no one can be certain of being a winner. Still, many questions remain regarding the background and consequences of the Helms-Burton Law.

Curiously, most of the parties involved with the Helms-Burton process can claim some degree of success, or at least some collateral benefits. Canada and Mexico have made their positions clear. The European Union has explicitly opposed the law while approving the resolution, the joint action, and the Common Position on Cuba, and awaiting the development of the 1998 agreement. Castro can boast that he did not collapse under pressure or compromise Cuba's independence. Meanwhile, the U.S. government has kept Title IV activated, and the threat of Title III still looms over the heads of investors, in spite of the 1998 understanding. The Spanish government has shown firmness toward the law, while appearing as a major advocate of the Common Position on Cuba. Even when one considers that the Cuban government has hardened its internal policies (an example is the measures designed to harass dissidents adopted in 1997), the Spanish Socialists may also claim some success. They could argue that more satisfactory results could have been obtained with their "carrot" policy of inducements to Castro. By the end of 1997, no benefits had yet been obtained by the "stick" brandished by the government of José María Aznar, or the more diplomatic pressures devised by the European Union through its Common Position.

Electoral Benefits

One need not be a cynic to recognize that the clearest and more lasting consequence of the Helms-Burton Law may be at the polls. In an apparent affirmation of their efforts, *all* its most vocal legislative supporters won reelection to the U.S. Congress in 1996 and strengthened their positions for subsequent electoral challenges, as the 1998 elections confirmed. Their 1998 successes came despite the failure of Republicans to profit from the impeachment difficulties experienced by President Clinton and the Democrats.

In one exception, although he was not directly involved with Helms-Burton, New York's Republican Senator, Alfonse D'Amato (the main backer of ILSA), lost his reelection bid in the fall of 1998 to Democrat Charles Schumer. To be sure, the politicians' support of Helms-Burton cannot be considered the only reason for their success, since they all enjoy the comfortable backing of their respective constituencies. It can at least be argued that their support for the law did not generate a *loss* of votes. What their experience may prove is that the Cuba question was inconsequential. In any case, the sponsors of the bill, Senator Jesse Helms (North Carolina) and Congressman Dan Burton (Indiana), as well as noted Helms-Burton backers Robert Menéndez and Robert Torricelli (both from New Jersey), were reelected, as were Ileana Ros-Lehtinen and Lincoln Díaz-Balart, both Cuban-American representatives from South Florida. According to polls taken in 1996, President Clinton also dramatically increased his support in the Cuban-American community, from 22 percent in 1992 to almost 41 percent in his reelection bid, a level never before enjoyed by a Democrat.[69]

The lesson of not losing votes by espousing hard-line measures against Cuba had been absorbed by Vice President Al Gore on his path to the Democratic Party nomination in the 2000 presidential election. More favorably regarded in the Cuban community than President Clinton because of his conservative views, Gore did not want to make any unnecessary moves that might cost him a fraction of the Cuban vote in the primaries and in the final contest. This logic can also be applied to the State Department staff. Even if they are inclined to espouse liberal measures, there is an understanding that Cuban policy can be better managed "from the right."[70]

Claims of Impact on Investment

In March 1997, a year after the approval of the law, its main advocates felt called upon to issue statements. Senator Jesse Helms addressed the Cuban people through Radio Martí, claiming that "one by one, foreign investors that fill the pockets of Fidel Castro and keep his regime afloat are fleeing."[71] However, *Miami Herald* correspondent Christopher Marquis reviewed the pressures experienced by foreign companies after one year of the law. His research revealed that (perhaps under instructions by the White House to the State Department to "go slow") executives of only two companies had been barred from entering U.S. territory under the provisions of Title IV. The main problem seemed to be that potential claimants of confiscated property were not providing hard data to the U.S. government, preferring to withhold their lawsuits until Title III went into effect.[72]

On March 12, 1997, the first anniversary of H-B, Congresswoman Ileana Ros-Lehtinen addressed the House of Representatives, claiming that "dozens of companies have suspended operations in Cuba while others are postponing their plans for investment in the slave economy of Castro."[73] She listed some of the companies that, according to her sources, had left Cuba: Bow Valley Industries of Canada, Vitro and Pemex of Mexico, and Guitart of Spain. It is a fact that some investment projects were put on hold, while some companies announced they were leaving Cuba because of the uncertainties facing foreign investors. Additional companies were named in press reports: Gencor (South Africa), Heenan Blakey and York Medical (Canada), Vitro (Mexico), and Wiltel (United States).[74] Ros-Lehtinen claimed that two companies had delayed their operations: the United Kingdom's BAT and Beta Gran Caribe of Canada.[75] Cuba Business reported to the European Parliament that, among others, three British engineering firms had backed out of contracts to build industrial plants in Cuba. Redpath, a Canadian subsidiary of Tate and Lyle, also stopped buying Cuban sugar, and a European chemical trading company confirmed that a Mexican company would no longer supply products to Cuba "for fear of pressure from the U.S."[76] Sources in the Spanish government and the European Commission revealed that about twenty European companies received requests for information from the U.S. Department of State regarding their operations in Cuba.[77] However, a final assessment of all these responses, including their real motivations and linkages to the provisions of Helms-Burton, remains to be done.

Ironically, the embargo has proved beneficial for several economic sectors in the vicinity of Cuba. For example, the Florida citrus industry would be seriously damaged by the end of the embargo,[78] while cigar makers in the

Dominican Republic would also suffer considerably from the competition created by an open market economy in Cuba. The hotel industry in the Caribbean is already preparing for the normalization of relations between the United States and Cuba, especially in the Dominican Republic, Puerto Rico, and Jamaica.[79] Iberia Airlines, the Spanish company that maintains a hub in Miami for its operations with Central America, would consider switching to Havana, making South Florida a loser.

Energies Wasted

The 1997 compromise between the United States and the E.U. was not the end of the story as far as some diehards were concerned. In June 1997 several new measures were introduced in Congress. Among them was a bill by Senator Robert Torricelli that would make foreign companies using confiscated American property liable for the dollar amounts that U.S. claimants had written off as a loss on their tax bills. While this figure is estimated to total over $2 billion, the proposed law would have been virtually unenforceable. Representative Bill McCollum planned to present another bill to strip Clinton of his ability to waive Helms-Burton's Title III. Other legislative proposals would have withheld U.S. assistance to Russia and other countries that continued their aid and cooperation programs with Cuba.[80]

These new anti-Cuban initiatives were countered by short-lived legislative measures that suggested a Puerto Rican–Cuban feud. This was the case of a proposal presented by New York's Democratic Congressman José Serrano, demanding that quarterly reports be compiled by the State Department regarding the diplomatic protests presented by Cuba. This was supposed to mirror a measure sponsored by Cuban exiles that would force the State Department to report on individuals and companies not complying with Helms-Burton.[81] Serrano's amendment was passed on a day when the House had a very low attendance but was later defeated by 287 votes to 141.[82] The confrontation with Serrano was a microcosm of the imperfect relations between the Cuban-American congressional delegation and the rest of the Hispanic caucus. They are similar to the uneven relations between Cuban-Americans and African-Americans in Congress, for reasons that include disagreements over discriminatory immigration policies applied to Haitians.[83]

As a whole, these rearguard moves did little either to further the Helms-Burton strategy or to strengthen the opposition. Instead, these futile partisan efforts inflicted considerable damage on the already damaged reputation of the U.S. Congress in the eyes of the U.S. electorate, and in the perception of the rest of the world.

Evidently unsatisfied with the State Department and White House actions regarding the implementation of Title IV, Senator Helms pursued his own campaign against foreign companies having investments in expropriated properties. While the White House and the European Union were busily trying to create a mutually acceptable pact, Senator Helms pressed the president and secretary of state for action and information regarding the following, inter alia:

- memoranda, cables, minutes, electronic mail, messages, telefaxes, drafts, relating to past or pending investigations or decisions under Title IV of the Libertad.

- a list of State Department personnel who have participated directly in investigations and decisions under Title IV.

- memoranda, cables, electronic mail, etc., relating to the policies of third countries or international organizations (including, but not limited to, the European Union and each of its member states) toward the regime of Fidel Castro in Cuba, since March 12, 1996.[84]

Further Reverberations in the Backyard and Europe

Congressional prestige also suffered a setback when Representative Ileana Ros-Lehtinen sponsored a bill intended to punish the Caribbean nations for promoting the eventual membership of Cuba in CARICOM. The pressure seems to have given Caribbean leaders a new incentive to expand their links with Cuba. The list of oddly coincidental subsequent events includes the commemoration of twenty-five years of relations between Barbados and Cuba; the visits to Cuba of prime ministers P.J. Patterson of Jamaica, James Mitchell of Saint Vincent, and Keith Michell of Grenada; the holding of a joint CARICOM-Cuba meeting; and the meeting *in Havana* of the Caribbean Council for Europe, which was attended by Barbadian Prime Minister Owen Arthur and high officials of the European Commission.[85] The possibility of Cuba's eventual membership in the Lomé Convention was the talk of the town, a prospect that was confirmed when Cuba was granted observer status in the ongoing negotiations. The unofficial agenda of the Havana meeting included the following significant questions:

- Which mechanism, the ACS[86] or CARICOM, will facilitate the integration of Cuban trade in the Caribbean, or is a new approach needed?

- In what way would Cuba benefit from being an observer at Caribbean Forum [CARIFORUM, the institutionalized structure of the Caribbean nations benefitting from the Lomé Convention]?

• Is the establishment of bilateral agreements with individual Caribbean states the best long-term strategy for Cuba, or should it seek inclusion in multilateral agreements such as the Lomé Convention?[87]

In the course of the meeting, Carlos Lage, as Cuba's minister of economy, cited figures indicating the increased linkage of Cuba with the Caribbean. By 1997 more than a thousand Caribbean students had graduated from Cuban universities and institutes, while 166 Cuban technicians and doctors are working in the area. And although just 8 percent of Cuban trade is carried on with its Caribbean neighbors, the figure represents an increase of 300 percent since 1992.[88]

To top off these gestures of good will, 1997 ended with the landing of the French-British Concorde in . . . Havana. More than a hundred British and French businesspeople and tourists thought that was the fastest way to arrive in the Cuban capital, just by expanding the route that British Airways maintains to Bridgetown, Barbados.[89] Fidel Castro himself entered the cockpit for a photo opportunity.[90]

The sponsors of Helms-Burton are not the only members of Congress capable of provoking friction between the United States and the rest of the world. One incident featured Congressman Benjamim William (R-New York), chairman of the influential House International Affairs Committee. It all started when the forty-nation Council of Europe—not to be confused with the European Council, the European Commission, or the Council of Ministers of the European Union, all institutions of the E.U.—decided to issue a report critical of Helms-Burton. In a way it was a repetitious exercise since all the European Union members are also members of the inter-governmental Council of Europe. However, it was an opportunity for the twenty-five other nations who are not yet members of the E.U., among them Russia, to vent their anger at the U.S. legislation. "It is disheartening that others in Europe have, for different reasons, stepped in to resuscitate the Cuban economy just as it began to feel the effects of our embargo," the U.S. congressman wrote in response. His justification for his move was that "these critics are among those who trade with the Castro regime in a manner that has the effect of undermining our well-founded policy of isolation."[91] Not surprisingly, the reaction from the Parliamentary Assembly of the Council of Europe still echoes in the Strasbourg chamber.

With respect to the NAFTA partners, there are just two known examples of a direct impact of Helms-Burton. Visas were denied to one company, and another abandoned its management of the Cuban telephone system. Sherritt International, a Canadian enterprise dealing with mineral resources, received warnings from Washington as early as July 1996, with the result that several of its executives were denied visas to enter the United States.[92] Executives of the Mexican conglomerate Domos also received letters from the State Department telling them that they could not travel to the United States and that they could become the subject of lawsuits. Domos announced that it was abandoning its investment in Cuba's telephone system, which had once belonged to ITT.[93] As we have seen in chapter 5, an Italian company, STET, rushed to fill Domos's place, forming the Empresa de Teléfonos de Cuba (ETECSA), with an investment of $700 million. Subsequently, the U.S. Department of State reinstated visa privileges for the Mexican company.[94]

The Pain in Spain

The Spanish business press has often expressed concern that Helms-Burton has caused the loss of profitable investment opportunities that other countries have then taken advantage of. This worry has been shared by the political opposition to the PP government. Ironically, Spain, one of the world's most active commercial partners with Cuba, was not part of this "telephone connection," although Cuban-American interests are heavily invested in Spain's telecommunication networks.[95] Companies owned by Jorge Mas Canosa purchased SINTEL (Sistemas e Instalaciones de Telecomunicación, S.A.), a Spanish subsidiary of the Telefónica conglomerate. Although this giant has been without a presence in Cuba, it nonetheless had considerable interests in the rest of Latin America, especially Argentina, Chile, and Peru, and more recently in Brazil. Subsequently, after the death of Mas Canosa, his son sold 85 percent of the stock of Sintel and its subsidiaries.[96]

Helms-Burton's supporters could correctly claim that the combination of the U.S. legislative measures and the political change in Spain produced uncertainty in Spanish business circles. As early as June 1996, reports filed by the Spanish press in Havana reflected significant concern about Helms-Burton. Spanish companies were suddenly divided into three categories: those having ties to the United States, those with no U.S. economic ties, and those having significant links with the United States but no investments in Cuba. Hotel chains such as Sol Meliá, tobacco enterprises such as Tabacalera, and the banking conglomerates Banco de Bilbao-Vizcaya (BBV) and Argentaria belong to the first group. Businesses like the popular Freixenet, with a sizeable market in the United States as well as some sales in Cuba, became apprehensive about the potential for retaliation spearheaded by Cuban interests that controlled food distribution in Miami. Tabacalera decided to abandon its plans to invest in Cayo Coco and began to look for safer locations than Cubanacán, for fear of retaliation from the United States. Argentaria had second thoughts about investing in the renovation of buildings in Havana. BBV wondered about financing the sugar harvest on lands that might be claimed by Cuban-Americans.[97] Occidental Hoteles announced that it was withdrawing from a project to build a resort in Varadero, in conjunction with the Cuban company Gaviota.[98] Later on, the Spanish government announced the suspension of plans to build eight ho-tels to be managed by a consortium formed by the Cuban government agency Gran Caribe and the Spanish public company Paradores de España, with an investment of $16 million.[99] In a rare public admission of difficul-ties, Foreign Minister Abel Matutes ended his early 1997 report to the Spanish Congress declaring that Spanish investments had "stagnated" be-cause of the "climate generated by the Helms-Burton law."[100] With no de-tails given, this statement was viewed as self-protective in view of the criti-cism by the political opposition regarding the government's hard-line policies toward Cuba and its curtailment of investment incentives.

Other business signals were more mixed. Independent analysts acknowl-edge that the U.S. policy has generated a certain degree of caution among large corporations having investments in both Cuba and in the United States, but it has not derailed the medium-sized or small companies with no economic links in the United States. Further, most of the largest Spanish firms openly operating in Cuba did not decrease the level of their operations or the public visibility with which they undertook their investments, espe-cially in the field of tourism. One example is the Mallorca-based company Meliá, led by Gabriel Escarré, a vocal critic of Helms-Burton. A presence in Cuba since the 1990 opening of its Sol Palmeras Hotel, Meliá expanded its position by opening the five-star Meliá Confort Habana in July 1998. Meliá currently operates more than 4,500 rooms in Cuba, close to 12 percent of the whole hotel industry there, although the Cuban operation is just a frac-tion of its 245 hotels doing business in twenty-five countries.[101]

Overall, Spanish exports to and investments in Cuba have risen, al-though Cuba accounts for only 0.12 percent of the total Spanish investment in the world. Nevertheless, as we have seen, by 1996 Spain had become the second most important trading partner of Cuba (up from sixth place in 1994),[102] and had captured first place in 1997. During the first half of 1998, a sizable number of Spanish political leaders accompanied important trade missions to Cuba. Among them were the presidents of the autonomous communities of Andalusia, the Basque Country, and Extremadura. The lat-ter raised eyebrows within the Spanish government when he invited Fidel Castro to visit the region on the occasion of his scheduled trip to Oporto, Portugal, to attend the fall 1998 Ibero-American summit.[103]

An impressive delegation representing more than a hundred Spanish companies visited Cuba in April 1998 for the purpose of increasing investment and trade.[104] Josep Piqué, minister of industry and energy, became the first member of the Conservative cabinet to visit Cuba. Accompanied by leaders of the most important public-sector companies of Spain, he was warmly received by Castro and announced a new program of Spanish investments.[105] In February 1999 Cuban vice president and minister of economics, Carlos Lage, traveled to Spain to prepare for the Spanish monarchs' visit to Cuba and also to encourage increased Spanish investments. In 1998, total trade between the two countries had surpassed the $600 million mark, while nearly 150,000 Spanish tourists visited Cuba.[106]

These overtures by Spain, in addition to its continuing provision of development and humanitarian aid and scholarships, reveal the disproportion between the attention given by Spain to Latin America and Cuba specifically, and the region's real trade and investment value in the context of Spain's global interests. As we have seen, Latin America and Cuba are important to Madrid for reasons not limited to economic considerations. Cultural dimensions and mutual perceptions are to be considered when attempting to interpret a contradictory and confusing pattern of behavior. The institutions of the E.U. and the U.S. government should pay close attention to this special profile of relations between Spain and Latin America, especially when incidents such as the ones generated by the Helms-Burton law are considered.

Aftershocks in Cuba

Loser or Winner?

The opposing points of view expressed in a private colloquium attended by representatives of most of the parties in this conflict (the United States, Canada, Mexico, and the European Union) can be summarized as two poles of frustration. On one hand, the European Commission felt that "Fidel Castro has not been affected by this law; it is the Cuban people who suffer." On the other, the U.S. government believed that "European indecisiveness in their model of relations with Cuba does not lead anywhere" and that "the conflict unchained by the E.U.'s demand in the World Trade Organization does not benefit anybody."[107]

Let us recall the two measures geared to exert influence on the behavior of the Cuban government. As discussed in chapter 6, one was the initiative of the U.S. government in the form of an offer known as "Support for a Democratic Transition in Cuba." The other was European in origin, the

"Common Position." It had an unprecedented impact on Cuba because it was the first of its kind taken by the E.U., collectively passed for a Latin American country. Its purpose was to offer a cooperation agreement with Cuba conditional upon Cuba's taking steps toward democratization. This was one of the first experiments in the incipient Common Foreign and Security Policy (CFSP), known as the "second pillar" of the E.U. structure. Naturally, the Common Position was interpreted in Havana as a sign that the E.U. had caved in to pressure from the United States and a payoff for taking a hardline approach to H-B, as expressesd in the other two major decisions on Cuba, the blocking statute and the Joint Action. When the E.U. confirmed the spirit and the specific requirements of its Common Position in mid-1997, the Cuban government reacted with a blistering letter addressed to the president of the European Council.

When the 1997 understanding between the E.U. and the United States was announced, Cuba reminded the parties that they had no right to negotiate its sovereignty. Then Castro shifted his policy focus to reinforcing Cuba's positive new links with Spain in support of Cuba's bid to become a member of the group of the ACP countries as beneficiaries of the Lomé Convention. This commonly binding treaty provides substantial trade and aid packages for the former colonies of European powers. Until the admission of the Dominican Republic, no former Spanish colony was a member. Cuba now seeks a similar status. After the announcement of the process toward granting Havana observer status, E.C. officers rushed to clarify that this status did not mean guaranteed membership. Internal confidential documents indicate that Cuba was advised that it needed to make substantial changes, although the E.U. preferred the path of dialogue and constructive engagement toward this end. This status is seen as a process that considers Cuba's location in the Caribbean but makes it still subject to conditions. The 1996 Common Position is then consistent with article 5 of the Lomé Convention making it incumbent on Cuba to adapt to the rules. Simultaneously, the General Affairs Council of the E.U. took note but announced as its expectations for Cuba "substantial progress on human rights, good governance, and political freedom"—an explicit reminder of displeasure with the latest Cuban actions regarding human rights. As one of the approved measures, the E.U. had put in place a sort of committee of diplomatic representatives in Havana to supervise human rights in Cuba and to maintain contact with the dissidents. The council declared that "obstruction" of the Havana Ambassadors Human Rights Working Group should end and that the members of the Dissidents' Working Group in prison should be released.

Just days before, a communiqué of the Cuban government, addressed to all foreign embassies in Havana, warned of the "illegal" nature of any measure that might be seen as cooperating with the provisions of the Helms-Burton Law.[108] Cuba elected to brand the E.U.-U.S. agreement as damaging to Cuban interests, although the process may end in a compromise that is ultimately to Cuba's benefit.[109] However, when Cuba became aware that new, hardline measures were under consideration in Congress, the Cuban government denounced them on live television (via CNN) in a press conference given by the president of the Popular Assembly, Ricardo Alarcón.[110] By way of follow-up, Foreign Relations Minister Roberto Robaina visited several Central American and Caribbean capitals denouncing the new U.S. measures and delivering a personal message from Castro. Simultaneously, his deputy Isabel Allende visited Europe, while the minister of foreign investment, Ibrahim Ferradaz, traveled to South America. Cuba's vigorous response surprised Washington.[111]

Upon the signing of the 1998 understanding between the United States and the E.U., Cuba reminded the involved parties that they had no right to negotiate its sovereignty. Then Castro shifted his policy focus to reinforcing Cuba's positive new links with Spain, in support of Cuba's bid to become a member of the group of the ACP countries as beneficiaries of the Lomé Convention. As in the case of the May 1998 understanding with the United States, European Commission officers rushed to clarify that Lomé observer status did not guarantee membership. Internal documents indicate that Cuba was advised that it needed to make substantial changes, although the E.U. preferred the path of dialogue and constructive engagement toward this end. The Lomé status is then seen as a dynamic process considering Cuba's geographical location. The 1996 Common Position is consistent with Article 5 of the Lomé Convention, making it incumbent upon Cuba to adapt to the "rules of the club." Simultaneously, the General Affairs Council of the European Union took note of the project but announced its expectations for Cuba: "substantial progress on human rights, good governance and political freedom." In particular the Council indicated its expectation "that the obstruction of the Havana Ambassadors Human Rights Working Group shall cease, and that the four members of the Dissidents' Working Group now in prison shall be released."[112]

Nevertheless, as a follow-up of this diplomatic accomplishment, Castro embarked on an unprecedented tour around the Caribbean. He traveled to the Dominican Republic, Jamaica, Barbados, and, most significantly, Grenada—the site of one of his most spectacular defeats when, in 1983, President Reagan ordered the invasion of the tiny island that had become an ally of the Cuban regime. These trips and Cuba's observer status in the Lomé Convention revealed El Salvador and Costa Rica to be the only countries in Central America or the Caribbean without full diplomatic relations with Cuba. Costa Rica announced in January 1999 that it would open a consulate in Havana.[113]

The perception in Brussels is that Cuba has been a "serious and active" participant in the meetings of the ACP countries.[114] Its willingness to cooperate and demonstrate progress in the field of human rights, one of the preconditions for membership, was rewarded by the 1998 UN Human Rights Commission vote, when the U.S.-sponsored measure to condemn Cuba was defeated. However, whether Cuba can attain full status in the Lomé Convention is still not clear. It would not be surprising, when the time comes to distribute funds, if the same Caribbean countries that now endorse Cuba became difficult negotiators, as the experience of the admission of the Dominican Republic shows. Still, Cuba has the advantage that a coherent Caribbean diplomatic presence needs the full participation of the largest state. In the words of Fidel Castro himself, during the meetings of the CARIFORUM, "without Cuba the Caribbean is not complete."[115]

The Overall Impact of Helms-Burton

As the preceding chapters have discussed, when it lost the support of the Soviet Union, Cuba sought to strengthen its economic ties with other countries. Observers have pointed out that if such efforts succeed, the embargo and the Helms-Burton Act may, in the long run, actually strengthen Castro economically while Cuba gains the moral high ground in public opinion as well.[116] Following the 1991 collapse of the Soviet Union, the Cuban economy hit bottom in 1993. It began to recover in the 1994–96 period, a fact that pleased Cuban officials. Data for 1997, 1998, and 1999 have to be interpreted with extreme caution.

From the time Helms-Burton was announced until Cuba passed its own protective legislation late in 1996, Cuban officials responded in two apparently contradictory ways. First, they insisted that foreign investment was continuing to grow. Second, while admitting that the codification of the embargo had done considerable damage to the Cuban economy, they characterized the trend as temporary. Ibrahim Ferradaz, minister of foreign investment, indicated that the number of joint ventures during the first four months of 1996 was the same as in 1995. He suggested that the real victims of Helms-Burton were U.S. businesspeople, whose claims would not be negotiated by the United States and who could not compete with the rest of the world in the Cuban economy.[117] Octavio Castilla, vice minister for foreign investment, caustically remarked that Helms-Burton gave "the impression that the entire country was a former U.S. property." He minimized the importance of the law's sanctions because out of the 236 joint ventures in existence, only 4 involved "properties under U.S. litigation."[118]

Carlos Lage predicted that the law would not interefere with the economic recovery of Cuba. Forty-three nations had invested in thirty-four areas, with 143 new ventures under negotiation.[119] Tourism grew 46 percent in the first part of 1996, over the revenues of $1.1 million for 1995. Lage stressed that many investments could be made in Cuba without involving confiscated properties, but he acknowledged that some enterprises had postponed their plans because of the "climate of uncertainty." In sum, he admitted that the law caused "irreparable harm." After all, he claimed, foreign joint ventures employed only 5 percent of the Cuban workforce and generated only 3 percent of the net income in 1995.[120] Whatever the negative economic effects of Helms-Burton, Lage argued, there was a corresponding political benefit. It "has played a role in unifying the Cuban people, has unified the international community, has increased our adrenaline flow, and has allowed the Cuban people to confirm that the success of the U.S. policy toward Cuba would mean hunger and misery for our people."[121] He also mentioned the impact of the embargo on Cuba's international credit status. Blaming the United States for proclaiming itself as a "major stockholder" in the IMF, the World Bank, and other financial institutions, Lage complained of the "discriminatory treatment" imposed on Cuba and its creditors.

As evidence that Cuba was working to meet some of the international requirements for reform, Lage mentioned changes in the tax system, the increased availability of consumer goods at market prices, the modification of wages and incentive systems, the reorganization of the banking system, new laws on free zones and real estate investments, and the signing of investment-promotion agreements with eighteen countries. He pointed out that Cuba had always been willing to negotiate with the United States over the expropriations issue, but the offer was rejected most explicitly by laws such as Torricelli and Helms-Burton.[122] Cuban officials ended 1996 with satisfaction, in view of the success of the Havana International Fair. With 240 joint ventures from forty-three nations already in place (40 of them formed in 1996), 17 business and government delegations and 281 companies attended the fair. While in 1983 Spain was the sole foreign participant, first-time attendees in 1996 included companies from Indonesia, Namibia, South Korea, Barbados, and Haiti.[123]

By early 1997, the number of joint ventures formed after Helms-Burton had jumped to forty-two.[124] Cuban officials acknowledged the high cost of risk insurance caused by the uncertain investment climate. In spite of that difficulty, financial institutions established in Cuba still granted $440 million in loans for Cuban projects.[125] At the end of the year, an official report showed a 2.5 percent increase in the economy, despite restrictions on international financing for the sugar harvest. Cuba's foreign exports increased only .6 percent, a reflection of sugar and nickel prices. Imports grew 19.9 percent. Foreign debt at the end of 1996 decreased .38 percent compared to 1995. Tourism reached nearly 1.2 million visitors, an increase of 17 percent. Investment grew 7.6 percent.[126]

Notwithstanding these positive indicators, Cuban officials have made use of Helms-Burton to explain real or anticipated economic problems. According to Carlos Fernández de Cossío, a Foreign Ministry official, "the effects of Helms-Burton are real. . . . It is not what [Senator Jesse] Helms said, that the law would bring this government to its knees in a year, but it has made our lives more difficult. . . . As a result of the law, many people are afraid to invest here."[127] The same spokesman had this opinion about the law's inhibition of investment: "There's people that were supposed to come at some point, start investments, and they have not come. And also there's an effect that we will never be able to measure because we will never know how many foreign investors could have approached Cuba to invest their capital here and yet never came because of the threat of this law. . . . The decision taken by Clinton in no way diminishes the kind of impact that the law is already having in the Cuban economy."[128]

In addition to its efforts within the United Nations to condemn the U.S. embargo, Cuba has tried to challenge the embargo in the public opinion wars. While the United States defines Helms-Burton as a matter of national security and has emphasized the issue of confiscated property, Cuba has stressed the humanitarian dimension, and especially the public health effects. Cuba's education system and its energy resources have also been affected.

Numerous private organizations in the United States have sided with Cuba, focusing on the shortages of food, medicine, and school supplies for children. A group called Pastors for Peace staged a "fast for life" to persuade the U.S. government to allow the shipment of computers for use in Cuban hospitals. "Caravans for the children of Cuba" were organized to collect "friendshipments" containing toiletries, school supplies, medicine, sports equipment, educational toys, musical instruments, and the like for Cuban children. Orgnizers justified their actions arguing that the U.S. embargo in effect uses hunger and disease as political weapons. Some members of Congress tried to get an amendment approved that would permit the trade of U.S. food and medicine.[129] This debate was reopened following the visit of John Paul II to Cuba, and it was revived at the end of 1998 under pressure of a task force formed by the Council on Foreign Relations, with the result of the announcement by the White House of liberalization measures of the general embargo in 1999.

Meanwhile, the Cuban government submitted what can be described as a bill to the United States for losses suffered under the embargo. The Cuban government has suggested figures of $40 billion (until 1993) and $60 billion (until 1998) as the cost of the U.S. measures since 1962.[130] While admitting the true cost of the embargo would be impossible to measure, Carmelo Mesa Lago points out that its end will not solve all the problems caused by Cuba's "disastrous economic model," the collapse of the Soviet bloc, and the loss of trade and aid. Gillian Gunn estimates the embargo drags the Cuban economy 10 to 15 percent.[131] Cuban authorities claim that the embargo had cost $2 billion from 1990 to 1993, at the crucial time of the discontinuation of Soviet aid. The Cuban Democracy Act caused a loss of another $1 billion in 1992–1993. In the area of health, the damage claimed by the Cuban government has reached $1.2 billion.[132] Using recent claims, for 1998 only the costs of the embargo was estimated as $800 million.

Cuban authorities itemized the annual loss as follows: $130 million in additional transportation costs; $155 million for credit restrictions; $200 million for higher costs of imports; $55 million for losses in exports; and $260 million in currency exchange losses.[133] That means that the Cuban economy has "to expend about 20 percent more funds than it would have to otherwise" without the embargo, and this figure does not include the loss of income from missing U.S. tourists, flights, investment, and financing.[134] However, Ibrahim Ferradaz, minister of foreign investment, admitted in May 1999 that it is impossible to measure Helms-Burton's impact with accuracy.[135]

In off-the-record settings, Cuban scholars, officials, and diplomats will often indicate, tongue in cheek, that H-B has been *un regalo* (a gift) to Cuba.[136] Most Cuban studies and reports exult in describing the embargo and H-B as *un fracaso* (a failure).[137] But while they acknowledge that the U.S. embargo and H-B have supplied Cuba with a political excuse, on balance these Cuban professionals would have preferred to operate without the political and especially the economic limitations imposed by the United States.[138]

Dollars and Sense

Damage Control: Why?

The most visible international effect of Helms-Burton has been to foster unity and galvanize opposition on the part of all the governments of Europe and Latin America, who have condemned the law in various forums since its inception. In addition, the General Assembly of the United Nations has witnessed a steady decline in the number of governments abstaining when matters concerning the U.S. embargo come up for a vote.

The law illustrates a negative dimension in the international image of the United States, which has been the subject of criticism from respected sectors that cannot be considered favorable to Castro. As one of the numerous examples, Georgie Anne Geyer, the Universal Press Syndicate columnist and author of books on Castro, summarized the frustration of many who sense that the U.S. government is actually contributing to the survival of the Castro regime. According to her, the Helms-Burton Law has poisoned relations with the main allies of the United States and caused them to take actions, some of which could be unpleasant, with effects lasting for decades. American actions have made U.S. allies side with Castro, pretending that his shortcomings do not exist.[139] Observing the influence of domestic political forces on U.S. foreign policy, Samuel Huntington notes, "foreign governments have learned not to take seriously administration statements of its general policy goals and to take very seriously administration actions devoted to commercial and ethnic interests."[140]

This new political reality reflects the U.S. shift from a multilateral policy (whereby actions were taken in accordance with international laws and conventions) to a unilateral one, derived from the concept of "exceptionalism." With the Cold War ended, the United States sees itself as the sole superpower, with a right to impose its perspectives and priorities on the rest of the world. Helms-Burton is perceived abroad as evidence of the gradual loss of interest in international affairs among many sectors of U.S. society. At the same time, it results from the rise of an ideology that seeks to impose a local agenda with little regard for the impaired international image of the United States, because the cost is not considered significant.

Some foreign relations experts also detect in Helms-Burton evidence of an evolution from interdependence to globalism. While interdependence strengthened the power of the traditional nation-state and provided governments with novel avenues to survive, globalism has tempted states to search for alternatives. According to Wolfgang H. Reinicke of the Brookings Institution, Helms-Burton is an example of an "offensive intervention" undertaken by "policy makers to broaden the reach of internal sovereignty to match the economic reach of corporate networks." In this scenario, jealous of the autonomy enjoyed by foreign companies, the U.S. government retaliates. However the problem may worsen, because "protectionism by one country, irrespective of its intentions, leads to retaliation and jeopardizes the world economy."[141]

Some observers disagree that the American public has lost interest in international topics, however. Instead, they suggest, since the end of the Cold War, international issues are perceived differently, with drug trafficking, immigration, the global environment, and energy problems getting the most attention. Research shows that the U.S. citizen is more idealistic and concerned with global issues and the proper role of their country in the world than what politicians prefer to believe. This allows them to justify their often-parochial voting patterns.[142] Ultimately, what Helms-Burton has shown is a chasm between the political class and academia, between an influential political sector and the media, between a narrow view and a broader perspective.

Sources of Pressure to Compromise

Two powerful sectors have been exerting their influence on the White House. On one hand, U.S. military circles have quietly suggested the need for a U.S. policy aimed at a "soft landing" transition in Cuba. The objective would be to minimize the threat of sudden out-migration and to reduce the political pressure to intervene in a catastrophic collapse of the Castro regime. In the aftermath of the papal visit to Cuba, the head of the U.S. Southern Command, Marine General Charles Wilhelm, admitted that the Cuban armed forces posed no threat to the region.[143]

On the other hand, large U.S. corporations have anchored their future on the expansion of world trade, and they have expressed growing impatience over economic sanctions that impede trade with Cuba. Since the beginning of the U.S. embargo, many in the business community have criticized the official approach because they saw themselves losing opportunities in sectors as diverse as sports, construction, and sales of a myriad of products.[144] Moreover, the business community resents that the economic sanctions were executed without the consent of important corporate powers. Among other economic groups, the National Association of Manufacturers has expressed concern that Helms-Burton may endanger future sales, and that U.S. actions may have the effect of ceding American jobs to foreign firms. American companies also risk being branded in other markets as "unreliable suppliers."[145] In March 1998, representatives of the the the U.S. Chamber of Commerce participated in a congressional hearing held for the second anniversary of Helms-Burton, where they expressed their collective opposition to the U.S. embargo.[146]

The law has had other effects apart from its original objectives. For example, the protests made by U.S. trading partners (Mexico, Canada, and the European Union) have strengthened U.S. sectors that oppose free-trade agreements. (Countries that openly resist the imperatives of U.S. law appear to be undeserving of the confidence of the guardians of American sovereignty, which may seem to be curtailed by the signing of trade agreements.) For example, to dramatize its protest against the law and to emphasize its distance from U.S. interests and policies, Canada intensified its links with Cuba through high-level diplomatic visits. This clear message of defiance produced considerable displeasure in Washington circles opposed to NAFTA. Mexico maintained its own independent stance toward Cuba, despite receiving a number of favors from the United States, including certification for its efforts in the war against drug trafficking. In these circumstances, popular expressions come to mind: "With friends like these, who needs enemies?"[147]

What Really Counts: WTO and NAFTA

Some observers combine cautious criticism with a call to avoid further damage to international relations. William Dodge expressed concern about the law's impact on still-fragile international judicial processes:

> The final pages of the Helms-Burton story have yet to be written. It may end happily with the conclusion of a multilateral agreement governing investment in expropriated property and the indefinite suspension or even the repeal of the Helms-Burton Act. Or it may end with the U.S. withdrawing from the WTO dispute resolution system as it withdrew from the compulsory jurisdiction of the International Court of Justice in the 1980s. Whatever the ultimate resolution of the Helms-Burton dispute, it will stand as an important chapter in the development on International Law and of transnational legal process.[148]

In the event that the United States and the E.U. cannot avert a confrontation in the WTO forum, and if the dispute ultimately wrecks the WTO mediation procedures, congressional "meddling" in foreign affairs will inevitably be blamed. The argument that the president should conduct foreign policy more effectively will grow stronger.[149]

Meron and Vagts warn that "putting Helms-Burton into application would unnecessarily burden these still fragile institutions with divisive controversies."[150] In the opinion of other experts, the damage has already been done, to echo the subtitle and the central thesis of Kinka Gerke's study. In a blunt piece published in the Italian journal *International Spectator,* Gerke recalls that the WTO dispute-settlement procedure was, ironically, an objective of the United States, which sought a quasi-judicial procedure, judging the old approach ineffective. The new system has eliminated de facto veto, and now the United States cannot block the appointment of a panel to look into the matter. It is for this reason that in the event of a call by the E.U. to form a panel, the United States has no other recourse but to claim that the issue is a matter of national security, an option that in the former commercial agreements has not been invoked since 1948. The problem is that Helms-Burton is "an example of a dispute that does not lend itself to judicial-style arbitration because at the core of it lies a deeply political question."[151] The fact remains that the E.U. and the United States are fundamentally divided over the question of what the GATT law is in this case, and how widely the security clause should be interpreted.

Gerke warns that if both parties are unwilling to accept its ruling, the WTO will be the loser, a failure for which both will be responsible. The E.U. is at fault, Gerke asserts, because "it lodged a complaint to the WTO— justified in legal terms—asking the organization to do precisely what it cannot do: bring about a political consensus by legal terms." By putting the power of the organization to the test over a question it is "inherently unqualified to resolve," the European Union was making the new organization look "weak and ineffective," and this could lead to the break-up of the fragile consensus. On the other hand, she points out that "should the panel decide—however absurd this may seem in the case of Cuba—that the use of secondary sanctions to protect U.S. national security accords with the rules of the trade regime, this would be deleterious to the regime. The floodgates would be open for invocation of Article XXI for purely internal political and/or protectionist reasons."[152] For that reason, the United States is the party to be blamed for the destructive result.

While on the surface Gerke may seem to agree with those who suggest that "both parties are to be lauded for averting the immediate threat of a further escalation of the conflict," she stresses that the "damage to the authority of the WTO is irreparably done."[153] Therefore, the only remaining avenue is to persuade Congress to revoke the law. However, the source of the E.U. irritation is still intact, and she asks "how the Europeans can protect themselves against blackmail." The E.U. cannot relinquish its right to reinstate its case, while persuading Congress to lift or revoke the sanction of the law. In addition, she sums up, "the EU should seek to exert influence on the internal political decision-making process in the United States structure."[154]

This development would confirm a central thesis of this book. The actions taken by other parties (Canada, Mexico) would be considered secondary to the paramount goal of avoiding a major economic confrontation between the European Union and the United States. In this conflict between

Brussels and Washington, a limit has been set on the potential damage inflicted upon the World Trade Organization. In the triangular relationship formed by the United States, Canada, and Mexico, the parallel limit has been presented by the fragility of NAFTA, and the overall free-trade network that was born in the 1994 Miami Summit of the Americas. However, Europeans may still suspect that the 1998 agreement meant an acceptance of U.S. dominance through the insertion of its original claims into the projected (and later failed) MAI code.

The Relative Value of Cuba

It is important to keep one's perspective about Cuba. The fact is that the repercussions provoked by the Castro government may be disproportionate to the objective value and impact of this nation in the global arena. The importance that Cuba has for the United States and Spain (each one a special case) is different from its significance for Europe as a whole. It is mainly for this reason that the European-U.S. disagreements on this matter have avoided passing the point of no return. Few would admit it publicly, but the reality is that Cuba (in isolation from other issues) is not worth a commercial or political war between Washington and Brussels. This explains the ambiguity that has characterized so many actions by the European Union and its member states, as well as some of the contradictory signals from the White House. Chief among the latter is President Clinton's decision to sign Helms-Burton into law, then partially suspend it, and finally neutralize it with the 1997 and 1998 compromises with Brussels. Let us also remember that in mid-1996, when the European Union announced a delay in negotiations for a cooperation-aid agreement with Cuba, its opposition to the Helms-Burton Law remained undiminished.

The reasoning proposed by the protection of a free-trade scenario is also applicable to the U.S. partners in NAFTA. As a consequence, for Brussels, Washington, Ottawa, and Mexico City, the relative weight of Cuba reveals itself in all its limitations within the global context. An Associated Press (AP) list of pending issues that President Clinton had left behind during his short 1998 winter vacation in Saint Thomas did not include Cuba.[155] Complementing the U.S. lack of concern about Cuba, frequent reviews of issues affecting the U.S.-E.U. agenda omit the feud over Helms-Burton.[156] A survey of the problems that the United States and the E.U. face because of the erratic behavior of "difficult" states did not place Cuba in the company of Iraq, Iran, and Libya.[157] The *Miami Herald*'s Latin America commentator, Andrés Oppenheimer, has characterized Cuba as simply "a once hyperactive Caribbean island that has become virtually insignificant in the world scene."[158] To paraphrase the famous comment attributed to Henry IV of France, "Havana is not worth a mess."[159]

In contrast, the trade in bananas has become a cause for transatlantic conflict. While the United States and the E.U. withdrew from confrontation over H-B in the context of the WTO, they were adamant on the subject of the market allotted for the so-called dollar bananas of mostly Central American origin (controlled by the U.S. growers) and the Caribbean bananas. Under the threat of tariff retaliation on European luxury products, round one of the "banana war" was won by the United States. The lesson from this episode is that Cuba is less important for the United States and the European Union than the banana market—they risked confrontation at the WTO over this agricultural marketing disagreement, but they avoided a clash in the same place because of Cuba.[160]

The "Nuclear" Solution

In the post-Soviet era, the United States is facing other adversaries in its bid to control the global economic order. Josep Joffe, in the seventy-fifth anniversary issue of *Foreign Affairs,* summarized it this way: "Today, Europe and America threaten each other with economic warfare when negotiations stall. But threats are where the conflict usually stops because everyone is deadly afraid of destroying the global trading system." Thus common sense comes into action and exerts pressure for a responsible compromise: "Shoring up the World Trade Organization, even when it pronounces against Washington, is still good for America because, as the world's largest exporter, it has the greater interest in free trade."[161]

Today's threats to unleash commercial wars in the theaters of the WTO and NAFTA are like the old-time nuclear threats during the Cold War. Both parties hope that the unthinkable (firing the intercontinental missiles or wrecking the free-trade networks) will never happen. That is why deadlines for the expiration of the truce between the United States and the European Union are dramatic, with urgent "eleventh hour" meetings predictably producing a compromise. Complicating the search for mutually acceptable solutions has been the fact that the Helms-Burton controversy is mixed with other U.S. legislation that seeks similar objectives regarding investments in Iran and Libya. In a seminar held in Washington at the beginning of 1998, Stuart Eisenstat reiterated the U.S. policy.[162]

A second problem derives from some issues to be inserted in the planned (and mostly failed) Multilateral Agreement on Investment (MAI), to be negotiated under the auspices of the Organization for Economic Cooperation and Development. Before the May 1998 agreement, the United States maintained that this pact should cover properties expropriated in the past.[163] The E.U. resisted negotiating under the threat of the Helms-Burton and D'Amato laws,[164] and finally accepted a compromise agreeing to discourage "questionable" investments and to prohibit future illegal expropriations. The end result was that the "nuclear weapon" was not used.[165]

In the Aftermath of the Pope's Visit

The visit of Pope John Paul II to Cuba has had a double effect. First, it accelerated the expectations for change in Cuba and strengthened the sectors opposed to the U.S. embargo. Second, the visit gave some breathing room to the Castro regime. Contrary to what some hard-liners might think, it would not have been in the best interest of the United States if, soon after the return of the Pope to the Vatican, the Castro government had collapsed. After almost four decades of harassment, embargo, and pressuring of allies, it would be an affront to the United States if the papal visit had had such immediate consequences. Further, the Cuban Catholic Church and the United States needed more time to position themselves in the new circumstances. The Cuban exile community has shown signs of being more divided than ever, over such issues as humanitarian aid to Cuba and a sense of national reconciliation.[166] Nevertheless, the effect of John Paul's visit on the U.S. embargo was unequivocal. His own words were "let the world open up to Cuba"—and Cuba in turn was called on to open itself to the world, in the form of political change. The Pope's appeal made the U.S. isolation more evident. Hard-liners in Congress rushed to regain the initiative, struggling to counter the demands from the business and church communities and the liberal proposals presented by Representative Esteban Torres (D-California) and Senator Bob Graham (D-Florida).

Senator Jesse Helms, in conjunction with the Cuban-American National Foundation, elected to take the counteroffensive with a plan for humanitarian aid for Cuba.[167] In a rare case of disagreement with their long-time allies, Cuban-American members of Congress Ros-Lehtinen and Díaz-Balart expressed their opposition to the plan. Reflecting the feelings of a coalition of exile organizations,[168] they argued that sending humanitarian aid to Cuba was not banned by the embargo, and they estimated that more than $1 million in U.S. aid had already reached the island.[169] Ultimately, both groups reached a compromise[170] in recognition of the fact that various organizations were making plans to send aid to Cuba.[171] Naturally, Castro blasted the plan of CANF and Senator Helms and any attempt to impose conditions on the sending of humanitarian aid.[172] As this controversy was developing, a score of political prisoners were released by the Castro government in response to the pleas of the Pope.[173]

Former White House adviser Richard Nuccio pressed the president for action in an open memorandum, suggesting that he must still regret the day that he signed the Helms-Burton Bill. As Nuccio put it, the president must lament "a straitjacket" that "in effect commits the U.S. to a violent, not a peaceful, transition in Cuba."[174] As a remedy, Nuccio proposed the following measures:

- challenging Castro to conduct an experiment in free and fair elections on a municipal or provincial level;

- announcing that the United States would establish a fund through the OAS to provide technical assistance to Cuba in support of free elections;

- creating a general license for sales of medicines that are monitored by nongovernmental organizations in Cuba;

- reestablishing direct flights from the United States to Cuba for licensed activities such as family visits and scientific, educational, and cultural exchanges.[175]

The chain of events following the visit of Pope John Paul also includes interesting responses from other actors. As discussed above, Spain decided to accelerate its policy of rapprochement, announcing that a new ambassador to Havana would soon be named. While a royal visit to Cuba had long been out of the question, now the Spanish government announced that it could become a reality in 1998. Subsequently, however, disagreements between the Spanish Ministry of Foreign Affairs and Prime Minister Aznar's advisers, plus the hardening of Cuba's policies, complicated the plans for this visit. Argentine president Carlos Menem, a public critic of Fidel Castro, offered to serve as an intermediary between Cuba and the United States, and declared himself ready to go to Cuba if invited.[176]

The liberalizing trend was to continue for the rest of 1998, and the prospects for more diplomatic engagement grew in 1999. Reinforcing the traditionally strong relations between Cuba and Canada, the Cuban government extended an invitation to Canadian premier Jean Chrétien to visit Havana.[177] Meanwhile, it was speculated that a number of released political prisoners would use Canada as a destination. Nonetheless, not all was rosy for the Cuban government, because new repressive measures taken in 1999 once again derailed the royal visit.

8

Conclusion

Lobbyists are fighting for business as usual with thugs, tyrants,
and terrorists; the Castro regime is teetering; unless America gives
up its leverage by unconditionally lifting [the embargo], his successors
will be anxious to exchange normalized relations with the United States
for a democratic transition in Cuba.
Senator Jesse Helms, January 1999

Crumbs. Subversive, counterrevolutionary, and injerencista.
Comments on the U.S. plan to soften the embargo
by José Luis Rodríguez, Cuban economy minister, and Ricardo Alarcón,
president of Cuba's National Assembly, January 1999

The Revolution has not yet started.
Fidel Castro, January 1, 1999

New Times

With the Soviet Union now gone, scholars have begun to analyze the factors
that have contributed to the lengthy survival of the Castro regime.[1] Aggre-
gating points of view that include those of hard-liners in the Cuban exile
community, one concludes that, first, the Cuban Revolution was not imposed by Soviet tanks, unlike what happened in Central and Eastern Europe. It was originally "made in Cuba," and strongly endorsed by a sizable,
multiclass sector of the Cuban population. Paradoxically, the fact that the
Castro regime was initially backed by sectors that have become his irreconcilable enemies in exile makes rapprochement an impossible task.

Second, the Cuban Revolution might have been one of the most significant fusions in Latin American history of two of the continent's most genuine political characteristics: a thirst for nationalism and the role of the
caudillo. Fidel Castro will certainly have a place in history for his acute
understanding of these cornerstones of Latin American political identity.
Third, the survival of the Cuban Revolution has an obvious debt to two

external factors. For the first three decades, the alliance with the Soviet Union signified a guarantee for Havana, and it placed the U.S.-Cuban feud in the context of the East-West confrontation. Additionally, observers point out that the erratic U.S. policy provided both excuses and political weapons for Castro. European and even some Latin American observers have not fully grasped the depth of this "philosophical" factor. Thus, they at times do not help in contributing to the solution, but make it worse. Unless one comes to terms with the significance of these factors, a full understanding of the Helms-Burton controversy is, if not impossible, very difficult.

Finally, one other detail may be a factor in the immediate future. In an era of globalism and as traditional political ideologies seem to fade away, nationalism has persisted (at times taking the forms of ethnic revival, regional unrest, and religious hostilities). In a continent where the national identity is still a project to be completed, Latin American and Caribbean national sentiment may act as a stabilizing mechanism in a time of confusion. Cuba was an incomplete national entity when the Cuban Revolution exploded. Nation-building and reconstruction are still pending matters on the Cuban agenda, no matter who is in power.

The sheer survival of the Castro regime—despite forty years of pressure from the world's leading superpower and the infliction of real damage on the Cuban economy—should serve to convince any reasonable observer of the failure of U.S. policy. Kaplowitz has listed some reasons for this result. First is that Cuba found alternative sources (the Soviet Union until the 1990s, Europe in more recent times) to make up for the lack of U.S. goods. Second, Cuba managed to implement "effective countermeasures," especially in the astute use that Castro has made of the U.S. pressure. Additionally, the goals of the embargo itself have been unrealistic, from suddenly ending Castro's regime to obstructing his international adventures. As this book has shown, the embargo has spurred U.S. allies to propose an alternative to the U.S. policy, at the same time that domestic backing for the measures has continued to erode. Finally, analysis shows that short-term sanctions have a higher expectation of success than long-term policies, which can be weakened as supporters lose interest and their priorities change.[2]

All these factors have increasingly isolated the U.S. attitude toward Cuba. The relative importance of Cuba in a global scenario dominated by serious crisis (Iraq, Kosovo) and the personal problems afflicting the U.S. president make a bold move unlikely. Indeed, inertia and the buying of more time after the papal visit might be the best outcome. Everybody needs more time. The Cuban Catholic Church needs time to recover the ground it has lost. The Cuban exile community, a microcosm of the Cuban nation, needs a period of reassessment and critical rapprochement with the domestic

Cuban population.[3] The potential new Cuban leadership needs time to prepare itself for the transition period. Granted, all this means that most parties have to accept the continuation of the Castro regime, at least for a while. Is there any other alternative to a sudden and unpredictable change?

In fact, the strategic and economic interests in close proximity to Cuba, and well beyond, are the best allies for those who oppose extreme measures against Castro. A freezing in time is working in his favor, considering worse alternatives. For the Caribbean countries, Cuba today is the best of both worlds: it is not a threat, and it is not yet the formidable competitor in tourism or investments that it could be when fully liberalized, both economically and politically. The same logic can be applied to certain sectors of political influence in the United States (such as the military and the Coast Guard), for which uncertainties are minimized by a Cuban regime willing to behave reasonably. For the European trading partners, Cuba is a secure market for the kinds of investments that have been made, based on short-term profits with small risks and a loyal labor force, unable to cause unwanted problems.

However, the new millennium is riddled with risks and uncertainties. The compromise crafted between the E.U. and the United States is fragile and temporary, although it confirms the steady engagement of the E.U. and its member states with Cuba. But we should not forget the historical pattern that often recurs just as the actors in the U.S.-Cuban quarrel seem ready to moderate their antagonistic positions. As Richard Nuccio noted in "Cuba: A U.S. Perspective," the radicals in the United States and Cuba seem to work in unison to derail a process that would deprive them of their roles.[4] While a comparison of Cuba and Spain may not be exact, it is instructive to recall a couple of expressions associated with the political evolution of Spain in the latter part of the 1970s. When Franco's backers saw power vanishing after the death of the dictator, they sighed in melancholy, "With Franco we used to live better." Two years after the transition, the communists claimed that "*Against* Franco we used to live better." When the Castro regime disappears, some may say that "with Castro we used to live better," while on the opposite side others may regret that "against Castro we used to live better."

Unsolved Mysteries

The way events unfold will depend on actions yet to be taken by the protagonists of both the Helms-Burton Law and the compromise agreements, and the extent to which they perceive themselves to be disadvantaged by the options open to them. At face value, the disappearance of the most drastic aspects of the law by virtue of the 1998 understanding was a setback for H-B's most ardent backers in the U.S. Congress. If Title IV was to be effectively suspended, the law would be virtually devoid of any content, even though both the European Union and the United States would keep their options open as they awaited each other's moves. The agreements to neutralize the law have also been detrimental to Cuba in that they have deprived the Cuban government of a useful scapegoat. However, the Brussels-Washington commitment to work together toward Cuban democratization, as an expansion of the E.U.'s November 1996 Common Position, is a new excuse for Castro to claim harassment and decry foreign meddling in Cuba's internal affairs.

The agreement crafted by British commissioner Leon Brittan is seen by many in Europe as a concession to the United States. Governments and opposition parties could easily use a critical attitude toward this deal for their own political benefit, especially in countries where maintaining a distance from the United States is a prudent attitude. The trend toward Social Democratic governments in most of the E.U.'s countries culminated with the 1998 German election and the naming of a former communist as Italy's prime minister. In view of the opposition to Helms-Burton even when conservatives were in command, it is predictable that socialist-led governments will be pressed to denounce the many loopholes in the understanding. An added uncertainty is the stance to be taken by the Canadian and Mexican governments, pressed to duplicate the European agreement—or in contrast, to take isolated, unilateral actions.

Considering that the U.S.-Cuban confrontation has its historical roots in the Spanish-Cuban relationship, it may be useful to resort to some Spanish understandings to shed light on this seemingly intractable enigma. Observers agree that, in spite of many recent transformations in the world scene, the mutual hostility between the United States and Cuba remains intact. In the absence of a seemingly rational justification for the continuing stalemate in the post–Cold War era, frustrated observers are tempted to embrace what seems to be the only other option: irrationality. If this is the case, a methodology based on rational arguments may be a futile exercise.

Commenting on the sarcasm expressed in one of my papers delivered at a symposium at the City University of New York on the Spanish-Cuban relationship, Eusebio Mujal León, a Cuban specialist on political transitions, offered an interesting comment. Born of Spanish parents and familiar with Spanish culture, Mujal ventured that the scenario I had outlined reminded him of Luis Buñuel's films, where surrealism and lack of rationality prevail, leaving the Spanish reality unexplained.[5] Perhaps, then, the U.S.-Cuban dilemma may most aptly be compared with Buñuel's *The Extermi-*

nating Angel. Readers will recall that the plot revolves around the inability of the attendees at a party to leave the room. They remain confined for days, unable to cross an invisible barrier that divides them from the outside world. It is an apt description of the situation that the United States and Cuba have created, each one unable to cross the line, as most of the "guests" of the *fiesta* survive, some get sick, and a few die.

Returning to the real world of scholarship, we find that traditional historical explanations have been incapable of explaining, in the first place, how Cuba could be converted into a Soviet satellite just ninety miles from U.S. shores. And today, as Jorge Domínguez outlined and Lars Schoultz has elaborated, political analysts seem unable to explain why the United States is still fighting the Cold War with Cuba.[6] David Bernell, reviewing the studies of dozens of scholars, asks, "How do we explain the bitter and uncompromising position toward Cuba that has characterized U.S. policy toward that country ever since Fidel Castro came to power? Or, more simply: Why has Cuba posed such a special problem for the U.S. for [so many] years?"[7] Frustrated by the lack of an existing satisfactory answer, he observes, "What is unusual about this particular period of anti-Cuban sentiment, however, is that it has coincided with the end of the Cold War." Competing explanations for the unwillingness of the United States to come to terms with the Cuban Revolution have been proposed by scholars who see imperialism and hegemony as the essential issues, and those who argue that resistance to the spread of communism is the fundamental cause. Bernell discusses a third group of scholars, who have been seeking a middle ground to explain the persistence of acrimony in the post–Cold War era.

In approaching this enigma, we may do well to come back to Spanish understandings and make use of a concept coined by the eminent Spanish essayist, poet, and novelist Miguel de Unamuno. As members of the Generation of '98, Unamuno and his colleagues took upon themselves the task of searching for the lost soul of Spain. He made the distinction between *historia* and *intrahistoria.* The first is most typically a compilation of facts: wars, regimes, battles, a succession of presidents and kings. Unamuno proposed that the daily life of nations and peoples takes refuge in the pages of novels, essays, dramas, and even poetry. This *intrahistoria* is what explains the irrational, the unexplainable.

More than half a century later, General Francisco Franco, a contemporary of the Generation of '98, ruled Spain with an iron fist. Instead of maintaining an "In" box and an "Out" box on his desk, so the story goes, the dictator kept two trays labeled "Matters That Time Will Solve" and "Matters That Time Will Never Solve." Ever patient, he kept changing items from one tray to another. This is why Spain today still has an intractable *independentista* problem, has to cope with Basque terrorism, and endures a regional disparity and economic gaps. The apparent unsolvable enigma of the U.S.-Cuban relationship, meanwhile, is part of the *intrahistoria* of both nations, shackling their political elites. The nature of the Cuban regime, the embargo, and the special relationship between Havana and Washington are matters that Franco would have loved to keep shifting from one tray to another.

If one combines this insight with the analysis offered by Bernell, the picture acquires new depth. The "Cuba problem" would be a clear case of intrahistoric constraints and unwillingness to solve the problems in the "In" box. First, as Bernell observes, "The government of the U.S. has little incentive to change its relationship with Cuba as long as Castro remains in power. . . . His continued hold on power not only defies the wishes of the U.S. but also represents a challenge to its role as unimpeded regional hegemon." The unredeemed and the intrahistorical original sin represented by the Cuban Revolution remains the main obstacle. Any change on the part of the United States will not provide any benefits: "Accepting the Cuban Revolution and making peace with Castro—ending the embargo, allowing travel, and ceasing to demand free elections and free markets as a precondition for normalizing relations—means giving in to the individual who defied the U.S. and got away with it. So the U.S. will not, almost cannot, accommodate him. To do so would mean that, once again, history would have absolved Fidel. This would represent the ultimate failure of U.S. policy toward Cuba."[8]

This same conceptual framework can be applied to the allies of the United States with respect to a variety of pressing issues (free trade, security, drug dealing). While they adhere to a common policy on these important items, the U.S. partners find in the Cuban-U.S. confrontation and such laws as Helms-Burton an opportunity to display their independence. The European partners and Canada, and to a lesser extent most of the Caribbean and Latin American states, have much to gain and little to lose by resisting the U.S. mandates on Cuba. They manage to exhibit a certain degree of autonomy when it is politically and economically affordable. They sell it very well in the international area, and they find it also rewarded in the domestic context. Standing up to the United States today is a easy and safe policy because it does not mean siding with the Soviet Union.

Finally, the same logic can be applied to another issue "that time will never solve": the confrontation between the hard-liners in the Cuban exile community and the Castro government. In fact, both sides have little to gain from a rapprochement. Its opposition to the Cuban dictatorship gave the

Cuban community its most genuine sign of identity. To cave in now would mean to admit failure when the majority of the exile community has long espoused the correctness of the embargo policy. The ultra-hard-liners have claimed that the U.S. measures have been the cause of the current economic and social ills of the Cuban Revolution, ranking much higher than the end of the Soviet subsidies and even the evident internal incapability of a bankrupt regime. It is, in general terms, the same logic that explains the collapse of the Soviet Union as generated almost solely by U. S. strategic pressure, without taking into account the internal deficiencies of Soviet society. The practical application of this logic seems to be apparent in the aggressive denials issued by the backers of Helms-Burton when rumors of a change in U.S. policy were spread in the aftermath of the death of Jorge Mas Canosa.[9]

However, contradictions survive. On one hand, there is the futility of the compensatory or punitive aspects of the Helms-Burton law, added to the complete absence of any agreement on the expropriations. On the other hand, it seems odd that a U.S. court awarded more than $187 million in damages to the families of the victims of the criminal shooting-down of the Brothers to the Rescue planes.[10] In addition to the fact that the prospects for receiving the court-ordered compensation were bleak, the U.S. Justice Department stated its opposition to using frozen Cuban funds or diverting payments by ATT and MCI for phone services, under threat from the Cuban government to suspend the service between the two countries.[11] Subsequently, a Miami federal court issued a ruling mandating the payment of $6.2 million (to be drawn from the phone assets) to the families of the three pilots who were U.S. citizens. Since the Cuban government had not been paid for months for the calls made, it cut off communications to and from Cuba, a problem that could be alleviated by using intermediary connections, although at a higher cost.[12] Subsequently, in a climate of tit-for-tat, the Cuban government announced that it would file a $181 *billion* suit as compensation for the victims of U.S.-sponsored attacks since 1959. The itemized bill included a claim of $30 million for each of the alleged 3,476 people killed and $15 million for each of the 2,099 who were allegedly disabled, in addition to $45 million for "general hardship."[13]

In these circumstances, Castro too appears to be faithful to a durable logic. Why capitulate and make concessions when Cuba's opposition to U.S. hegemony has been the trademark of his regime and allegedly the talisman for its survival? On the other side of the fence, Florida's new governor, Jeb Bush, is expected to play a key role in the 2000 presidential election and, with 72 percent of Miami Cubans still supporting the embargo, cannot afford any changes. Inter-American Dialogue's Luigi Einaudi comments that, similar to the circumstances of the trapped party-goers in *Exterminating Angel,* "The dynamics between us and Cuba looks dated, it looks sterile, and yet no one can find a way around it." The reason is, in the metaphor of Richard Nuccio, because Cuba has been always a "third rail" of U.S. policy. "Touch it and you die," the former White House adviser often states when asked to describe the dangers of dealing with this portion of U.S foreign policy.[14]

Casualties and Balance

A final review of the events and arguments that have developed around the rise and (predictably) the fall of the Helms-Burton Act reveals some interesting lessons. First is the obvious isolation of the United States in the world. This is a paradoxical development at a time when the United States has become the only global superpower. The essence of this contradiction may be that being a "power" does not bestow the trappings of *auctoritas.* The rest of the world perceives the U.S. national identity to be in question, as foreign policy concerns take a back seat to local, regional, and ethnic priorities. Most alarming is the fact that a dual government, whose checks-and-balances mechanism has been an effective guarantor of democracy, has been compromised by a sector of the U.S. Congress that has little concern for sensitive global issues, and is ignorant or disdainful of international law and U.S. commitments. Ironically, foreign governments are still not prepared to deal with this fractured power structure, and lack the resources to address the many different layers of governance in the United States. Even the European Union is not prepared to present a common strategy because of the infancy of its foreign policy and security arrangement.

The most tragically contradictory dimension of the Cuban-U.S. drama, nevertheless, is the situation of Cuba on the fortieth anniversary of the revolution. Cuba received diplomatic messages of congratulations from such diverse leaders as Pope John Paul II, French president Jacques Chirac, China's leaders Jiang Zemin and Zhu Rongji, and India's Atal Behari Vajpayee.[15] After the papal visit, ten more heads of state or government (from Panama, Colombia, Ghana, Haiti, Canada, and elsewhere) visited Havana, and the epochal visit of the king of Spain was expected (but did not materialize). Castro was to host the 1999 Ibero-American summit, which, with the initial exception of Nicaragua's president, all Latin American and Iberian leaders were expected to attend. However, the presidents of Chile and Argentina threatened to boycott. Adding to such triumphs in the international sphere, Cuba became a member of the Asociación Latinoamericana de Integración (ALADI), received confirmation of its observer status within the ACP group, and reinforced its links with CARICOM.

But in economic terms, the picture was not as positive. The Cuban economy grew only 1.2 percent, the lowest level in the period 1994–98 and well below the expected rate of between 2.5 and 3.5 percent. The decrease was attributed to a variety of external factors such as drought, hurricanes, international financial crisis, and the U.S. embargo.[16] According to UN statistics, Cuba's Human Development Index ranks twenty-sixth out of thirty-five countries in the Americas. In the estimate of Hugh Thomas, author of a classic book on Cuban history, today Cuba has a "19th Century economy."[17] Ironically, while sugar harvesting increased in 1998 in terms of tonnage, income derived from this crucial commodity decreased $150 million in comparison to 1997 and $500 million compared to 1996. Changes in world climate and dropping prices were to blame.[18] Influential European governments have warned of Cuba's difficulties in paying its short-term debt and lacking credit guarantees.[19] Cuba owes $27 million to the U.K. in short-term debt, and still does not want to recognize its obligation to Germany for unsatisfied debts to the German Democratic Republic. In a circling-the-wagons reaction, the minister of foreign investment, Ibrahim Ferradaz, reiterated Cuba's refusal to allow the privatization of the sugar industry, especially in its production stages. Confirming reports of resistance to liberalization of the Cuban economy, Ferradaz also stated that the investment policy would focus on seeking suitable investors rather than waiting for them to come.[20] Fidel Castro himself affirmed pragmatism in investment, but added that Cuba would not be "sold" and that some national goods are "untouchable."[21]

Cuba's infant mortality is the lowest in Latin America (7.2 per 1,000 births, ranking among the twenty-five best in the world) and life expectancy is 75.3 (just one year behind the United States), Cuba has one doctor per 160 people and has eliminated a dozen infant diseases. However, the World Health Organization has reported that surgical procedures have dropped 40 percent since 1990 because of the shortage of medicines, while eyeglasses are perennially impossible to obtain and hypodermic needles are a rarity in hospitals. The percentage of people with access to safe drinking water dropped from 90 percent in 1989 to 40 percent in 1994. Per capita food consumption decreased from 2,800 calories in 1954–57 to less than 2,000 in the mid-1990s.[22] Cuba is the Latin American country with the highest percentage of people older than sixty.[23] Criminality, virtually absent in the past, has alarmed Cuban authorities, and resulted in spectacular police operations and harsh death sentences as punishment for assassinations of tourists.[24] Mafia operations have been detected in Havana, alarming Cuban and U.S. authorities alike.[25] Accusations of money laundering and drug trafficking are frequently made by the U.S. government.[26]

The dual economy created by the development of tourism and foreign investment has caused doctors and teachers with salaries in the range of $10–20 per month to pursue work in hotels instead. Cuba's social structure has come to resemble the pyramid characteristic of its neighbors in Central America and some parts of the Caribbean, where a minority composed of landowners, government officials, and the military occupy the top strata. In Cuba, in addition to the government elite, the sector with access to foreign currency (especially remittances from families in the United States) is now part of the privileged class.[27] The education system, another jewel of revolutionary accomplishment, is proud of having one teacher per 13.7 students and a 95.7 percent literacy rate. But this accomplishment has been compromised by a Marxist orthodoxy that corrupts the curriculum with useless content, while the best careers are reserved for students with the most distinguished "political" records.

For these reasons, more and more Cubans prefer not to wait for the few remaining legal ways to leave the island. Many proceed to marry foreign citizens, while others are fortunate to receive a visa through the U.S.-administered lottery (more than 40,000 Cubans applied in 1998). More desperate and less lucky, in 1997 406 Cubans (along with 587 Haitians) were intercepted by the U.S. Coast Guard as they sought to flee in overloaded rafts, small boats, and other unseaworthy craft. In 1998 the number of Cubans who were caught jumped to 1,025 (along with 1,206 Haitians).[28] By May 1999 more than 400 had been intercepted, provoking alarming CIA reports of an impending avalanche of uncontrolled *balseros* tragedies.[29] Using their own flimsy means, or with the help of professional smugglers, more than one hundred Cubans arrived in Florida on the eve of the revolution's fortieth anniversary.[30] Elizardo Sánchez Santacruz, a human rights dissident accused by exiled hard-liners of collaboration with the Castro regime, blames the crisis on "the failure of the totalitarian model."[31] In the words of Wayne Smith, "the Cuban Revolution, as we have known it over the past 40 years, is essentially dead,"[32] a theme reviewed by Mark Falcoff in "Reflections on a Dying Revolution."[33]

With the exception of his brother, Raúl, who was there from the early days, all of Castro's revolutionary *compadres* are dead or in silent retirement. Some are in exile (including Huber Matos and Eloy Gutiérrez

Menoyo),[34] along with more than 1.5 million Cubans living abroad—in the United States (1.2 million) as well as places as distant as Spain, Sweden, Peru, and Australia.

Meanwhile, as we enter the fifth decade of the Cuban-U.S. confrontation, both sides seemed to hold firm to their respective policies and ideologies. Speaking in Santiago de Cuba on January 1, 1999, the fortieth anniversary of his triumph, Fidel Castro announced that "the Revolution has not yet started," and he ended his speech with the customary phrase, "Socialism or death!" Looking toward the other side of the Florida Straits, in an era of spreading globalization, he denounced the "new economic order" and charged, "they have turned the planet into a giant casino." The price of progress of "free markets is paid in human misery, child labor, prostitution and drug traffic."[35]

Also timed to coincide with the anniversary of the revolution, Senator Jesse Helms published an article in *Foreign Affairs* titled "What Sanctions Epidemic?" For the most part, it was a clear call to stay the course with respect to Cuba. While lambasting those who perceive the U.S. sanctions to be excessive and denouncing "lobbyists who are fighting for business as usual with thugs, tyrants, and terrorists," Helms asserted that "Castro's regime is teetering; unless America gives up its leverage by unconditionally lifting it, his successors will be anxious to exchange normalized relations with the United States for a democratic transition in Cuba."[36] Helms was referring to the pressures toward normalization being exerted by the powerful U.S. business sector, increasingly irritated by the loss of investment opportunities in Cuba, in combination with a project announced by the Council on Foreign Relations (the publisher of *Foreign Affairs*) whose objective was also to ease the embargo.[37]

The failure of this project has been identified as a possible cause for the hardening of the Cuban government's measures against internal opposition, as expressed in Law No. 88, officially titled "Protection of National Independence and the Economy of Cuba" but immediately labeled the *ley mordaza* (gag law). Although it was not a direct application of this law, the evident connection with the trial against a group of dissidents who, among other activities, had issued the famous manifesto "The Fatherland Belongs to All,"[38] was not lost to international opinion.[39] Some of the consequences were a rash of critical comments in the European and Latin American press,[40] diplomatic protests, questions about expanded agreements with the Rio Group and other networks,[41] calls for the suspension of the Ibero-American summit to be held in Havana in the fall of 1999,[42] and another delay in the scheduled visit of King Juan Carlos I to Cuba.[43]

Simultaneously, Senator Helms held hostage an important diplomatic nomination, with serious consequences in the Americas. The confirmation of Peter Romero, a former ambassador to Ecuador and the first Hispanic ever to be named assistant secretary of state for inter-American affairs, was blocked on the grounds that Romero had been slow in implementing the conditions dictated by H-B.[44] However, Helms's obstructionism has not been limited to Cuban affairs. He also managed to delay or derail diplomatic appointments to Brazil, Panama, Mexico and the United Nations.[45] His main arguments were stated in an article published in the controversial June 1999 special issue of the magazine *Cigar Aficionado*.[46]

The expectations of the Council on Foreign Relations lobby were not fulfilled by the offer announced by President Clinton on January 5, 1999. It included facilitating communications with Cuba, especially by expanding air and mail links, remittances, and the sale of food and agricultural products to "independent entities." The offer also included an increase of funding for the beaming of radio and television signals via Radio and Televisión Martí.[47] In the context of continuing domestic pressure to preserve the embargo, and the heightened international attention focused on Cuba in the anniversary year of the revolution, Clinton's move was seen as an attempt to counter the increased isolation of U.S. foreign policy.[48] The U.S. international initiative was slipping while Castro was about to bask in a series of triumphal international appearances and serve as host for an impressive number of distinguished foreign visitors. First in line were his scheduled trips to Saint Lucia for the twentieth anniversary of its independence and to Caracas for the inauguration of President Chávez. At the same time, the new Colombian president, Andrés Pastrana, expressed to Castro his commitment to the peace process of his country.[49] Chávez and Pastrana spent a weekend in Havana, with Castro as host, power broker, and intermediary in the negotiations between the Colombian government and the guerrillas. The VIP visits to Havana continued with Jules Wijdenbosch, president of Surinam. Later in the year, Castro would attend the European–Latin American summit to be held in Rio de Janeiro, an idea espoused by President Chirac of France.

As a countermeasure, the ball was again in Cuba's court as to what to do with Clinton's offer of food and medicine, simultaneously with complaining about shortages. After a brief pause, while the Cuban government initially adopted a cautious wait-and-see attitude, the reaction to the U.S. offer fell into the customary pattern, with moderates expressing hope and the extremists embracing irritation and rejection. For different reasons, H-B backers and the Cuban government once again crafted their "coalition" in defense against what they considered the threat of moderation and compromise.[50]

Some observers saw the Clinton measures as simply a concession to the members of Congress who were pressing for reforms and an attempt to find a balance between the hard-liners and moderates in the White House and the State Department. Others viewed it as a serious effort to weaken the embargo.[51] In this vein Congressman Díaz-Balart vouched for the continuation of the policy, outlining the major accomplishments of 1998. Most of the items on his list were negative: blocking proposals for liberalization made by his colleagues, increase of funding to monitor "illegal business travel to Cuba," the suspension of a U.S. contribution to the UN food program, the opposition to Clinton's plans to "gut Titles III and IV," and the delay in confirming the appointment of Peter Romero.[52] He rightly reminded readers that, with Title II still operative, a more ambitious plan to dismantle the embargo would have to meet the law's requirements for a "transitional government."

Other backers of H-B announced an energetic opposition to Clinton's proposal. Besides the expected complaints from Senator Helms and Congressman Burton, Ben Gilman, chairman of the House International Affairs Committee, and Congresswoman Ileana Ros-Lehtinen, reaffirmed their concerns, predicting considerable controversy over the proposal to sell food and medicine, seemingly in violation of the provisions of Title II of the law. Other observers wondered if the real objective of the measure was something other than the implementation of the difficult mechanism to channel products selectively and directly to the Cuban people.

U.S. partners received the measure with optimism. Canada's foreign minister and Spain's chambers of commerce called the move positive.[53] While the Cuban Catholic Church welcomed the move, pro-regime Cuban exiles residing in Miami issued a condemnation, sharing the view of hard-liners.[54] Dissidents in Cuba predicted that the government might reject the offer, and in fact Cuban authorities issued a series of declarations refusing the U.S. initiative. Economy Minister José Luis Rodríguez called the offer "crumbs."[55] Ricardo Alarcón went further, calling the offer "subversive, counterrevolutionary, and *injerencista*" (meddlesome).[56] He especially denounced the attempt to make the Catholic Church an "accomplice" of U.S. foreign policy, and stated that during previous so-called openings Cuba had not been able to buy even "an aspirin" from the United States.[57]

The Cuban government had to respond to the modified U.S. policy with either stiff resistance or acceptance. Predictably, Castro chose resistance. One informed Cuban source frequently quoted by the *Miami Herald*'s Juan

Tamayo in his perceptive reports, offered an insightful image: "When you come at me with a saber in your hand I have to defend myself any way I can. But when you put away that saber and try to embrace me, you put me in a difficult situation."[58] The apparent disappearance of the enemy had to be replaced a new threat.

The actions and reactions in the sphere of official government policy were followed by two historic cultural exchanges, whereby the Baltimore Orioles baseball team played in Havana and the Cuban national team visited Baltimore. Meanwhile, business interests in the United States increased the pressure to lift the embargo during an important convention held in Cancún, Mexico, that was attended by high-ranking Cuban officials.[59] Influential members of Congress such as Senator Christopher Dodd also pressed for a change in U.S. policy toward Cuba.[60] Business leaders who favor lifting the embargo cite economic arguments such as Commerce Department estimates that convert each $1 billion in U.S. exports into twenty thousand additional jobs. With expected U.S.-Cuban trade projected to be worth $3–6 billion following normalization, the continuing cost to the U.S. economy is evident.[61] Meanwhile, a Gallup poll revealed that 71 percent of Americans favored diplomatic ties with Cuba, with just 25 percent opposed.[62] In response to these arguments, hard-line sectors of the Cuban exile community denounced what they perceived as moderate moves of the U.S. government toward Cuba.[63]

As we have seen, the third anniversary of Helms-Burton took place in a climate clouded by the repressive laws passed by the Cuban government against dissidents and alleged "collaborators" with the U.S. embargo. All sides in this drama adopted the same rigid positions they have always favored. U.S.-Cuban relations continued on the customary roller coaster, combining music and sports exchanges with discoveries of spy rings in the United States and assassination plots. Foreign governments, while maintaining opposition to the embargo, were extremely critical of Cuba's closed judicial proceedings against the dissidents (Félix Bonne, Vladimiro Roca, Marta Beatriz Roque, and René Gómez Manzano), who were in jail for months and eventually sentenced to harsh jail sentences. The Cuban Catholic Church openly criticized the measures, on the grounds that they would not reduce political opposition nor decrease criminal activity.[64] Reports of a rise in the number of death sentences (including those imposed on the perpetrators of the terrorist activities against tourist hotels) and executions alarmed observers.[65] Rumors of arrests and important staff changes in the high ranks of the Cuban Ministry of Interior[66] coincided with reports in the official press of conflicts of opinion in the Communist Party, with the hard-liners getting the upper hand.[67] Expecting to receive little sympathy for Cuba's demands for better treatment in the aftermath of the April 1999 decision issued by the UN Human Rights Commission, Foreign Minister Roberto Robaina canceled scheduled trips to key European capitals in May 1999.[68]

The Fall of Roberto Robaina: A Change of Course?

Rumors about Robaina's fall from grace were confirmed when on May 28, 1999, he was replaced by Felipe Pérez Roque, a thirty-four-year-old personal aide to Fidel Castro. The change prompted more questions than answers about Cuba's foreign-policy agenda in view of the important issues pending for 1999 (among them, Cuba's status in the Lomé Convention and the Rio Group and Ibero-American summits).[69] It became the immediate subject of front-page articles, commentaries, editorials, and news dispatches.[70]

Roberto Robaina had been heralded as the architect of Cuba's most effective foreign-policy accomplishments since his appointment in 1993, and for this reason his dismissal caught observers by surprise. A careful consideration of Cuba's foreign relations record of 1998, together with the developments of 1999, suggests an explanation for the dismissal. First of all, Robaina's term ended with Cuba having established an impressive number of international diplomatic links. Havana maintains direct relations with 166 countries and has diplomatic representation in 116. In 1998, 173 foreign dignitaries visited Cuba, among them 12 heads of state or government, 114 ministers (among them 24 ministers of foreign relations), and 21 presidents of parliaments.[71] Simultaneously, the *International Who's Who* lists Fidel Castro among the one hundred most influential figures of the century. This impressive record contrasts with the context of the dismissal.

The formality used in announcing the change in the wake of another trip that Robaina had scheduled (and later canceled) to several Caribbean and Latin American capitals and the foreign-policy inexperience of Pérez Roque initially caused puzzlement. However, the youthfulness of Robaina's successor need not be a major concern. Robaina himself was appointed to the post when he was only thirty-seven. Both men also initially lacked a background in economics, diplomacy, or law, coming from technical disciplines such as mathematics and engineering. Both appointments suggest an official distrust of the diplomatic career establishment.

A more important issue is the fact that the announcement, made on the front page of *Granma,* implied a critical view of Robaina's foreign-policy accomplishments in recent months. The announcement spoke of "the current complexity of the tense international situation, its growing importance for the future of our country and of the world and the need for deeper, more rigorous, more systematic and more demanding work in this area."[72] Among the issues contributing to the "complexity of the tense international situation," commentators pointed to the crisis in Kosovo (in which Cuba sided with Milosevic) and the progress of Britain's extradition efforts against the former Chilean dictator Augusto Pinochet. These two developments were seen by Cuba as new threats to itself. In an apparent overreaction, the Cuban leadership appeared concerned by efforts to extradite a foreign leader and by the new NATO doctrine of intervening in peripheral areas in extreme crisis. Stretching the point, Cuban officials detected similarities between the U.S. intervention in Cuba in 1898 and in Yugoslavia in 1999, believing in the ever-present potential for a new involvement in Cuba. While U.S. sources declared that they did not expect major changes in relations with Cuba, and Cuban diplomats in Europe reassured governments and European Union officials that Havana's agenda would remain the same with the new foreign minister, one of Pérez Roque's first declarations was to demand the trial of NATO Secretary-General Javier Solana as a "war criminal."[73]

Naturally, more specific events have been credited for the exhaustion of Robaina's political credit. First was the condemnation of Cuba by the UN Human Rights Commission. Then, as an indirect result of the repressive laws, the projected official visit of King Juan Carlos of Spain was delayed indefinitely, and reduced to the possibility of an appearance at the Ibero-American Summit scheduled for November 1999, with an extended stay in Havana afterwards. "Unfortunately, proper circumstances were absent," said the official declaration of Spain, avoiding the admission that the conditions presented by the Spanish government (media access, meetings with dissidents) had been rejected by Cuban authorities.[74] The summit, in turn, increasingly fell under the threat of boycott by several Latin American leaders. None of these failures could be attributed to Robaina. "Robertico," the "salsa minister" (as his detractors in Cuba and his foreign colleagues used to call him), faced a formidable task. A U.S. businessman quoted by the *Miami Herald*'s Juan Tamayo accurately depicted his mission impossible: "Robaina's ability to 'sell' Cuba has been harmed not by his salesmanship but the fact that the product he was trying to sell changed."[75]

Former U.S. envoy to Cuba Wayne Smith had this to say in assessing the accomplishments of the former foreign minister: "He really traveled around and used Helms-Burton effectively against the U.S. to a point where the U.S. was more isolated by it than Cuba."[76]

Granma's announcement contained a significant prediction about the "new" Cuban foreign policy. It was imbedded in the justification for the appointment of Pérez Roque: "he is familiar as few other people are with the ideas and the thought of Fidel Castro." Only time will confirm whether this is a signal that Castro himself will be at the helm of Cuba's day-to-day foreign policy. However, the enigmatic phrase alarmed a number of readers, who called the *Granma* office inquiring about the apparent scarcity of ideological affinity among the Cuban citizenry. In an unprecedented editorial, *Juventud Rebelde* rushed to clarify that the notation was not exclusionary but a sign of Pérez Roque's outstanding capabilities, as *more* familiar with Fidel's thinking.[77]

As one reviews the events of the first half of 1999, a wider question arises: Why did Castro elect (or why was he forced) to waste such impressive political capital shortly before he was to achieve unprecedented foreign policy triumphs? Why did the Cuban government change course just as it was enjoying a prolonged truce and a period of tolerance in the global community, including some moderating overtures from the United States?

There are two possible explanations. The first one emphasizes the overwhelming pressure exerted by the international community and the deterioration of Cuba's economy, which increased the threat of internal dissension. The system was then forced to protect itself in bunker fashion. The second explanation suggests that the Castro regime perceived the greatest threat as coming from the expanded climate of liberalization, especially in the economic terrain, and anticipated a spillover into the social realm that would ultimately threaten its political monopoly. This scenario would explain, in part, the conditions imposed on investment and the harsh terms of the repressive new laws. It would also explain Castro's objective of detecting or inventing an atmosphere of harassment against Cuba, as exemplified by imposition of requirements for political reform (denounced as technical violations of sovereignty) as conditions imposed on the projected visit of the king of Spain and for the revision of a cooperation aid agreement granted by the European Union. Put in blunter terms, the price to be paid by the cancellation of the Ibero-American Summit, the ACP observer status, or a royal visit was seen by the Cuban leadership as insignificant when compared with the risk to its continuing in power. This would confirm, once again, that one party in the drama elected to make a bold move to revive a climate of uncertainty and tension.

Future Research and Policy Suggestions

It is important to consider, before concluding this discussion, the way the academic community has responded to Helms-Burton and to the attendant broad questions of America's relations with Cuba, Europe, and its NAFTA partners. Two issues in particular seem in urgent need of redress. First is the limitation imposed by conventional disciplinary divisions, with the result that the legal dimensions of the Helms-Burton Law are consistently overlooked in the analyses of political scientists and economists. This omission may be the result of the attitude of the realpolitik that dominated research in international relations during the Cold War. However that may be, political commentaries are typically part of the legal experts' scholarly dissections of the law. Closer communication between the two fields is urgently needed.

Second is the fact that the huge impact of the Helms-Burton fiasco has transcended the convenient disciplinary boundaries erected by Latin American studies and European studies. Although globalism may be viewed as a formidable threat to regionalism and area studies, in this instance an analysis that tackles both sides of the ocean is not only appropriate but unavoidable. An erroneous perception of the European Union as a simple free-trade pact has generated, among those engaged in non-E.U. regional studies in the United States, a regrettable lack of understanding of the internal culture of the European Union. Moreover, the notion that all politics are local (as illustrated by the local origin of the Helms-Burton Law) is also applicable to the reality that H-B has become a domestic affair in some countries, as in the case of Spain. An understanding of the internal culture of these countries is imperative. During the Cold War secondary actors were considered expendable, but this is not possible today. Again, the case of Spain is paradigmatic because it has moved from pariah status in the 1950s into one of the causes for the development of the Helms-Burton Act, by virtue of its close economic and cultural links.

With respect to the relations between the United States and the rest of the world, some special attention should be given to the problems caused by the conflicting judgments regarding alternate policies. This suggests some final recommendations and considerations.

First of all, the U.S. government and Congress should take into account the assessments of independent scholarly voices, individuals who are detached from the Cuban-American exile community, the centers of power in Washington, and from the Cuban government. With no personal or political agenda at stake, numerous voices in Latin America, Canada, and Europe have expressed alarm. An objective analysis of the effects of U.S. policy on Cuba has clearly shown damage to the alleged goals of democratization. The British-trained Italian scholar Maurizio Giuliano has demonstrated the link between each one of the most recent U.S. measures and Cuba's use of them for domestic political purposes. Reflecting a wide European consensus, his judgment is that the U.S. embargo is counterproductive because the policy "helps legitimise the Cuban regime in the eyes of the population. . . . It persuades elites to refrain from making much political reforms, it provides the regime with a convenient explanation of the country's economic crisis, and gives the government a rationale for imposing repressive measures and resisting calls for democratic opening." Morever, if the U.S. embargo were to cease, Castro would be forced to ask Cubans "to remain united in order to resist 'ideological poisoning.'" In such a case, European and Latin American governments would not continue to back him.[78]

With regard to the economic relationships of the United States, its partners and allies should make every effort to convince U.S. leaders that any serious confrontation over trade and investment in Cuba should first be weighed against the relative importance of the case. Irreparable damage to global relationships should be avoided. Although complete success is doubtful, this message should be systematically and publicly expressed, if only for the record.

On the other hand, Europeans (and other partners) should not entirely disregard the concerns of the United States. This is essential if a shared goal is to make the Cuban transition as painless and peaceful as possible. Among other possibilities for compromise is the projected Multilateral Agreement on Investment, which should be carefully considered; or it should be revived if seriously damaged, as appeared to be the case in early 1999.

Meanwhile, European policy toward Cuba should continue to be implemented with a high degree of transparency, both for domestic purposes and for the benefit of the United States. This will also be useful to the U.S. neighbors in the Western hemisphere. In the absence of security concerns, European and Western hemisphere governments cannot afford to give the impression that they are concealing a special policy toward Cuba that may be interpreted by Washington as hostile.

As far as the E.U. network is concerned, while maintaining all the previously approved measures (Regulation, Common Position, Joint Action), a cautious attitude (on both Cuban and U.S. policies) should continue. This may not be the most ambitious policy, but it is the most advisable in view of the unpredictable course that the Cuban regime might take and the uncertain U.S. response, which is subject to the complex constraints that have been reviewed in this work.

Coordination of policies, especially within the E.U. structure, should be a priority in order to deter the U.S. and Cuban protagonists from taking advantage of divisions in the European front. When possible, apparent contradictions or violations of E.U. mandates (such is the case of STET) should be avoided.

Regarding the evolution of Cuban society, foreign interests will be ill served if they add to the extreme hardships of the Cuban people by unnecessarily limiting the current engagement. The European and Canadian governments should maintain the policies that have been implemented until now. However, while economically engaging the Cuban society, trading partners should be alert to the danger of contributing to the formation of a dual economy in Cuba. The division of Cuban society into two sectors, composed of those who have access to foreign currency and the rest who have to survive in the still-centralized economy, may change the image of the "ugly American" into the "ugly European," with serious consequences in the future.

Europeans should pay attention to the observers, both in the United States and in Europe—and not necessarily defenders of U.S. policy—who question the efficacy of European policies toward Cuba. Not all of them share the European enthusiasm for unconditional engagement. According to Richard Haass, while Europeans may view U.S. policy as "all stick and no carrot," they should be prepared to be criticized for a policy that is "all carrot and no stick." In contrasting the differing approaches of the United States and its allies, the metaphor of "good cop, bad cop" is useful. The contributions of the "good" cop (Europe, Canada, some Latin American and Caribbean states) may be effective "if the good cop is willing to get tough and join hands with the [bad cop] if incentives fail to bring about the desired results."[79] Cautious observers have expressed doubt regarding the efficacy of the engagement policy in the democratization process of Cuba.[80]

While the rest of the E.U. member states do not have a "special relationship" with Cuba and can therefore afford a detached policy, Spain has a very special historical role to play in Cuba. This became evident when the centennial of the end of colonial rule was commemorated in 1998. This special relationship should be pursued with a high sense of responsibility, and it deserves the full cooperation of its European partners. The U.S. government should take this special relationship into account as well.

As in the cases of the United States and its partners, linking aid to the improvement of human rights conditions should be an aim but not a fixed precondition. The distribution of aid through NGOs, although not entirely free from obstacles imposed by the Cuban government, may still be the best guarantee of success.

The European opposition to the U.S. embargo, coupled with a coordinated policy toward Cuba regarding human rights, will be judged by history to have produced more benefits than costs. The goal of fostering democracy in Cuba is an objective shared by all the U.S. partners and allies.

The current intriguing chapter of Cuban history is still open to analysis. The time frame for a future evaluation will include the consecutive terms of unofficial "truce" agreed upon by the European Union and the United States in 1997, and confirmed by the apparent permanent status of the Understanding of 1998. This arrangement should last at least until President Clinton leaves office in January 2001. Until then, in the event that the Cuban regime comes to an end by virtue of natural evolution (as a consequence of Castro's death), the Helms-Burton Law will claim a place in history—with a balance sheet showing more harm than good. Its central objective, Castro's exit under the effect of economic pressure, will not have been accomplished. The law then will go on record not as a simple attempt to promote democracy in Cuba but rather as an expression of what I have called the Helms-Burton doctrine. As discussed, in essence the law is seen as an an expansion and an update of the Monroe Doctrine and its corollaries as applied to Cuba. The main problem with international repercussions is that H-B was not only destined to impose conditions on Cuba for the lifting of the U.S. embargo (as Title II states). It is also a revival of the Monroe Doctrine when it tries to dictate rules (Titles III and IV) to other countries regarding their economic relations with Cuba.This is a side effect that the United States and Europe hardly need in this complex and confusing new world order, which in the case of the U.S.-Cuban relations so much resembles the old order.

APPENDIX: BIOGRAPHICAL SKETCHES

Lincoln Díaz-Balart

Born in Havana in 1954, Representative Lincoln Díaz-Balart received his secondary education in Madrid. He holds a B.A. from New College of the University of South Florida and a law degree from Case Western Reserve University Law School. An attorney, he was elected as a Republican to the Florida House (1986–89), the Florida Senate (1989–92), and the U.S. House of Representatives (1992, 1994, 1996). (Ironically, Lincoln Díaz-Balart is related to Fidel Castro, who was once married to his aunt Mirta Díaz-Balart. From this marriage, which ended in divorce after five years, came "Fidelito" Castro Díaz-Balart, the only child explicitly recognized by the Cuban leader, although he has acknowledged being the father of Alina Fernández-Revuelta, a daughter he had as the result of an extramarital relationship.) Lincoln Díaz-Balart is married and has two children.

Ileana Ros-Lehtinen

Born in Havana in 1952, Representative Ileana Ros-Lehtinen holds B.A. and M.S. degrees in educational leadership from Florida International University. She is a certified teacher and the founder and former owner of Eastern Academy. Her political career includes election as a Republican to the Florida House (1983–87), the Florida Senate (1987–89), and the U.S. House of Representatives (1989, 1994, 1996).

Robert Torricelli

Born in 1951, Senator Robert Torricelli holds a law degree from Rutgers University and a master's degree in public administration from Harvard University. After a stint as deputy legislative counsel to New Jersey governor

Brendan Byrne, Torricelli served as an adviser to Vice President Walter Mondale. In 1982 he was elected to the House of Representatives for the Ninth Congressional District, where he served for seven terms, until 1996, when he became a U.S. senator.

Jorge Mas Canosa

In a report ranking Hispanics in the United States by wealth, Jorge Mas Canosa and his son, Jorge L. Mas, appeared in fifth and fourth place, with net worths of $257 million and $329 million, respectively. Their combined fortunes made them the second wealthiest Hispanics listed, behind only Roberto Goizueta, the late chief executive of Coca-Cola. Born in Havana in 1939, Jorge Mas Canosa came to the United States in July 1960 as a refugee. He purchased a construction company where he had been an employee and changed its original name (based on the founders' names, Iglesias and Torres) to Church and Tower. Disillusioned with the U.S. policy toward Cuba, he founded the Cuban-American National Foundation (CANF) in March 1981, modeled on the American-Israeli Political Action Committee (AIPAC). In 1981 CANF lobbied for the creation of Radio Martí. After President Ronald Reagan visited Miami in 1983, the U.S. government backed the project sponsored by CANF. Radio Martí was created, and Mas Canosa was named to chair its advisory board. After supporting the Torricelli bill, CANF became the force behind the development of the Helms-Burton Law in 1995. Mas Canosa's most spectacular triumph was his September 1996 televised debate with Ricardo Alarcón, president of the Cuban National Assembly. After revealing that he had a disease, Mas disappeared from public appearances and died on November 23, 1997.

Jesse Helms

Senator Jesse Helms was born in 1921 in Monroe, North Carolina. He was educated at Wingate College and Wake Forest University. Following service in the U.S. Navy (1942–45), he was city editor of the *Raleigh Times* and executive director of the North Carolina Bankers Association (1953–60). Elected to the Raleigh City Council (1957–61), he became a U.S. senator in 1972. He is married and has three children.

Dan Burton

Born in Indianapolis, Indiana, in 1938, Representative Dan Burton attended Indiana University (1958–59) and Cincinnati Bible College (1959–60). He served in the U.S. Army Reserve (1957–62) and was a businessman in insurance and real estate. He has served in the Indiana House (1967–69 and 1977–81) and the Indiana Senate (1969–71 and 1981–83). Since 1982 he has represented Indiana District 6 in the U.S. Congress. Burton is married and has three children.

Robert Menéndez

Representative Robert Menéndez was born in New York City in 1954 of Cuban parents. He holds a B.A. from Saint Peter's College in Jersey City, New Jersey, and a law degree from Rutgers University. Before becoming a member of Congress from the 13th District of New Jersey, he was state senator (1991–92), New Jersey state assemblyman (1987–91), and mayor of Union City (1986–91). He is married and has two children. A member of the Foreign Relations Subcommittee of the House, he is the only Cuban-American congressman who is a Democrat. According to unconfirmed sources, in exchange for Menéndez's help, the White House agreed to change its moderate Cuban policies and terminate several advisers, among them Morton Halperin, Richard Nuccio, and Richard Feinberg. Naturally, this is denied by other observers.

Bacardí

The company was founded in Santiago de Cuba in 1862 by Facundo Bacardí y Masó, a Catalan immigrant born in 1813 in Sitges, a town near Barcelona. He retired in 1876 and left the company in the hands of his three sons, Emilio, Facundo, and José Bacardí Moreau. They in turn expanded the company with financial backing from Enrique Schueg. Emilio Bacardí (1844–1922) became the most well known member of the family for his dedication to the independence of Cuba and his impressive scholarly productions (among them the *Crónicas de Santiago de Cuba, 1908–24*). He became mayor of Santiago (initially appointed by the U.S. authorities and later democratically elected) and a Cuban senator. The internationalization of the company began in 1910 with the establishment of a bottling plant in Barcelona, Spain, just north of the original birthplace of the founder. In 1916 the company's first plant was built in New York City. In 1960 the company was nationalized. Its value was set at $76 million, which included the famous headquarters building in Havana and the Santiago distillery. With its trademark intact, the company was rebuilt in the Bahamas, with three additional distilleries in Mexico, Puerto Rico, and Brazil. Company CEO Pepín Bosch aggressively and successfully contested in several national courts the attempts of the Cuban government to use the trademark. Indeed, his string of legal victories may be viewed as the first significant triumphs of a Cuban exile over the Castro regime. The Bacardí product is now sold in 170 countries, and annual sales amount to 20 million cases. Ironically, the expropriation of the company may be considered the initial impetus for the worldwide success of the business through its rebuilding in other countries. "Some people say that Castro is the best thing that happened to Bacardí," says Juan Prado, a member of the corporate family.

NOTES

Author's Note on Newspaper Sources

Readers may notice that at times newspaper sources have no page numbers. In these cases the reference comes from the text found in Internet editions that at the time of access did not contain the page numbers of the original edition. In other cases, references are to photocopies of the articles as provided by European Union agencies and the Spokesman Service of the Ministry of Foreign Affairs of Spain, especially through its daily service *Prensa de la mañana* and the monthly compilation *La política internacional en la prensa*. In addition there are references to wire dispatches originating in the major news agencies, such as the Associated Press, Agence France Press, and, especially, the Spanish news agency EFE. This information is provided as an "anchor" in time for an event or a declaration as reported by reputable news agencies. It is expected that the basic information of the corresponding wire services was printed by literally dozens of newspapers subscribing to the service. When a sample is actually available in the author's files, data are provided.

1. Background and Development

1. Domínguez, "U.S.-Cuban Relations," 58.
2. Huntington, "The Erosion of American National Interests."
3. Ibid., 37, 48.
4. The literature on the relations between the United States and Cuba is voluminous. Besides the studies referenced in the notes and bibliography, a useful starting point is a review article by Lynn Stoner, "Recent Literature on Cuba and the United States." One of the most recent accounts of the pending items is the article by Pamela Falk, "The U.S.-Cuba Agenda: Opportunity or Stalemate?"
5. For a review of the interconnection between the legal aspects involved, see works by the Bar Association of New York, Bourque, Cain, Donner, Porotsky, Wong, and Zipper, cited in the bibliography.
6. Kaplowitz, *Anatomy of a Failed Embargo*, 35.
7. Wayne Smith, *The Closest of the Enemies*, 47, 49.
8. For a review of these measures, see the monograph by Francisco García Amador, *La cuestión cubana en la OEA*.

9. See Carmelo Mesa Lago and June S. Belkin, *Cuba in Africa.*

10. Decreto Legislativo no. 50 (Feb. 15, 1982).

11. For a broad analysis of the reforms, see Carmelo Mesa Lago, *Are Economic Reforms Propelling Cuba to the Market?* See also Vivian del Rosario Hernández, "España-Cuba: Empresas mixtas," for a Cuban perspective on the prospects for reform.

12. Combined data provided by Consultores Asociados (CONAS) (Havana), as quoted and processed by Jorge Pérez-López, "Foreign Direct Investment in the Cuban Economy"; Christian Freres, "The Role of the European Union"; IDB/IRELA, *Direct Foreign Investment in Latin America: The Investor's Perspective.*

13. CONAS, 1995.

14. Pérez López, "Foreign Direct Investment in the Cuban Economy."

15. Ana Julia Jatar-Hausman, "What Cuba Can Teach Russia," 95.

16. CONAS, "Cuba: Inversiones y Negocios 1995–96," in Argentaria / Club del Exterior, *Cuba: Guía de Negocios,* 75.

17. Evaluation provided by Wolf Grabendorff, director of IRELA, to author, Dec. 1998.

18. Miguel Ángel de la Guardia, Havana Radio, Jan. 5, 1997, Foreign Broadcast Information Service (FBIS-LAT-004).

19. Robert C. Helander, "Creditors' Rights: Claims against Cuban Confiscated Assets," 40.

20. Ibid.

21. See Rolando Castañeda and George Plinio Montalván, "Economic Factors in Selecting an Approach to Confiscation Claims in Cuba," 228.

22. Robert C. Helander, "Creditors' Rights."

23. Banco Nacional de Cuba, Annual Report 1994.

24. CONAS, "Inversiones y negocios, 1995–96."

25. Iraida Calzadilla Rodríguez, "Otro año que va concluyendo con buenos resultados," *Granma,* Dec. 30, 1998; Miguel Comellas, "1.14 million tourists," *Granma International,* Dec. 30, 1998.

26. Books exploring these issues include Carlos Alberto Montaner, *Cuba hoy: La lenta muerte del castrismo,* and Andrés Oppenheimer, *Castro's Final Hour: The Secret Story behind the Coming Downfall of Communist Cuba.*

27. Domínguez, "U.S.-Cuban Relations," 55.

28. LeoGrande, "From Havana to Miami."

29. Domínguez, "U.S.-Cuban Relations," 55.

30. "America's Culture War and the Cuban Revolution," 169–86.

31. Grenier and Gladwin, *FIU Cuba Poll* (1997).

32. "Reproducción generacional del discurso tradicional," *El Nuevo Herald* (Miami), Jan. 17, 1999, 25A.

33. Memorandum for Assistant Secretary of State for Inter-American Affairs Alexander Watson, Aug. 1, 1993, quoted by Richard Nuccio, "Cuba: A U.S. Perspective," 10.

34. Ibid.

35. For commentary on this aspect of U.S. policy under the Torricelli law, see David Reiff, "Cuba Refrozen," 73.

36. One example: Peter Kornbluh, "Killing Castro Softly," *The Nation,* March 18, 1996, 4.

37. Abi-Mershed, Krinsky, and Golove, *United States Economic Measures against Cuba,* 868.

38. Bar Association of the City of New York, "The Legality of the Extraterritorial Reach of the Cuban Democracy Act of 1992."

39. Jerry W. Cain, Jr., "Extraterritorial Application of the United States' Trade Embargo against Cuba," 389–90.

40. Kaplowitz, *Anatomy of a Failed Embargo,* 1–10.

41. Bourque, "The Illegality of the Cuban Embargo," 212.

42. Ibid., 215.

43. Cain, "Extraterritorial Application," 389.

44. Bourque, "Illegality," 209.

45. Wong, "The Cuba Democracy Act of 1992," 681, 659, 660.

46. Congressional Record H9086. For an earlier statement by Rangel opposing U.S. policy toward Cuba, see "Should the United States Lift Its Embargo against Cuba?" *Congressional Quarterly Researcher* 4, no. 40 (Oct. 28, 1994): 953.

47. Donner, "The Cuban Democracy Act of 1992," 261–62.

48. Wong, "The Cuba Democracy Act," 681.

49. Donner, "The Cuban Democracy Act," 267.

50. Rep. Charles Rangel, Congressional Record H9086, as quoted by Wong, 657n.33.

51. Wong, "The Cuba Democracy Act," 681.

52. "Canada Issues Order Blocking U.S. Trade Restrictions," External Affairs and International Trade Canada news release no. 199, Oct. 9, 1992; see also Wong, 670.

53. Donner, "The Cuban Democracy Act," 265.

54. Ibid.; David Owen, "UK Rejects Trade Ban on Cuba by U.S.," *Financial Times,* Oct. 21, 1992.

55. Donner, "The Cuban Democracy Act," 266.

56. Ibid., 267.

57. *A Road Map,* xv, 3, 19, 21.

2. Getting Their Act Together

1. Ondetti, "Western European and Canadian Relations with Cuba," 1.

2. Domínguez, "U.S.-Cuban Relations."

3. Celia W. Dugger, "Leader's Zeal Powers Exile Lobby," *Miami Herald,* April 10, 1988, 1A; Mimi Whitefield, "Cuban Americans Top List of Rich Hispanics," *Miami Herald,* March 5, 1997; "El club de los millonarios hispanos," *El Nuevo Herald,* March 5, 1997. For detailed comments on his life and enterprises, see the *Miami Herald, El Nuevo Herald,* and *Diario las Américas* in the days following his death, especially the article by Christopher Marquis, "Jorge Mas Canosa, 1939–1997," *Miami Herald*, Nov. 24, 1997, 1A.

4. "Exile: Cuba Investments 'An Act of Collaboration'," *Miami Herald,* Dec. 22, 1994.

5. Dispatches of AP and other news agencies for Feb. 9, 1995.

6. Eric Green, "Helms-Burton Bill 'Godsend' to Castro Regime," U.S. Information Agency, U.S. Mission in Italy, July 13, 1995.

7. Betancourt, "Potential Impact of the Helms/Burton Act," 425.

8. "Bill Would Tighten Cuba Embargo," *Congressional Quarterly Weekly Report* 53, no. 28 (July 15, 1995).

9. Carroll J. Doherty, "Senate GOP Falls Short in Bid to Tighten Screws on Castro," ibid., no. 40 (Oct. 14, 1995): 3156.

10. For a succinct review of this process, see Renee G. Scherlen, "The Politics of Helms-Burton."

11. Among other commentaries, see Jorge Domínguez, "U.S.-Cuban Relations," 64

12. Carl Nagin, "Backfire," *New Yorker,* Jan. 26, 1998, 30–35.

13. "Remarks Announcing Sanctions against Cuba Following the Downing of Brothers to the Rescue Airplanes," *Weekly Compilation of Presidential Documents* 32, no. 9 (March 4, 1996): 381.

14. For a sample of U.S. media commentaries, see Tara Sonenshine and Tom Masland, "Troubled Waters: Clinton's Carefully Crafted Policy Was Shot Down along with the Planes," *Newsweek,* March 11, 1996, 48; Kevin Fedarko, "This Cold War Is Back (U.S. vs. Cuba)," *Time,* March 11, 1996, 36; Linda Robinson, "Honking at Havana: Cuban Exiles Vow to Keep Up the Pressure on Castro—and Washington," *U.S. News & World Report,* March 11, 1996, 35.

15. For selected direct reporting, see these two notes by Carroll J. Doherty: "Clinton Fires Warning Shot in Cuba Trade Crackdown," *Congressional Quarterly Weekly Report* 54, no. 28 (July 13, 1996): 1983; "Clinton Delays but Allows Suits over Confiscated Property," ibid., no. 29 (July 20, 1996): 2063.

16. "Let's Try Dialogue, Not Embargo, as Cuba Policy," *Miami Herald,* June 30, 1995, 17A.

17. Combined wires of AFP, AP, DPA, Reuters, and EFE, during the first week of March 1996.

18. Prensa Latina, March 2, 1996 (FBIS-LAT-96-043).

19. Prensa Latina, March 7, 1996 (FBIS-LAT-96-047).

20. "Robaina States Position," Radio Rebelde, March 19, 1996 (FBIS-LAT-055).

21. Radio Havana, March 11, 1996 (FBIS-LAT-96-049).

22. Nuccio, "Cuba: A U.S. Perspective," 27n.9.

23. Nuccio's expanded comments were made in the course of the question and answer period in March 1998 at a Brookings conference, where his "Cuba: A U.S. Perspective" originated.

24. LeoGrande, "From Havana to Miami," 81.

25. Albright, "The Testing of American Foreign Policy," 62.

26. See Nuccio, "Cuba: A U.S. Perspective." For a specific comment on this aspect of the law, see Muse, "A Public International Law Critique."

27. For a review of Menéndez's role, see comment by Daniel A. Restrepo (staff member of the House International Affairs Committee, July 1993–June 1996), "Helms-Burton: The Political Context."

28. Cynthia Corzo, "Halla eco en Clinton voz de Bob Menéndez," *El Nuevo Herald*, April 7, 1996, 18A; Ariel Ramos, "Explica Menéndez detalles," *Diario las Américas*, March 9, 1997, B1.

29. Domínguez, "U.S.-Cuban Relations," 57.

30. Schoultz, *Beneath the United States*, 367.

31. Ibid., 374.

32. Ibid., xvi.

33. Ibid., xvii.

34. Ibid., 151.

35. "Alarcón Discusses Helms-Burton," Havana radio and television networks, March 21, 1996 (FBIS-LAT-96-059).

36. Ibid.

37. See Nuccio, "Cuba: A U.S. Perspective."

38. Sorel, *Nacionalismo y revolución en Cuba*, 129–30.

39. "Alarcón discusses Helms-Burton."

40. Ibid.

41. "The Helms-Burton, Cubans, and Housing," *Prensa Latina*, April 3, 1997 (FBIS-LAT-97-093).

42. For one of the most complete legal and economic commentaries on this issue, see Robert Muse, "A Public International Law Critique."

43. Castañeda and Montalván, "Economic Factors," 239.

44. Consuegra-Barquín, "The Present Status Quo of Property Rights in Cuba," 206.

45. Domínguez, "U.S.-Cuban Relations," 58.

46. This expression is attributed to Wayne Smith; see Ken Silverstein, "The 1995 Lobbying of Shame," *Multinational Monitor* 17 (Jan.–Feb. 1996), 1–2.

47. This label is attributed to Gary Jarmin, chairman of the conservative U.S.-Cuba Foundation, who lobbied against H-B; see Robert Stone, "The High Cost of a Good Drink," *New Yorker*, Jan. 26, 1998, 7.

48. By Gary Jarmin, chairman of the U.S.-Cuba Foundation; see "Helms-Burton Would Benefit Castro, Rich Cuban Americans," *Miami Herald*, Oct. 9, 1995, 13A.

49. Based on information provided by Ignacio Sánchez, attorney for Bacardí and a director of CANF, during an interview on Jan. 14, 1999, granted through the good services of Jurge Rodríguez Márquez, a vice president of Bacardí.

50. Mimi Whitefield, "Stakes High in Cuba Claims Bill," *Miami Herald*, Oct. 2, 1995, 13B.

51. Samuel Gallo, *Bacardí, 1862–1962*; Nicolás Torres Hurtado and José Limia González, *Orígenes de la Compañía Ron Bacardí*; Alejandro Benes, "The Spirit of the Bat"; Bacardí, *Key Historical Facts*, pamphlet, n.d. For a complete history of the company, see Peter Foster, *Family Spirits, The Bacardi Saga: Rum, Riches, and Revolution.*

52. For background on this rum, see Félix López, "La 'catedral' del Havana Club," *Granma, Diario Digital*, May 28, 1999.

53. Testimony of Ignacio Sánchez for Bacardí-Martini before the House Judiciary Subcommittee on Courts and Intellectual Property, May 21, 1998.

54. Juan Tamayo, "Juez prohibe a Cuba vender marca de ron," *El Nuevo Herald*, Aug. 12, 1997.

55. Gail Appleson, "El fallo a favor de Bacardí puede provocar represalias," *El Nuevo Herald*, April 28, 1999, 10A; José de Córdoba, "Bacardí se anota una victoria por una marca clave," *World Street Journal / Cinco Días* (Madrid), April 19, 1999, 39; Juan Tamayo, "Fidel Threat: We'll Make Our Own Coke," *Miami Herald*, May 11, 1999, 1C; "Castro amenaza con producir una Coca-Cola cubana," *El Nuevo Herald*, May 11, 1999; "Cuba Loses Trademark Suit," *Miami Herald*, April 16, 1999, 12A.

56. For a sample of reactions in the Cuban press, see Félix López, "De cómo el ladrón fue declarado inocente"; "Apela Havana Club fallo de un tribunal de Nueva York"; and "A Bacardí le hace daño el Havana Club"; all are in *Granma International Digital*, May 25–31, 1999.

57. Nuccio, "Cuba: A U.S. Perspective," 29–30.

58. Ibid., 30.

59. Ariel Remos, "Suspende de nuevo Clinton el Título III," *Diario las Américas*, Jan. 16, 1999.

60. Morici, "The United States, World Trade, and the Helms-Burton Act," 87.

61. Statement by Senator Thomas Dodd, Feb. 28, 1996, press release.

62. Jimmy Carter, quoted by James Canute, "Carter Assails Helms-Burton," *Journal of Commerce*, Jan. 28, 1997.

63. "Helms-Burton Bill: A Sound Solution." *New York Law Journal* 215, no. 33 (Feb. 20, 1996): 81.

64. Amaya Ledesma, "Cuba: José Ignacio Rasco," *ABC*, July 23, 1996.

65. Smith, *Cuba after the Cold War, The Travel Ban to Cuba*, and *Our Cuba Diplomacy;* Center for International Policy, *Helms-Burton: A Loose Canon?*

66. Lisio, "Helms-Burton and the Point of Diminishing Returns," 691–93, 709–10.

67. LeoGrande, "Enemies Evermore," 211–21.

3. Lawyers Meet the Law

1. Noreen Marcus, "Attorneys Capitalize on Anti-Castro Law; Helms-Burton Sparks Suits," *Legal Times* 18, no. 47 (April 8, 1996): 2.

2. This study considers only the scholarly publications abstracted or indexed by two of the most used search indexes: Wilson's *Index to Legal Periodicals* and the *Legal Resources Index*. The only exceptions are unpublished papers made available to the author by legal practitioners.

3. Alberto Luzurraga, "Castro Must Open Regime before U.S. Opens to Cuba," *New York Law Journal* 215, no. 33 (Feb. 20, 1996): 81.

4. Susan Kohn Ross and John W. Shi, "Sovereignty Matters: The Expanded Embargo against Cuba," *Los Angeles Daily Journal* 109, no. 185 (Sept. 24, 1996): 7.

5. See, for example, Cecil Johnson, "Congress, Isn't This a Parody? Helms-Burton Law Takes Foolish Approach to International Trade," *Los Angeles Daily Journal* 109, no. 214 (Nov. 4, 1996): 6; "Law against Cuba Will Backfire," ibid. 105, no. 143 (July 23, 1992): 6; Evelyn F. Cohn and Alan D. Berlin, "European Community Reacts to Helms-Burton," *New York Law Journal* 218, no. 24 (Aug. 4, 1997): S2.

6. Solís, "The Long Arm of U.S. Law: The Helms-Burton Act," 740.

7. Gierbolini, "The Helms-Burton Act."

8. Meron and Vagts, "The Helms-Burton Act," 83–84.

9. Clagett, "A Reply to Professor Lowenfeld," 436, 437.

10. Muse, "Legal and Practical Implications of Title III," 5.

11. Lowenfeld, "The Cuban Liberty . . . Act," 425.

12. Ibid., 433.

13. Ibid., 423.

14. Altozano, "La Ley Helms-Burton y la protección de las inversiones españolas en Cuba," 12.

15. Muse, "Legal and Practical," 8.

16. Lowenfeld, "The Cuban Liberty . . . Act," 431.

17. Ibid., 429.

18. Álvarez-Mena and Crane, "From the Commerce Clause to Café Cubano," 13.

19. Clagett, "A Reply to Professor Lowenfeld," 137.

20. Clagett, "Title III of Helms-Burton," 439.

21. Betancourt, "Potential Impact of the Helms/Burton Act on Castro's Regime," 426.

22. Freer, "Helms-Burton Myths and Reality," 429.

23. Ibid., 430.

24. Ibid.

25. Ibid.

26. See Muse, "Legal and Practical," 11.

27. Ibid.

28. The expectations of Cuban-Americans were not overlooked in the legal commentaries and reporting. See, for example, Ann Davis, "Helms-Burton's First Test Comes Soon: Cuban-Americans Lining up to Sue Foreign Investors in Cuba under New Act," *National Law Journal* 18, no. 31 (April 1, 1996): A6.

29. Christopher Marquis, "Republicans Revise Bill," *Miami Herald,* Nov. 11, 1995, 16A.

30. John D. McKinnon, "Exiles Unlikely to Get Damages Any Time Soon," *Miami Herald,* March 6, 1996, 15A.

31. Estimate by Miami attorney María Elena Prío, quoted by Noreen Marcus, "Attorneys Capitalize," *Legal Times,* April 8, 1996.

32. Muse, "The Nationality of Claims Principle," 783.

33. Ibid., 797.

34. Ibid., 785.

35. Ibid., 783.

36. Jorg Paul Müller and Thomas Cottier, "Estoppel," 116.

37. Quoted by Muse, "The Nationality of Claims," 795.

38. Müller and Cottier, "Estoppel," 116.

39. International Court of Justice (ICJ) Reports (1962), 143–44, quoted by Müller and Cottier, 116.

40. Muse, "The Nationality of Claims," 795.

41. Ibid.

42. Ibid., 797.

43. Muse, "Legal and Practical Implications," 6.

44. Claim no. IT-10,252, ibid.

45. Muse, "The Nationality of Claims," 779.

46. Clagett, "Title III," 435.

47. See Quickendon, "Helms-Burton and Canadian-American Relations at the Crossroads," 749; Robert Kelso, "Espousal."

48. Álvarez-Mena and Crane, "From the Commerce Clause to Café Cubano," 14–15.

49. Ignacio Sánchez, testifying before the U.S. Senate, quoted by Muse, "The Nationality of Claims," 779.

50. Solís, "The Long Arm," 725.

51. See Álvarez-Mena and Crane, "From the Commerce Clause to Café Cubano," 18.

52. See Lowenfeld, "The Cuban Liberty," 433.

53. For a Chilean view on this issue, see Torres Macchiavello, "Antecedentes de la ley Helms-Burton," 54–66.

54. Solís, "The Long Arm," 711.

55. Lowenfeld, "The Cuban Liberty," 422.

56. Ibid., 433.

57. See Yoo, "Federal Courts as Weapons of Foreign Policy," 776.

58. Sumner, "Due Process and True Conflicts," 960–61.

59. Yoo, "Federal Courts as Weapons of Foreign Policy," 776.

60. Lowenfeld, "The Cuban Liberty," 428.

61. Solís, "The Long Arm," 724.

62. Álvarez-Mena and Crane, "From the Commerce Clause to Café Cubano," 16–18.

63. Among other papers, see ibid. and Clagett, "Title III."

64. Muse, "The Nationality of Claims," 779.

65. Solís, "The Long Arm," 740.

66. Lowenfeld, "The Cuban Liberty," 434.

67. Ibid., 426.

68. Ibid., 424.

69. Mallett, "The Application in the United Kingdom," 1.

70. Lucio, "The Cuban Liberty and Democratic Solidarity (LIBERTAD) Act," 342.

71. Altozano, "La Ley," 11.

72. Lowe, "U.S. Extraterritorial Jurisdiction," 385.

73. Lowenfeld, "The Cuban Liberty," 429.

74. Ibid., 434.

75. Lowe, "U.S. Extraterritorial Jurisdiction," 378.

76. Solís, ""The Long Arm," 723.

77. 168 US 250 (1897).

78. De Falco, "Comment," 126.

79. Altozano, "La Ley," 19.

80. 37 US 398 (1964).

81. Lowe, "U.S. Extraterritorial Jurisdiction," 428.

82. Long, "A Challenge," 496.

83. Solís, "The Long Arm," 722.

84. Álvarez-Mena and Crane, "From the Commerce Clause," 9.

85. See Clagett, "Title III."

86. Meron and Vagts, "The Helms-Burton Act," 84.

87. Altozano, "La Ley," 6.

88. Ibid., 7.

89. Lowenfeld, "The Cuban Liberty," 423.

90. Dattu and Boscariol, "GATT Article XXI."

91. Welke, "GATT and NAFTA," 378.

92. Kaye, "The Helms-Burton Act," 745.

93. Lowe, "U.S. Extraterritorial," 390.

94. Muse, "Legal and Practical," 11.

95. Ibid., 13.

96. Lowe, "U.S. Extraterritorial," 388.

97. Auge, "Title IV," 575.

98. Solís, "The Long Arm," 711.

99. Ibid., 741.

100. Ibid., 389.

101. Lowe, "U.S. Extraterritorial," 389.

102. Solís, "The Long Arm," 710.

103. Dodge, "The Helms-Burton Act," 726.

104. Quickendon, ""Helms-Burton and Canadian-American Relations," 766.

105. Ibid.

106. Welke, "GATT and NAFTA," 378.

107. Ibid., 1996.

108. Gierbolini, "The H-B Act," 321.

109. Muse, "The Nationality of Claims," 798.

110. Fairey, "The Helms-Burton Act," 1335.

111. Solís, "The Long Arm," 712.

112. Quickendon, "The Helms-Burton Act," 762–63.

113. Fairey, "The Helms-Burton Act," 1333.

114. Quickendon, "The Helms-Burton Act," 763.

115. Maria L. Pagan, "U.S. Legal Requirements Affecting Trade with Cuba," 317.

116. Fairey, "The Helms-Burton Act," 1334.

117. Solís, "The Long Arm," 739.

118. Ibid., 740.

119. Fairey, "The Helms-Burton Act," 1335.

120. Hans, "The United States' Economic Embargo of Cuba," 346.

121. De Falco, "Comment," 154.

122. Hans, "The United States' Economic Embargo of Cuba," 345.

123. Fidler, "Libertad v. Liberalism," 352–53.

124. Solís, "The Long Arm," 729.

125. Muse, "A Public International Law Critique," 267–68.

126. Ibid., 269.

4. The World Response

1. Kirk, "Descifrando la paradoja," 571.

2. Kirk and McKenna, *Canada-Cuba Relations,* 17.

3. Ibid., 176, 178.

4. Ibid., 178. For Canadian interests in the phone business in Cuba before the passing of Helms-Burton, see "Cuba," *Business Latin America,* Oct. 11, 1993.

5. Kirk and McKenna, *Canada-Cuba Relations,* 177.

6. Ibid.

7. Ibid., 179.

8. Ibid., 180.

9. "Computers for Cuba," *Maclean's,* June 3, 1996.

10. D'Arcy Jenish, "Staking a Claim: Canadians Prepare to Fight a U.S. Ban on Trade with Cuba," *Maclean's,* June 24, 1996, 30. For a selected review in U.S. sources, see Charles Lane, "Canada Sly: National Insecurity," *New Republic,* Aug. 5, 1996, 11.

11. John Kneale, "Tightening the U.S. Embargo," 1.

12. John DeMont, "A New 'Opening': Canada's Cuba Visit Annoys Washington," *Maclean's,* Feb. 3, 1997, 34; "Canada Fails to Confront Dictator," *New York Times,* Jan. 25, 1997.

13. "Confrontation over Cuba: Canada and Mexico Have Filed a Complaint under NAFTA," *Maclean's,* July 1, 1996, 32.

14. For a complete legal and political analysis of the Canadian-U.S. confrontation, see Quickendon, "Helms-Burton and Canadian-American Relations at the Crossroads."

15. "Barred at the Border?" *Maclean's,* June 10, 1996, 47.

16. "The Cuban Pajama Crisis," *Maclean's,* March 17, 1997, 33; Agence France Press (AFP), "Pijamas cubanos son eje de pesquisa canadiense," *El Nuevo Herald,* March 6, 1997.

17. Christopher Moore, "Writers of History: Helms-Burton Meet Godfrey-Milliken," *The Beaver*, Feb. 1, 1997, 52.

18. *60 Minutes*, Oct. 20, 1996.

19. "Pay Native Americans, Too," *Miami Herald*, March 12, 1997.

20. "U.S. Responds in Kind to Canadian Bill Mocking Helms-Burton," Agence France Press, Oct. 23, 1996. See complete context in Anthony Solís, "The Long Arm of U.S. Law," 722.

21. "Desde Washington: Estudio demuestra la falsedad de la legislación de parlamentario canadiense," *Diario las Américas*, March 9, 1997.

22. Carol Rosenberg, "Canada's Pro-Cuba Boycott: Is Florida Hurting?" *Miami Herald*, March 9, 1997.

23. "Canadian Anglicans Boycott U.S. Resorts," *Christian Century*, Jan. 15, 1997, 44.

24. Barbara Amiel, "Canada—The Guilt of Having Stolen Goods," *Maclean's*, April 14, 1997, 9; "Canada's Chastised: European Union Criticizes Canada for Breaching Informal Agreement to Challenge Helms-Burton Act," *Maclean's*, May 12, 1997.

25. Kim Campbell, "Helms-Burton: The Canadian View," 799.

26. Heather Scoffield, "Ottawa in No Rush to Back U.S.-E.U. Deal," *Globe and Mail* (Toronto), May 20, 1998, B5, as quoted and contextualized by Kirk et al., "Canada, Mexico, and Helms-Burton," 1.

27. Kirk et al., "Canada, Mexico and Helms-Burton."

28. John D. Harbron, "Will Canada's 'Snowbirds' Go to Florida, or Cuba?" *Miami Herald*, Jan. 2, 1999, 17A.

29. Geri Smith, "Salinas' Sweet Deal with Castro Is a Bitter Pill for the U.S.," *Business Week*, June 27, 1994, 47.

30. Mexican government press release, May 28, 1997.

31. Resolution of Congress, May 29, 1996. A communiqué of the foreign affairs secretary stated that the letter sent to Domos was an attempt to apply extraterritorial jurisdiction in Mexico. Mexican government press release, May 29, 1996.

32. Mexican government press release, June 17, 1996.

33. Ibid., Aug. 20, 1996.

34. See paper by Hernán de Jesús Ruiz Bravo and Manuel Morán Rufino, "La Ley Helms-Burton."

35. "Position Taken by Mexico on the Helms-Burton Law and the Question of Cuba," Mexican government press release, Aug. 28, 1996. Official text in English published in the *Hastings International and Comparative Law Review* 20, no. 4 (Spring 1997), 809–14. A meeting of Mexico's Secretary of State José Angel Gurría and U.S. envoy Stuart Eisenstat was held the same day.

36. Mexican government press release, Oct. 23, 1996.

37. *Mexico and Nafta Report* (London), July 18, 1996, 2.

38. Ibid.

39. Confirmation of facts provided by Oscar Elizundia, consul general of Mexico in Miami, through the good offices of Alberto Gaytán.

40. Andrés Oppenheimer, "Mexico Says NAFTA Visas Don't Cover Nude Dancers," *Miami Herald,* Dec. 18, 1997, 24A.

41. Organization of American States, Opinion of the Inter-American Juridical Committee following the mandate of the Resolution AG/DOC.337/96 of the General Assembly of the Organization of American States, titled "Freedom of Trade and Investment in the Hemisphere" (Aug. 23, 1996).

42. Roberto Robaina, interview with *Prensa Latina,* Aug. 26, 1996 (FBIS-LAT-96-167).

43. From combined news wires as reported during the first two weeks of June 1997.

44. "La ley Helms-Burton frena la integración," AFP, June 16, 1997.

45. Sistema Económico de América Latina (SELA), *Implicaciones jurídicas y económicas de la ley Helms-Burton.*

46. Rio Group, Final Declaration of the Summit, Sept. 6, 1996.

47. Berrios, "Why America Should Lift Its Cuban Embargo"; Berrios and Thomas, "Taking Orders from Little Havana."

48. AFP, Dec. 30, 1997.

49. For a sample of studies on the development of the ACS and the position of Cuba in the area, see Alzugaray, "Cuba y el Sistema Internacional en la década de 1990" and "La Asociación de Estados del Caribe (AEC) y la Unión Europea (UE)"; and Bryan and Bryan, *The New Face of Regionalism in the Caribbean.*

50. Erisman, "Cuba and the Caribbean Basin."

51. Christopher Marquis, "Correspondent's Letter: Son of Helms-Burton," *Miami Herald,* Aug. 28, 1997, 24A.

52. "Proposed Ros-Lehtinen Bill: A Helms-Burton for the Caribbean?" U.S. Information Agency, Aug. 28, 1997.

53. *Nation* (Barbados), Aug. 8, 1997.

54. *Sunday Herald* (Jamaica), Aug. 10, 1997.

55. *Nation,* Aug. 6, 1997.

56. Ibid., Aug. 18, 1997.

57. Ibid., Aug. 8, 1997.

58. *Granma,* Aug. 21, 1997.

59. Torres Macchiavello, quoting opinion by Carmen Luz Guarda, Chile's ambassador to the WTO, in "Antecedentes de la ley Helms-Burton," 64.

60. Ibid., 64, 66.

61. Ibid, 60.

62. Douglas Farah, "Cuba Slows Free-Trade Changes and Reemphasizes Marxist Ideology," *Washington Post,* April 29, 1996, A10.

63. Maurizio Giuliano, *El caso CEA;* "Cuba Attacks Reformists' 'Fifth Column'," *Miami Herald,* March 28, 1996, 12A; see also text of critical comments by Raúl Castro published in *Granma,* March 27, 1996.

64. Roberto Robaina's interview, *Prensa Latina,* March 19, 1996 (FBIS-LAT-96-055).

65. *Granma,* March 22, 1996.

66. *Granma,* March 23, 1996.

67. *New York Times,* May 2, 1996.

68. Communist Party of Cuba, "The Meaning of Helms-Burton."

69. "Minister Reacts to President Clinton's Announcement," *Prensa Latina,* July 16, 1998 (FBIS-LAT-96-138).

70. *Prensa Latina,* July 18, 1996 (FBIS-LAT-96-139).

71. "ANPP to Begin Discussion of Antidote Bill," Tele Rebelde, Dec. 23, 1996 (FBIS-LAT-96-249); "Parliament Approves Bill," Cubavisión, Dec. 25, 1996 (FBIS-LAT-96-249).

72. For an exhaustive study of the treatment of the embargo at the UN General Assembly, see Porostky, "Economic Coercion and the General Assembly."

73. For a detailed commentary, see Viñas, "La Unión Europea y Cuba."

74. "A Lonely Stand against Castro," *U.S. News and World Report,* Nov. 25, 1996.

75. "Robaina Addresses U.N. General Assembly," Havana Radio, Oct. 1, 1996 (FBIS-LAT-192).

76. "Intervención de Carlos Lage," *Granma,* Nov. 14, 1996.

77. Ricardo Alarcón, "Necessity of Ending the Economic, Commercial, and Financial Embargo," Nov. 5, 1997.

78. News wires, Nov. 5, 1997. Naturally, the official Cuban publications reflected this voting pattern. See, for example, "Cuba Is Not and Never Will Be a Colonial Possession of the United States," *Granma International,* Nov. 2, 1997. Fernando Remírez de Estenoz, chief of the Cuban Interest Section in Washington, D.C., issued a letter, dated Nov. 12, 1997, stressing the same facts and noting that Japan for the first time voted for the resolution.

5. The Washington-Havana Feud as Seen from Brussels

1. Scherle R. Schwenninger, "The Rift over Rogues," *The Nation,* Oct. 7, 1996, 21–23.

2. Granell, "Conflicto y cooperación."

3. *European Union News* (Washington, D.C.), Dec. 17, 1998.

4. "Slippery Business," *Miami Herald,* Dec. 26, 1998; Don Bohning, "Banana Wars Snag Caribbean Island Nations," *Miami Herald,* Dec. 23, 1998; Robert Batterson, "Banana Battle," *Miami Herald,* Jan. 20, 1999.

5. Hennessy and Lambie, *The Fractured Blockade,* iii.

6. United Kingdom, Order no. 2449, Oct. 1992.

7. *The Economist* (editorial), Sept. 3, 1994, 19.

8. Ibid., March 2, 1996, 20.

9. Ibid., June 3, 1996.

10. Ibid., July 20, 1996, 16.

11. Ibid., Aug. 10, 1996, 37–38.

12. For a comprehensive treatment of this relationship, see Lambie, "Anglo-Cuban Commercial Relations in the 1960s: A Case Study of the Leyland Motor Company Contracts with Cuba," in Hennessy and Lambie, *The Fractured Blockade,* 163–97.

For a shorter review of the same topic, see Jenkins, "Trade Relations between Britain and Cuba." For a more recent review, see Grabendorff, "The Relationship between the European Union and Cuba."

13. "La ley Helms-Burton sólo logrará que Castro se sienta como fortaleza aparte," *El Universal* (Caracas), June 1, 1996.

14. See Grabendorff, "The Relationship between the European Union and Cuba." For a standard view of Cuba in academic and general books, see Jean Lamore, *Cuba.*

15. AFP and other news agencies, April 25; Octavi Martí, "Francia reta a EE.UU.," *El País* (Madrid), April 26, 1997.

16. Associated Press, April 4, 1997.

17. AFP, Nov. 17, 1997. Following in the steps of different French publications led by *Le Monde,* the weekly *L'Express* dedicated a special issue to Cuba with a full disclosure of the numerous links between France and Cuba (Dec. 5, 1997).

18. "France Threatens to Veto Free-Trade Pact," *Washington Post,* March 13, 1998.

19. Comments made by French Embassy sources during interviews on March 13, 1998.

20. For a commentary on this relationship, see the section on Germany in Grabendorff, "The Relationship between the European Community and Cuba."

21. See Florentino Graupera, "Cuba and Germany in the 1990s: Towards a New Opening?" and Grabendorff, "Germany and Latin America."

22. For a complete review from a Cuban perspective, see Roque Valdés, "Italian-Cuban Relations in the 1990s."

23. Incidentally, since the Costa Cruise Line was bought by the U.S. company Carnival, Costa ships no longer visit Cuban ports.

24. Juan Tamayo, "Talks to Deter Cuba Investment Falter," *Miami Herald,* Aug. 17, 1997; AFP, "EU y Europa en nueva ronda sobre ley Helms," *El Nuevo Herald,* Oct. 15, 1997.

25. Juan Tamayo, "Firma italiana se burla de ley Helms," *El Nuevo Herald,* March 6, 1997; Christopher Marquis, "New Test Looms in Wrangle over Property Cuba Seized," *Miami Herald,* April 26, 1997; "Empresa podría evitar efecto de ley Helms," *El Nuevo Herald,* April 26, 1997.

26. *New York Times,* "ITT in Deal for Property Cuba Seized in '61," July 24, 1997.

27. AP, April 28, 1997.

28. "CANF Statement on STET-ITT Settlement Announcement," press release, July 23, 1997.

29. EFE, "Comisión Europea no actuará contra STET por compensación a ITT," July 25, 1997.

30. As an example of the justifications endorsed by the main advocates of the law, see Bill McCollum, chairman of the Judicial Subcommittee of the House, "El cumplimiento de la ley Helms-Burton," *El Nuevo Herald,* Oct. 13, 1997.

31. Granell, "Conflicto y cooperación," 49.

32. Floyd Norris, "What ITT and Castro Have in Common," *New York Times,* Dec. 7, 1997, B1.

33. This may seem to contradict Cuban-American sources that claim that the whole Cuban-American system was owned by U.S. interests. The reality is that the predominantly U.S. ownership was backed with private Cuban capital.

34. For a complete review of this logic, see Susan Long, "A Challenge to the Legality of Title III of LIBERTAD and an International Response."

35. *El País,* Oct. 19, 1996.

36. AFP, Sept. 20, 1997; Richard W. Stevenson, "Israelis Penalized for Dealing with Cuba," *New York Times,* Nov 18, 1997, A9.

37. Interview with Dore Gold, Israel's ambassador to the UN, by Roberto Fabricio, *El Nuevo Herald,* Jan. 24, 1999, 22A.

38. The European Union declarations have generally referred to the U.S. measures against Cuba as an *embargo*. On at least one occasion the term *blockade* has been used by the European Parliament. See, as an example, the resolution of Sept. 29, 1994.

39. See resolutions of the European Parliament for 1987, 1988, 1990, 1992, 1993 and 1996, listed in the bibliography. For a complete, chronological review see the compilation published by the Instituto de Relaciones Europea-Latinoamericanas (IRELA) (*Veinte años,* 1996, 769–803) regarding documents generated in the last twenty years of European Union–Latin American relations.

40. Agenda Item 24, "Necessity of Ending the Economic, Commercial and Financial Embargo Imposed by the United States of America against Cuba," "Explanation of Vote" (New York, Oct. 26, 1994).

41. See Ángel Viñas, "La Unión Europea y Cuba."

42. Richard Nuccio, then White House special adviser for Cuba, put the blame exclusively on Castro in an article distributed by a *Los Angeles Times* service. See, for example, "Es Castro quien aisla al país," *El Nuevo Herald,* Jan. 22, 1998.

43. The Spanish expression to illustrate this would be, "Si no quieres caldo, toma dos tazas." Roughly translated into English it would be "the less you want to accept, the more we are going to demand." (Interpretation from anonymous sources of the E.U. Commission and Parliament.)

44. See Nuccio, "Cuba: A U.S. Perspective."

45. Perera Gómez, "Cuba and the European Union."

46. For a detailed review of these events, see IRELA, *Cuba y la Unión Europea.*

47. EFE and other news wires, "Firme la UE frente a Cuba," reprinted in *Diario las Américas,* Dec. 9, 1997.

48. "Estados Unidos pide un gesto," *ABC* (Madrid), March 9, 1996.

49. "La organización se limita a pedir," *Expansión* (Madrid), May 23, 1996; "Matutes critica la actitud de Washington sobre Cuba," *Gaceta de los Negocios* (Madrid), May 23, 1996.

50. See documents detailed in the bibliography, especially the resolutions of the European Parliament of 1992, 1993, and 1996, and the declarations of the council and the presidency of the European Union of 1995. Complete texts are available in the compilation by IRELA, *Europa–América Latina: Veinte años de documentos oficiales.*

51. Council Regulation (EC) No. 2271/96. Earlier in the process, the Canadian and

British press were following the preparations. See, for example, "Europe's Cuba Law," *Maclean's,* Nov. 11, 1996, 36; "A Façade of Unity: Europe's Foreign Policy," *The Economist,* Nov. 2, 1996, 49.

52. An appendix specifically listed all U.S. legal measures that the European Union considered unacceptable, including the Iran-Libya Sanctions Act of 1996. See Hebert, "Unilateralism as Defense Mechanism."

53. Huber, "The Blocking Statute of the European Union," 705, 707.

54. Ibid., 710.

55. Ibid., 716.

56. "EU to Move Helms-Burton to WTO Dispute Settlement Panel," *European Union News,* Oct. 1, 1996.

57. See "Desde Washington: La irritación europea con la ley Helms-Burton," *Diario las Américas,* March 2, 1997.

58. For a detailed analysis of the evolution of this U.S. measure, see IRELA, *La posición común.*

59. Juan Tamayo, "Europeans Get Tough in Policy on Cuba," *Miami Herald,* Dec. 3, 1996.

60. Perera Gómez, "Cuba and the European Union," 113.

61. State Department communiqué, Dec. 3, 1996.

62. EFE, "Banco de Cuba, con grandes expectativas ante el euro," *El Nuevo Herald,* Jan. 1, 1999.

63. President Clinton's statement on the Helms-Burton waiver, Jan. 3, 1997.

64. *Washington Post,* Jan. 5, 1997.

65. Ibid., April 12, 1997; Christopher Marquis, "Europe, U.S. Make Cuba Deal," *Miami Herald,* April 12, 1997; Cynthia Corzo, "EU y Europa pactan sobre Ley Helms," *El Nuevo Herald,* April 12, 1997.

66. News agencies (among them AFP) leaked the agreement on March 25, 1997.

67. News wires of AP, EFE, and other news agencies, April 11, 1997. On April 18, the Committee of Permanent Representatives (COREPER) confirmed the agreement.

68. "Empresario español se declara inocente," EFE, April 11, 1997.

69. AFP, April 3, 1997. The resolution was passed with 37 votes in favor and 8 against.

70. Robert Evans, Reuters, April 17, 1997.

71. Xavier Vidal-Folch, "Los negociadores de EE.UU. y la UE alcanzan un pacto para desactivar su litigio sobre Cuba," *El País,* April 12, 1997.

72. Understanding, April 11, 1997, press release of the European Commission.

73. Xavier Vidal-Folch, "La UE no ha perdido nada," *El País,* April 27, 1997.

74. Statement released by the State Department on "Multilateral Agreement on Property Rights," transcribed under the title of "Enfoque multilateral a los derechos de propiedad," in *Diario las Américas,* April 27, 1997.

75. David Marens, *New York Times* service, April 12, 1997, as transcribed in a report titled "Suavizan diferendo en ley Helms-Burton," *Diario las Américas,* April 13, 1997.

76. Ileana Ros-Lehtinen, "La administración Clinton se rinde ante las demandas europeas," *Diario las Américas,* April 20, 1997.

77. "Eurodiputados prevén el Congreso se niegue a suavizar Helms-Burton," EFE, April 18, 1997.

78. Associated Press, April 18, 1997.

6. The Ever Faithful Island

1. This information is based on anonymous sources.

2. Lambie, "Franco's Spain and the Cuban Revolution," in Hennessy and Lambie, eds., *The Fractured Blockade,* 253.

3. "Declaraciones a *El País* de Fidel Castro," *El País,* Jan. 20, 1985, 4.

4. Paraphrasing of Castro's words offered by White in a letter to this author dated Nov. 25, 1997.

5. From confidential first-hand diplomatic sources.

6. See the contrasting views of Izquierda Unida's Diego López Garrido, "Sobre Cuba y la UE," *El País,* Jan. 3, 1996, and Cuban exile Carlos Alberto Montaner, "Aznar, la ley Helms-Burton y los cubanos," *El País,* June 5, 1996. For a more detailed analysis, see the following articles: Inocencio Arias (defending the Spanish government's position), "La bula progresina"; Antonio Remiro Brotons (criticizing it), "Cuba, las amistades peligrosas"; and Felipe Sahagún, "Cuba: Un asunto interno español," presenting a balanced approach.

7. A classic example was the article written by former minister of culture Jordi Solé-Tura, in *El País,* titled "Cuba y nosotros," Aug. 11, 1994. For a complete discussion, see Roy and Galinsoga *The Ibero-American Space,* 240.

8. Read Sahagún's article, "Cuba: Un asunto interno español," in this context.

9. See, for example, the statements by Alex Penelas, mayor of Dade County, to Paloma Galán, "Nos sentimos muy agradecidos por la posición de Aznar hacia Cuba," *ABC,* July 28, 1997; and quotes of Secretary of State Madeleine Albright in Alberto Míguez, "Agradece a España su ayuda en la política hacia Cuba," *Diario las Américas,* July 8, 1997.

10. For a critical view, see column "Cuba ausente," by Antonio Elorza, *El País,* Dec. 26, 1998.

11. See, for example: "Ardanza, tras visitar a Castro, dice que pronto se podrán normalizar las relaciones con Cuba," *ABC,* June 24, 1997; "Se reúnen Castro y Ardanza," *El Nuevo Herald,* June 23, 1997; "Ardanza estrecha lazos con Cuba," *Diario16,* June 23, 1997; Mauricio Vicent, "Ardanza lima asperezas en Cuba entre Castro y el gobierno de Aznar," *El País,* June 24, 1997; "Líder vasco optimista sobre nexo Cuba-España," *El Nuevo Herald,* June 24, 1997.

12. Alberto Pérez Giménez, "El Gobierno prepara medidas con la Ley de EE.UU.," *ABC,* May 23, 1996.

13. "Sancionará España a quien cumpla la Helms-Burton," *Diario las Américas,* Feb. 14, 1998, 1A. For the complete text of the bill, see Congreso de los Diputados, Proyecto de Ley, *Boletín Oficial de las Cortes Generales,* March 3, 1998, 1–3.

14. Jesús García Becerril, "Cumbre confirma Cuba diferencia acción exterior," EFE, Nov. 10, 1996.

15. EFE, "Cumbre Iberoamericana: España se une a petición general para que la democracia alcance a toda América," Nov. 10, 1996.

16. EFE, "Cumbre Iberoamericana: Aznar y Menem coinciden en petición de elecciones en Cuba," Nov. 11, 1996.

17. EFE, "Aznar: Castro quiere seguir siendo dictador," Nov. 25, 1996.

18. Mauricio Vicent, "Castro: 'La mafia de Miami ayudó con dinero al "caballerito" Aznar,'" *El País,* Nov. 25, 1996. The expression is open to interpretation. Sometimes translated as "little man," in this case it conveyed a sort of class distinction and disdain. It usually means that someone is not likely to be worthy of becoming a *caballero.*

19. Mauricio Vicent, *El País,* Nov. 20, 1996.

20. *Cinco Días,* Aug. 22, 1997.

21. José Antonio Sorzano, "Asuntos Exteriores, la casa de los líos," *El Siglo,* June 8, 1998.

22. From sources in the PSOE, Spanish Ministry of Foreign Affairs, and the European Parliament (July 1998). For the perspective of someone who was then Aznar's potential contender in the next elections, see Josep Borrell, "Entre la Habana y Jerusalén," *El País,* July 24, 1998.

23. For the evolution of the E.U. policy toward Cuba, see Ángel Viñas, "La Unión Europea y Cuba."

24. Alberto Míguez, "Mas Canosa y Montaner dimiten en la Fundación Hispano-Cubana," *Diario las Américas,* June 20, 1997.

25. See my commentaries "Tensión lingüística entre Madrid y La Habana," *Diario las Américas,* March 28, 1997, and *La Opinión* (Los Angeles), March 26, 1997.

26. For a complete review of this incident, see Manuel de Paz-Sánchez, *Zona rebelde.*

27. AFP, June 11, 1997.

28. AFP, June 3, 1996.

29. *Diario las Américas,* June 13, 1996.

30. For example, Gencor (South Africa), Heenan Blakey and York Medical (Canada), Vitro (Mexico), and Wiltel (United States), among others. See Pablo Alfonso, "Rechazo europeo oscurece el horizonte económico," *El Nuevo Herald,* May 18, 1996.

31. José María Triper, "El capital español apuesta por Cuba," *Cinco Días,* Feb. 11, 1997.

32. Ministry of Economy, "Crece la inversión española," *Expansión,* April 15, 1997.

33. Pablo Pardo, "Pese a Helms y a Burton, España exporta más a Cuba," *Expansión,* Aug. 3, 1996.

34. Mauricio Vicent, "Cuba sí, a pesar de la cuarentena política," *El País,* Aug. 10, 1997.

35. See Armando Correa, "Fase difícil entre España y Cuba no afecta inversiones," *El Nuevo Herald*, Aug. 12, 1997.

36. However, in comparative terms, this figure represents only 12 percent of the total Spanish investment in the world.

37. Mauricio Vicent, "El gobierno de Aznar cancela un crédito," *El País*, Feb. 2, 1997.

38. *El País*, Jan. 8, 1997.

39. AFP, EFE, Feb. 28, 1997.

40. Alberto Míguez, "Cuba es el país con más impagos a España," *Diario las Américas*, Sept. 18, 1997.

41. Enrique G. Acevedo, "Lage busca más inversiones en Madrid," *El Nuevo Herald*, Feb. 2, 1999, 7A.

42. For a more detailed analysis, see my chapter in Roy and Galinsoga, *The Ibero-American Space*, on the nature of Spain's relations with Latin America.

43. This story was related by anonymous sources from the Ministry of Foreign Affairs.

44. "Entre la Habana y Jerusalén," *El País*, July 24, 1998.

45. "Razón de gobierno," *El País*, Feb. 5, 1999.

46. Juan Tamayo, "Castro Condemns US," *Miami Herald*, Jan. 30, 1997, 21A; "Castro dice que Clinton quiere comprar Cuba," *El Mundo*, Jan. 30. 1997; "Veneno cubano para el 'Tío Sam'," *Diario16*, Jan. 30, 1997.

47. "A Promise of Help," editorial, *Miami Herald*, Jan 29, 1997, 14A; Ariel Hidalgo, "El Plan de Clinton de Apoyo para Cuba: Nuestra soberanía no está en venta," *El Nuevo Herald*, Feb. 17, 1997, 11A; Jorge Sanguinetti, "¿Cómo ayudará EU a Cuba?" *El Nuevo Herald*, Feb. 17, 1997, 11A; José Ignacio Rasco, "¿Quién le pone el cascabel al gato?" *Diario las Américas*, Feb. 7, 1997, 5A; Carlos Alberto Montaner, "Cuba: el documento de la esperanza," *El Nuevo Herald*, Feb. 2, 1997, 18A.

48. Alejandro Armengol, "Cuba en venta," *El Nuevo Herald*, Feb. 5, 1997, 12A.

49. "Déjà vu: Rebuilding Cuba," *Miami Herald*, Jan. 29, 1997, 15A.

50. Christopher Marquis, "Plan para Cuba sin Castro," *El Nuevo Herald*, Jan. 28, 1997, 1A.

51. Pablo Alfonso, "Economía va en picado," *El Nuevo Herald*, Oct. 10, 1997.

52. For an assessment of the impact of the Helms-Burton Law, see: "Balance provisional de la ley Helms-Burton," *Diario las Américas*, Aug. 22, 1997; "Balanç provisional de la llei Helms-Burton," *Avui* (Barcelona), Aug. 18, 1997; "La ley Helms-Burton, dos años después," *Diario las Américas*, March 11, 1998; "Cuatro décadas de la Revolución Cubana: Claves y predicciones," *Diario las Américas*, Dec. 29, 1998.

53. Alberto Míguez, "España no protestará," *Diario las Américas*, April 8, 1997.

54. "Ahora Felipe González acusa a EE.UU. de violar los derechos humanos," AFP, April 9, 1997; Alberto Míguez, "Ataca la izquierda a Aznar," *Diario Las Américas*, April 9, 1997.

55. EFE, "Albright acoge caso de español preso en Miami," *El Nuevo Herald*, May 1, 1997, 6A.

56. EFE, "Empresario es inocente de violar embargo a Cuba," *El Nuevo Herald,* Oct. 15, 1997.

57. Pedro Rodríguez, "EE.UU. excarcelará a un español condenado por 'traficar' con Cuba," *ABC,* June 12, 1998.

58. "Reconocen impacto de las explosiones en el turismo," *El Nuevo Herald,* Sept. 24, 1997.

59. The topic frequently dominated the press pages dedicated to Spanish-Cuban relations. For a sample, see Alberto Míguez, "España nombrará embajador en Cuba próximamente," *Diario las Américas,* June 26, 1997; Alberto Míguez, "Presionan a España para que nombre embajador en La Habana," *Diario las Américas,* June 14, 1997; AFP, "Próximo nombramiento del embajador español en Cuba," Aug. 28, 1997; Alberto Míguez, "España presentará a Cuba próximamente el nombre de su embajador en La Habana," *Diario las Américas,* Sept. 19, 1997; "Es prematuro hablar de embajador," *El Nuevo Herald,* Sept. 22, 1997. Rumors abounded that Cristina Barrios, chief of protocol for Abel Matutes, was going to be named ambassador ("La jefa de protocolo de Matutes se perfila como embajadora," *La Vanguardia,* Dec. 14, 1997).

60. This request was made explicitly by Foreign Minister Abel Matutes on the noted TVE program "Los desayunos de Radio 1." He was a guest on Oct. 22, 1997, part of a series of media appearances leading to the November Ibero-American summit in Venezuela.

61. Luis Ayllón, "El gobierno designa a Cuba, Colombia y Guatemala como prioritarias para la cooperación española durante 1998," *ABC,* Dec. 31, 1997.

62. Mauricio Vicent, "Tras complejas negociaciones, echa a andar en La Habana el Centro Cultural de España," *El País,* Dec. 22, 1997.

63. Trinidad de León-Sotelo, "El Cervantes premia a Cabrera Infante," *ABC,* Dec. 10, 1997.

64. "Cuba autoriza una delegación permanente de TVE en la isla," *El País,* Dec. 6, 1997. The office was officially opened just before Pope John Paul's visit.

65. José Miguel Arraya, "Cuba concede el plácet a un agregado militar español en La Habana," *El País,* Nov. 5, 1997.

66. Martin Arostegui, "Cuba Aided Rebels, Seized Files Reveal," *Miami Herald,* Dec. 27, 1997; "Exteriores no confirma que Otegui esté en Cuba," *Diario16,* Dec. 22, 1997; I. Cembrero, "Dos etarras que estaban deportados desde 1985 en Cabo Verde se han ido a Cuba," *El País,* Dec. 15, 1997.

67. José Borrell, "Entre la Habana y Jerusalén," *El País,* July 24, 1998.

68. Alberto Míguez, "Reyes de España visitarán si Castro hace algunas concesiones," *Diario las Américas,* June 28, 1997; "Estados Unidos no plantea ninguna objeción al viaje del Rey a Cuba," *El País,* June 17, 1997.

69. Mauricio Vicent, "Castro asegura que no quiso herir a España al criticar la colonización," *El País,* Feb. 4, 1998.

70. Declaration made to TVE on Feb. 6, 1998; EFE, "Matutes confirmó la posibilidad de viaje del Rey Juan Carlos a Cuba," Feb. 7, 1998.

71. Alberto Míguez, "Partido de Aznar quiere reconciliarse con el castrismo," *Diario las Américas,* Feb. 22, 1998, 1A.

72. "Sancionará España a quien cumpla la Helms-Burton," EFE, *Diario las Américas,* Feb. 14, 1998, 1A.

73. Ignacio Rupérez, "España y Cuba," *El País,* Aug. 22, 1994.

7. Disproportionate Influence Still Creates Outsized Problems

1. European Union Commission, "Understanding with Respect to Disciplines for the Strengthening of Investment Protection." For a detailed analysis of the evolution of the content and language of the agreement, see *Inside U.S. Trade* (May 1, 15, 1998) and *Americas Trade* (May 15, 1998).

2. Press release, Stuart Eisenstat, Washington, Feb. 1, 1998.

3. Interviews held in Brussels, July 5–9, 1998.

4. AFP, "Francia y España obstacularizaron trato," *El Nuevo Herald,* May 18, 1998; "Member States Poised in Fight to Accept U.S.-EU Agreement on Helms-Burton," *Inside U.S. Trade,* May 22, 1998; José Miguel Larraya, "Duro ataque de los socios del gobierno al acuerdo UE-EE.UU. sobre Cuba," *El País,* June 4, 1998.

5. Hermenegildo Altozano, "España, la ley Helms-Burton y el Acuerdo Multilateral de Inversiones," *Expansión,* May 14, 1998.

6. Thomas W. Lippman, "Politicians at Odds on Sanctions as Policy," *Washington Post,* May 19, 1998; Jonathan Miller, "How Europe Forced Cuba Deal," *Miami Herald,* May 24, 1998.

7. "Castro insta a la UE a rechazar el acuerdo sobre la ley Helms-Burton," *Expansión,* May 20, 1998; AP, "Castro Condemns Agreement," *Miami Herald,* May 20, 1998; AFP, "Castro califica el acuerdo entre EE.UU. y la UE de 'amenazante y no ético'," May 20, 1998; Mauricio Vicent, "Castro advierte que ningún entendimiento entre la UE y EE.UU. puede realizarse a costa de Cuba," *El País,* May 25, 1998.

8. "Helms Tells European Union: 'No Deal'," *United States Senate,* Committee on Foreign Relations, May 18, 1998; "Helms Aide Tells EU to 'Drop Dead' on Request for Helms-Burton Fix," *Inside U.S. Trade,* May 29, 1998; "Congress Strongly Criticizes U.S.-EU Agreement on Helms-Burton Law," *Inside U.S. Trade,* May 22, 1998; "Gingrich critica acuerdo de Clinton con Europa," *El Nuevo Herald,* May 23, 1998.

9. "Senators Urge Albright Not to Grant ILSA Waivers for Libya Projects," *Inside U.S. Trade,* May 29, 1998. For a comparative review of the Helms-Burton and ILSA controversies regarding "problem" countries, see Haass, ed., *Transatlantic Tensions.*

10. Krenzler and Wiegand, "EU-U.S. Relations: More Than Trade Disputes?"

11. European Commission sources and notes taken during personal interviews, June, July 1996.

12. Confidential notes of COREPER meeting, Brussels, June 23, 1998.

13. See Altozano, "Consideraciones sobre el entendimiento UE-EE.UU."

14. This view is shared by numerous sources in the Permanent Representations of the member states in Brussels. Interviews, July 5–9, 1998.

15. Subsequent drafts of the "side letter" signed by Brittan show that a statement

declaring that the commission was representing the European Union was finally deleted.

16. See complete texts of the debates: Congreso de los Diputados, *Boletín oficial de las Cortes Generales,* Acuerdo entre los Estados Unidos y la UE; Efectos del Acuerdo entre la UE y los Estados Unidos (Madrid: BOE).

17. Jenkins, "The Effects of Extraterritorial Laws."

18. As an illustration of the resistance to change expressed by the backers of the Helms-Burton Law on its second anniversary, see the report of the staff of the Senate Committee on Foreign Relations and the House Committee on International Relations, titled *Cuba at the Crossroads: The Visit of Pope John Paul II and Opportunities for U.S. Policy* (March 1998). In the same line, see the content of the hearing held by the Subcommittee on International Policy and Trade, conducted by Congresswoman Ileana Ros-Lehtinen, especially statements by Claudio Benedí of the Junta Patriótica Cubana, Francisco Hernández of the Cuban-American National Foundation, and Ralph Galliano, editor of the *U.S.-Cuba Policy Report.* In contrast, see the moderate declaration by State Department representative Michael E. Ranneberger and the explicit opposition to the U.S. embargo by Jorge Hernández of the U.S. Chamber of Commerce.

19. Domínguez, "U.S.-Cuban Relations," 65.

20. Letter of June 17, 1998.

21. Speech delivered at the WTO, Geneva, May 19, 1998.

22. Mauricio Vicent, "Castro advierte."

23. Press release, "Intervención en la sesión de la Delegación del Parlamento Europeo para las relaciones con América Central y México," July 2, 1998.

24. Horacio Ruiz Pavón, "Agridulce aniversario de la ley Helms-Burton," *Diario las Américas,* March 13, 1998.

25. Rafael Cañas, "Ley Helms cumple años," *El Nuevo Herald,* March 12, 1998.

26. Christopher Marquis, "Pope's Steps Producing D.C. Echoes," *Miami Herald,* March 12, 1998.

27. Pablo Alfonso, "Vaticano insiste en mediación Cuba-EU," *El Nuevo Herald,* March 30, 1998.

28. Olance Nogueras, "Sugieren ayudar a cubanos y mantener embargo," *El Nuevo Herald,* March 10, 1998. For a detailed critique of the human rights situation in Cuba and the argument for maintaining the embargo, see U.S. Senate Committee on Foreign Relations and House Committee on International Relations, *Cuba at the Crossroads.*

29. Olance Nogueras, "Congreso debate mañana más sanciones," *El Nuevo Herald,* March 17, 1998.

30. Olance Nogueras, "Cámara aprieta tuercas a Cuba," *El Nuevo Herald,* March 27, 1998; "Congresista Ros-Lehtinen busca que Rusia no colabore," *Diario las Américas,* March 11, 1998.

31. Ileana Ros-Lehtinen, "Grupos izquierdistas viajan a Washington," *Diario las Américas,* March 29, 1998.

32. Ros Lehtinen, "Mi testimonio ante la Comisión Interamericana de Derechos Humanos," *Diario las Américas,* March 15, 1998.

33. The flights resumed in mid-July of 1998, with considerable positive response from the Cuban exile community; see Pascal Fletcher, *El Nuevo Herald,* July 16, 1998; Mauricio Vicent, "La Habana, ida y vuelta," *El País,* July 26, 1998.

34. Christopher Marquis, "U.S. to Ease Cuba Restrictions," *Miami Herald,* March 20, 1998; Horacio Ruiz Pavón, "Anunciará Estados Unidos," *Diario las Américas,* March 20, 1998.

35. Christopher Marquis, "Albright Proposes New View," *Miami Herald,* March 21, 1998.

36. "Embargo on Cuba No Longer Needed," *Miami Herald,* March 25, 1998; "Adjustment in Cuba Policy Will Ease Tension, Help Island's Poor," *Sun-Sentinel* (Fort Lauderdale), March 22, 1998.

37. Larry Birns, director of the Council of Hemispheric Affairs, letter to the editor, *Miami Herald,* March 22, 1998, 2L.

38. Christopher Marquis, *Miami Herald,* March 29, 1998. General John Sheehan, former NATO commander, was in Cuba for a visit endorsing a normalization of relations; "Está en Cuba ex-jefe de la OTAN," *Diario las Américas,* March 14, 1998.

39. "Duda Hamilton que Cuba salga de la lista," *Diario las Américas,* March 25, 1998.

40. EFE, "Cuba constituye una amenaza," *El Nuevo Herald,* March 24, 1998.

41. Various news wires covered the story. See especially EFE, "Pentágono pospone el informe," April 1, 1998.

42. News wires, April 1, 1998; Ariel Remos, "Es altamente peligrosa la politización del Pentágono," *Diario las Américas,* April 1, 1998.

43. Tom Fiedler, "A Tale of Two Exile Leaders," *Miami Herald,* March 29, 1998.

44. See especially an unusually blunt commentary by Christian Democratic leader José Ignacio Rasco, "¡Eppur si muove!" *Diario las Américas,* March 31, 1998.

45. Ariel Remos, "Castro pretende un subsidio occidental," *Diario las Américas,* March 29, 1998.

46. Jaime Suchlicki, "The U.S. Embargo of Cuba." See condensed version in Spanish, *Diario las Américas,* March 29, 1998, and interview in edition of March 27, 1998.

47. AFP, "No a la ayuda de EU," *El Nuevo Herald,* March 28, 1998.

48. EFE, March 25, 1998.

49. "Cuba: U.S. Intruding in Havana-Vatican Ties," Reuters, March 28, 1998.

50. EFE, March 25, 1998.

51. "Castro comunica a Almunia su deseo de que los Reyes visiten Cuba," *El Mundo,* March 2, 1998; Mauricio Vicent, "Almunia insta al gobierno," *El País,* Feb. 28, 1998; Anabel Díaz and Mauricio Vicent, "El gobierno cubano desea que el rey visite la isla este año," *El País,* March 1, 1998.

52. José Miguel Larraya, "Aznar cree que en Cuba no se dan las condiciones para nombrar embajador," *El País,* March 3, 1998.

53. Mauricio Vicent, "Eurodiputados defienden normalizar relaciones con Cuba," *El País,* Feb. 24, 1998.

54. Alberto Míguez, "España exige libertad de acción para su futuro embajador," *Diario las Américas,* March 5, 1998.

55. Alberto Míguez, "Cuba desvincula el tema del nuevo embajador," *Diario las Américas,* March 26, 1998.

56. News wires, EFE, April 1, 1998.

57. Alberto Míguez, "España y Cuba: Deshielo," *Diario las Américas,* April 3, 1998.

58. José Miguel Larraya, "Aznar desbloquea por sorpresa," *El País,* April 2, 1998.

59. "A Cuba," *El País* (editorial), April 2, 1998.

60. Impressions gathered in various segments of the Spanish political spectrum and in the institutions of the European Union during the summer of 1998.

61. Henry Raymont, "Canciller canadiense insiste en reincorporar a Cuba a la OEA," *Diario las Américas,* March 10, 1998.

62. "Canada's Cuban Confusion," *Globe and Mail* (Toronto), March 11, 1998.

63. News wires, March 31, 1998; Pablo Alfonso, "Canadá niega asilo," *El Nuevo Herald,* March 31, 1998.

64. Guido di Tella, "La isla de la fantasía," *El Nuevo Herald,* March 28, 1998.

65. Pablo Alfonso, "Cuba de nuevo es tema de cita anual de la ONU," *El Nuevo Herald,* March 15, 1998.

66. Juan Tamayo, "U.S. Loses U.N. Vote," *Miami Herald,* April 22, 1998, 1A.

67. Ariel Remos, "Condena a Cuba," *Diario las Américas,* April 24, 1999, 1A.

68. Expression used by Caleb McCarry, staff member of the House International Relations Committee, during interviews with the author on March 13, 1998, when asked to describe the U.S. partners' policy toward Cuba.

69. Armando Correa, "Poll: For First Time, Many Dade Cubans Support a Democrat," *Miami Herald,* Oct. 5, 1996, 1B.

70. See Richard Nuccio, "Cuba: A U.S. Perspective."

71. "Helms a Cuba: Tiranía caerá pronto," *El Nuevo Herald,* March 13, 1997.

72. "Pulling Its Punches," *Miami Herald,* March 13, 1997.

73. See text published in Spanish in *Diario las Américas,* March 16, 1997.

74. Pablo Alfonso, "Rechazo europeo oscurece el horizonte económico," *El Nuevo Herald,* May 18, 1996.

75. Ileana Ros-Lehtinen, "Su primer año ha sido un éxito," *Diario las Américas,* March 16, 1997.

76. Jenkins, "The Effects of Extraterritorial Laws."

77. J. C. González, "Estados Unidos pide información," *El País,* Feb. 22, 1997.

78. Research undertaken under the direction of Tom Spreen (Institute of Food and Agricultural Sciences, University of Florida) and Alicia A. García (University of Havana), as discussed by Larry Luxner, "Cuba: ¿Futuro competidor agrícola?" *El Nuevo Herald,* April 27–May 3, 1998, 13N.

79. *Cuba Negocios* (Madrid), "Gran inquietud en diversos países del Caribe," June 1998.

80. Rafael Moreno, "Ros-Lehtinen feliz por alarma de Castro," June 2, 1997.

81. "Tema cubano inflama disputa," *El Nuevo Herald,* June 6, 1997.

82. EFE, June 12, 1997.

83. See in chapter 1 the criticism of the Torricelli and Helms-Burton legislation expressed by Representative Charles Rangel.

84. Letter to Secretary of State Madeleine Albright, Oct. 3, 1997, published in *Inside U.S. Trade,* Oct. 17, 1997, 27.

85. Larry Rohter, "Caribbean Nations Warming to Cuba," *New York Times,* Dec. 21, 1997, 8; Don Bohning, "Cuba corteja a sus vecinos del Caribe," *El Nuevo Herald,* Nov. 20, 1997, 19A; "Conferencia Europa-Caribe será en La Habana," *El Nuevo Herald,* Nov. 24, 1997; AP, "Países caribeños comerciarían con Cuba," *El Nuevo Herald,* Dec. 23, 1997, 9A.

86. For a consideration of this new regional integration scheme from a Cuban point of view, see Carlos Alzugaray Treto, "The Association of Caribbean States: A Challenge for the European Union."

87. Caribbean Council for Europe, "Integrating Caricom Trade and Other Relations with Cuba."

88. Press release, "Discurso a la VII Conferencia Europa-Caribe," Havana, Dec. 4, 1997.

89. EFE, "Volará a Cuba el 'Concorde,'" *Diario las Américas,* Dec. 31, 1997, 1A.

90. News wires, Jan. 1, 1998; *El Nuevo Herald,* Jan. 1, 1998, 1A; *El País,* Jan. 1, 1998. This was not an isolated occasion. Part of a campaign to offer evidence of good health, Castro made another unusual visit to the *Seward Johnson,* an American research vessel on a mission in Havana for the Discovery Channel; see "Castro Visits U.S. Research Ship," *Miami Herald,* Jan. 5, 1998, 7A.

91. "U.S. Slams Council of Europe Report on Cuba Trade," Reuters, Sept. 25, 1997.

92. State Department sources, reported by news agencies on March 15, 1997.

93. Andrés Oppenheimer, "U.S. Law Puts Cuba Investor on the Skids," *Miami Herald,* March 3, 1997.

94. Press release, statement by Cuban desk head Richard Rannenberger, May 17, 1998.

95. See, for example, Francisco Safont, "¿Qué nos jugamos en Cuba?" *Cinco Días,* Feb. 11, 1997.

96. Jane Bussey, "MasTec vende subsidiaria," *El Nuevo Herald,* Jan. 1, 1999.

97. Mauricio Vicent, "Una paranoya llamada Helms-Burton," *El País,* June 29, 1996.

98. *Diario las Américas,* June 13, 1996.

99. AFP, June 3, 1996.

100. "Informe sobre las relaciones con Cuba," Ministerio de Asuntos Exteriores, Madrid, press release, March 1997.

101. Manuel Hermógenes, "El imperio americano de Escarrer," *Tribuna* (Madrid), June 1, 1998, 39–40.

102. José María Triper, "El capital español apuesta por Cuba," *Cinco Días,* Feb. 11, 1997.

103. Alberto Míguez, "Rodríguez Ibarra elogió mucho a Fidel Castro," *Diario las Américas,* July 7, 1998.

104. "De visita numerosa delegación española," *El Nuevo Herald,* April 15, 1998.

105. *Cinco Días,* June 19, 1998; Mauricio Vicent, "Piqué viaja a Cuba," *El País,* June 21, 1998; "Josep Piqué, recibido por Fidel Castro," *ABC,* June 23, 1998.

106. Marcelo Aparicio, "Cuba pide mayores inversiones," *El Nuevo Herald,* Feb. 6, 1999.

107. Hugo Paeman, European Union ambassador in Washington, quoted in *La Gaceta de los Negocios* (Madrid), Feb. 12, 1997.

108. Pascal Fletcher, "Havana's 'Note' Creates a Puzzle for Embassies," *Financial Times,* April 15, 1997; "Sorprende a diplomáticos nota de la cancillería," EFE, April 11, 1997.

109. Christopher Marquis, "Cuba Blasts Embargo Proposals," *Miami Herald,* May 31, 1997. See also report by the office of Representative Ros-Lehtinen, "Congreso considera legislación," *Diario las Américas,* June 1, 1997; "Representantes de EU buscan apretar ley Helms-Burton," EFE, June 1, 1997.

110. CNN programs, May 30, 1997; "Canciller dice que Clinton es rehén del Congreso," Reuters, June 1, 1997.

111. "Cuba Lobbies against U.S. Embargo," *New York Times,* June 13, 1997, A4; Juan Tamayo, "Cuba Sets Off Blitz against Embargo," *Miami Herald,* June 13, 1997.

112. Press communiqué, June 29, 1998. The conditions were fully reflected by the international press. See, for example, AFP, "Cuba Becomes Observer," June 29, 1998.

113. "Costa Rica abrirá consulado en Cuba en los próximos días," *Diario las Américas,* Jan. 30, 1999.

114. Francesc Granell, "Cuba y la UE."

115. CARIFORUM, Aug. 20–24, 1998.

116. The scholarly literature on the impact of the embargo is huge. For a view favoring the U.S. actions, see Leyva de Varona, *Propaganda and Reality.* For a critical view, see Kaplowitz, *Anatomy of a Failed Embargo.*

117. Radio Habana, June 7, 1998 (FBIS-LAT-96-113).

118. *Prensa Latina,* June 18, 1996 (FBIS-LAT-96-119).

119. *Prensa Latina,* Aug. 19, 1996 (FBIS-LAT-96-163).

120. "Lage Discusses Economic Issues," *Prensa Latina,* Sept. 21, 1996 (FBIS-LAT-96-193).

121. Ibid.

122. *Prensa Latina,* Sept. 22, 1996 (FBIS-LAT-96-191).

123. Cubavisión, Tele Rebelde (FBIS-LAT-96-216).

124. Tele Rebelde, March 19, 1997 (FBIS-LAT-97-078).

125. Ramón Martínez, president of the Cuban Enterprise for International Insurance (ESICUBA), Havana Radio, March 10, 1997 (FBIS-LAT-97-069).

126. Informe Económico, Ministerio de Economía y Planificación, 1997.

127. Douglas Farah, *Washington Post* service, "La Habana lo admite: duele la Ley Helms," *El Nuevo Herald,* Jan. 27, 1997, 1A.

128. David Welna, National Public Radio / *New York Times*, "Some Cubans Prepare to Stick with Castro No Matter What," Aug. 7, 1996.

129. The topic has become the subject of frequent exchanges between backers of the U.S. legislative reforms and the hard-liners. See Ileana Ros-Lehtinen, "Castro, Not U.S., Imposes Embargo on Medicine," and Edward B. Atkeson, "Policy on Cuba Going Nowhere," *Miami Herald*, Jan. 2, 1998, 13A. For a response, see the letter by Wayne Smith and others in the Readers' Forum, *Miami Herald*, Jan. 8, 1998, 16A. A column by the *Herald*'s writer Soren Ziff, "Zona desmilitarizada" (*El Nuevo Herald*, Jan. 8, 1998, 12A), which argues the need for a safe mechanism to send medical supplies to Cuba, is representative of opinion in the moderate sectors of the Cuban exile community.

130. See Peter Schwab, *Cuba*, 88–89.

131. Mimi Whitefield, "Embargo Isn't What Ails Cuba," *Miami Herald*, Sept. 26, 1994, 10A.

132. Ricardo Alarcón, "An Economic War against Cuba," *Cigar Aficionado*, June 1999, 90.

133. Reuters, quoting Cuban government data as reported by *Trabajadores*, Jan. 5, 1999. The same figures were claimed by Ricardo Alarcón for 1997 (see his article in *Cigar Aficionado*, ibid.).

134. Ricardo Alarcón, "An Economic War," 90.

135. Andrew Cawthorne, "La Habana se ha hecho más selectiva en la búsqueda de inversiones," *El Nuevo Herald*, May 15, 1999, 15A.

136. Impression derived from a dozen interviews with representatives of foreign embassies and the media and with staff of Cuban think tanks and government agencies, in Havana, in late February 1999.

137. For one of the most representative samples, see Alzugaray, "El fracaso de la política de Estados Unidos."

138. From interviews conducted in Paris in April 1999.

139. "Estados Unidos ayuda a Castro a regresar al escenario mundial," *Diario las Américas*, March 6, 1997.

140. Huntington, "The Erosion," 49.

141. Wolfgang H. Reinicke, "Global Public Policy," 131.

142. See Barbara Crosette, "On Foreign Affairs, U.S. Public Is Nontraditional: Gap with Experts Continue," *New York Times*, Dec. 28, 1997.

143. Andrés Oppenheimer, "Cuban Forces Cut in Half, General Says," *Miami Herald*, Feb. 21, 1998, 14A.

144. For a sample of academic research, see Kirby Jones, *Opportunities for U.S.-Cuban Trade*. For a review of the attitude of U.S. business in the period immediately prior to the approval of Helms-Burton, see Pamela S. Falk, "Eyes on Cuba: U.S. Business and the Embargo."

145. Solís, "The Long Arm of U.S. Law," 738.

146. See statement by Jorge I. Hernández.

147. This point of view is represented by José Antonio Villamil, former U.S.

undersecretary of commerce, in his frequent columns. As an example, see "Peligran iniciativas sobre comercio internacional de los Estados Unidos," *Diario las Américas*, March 2, 1997.

148. Dodge, "The Helms-Burton Act and Transnational Legal Process," 728.

149. Ibid.

150. Meron and Vagts, "The Helms-Burton Act," 84.

151. Gerke, "The Transatlantic Rift over Cuba," 49

152. Ibid., 50.

153. Ibid., 51.

154. Ibid.

155. "President Ends Caribbean Escape: On New Year's Agenda: Budget, Elections, Mideast," *Miami Herald,* Jan. 5, 1998, 3A.

156. As an example, see the 1998 video produced by the delegation of the European Commission in the United States, "Ties and Tensions: EU-U.S. Relations in the Next Century."

157. See Haass, ed., *Transatlantic Tensions.*

158. "'Gore Factor' Will Hold the Line on Cuba," *Miami Herald,* Dec. 22, 1997, A14.

159. France's King Henry IV renounced Protestantism in 1593 in order to gain control of Paris, supposedly commenting, "Paris is well worth a mass."

160. "Going Bananas," *The Economist,* March 6, 1999, 18; "Londres pide a EE.UU. que retire las sanciones," *El País,* March 7, 1999; "EE.UU gana la 'guerra del plátano,'" *Expansión,* April 8, 1999; Luis Vázquez, "La OMC condena las sanciones," *El País,* March 9, 1999; *Le Monde,* "Isolés, les Etats-Unis intensifient leur offensive commerciale tous azimuts," March 10, 1999.

161. Joffe, "How America Does It," 25, 27.

162. "EE.UU. busca mayor efectividad," *Diario las Américas,* March 9, 1998.

163. *Americas Trade,* Aug. 7, 1997, 1, 19; *Inside U.S. Trade,* Oct. 17, 1997, 1, 26.

164. See *Inside U.S. Trade* 16, no. 6 (Feb. 13, 1998).

165. The "nuclear weapon" metaphor is often used by the professionals of the COREPER in referring to the dangerous opening of the WTO panel. French negotiators used the term during the discussions of COREPER on Oct. 16, 1997.

166. Christopher Marquis, "Plan for Food Aid to Cuba in the Works," *Miami Herald,* Jan. 28, 1998, 1A; Fabiola Santiago, "Cuban Exiles Rethink Options after Papal Visit," *Miami Herald,* Jan. 30, 1998, 1A; "Visita del Papa sacude posiciones del exilio," *El Nuevo Herald,* Jan. 30, 1998, 1A.

167. For a limited endorsement of the plan, see the editorial by the *Miami Herald,* "Toward Realistic Cuba Aid," Feb. 1, 1998, 2l.

168. Ariel Remos, "Exilio rechaza cambios sobre el embargo," *Diario las Américas,* Feb. 17, 1998, 1A.

169. See the statement issued by Ros-Lehtinen, Díaz-Balart, and Menéndez, "Existing Laws on Aid to Cuba Are Clear, Fair," *Miami Herald,* Feb. 9, 1998, 9A. For an individual statement by Díaz-Balart, see "Un instrumento fundamental," *Diario las Américas,* Feb. 13, 1998, 2B.

170. Christopher Marquis, "Lawmakers, Exile Lobby Reach Accord on Cuba Aid," *Miami Herald,* Feb. 14, 1998, 3A.

171. April Wit, "Católicos de EU envían $6 millones en medicinas," *El Nuevo Herald,* Feb. 20, 1998, 6A.

172. Christopher Marquis, "Lawmakers, Exile," Feb. 14, 1998.

173. Juan Tamayo, "Cuba to Free At Least 200 Prisoners," *Miami Herald,* Feb. 13, 1998, 1A.

174. Distributed by *Los Angeles Times* service, Nuccio's statements were reproduced in a number of U.S. newspapers. See "Mr. Clinton, Take the Lead in Shaping Up U.S. Policy on Cuba," *Miami Herald,* Feb. 1, 1998, 3L; "Memorando a Clinton," *El Nuevo Herald,* Feb. 4, 1998, 10A. Members of Congress Menéndez, Ros-Lehtinen, and Díaz-Balart issued a comment critical of Nuccio's proposal: "El síndrome Nuccio," *Diario las Américas,* Feb. 22, 1998, 4A.

175. This op-ed piece ("Mr. Clinton, Take the Lead") summarizes the arguments of Nuccio's paper "Cuba: A U.S. Perspective."

176. Andrés Oppenheimer, "Argentine President Seeks to Mend Ties with Cuba," *Miami Herald,* Feb. 7, 1998, 1A, 17A.

177. Ariel Remos, "Castro invita a que vaya a Cuba premier canadiense," *Diario las Américas,* Feb. 20, 1998, 1A.

8. Conclusion

1. Although we coincide in our opinions, I owe this assessment partially to comments made by David Thomas, former U.K. ambassador in Cuba, during our productive discussions at the conference held by the Center for International Policy in Miami on Oct. 16–17, 1997.

2. Kaplowitz, *Anatomy of a Failed Embargo,* 198–202.

3. For a sample of moderate discussion on the transition in Cuba, see "Friendly Prodding" by Mauricio Font and Francisco León.

4. Statements made by participants in hearing held by the U.S. Congress Subcommittee on International Policy and Trade, March 12, 1998.

5. City University of New York, Cuba Project, Sept. 28, 1998.

6. Jorge Domínguez, "U.S.-Cuban Relations"; Schoultz, *Beneath the United States.*

7. David Bernell, "The Curious Case of Cuba in American Foreign Policy," 69.

8. Ibid., 99.

9. For a sample of the press reports and public declarations, see Juan Tamayo, "Cuba-U.S. Meeting Cranks Up Rumor Mill," *Miami Herald,* Dec. 12, 1997, 34A; Horacio Ruiz Pavón, "Desmienten en Washington el rumor sobre contactos secretos en Cuba," *Diario las Américas,* Dec. 13, 1997, 1A; Emilio Guerra, "EU niega haya cambios en política hacia Castro," *El Nuevo Herald,* Dec. 13, 1997, 6A; Christopher Marquis, "U.S.-Cuba Policy Faces New Challenge," *Miami Herald,* Dec. 21, 1997, 1L; Ariel Remos, "Enfoque y presiones deben ser multilaterales," *Diario las Américas,* Dec. 19, 1997, 1A; Tom Fiedler, "EU amaga movida," *El Nuevo Herald,* Dec. 12, 1997, 1A; Lincoln Díaz-Balart, Robert Menéndez, and Ileana Ros-Lehtinen, "No

cambiará la política de EU hacia Cuba," *El Nuevo Herald,* Dec. 19, 1997, 24A; María Travieso, "Cuba Embargo Firm, Exiles Assured," *Miami Herald,* Dec. 19, 1997, 2B; Andrés Oppenheimer, "No parecen haber cambios hacia Cuba," *El Nuevo Herald,* Dec. 22, 1997, 1B; Ariel Remos, "No apoyará el Congreso limitaciones a la ley Helms-Burton," *Diario las Américas,* Dec. 21, 1997, 1B.

10. David Lyons, "A Claim on Cuba's Old Assets," *Miami Herald,* Dec. 1, 1997, 1B; "Juez otorga $187 millones," *El Nuevo Herald,* Dec. 18, 1997, 1A; "A Stunning Victory," editorial, *Miami Herald,* Dec. 18, 1997, 28A; David Lyons, "Cuba Must Pay," *Miami Herald,* Dec. 18, 1997, 1A. However, various voices warned of the minimal chances of ever receiving compensation. While José Basulto, the head of the Brothers to the Rescue organization, said that the Cuban funds frozen in the United States belong to the Cuban people, lawyers for the certified claimants state that they have the first claim to those assets.

11. "Justice for Whom?" *Miami Herald,* Jan. 30, 1999, 22A; Ariel Remos, "Se opone Departmento de Justicia a utilizar fondos congelados," *Diario las Américas,* Jan. 30, 1999, 1A.

12. David Lyons and Juan Tamayo, "Fliers' Kin Get a Way to Collect," *Miami Herald,* March 19, 1999, 1A; EFE, "Un juez de EE.UU. ordena indemnizar a anticastristas con fondos retenidos a Cuba," *El País,* March 19, 1999, 1.

13. Juan Tamayo and Meg Laughlin, "Cuba Files $181 Billion Claim," *Miami Herald,* June 2, 1999; "Cuba demanda al gobierno de EU," *El Nuevo Herald,* June 2, 1999; Mauricio Vicent, "Cuba reclama a Washington 181.000 millones," *El País,* June 2, 1999.

14. Juan Tamayo, "Castro's Vision Has a High Price: Democracy," *Miami Herald,* Dec. 27, 1998; Richard Nuccio, "Unmaking Cuba Policy: The Clinton Years," *Foreign Service Journal* 75, no. 10 (Oct. 1998): 24. See, among the many times he has been quoted, Tamayo, "Pressure Mounts on U.S. to Ease Sanctions," *Miami Herald,* Dec. 28, 1998, special report.

15. *Granma,* Dec. 30, 1998.

16. José Luis Rodríguez, minister of economy, declarations to Reuters, Dec. 22, 1998.

17. Quoted in a "The Isle of Broken Dreams," editorial, *Miami Herald,* Jan. 1, 1999.

18. Pablo Alfonso, "Cuba: más azúcar, menos ingresos," *El Nuevo Herald,* May 12, 1999, 1A.

19. D. Rousseau, "Insolvente la economía cubana," *El Nuevo Herald,* May 7, 1999, 1A.

20. Andrew Cawthorne, "La Habana se ha hecho más selectiva," *El Nuevo Herald,* May 15, 1999, 15A.

21. "Castro fija límites," *El Nuevo Herald,* May 19, 1999, 17A.

22. The figures are official or are generated by international organizations. See Juan Tamayo, "Castro's Vision Has a High Price: Democracy," *Miami Herald,* Dec. 27, 1998.

23. "La senectud marca," *El Nuevo Herald,* May 20, 1999.

24. Gerardo Tena, "Aplican una política de mano dura contra la delincuencia," *El Nuevo Herald*, Jan. 30, 1999, 16A; A. Cawthorne, "Condenan a muerte a los asesinos de dos turistas," *El Nuevo Herald*, Jan. 30, 1999, 18A.

25. Peter Katel, "Vuelve a Cuba la Mafia," *El Nuevo Herald*, May 17, 1999, 1A.

26. Pablo Alfonso, "La Habana lava dinero de drogas," *El Nuevo Herald*, May 14, 1999, 17A.

27. Mark Falcoff, "Reflections on a Dying Revolution," 563.

28. Andrés Viglucci, "35 More Cubans Reach U.S. Soil," *Miami Herald*, Dec. 30, 1998.

29. Peter Katel, "Peligro de avalancha de balseros," *El Nuevo Herald*, May 13, 1999, 1A.

30. AFP, Dec. 30, 1998.

31. Pablo Alfonso, "Sánchez culpa de crisis al totalitarismo," *El Nuevo Herald*, Jan. 1, 1999.

32. Juan Tamayo, "Castro's Vision Has a High Price: Democracy," *Miami Herald*, Dec. 27, 1998.

33. Falcoff, "Reflections on a Dying Revolution," 565–74.

34. Don Dorschner, "The Vanishing Revolutionaries," *Miami Herald*, Dec. 27, 1998.

35. *Granma International*, editorial, Jan. 2, 1999; John Rice, "40 Years Later, Castro Returns to Historic Spot," *Miami Herald*, Jan. 2, 1999; Serge Kovaleski, "Communist Cuba's Capitalist Contradictions," *New York Times*, Dec. 31, 1999; James McKinley, Jr., "Castro Talk Shows Him a Rebel And Prophet," *New York Times*, Jan. 3, 1999; James McKinley, "In City of Castro's Triumph, Most Still Back Him," *New York Times*, Jan. 2, 1999.

36. Helms, "What Sanctions Epidemic?" 5.

37. Rui Ferreira and Roberto Fabrizio, "El trasfondo de un forcejeo," *El Nuevo Herald*, Jan. 10, 1999.

38. For the text in Spanish, see, among other sources, *Diario las Américas*, March 21, 1999, 10A, and *El Nuevo Herald*, March 28, 1999, 18A.

39. Juan Tamayo, "Four Cuban Dissidents Convicted," *Miami Herald*, March 16, 1999, 1A; Mauricio Vicent, "Cuba condena a penas de hasta cinco años de prisión," *El País*, March 16, 1999, 9; John Harbron, "Will Canada Finally Chastise Castro?" *Miami Herald*, March 19, 1999, 23A.

40. "Condena cubana" (editorial), *El País*, March 17, 1999.

41. Pablo Alfonso, "Molesto el Grupo de Río con la ola represiva," *El Nuevo Herald*, March 19, 1999, 1A.

42. Luis Ayllón, "El Gobierno español intenta salvar la Cumbre Iberoamericana," *ABC*, May 11, 1999, 26.

43. José Miguel Larraya, "Aznar dice que las penas a 4 disidentes cubanos complican el viaje de los Reyes," *El País*, March 17, 1999, 23.

44. Andrés Oppenheimer, "Carta desde Washington," *El Nuevo Herald*, Feb. 1, 1999.

45. Andrés Oppenheimer, "Helms Derailing Key Clinton Appointments Abroad,"

Miami Herald, May 19, 1999, 1A; "Ambassadors Missing," editorial, *Miami Herald,* May 21, 1999, 26A.

46. Helms, "Tighten the Screws," *Cigar Aficionado,* June 1999, 80–84.

47. Frank Davies, "U.S. Easing Contacts with Cuba," *Miami Herald,* Jan. 5, 1999; Pablo Alfonso, "La Casa Blanca no revisará el embargo," *El Nuevo Herald,* Jan. 5, 1999.

48. Andrés Oppenheimer, "What Is Behind the Recent U.S. Measures?" *Miami Herald,* Jan. 7, 1999, 12A.

49. Interview with *El País,* quoted by EFE, "Pastrana confía en Castro," *Diario las Américas,* Jan. 8, 1999.

50. Floridano Feria, "Nueva política de Clinton con Cuba no afecta ley Helms-Burton: Opinan los doctores Ambler Moss y Joaquín Roy," *Diario las Américas,* Jan. 6, 1999; Ena Curnow, "Sigue debate en el exilio," *Diario las Américas,* Jan. 8, 1999.

51. Frank Davies, "Clinton Touts Food Sales, Flights to Ease Cuba Change," *Miami Herald,* Jan. 6, 1999; Rui Ferreira, "Cautelosa la reacción en La Habana," *El Nuevo Herald,* Jan. 6, 1999; Pablo Alfonso, "Ventas a sector privado impulsarían negocios," *El Nuevo Herald,* Jan. 6, 1999; "La Secretaria Albright y la nueva política hacia Cuba," editorial, *Diario las Américas,* Jan. 8, 1999.

52. "U.S. Lawmakers Rightly Oppose Castro's Tyranny," *Miami Herald,* Jan. 6, 1999.

53. AFP, "Cámaras de Comercio españolas creen positivo que EE.UU suavice el embargo a Cuba," *Diario las Américas,* Jan. 9, 1999.

54. Floridano Feria, "Líderes del exilio critican cambio de política hacia Cuba," *Diario las Américas,* Jan. 9, 1999.

55. Wilfredo Cancio Isla, "Critican medidas de la Casa Blanca," *El Nuevo Herald,* Jan. 9, 1999; Andrew Cawthorne, "Elogia anuncio de EU el canciller canadiense," *El Nuevo Herald,* Jan. 9, 1999; John Rice, "Cuba Dismisses U.S. Policy Shift," *Miami Herald,* Jan. 9, 1999; Pablo Alfonso, "La Habana rechazará comercio con EU," *El Nuevo Herald,* Jan. 8, 1999.

56. TV and radio interviews as reported by EFE, Jan. 9, 1999.

57. This graphic expression as also used by Alarcón in an article published in the special issue of *Cigar Aficionado,* titled "An Economic War against Cuba," June 1999, 89–90.

58. Juan Tamayo, "Robaina Is Dumped by Castro," *Miami Herald,* May 29, 1999, 1A.

59. AFP, "Cuba y empresarios de EE.UU hablan de negocios," May 20, 1999, 1A; EFE, "Empresas de EE.UU. desafían amenazas y siguen reunidas con funcionarios de Cuba," *Diario las Américas,* May 22, 1999, 1A; EFE, "En Cancún tintinean las monedas norteamericanas," *El Nuevo Herald,* May 21, 1999, 17A.

60. Among other declarations, see his article titled "End the Embargo," published in the controversial issue of *Cigar Aficionado,* June 1999, 81–88.

61. Dwayne O. Andreas, "Whose Embargo Is It, Anyway?" *Cigar Aficionado,* June 1999, 93–94.

62. Max Castro, "Americans Favor Diplomatic Ties with Cuba," *Miami Herald,* June 2, 1999, 17A.

63. Ena Curnow, "Denuncia la FNCA los intentos de la administración," *Diario las Américas,* May 22, 1999, 1B; Jaime Suchlicki, "Base 'New' Cuba Conversation on the Facts," *Miami Herald,* May 11, 1999, 10A.

64. AFP, "Revista católica critica las nuevas leyes represivas," *El Nuevo Herald,* May 11, 1999, 11A.

65. Rui Ferreira, "Fusilamientos en Cuba," *Miami Herald,* May 8, 1999, 1A.

66. Pablo Alfonso, "Informes de arresto," *El Nuevo Herald,* May 22, 1999, 11A.

67. Pablo Alfonso, "Prosigue la puja de reformistas y conservadores," *El Nuevo Herald,* May 23, 1999, 14A.

68. Pablo Alfonso, "El canciller Robaina, sus ausencias," *El Nuevo Herald,* May 5, 1999, 23A.

69. "Destituido el ministro cubano de Asuntos Exteriores," *El País,* May 28, 1999; "Designado Felipe Pérez Roque Ministro de Relaciones Exteriores," *Granma,* May 28, 1999, 1.

70. From a Spanish perspective: *ABC,* editorial, "Castro se enroca," *ABC,* May 29, 1999; A. Pérez Giménez, "Castro nombra canciller," *ABC,* May 29, 1999; Ángel Tomás González, "Castro destituye a Robaina," *El Mundo,* May 29, 1999; Joaquim Ibarz, "Fulminante destitución," *La Vanguardia,* May 29, 1999; Mauricio Vicent, "Fidel Castro destituye a Robaina," *El País,* May 29, 1999. In the Miami press: Santiago Aroca, "Robaina y el bunker," *Diario las Américas,* May 29, 1999, 5A; Ariel Remos, "Robaina purgado," *Diario las Américas,* May 29, 1999, 1A; Juan Tamayo, "Robaina Is Dumped," *Miami Herald,* May 29, 1999, 1A; "No Change in Cuba," editorial, *Miami Herald,* May 29, 1999, 26A. Additional accounts: "Purga política en Cuba," *El Nuevo Herald,* May 29, 1999, 1A; "Castro, Facing Outcry on Trials, Switches His Foreign Minister," *New York Times,* May 29, 1999; Carlos Bautista, "Ordenan un 'reajuste' al nuevo canciller," *El Nuevo Herald,* May 30, 1999, 19A.

71. Data from Cuba's Foreign Relations Ministry (Carlos Batista, *El Nuevo Herald,* May 30, 1999, 19A).

72. *Granma,* May 28, 1999, 1A; unofficial translation made by Serge F. Kovaleski, "Cuba Replaces Foreign Minister With Top Aide to Castro," *Washington Post,* May 29, 1999, A28.

73. Agence France Press, June 2, 1999.

74. Lisette Bustamante, "El Gobierno aplaza el viaje," *La Razón,* May 12, 1999; Luis Ayllón, "El gobierno español intenta salvar la cumbre," *ABC,* May 11, 1999.

75. Tamayo, "Robaina is Dumped," 16A.

76. Quoted by Kovaleski, "Cuba Replaces Foreign Minister."

77. "¿Qué significa 'como pocos'?" *Juventud Rebelde,* May 31, 1999.

78. Maurizio Giuliano, "The United States Embargo and Cuba's Foreign Relations." This text is a modification of chapter 3 of his book *La transición cubana y el bloqueo norteamericano,* 105–46.

79. Haass, "Conclusion," *Transatlantic Tensions,* 237.

80. Alexandra Barahona de Brito, "Promoting Democracy in Cuba?" in Pilar Alamos and Mauricio Font, *Integración económica y democratización,* 265–316.

BIBLIOGRAPHY

Author's Note

This bibliography is meant to provide complete citations to selected sources mentioned in the notes. It includes books, articles, and reviews of an academic nature, as well as government reports and statements by government officials. These reports and statements include, when possible, printed sources, but often documents cited have been available only as press releases or dossiers distributed in public hearings. Newspaper and magazine articles and other journalistic sources are cited only in the notes.

Abi-Mershed, Elizabeth, Michael Krinsky, and David Golove. *United States Economic Measures against Cuba.* Proceedings in the United Nations and International Law Issues. Reviewed in *American Journal of International Law* 89, no. 4 (1995): 868–69.

"Act of State Doctrine: Determining Its Viability in a Suit Involving an Expropriation by Cuba of Foreign-Owned Assets. *Banco Nacional de Cuba v. Chase Manhattan Bank*, 658 F.2d 875." *Lawyer of the Americas* 14 (Fall 1982): 337–53.

"The Act of State Doctrine and the Antitrust Laws: Time to Retreat from Sabbatino [*Banco Nacional de Cuba v. Sabbatino*, 84 S. Ct. 923 (1964)]?" *Saint Louis University Law Journal* 25 (1982): 867–89.

Alamos, Pilar, and Mauricio A. Font, eds. *Integración económica y democratización.* Santiago: Instituto de Estudios Internacionales, 1998.

Alarcón de Quesada, Ricardo. "Necessity of Ending the Economic, Commercial and Financial Embargo Imposed by the United States of America Against Cuba." Item 30, 52d Session of the United Nations General Assembly, New York, November 5, 1997. Press release.

Albright, Madeleine. "The Testing of American Foreign Policy." *Foreign Affairs* 77, no. 6 (October–December 1998): 50–64.

Altozano, Hermenegildo. "Consideraciones sobre el entendimiento UE-EE.UU. de 18 de mayo de 1998 respecto a medidas (disciplinas) para fortalecer la protección de inversiones." Paper presented at the seminar "Cuba: Nuevas perspectivas tras el acuerdo sobre la Ley Helms y el relajamiento del embargo," Cuba Negocios, Madrid, July 3, 1998.

———. "La Ley Helms-Burton y la protección de las inversiones españolas en Cuba." Paper presented at the seminar sponsored by IRELA on "The Strengthening of the U.S. Embargo against Cuba," Sitges (Barcelona, Spain), July 8–10, 1996.

Álvarez-Mena, Sergio, and Daniel A. Crane. "From the Commerce Clause to Café Cubano: The Constitutionality of Helms-Burton." Paper presented at the American Bar Association, International Law Section and Inter-American Law Committee, October 23–26, 1996.

Alzugaray Treto, Carlos. "La Asociación de Estados del Caribe (AEC) y la Unión Europea (UE): Los desafíos mútuos de una relación asimétrica." Paper presented at Seminar on European Union–ACS Relations held in Havana, June 1997. (Forthcoming from IRELA, 1999.)

———. "The Association of Caribbean States: A Challenge for the European Union." *Revista de Estudios Europeos* 11, no. 42 (April–June 1997): 28–49.

———. "Cuba y el sistema internacional en la década de 1990." In Emilio Duarte, ed., *Problemas actuales de teoría socio-política.* Havana: Editorial Félix Varela, 1999.

———. *De la fruta madura a la ley Helms-Burton: Auge, decadencia y fracaso de la política imperialista de Estados Unidos hacia Cuba.* Panamá: Editorial Universitaria, 1997.

———. "A dos años de la aprobación de la Helms-Burton: Las tribulaciones de una ley universalmente repudiada." *América Nuestra* (Nueva Época) 4, no. 2 (March–April 1998) (Havana, Asociación por la Unidad de Nuestra América [AUNA]): 40–44.

———. "El fracaso de la política de Estados Unidos hacia Cuba y la ley Helms-Burton." Paper presented at the Unión Nacional de Juristas de Cuba, Seminario Panamericanismo versus Latinoamericanismo, Havana, 1996.

American Association of Jurists. "Declaration of the American Association of Jurists on the United States Trade Embargo against Cuba." *National Lawyers Guild Practitioner* 49, no. 1 (Winter 1992): 1–3.

American Society of International Law. "Are the U.S. Treasury's Assets Control Regulations a Fair And Effective Tool of U.S. Foreign Policy? The Case of Cuba: A Panel." *Proceedings* 79 (1985): 69–89.

Argentaria / Club del Exterior. *Cuba: Guía de negocios.* Madrid, 1995.

Arias, Inocencio F. "La bula progresina." *Política Exterior 55*, 15 (Jan.–Feb. 1997): 21–28.

Association for the Study of the Cuban Economy (ASCE). *Cuba in Transition.* Papers and proceedings of the fifth annual meeting, Miami, Florida, Aug. 10–12, 1995.

Atlantic Council. *International Perspectives on U.S.-Cuban Relations.* Washington, D.C., 1998.

———. *A Road Map for Restructuring Future U.S. Relations with Cuba.* Washington, 1995.

Auge, Craig R. "Title IV of the Helms-Burton Act: A Questionable Secondary Boycott." *Law and Policy in International Business* 28 (Winter 1997): 575–91.

Bacardí Company. "Key Historical Facts." Pamphlet, n.d.

Bachman, Kenneth, Ricardo A. Anzaldúa, and Amy Deen Westbrook. "Anti-Cuba Sanctions May Violate NAFTA, GATT: Provisions of the Helms-Burton Bill Penalizing Dealers in Seized Property Would Impede Trade." *National Law Journal* 18, no. 28 (March 11, 1996): C3.

Banco Nacional de Cuba. Annual Report. 1994.

Barahona de Brito, Alexandra. "Promoting Democracy in Cuba? The European Union and Helms-Burton." In Pilar Alamos and Mauricio A. Font, eds., *Integración económica y democratización*, 265–315. Santiago: Instituto de Estudios Internacionales, 1998.

Bar Association of the City of New York. The Committee on Inter-American Affairs. "The Legality of the Extraterritorial Reach of the Cuban Democracy Act of 1992." *The Report* (May–June 1996).

Bayer, Stephen D. "The Legal Aspects of TV Martí in Relation to the Law of Direct Broadcasting Satellites." *Emory Law Journal* 41, no. 2 (Spring 1992): 541–80.

Benes, Alejandro. "The Spirit of the Bat." *Cigar Aficionado* (Autumn 1996).

Berlin, Alan D. "Business Opportunities in Post-Embargo Cuba: Cuban Legal System Will Have to Be Updated." *New York Law Journal* 215, no. 33 (Feb. 20, 1996): S2.

Bernell, David. "The Curious Case of Cuba in American Foreign Policy." *Journal of Interamerican Studies and World Affairs* 36, no. 2 (Summer 1994): 65.

Berrios, Rubén. "Why America Should Lift Its Cuban Embargo." *Contemporary Review* 265, no. 1545 (Oct. 1994):. 182.

Berrios, Rubén, and Lillian Thomas. "Taking Orders from Little Havana." *Bulletin of the Atomic Scientists* 50, no. 5 (Sept.–Oct. 1994): 20.

Betancourt, Ernesto F. "Potential Impact of the Helms/Burton Act on Castro's Regime." In ASCE, *Cuba in Transition* (papers and proceedings of the fifth annual meeting, Association for the Study of the Cuban Economy, Miami, Florida, Aug. 10–12, 1995), 410–28.

"Beyond Sabbatino [*Banco Nacional de Cuba v. Sabbatino*, 84 S. Ct. 923 (1964)]: The Exception That Consumes the Rule?" *University of Toledo Law Review* 17 (Fall 1985): 295–312.

Bourque, Shari-Ellen. "The Illegality of the Cuban Embargo in the Current International System." *Boston University International Law Journal* 13, no. 163 (Spring 1995): 191–228.

Bryan, Anthony T., and Roget V. Bryan. *The New Face of Regionalism in the Caribbean: The Western Hemisphere Dynamic.* Agenda Papers 35. North-South Center, University of Miami, March 1999.

Byron, H. Thomas, III. "Playing by International Rules." *Legal Times* 18, no. 45 (March 25, 1996): 28.

Cain, Jerry W., Jr. "Extraterritorial Application of the United States' Trade Embargo against Cuba: The United Nations General Assembly's Call for an End to the U.S. Trade Embargo." *Georgia Journal of International and Comparative Law* 24, no. 2 (1994): 379–96.

Campbell, Beverly L. "Helms-Burton: Checkmate or Challenge for Canadian Firms Doing Business in Cuba?" In ASCE, *Cuba in Transition* (papers and proceedings of the sixth annual meeting, Association for the Study of the Cuban Economy, Miami, Aug. 1996), 496–501.

Campbell, Kim. "Helms-Burton: The Canadian View." *Hastings International and Comparative Law Review* 20, no. 4 (Summer 1997): 799–808.

Canada. Foreign Extraterritorial Measures Act (United States) Order (FEMA). October 9, 1992.

Cañete, Frank Vera. "Relaciones Cuba-España en los 80s. Consideraciones y perspectivas." *Revista de Estudios Europeos* 12 (Oct.–Dec. 1989): 118–34.

Carayiannis, Peter P. "The Cuban Democracy Act: Success or Failure?" *Journal of International Law and Practice* 3 (1994): 195–204.

Caribbean Council for Europe. "Integrating Caricom Trade and Other Relations with Cuba and the DOM: The Role of the Post Lomé Arrangement with Special Reference to the ACS and Cariforum." Havana, December 4–5, 1997.

CARICOM and the Association of Caribbean States. "Declaration of CARICOM and the Association of Caribbean States." May 1996.

Carranza, Julio, Luis Gutiérrez, and Pedro Monreal, eds. *Cuba: La reestructuración de la economía.* Madrid: IEPALA, 1995.

Castañeda, Rolando H., and George Plinio Montalván. "Cuba: Cooperación internacional de emergencia y para la recuperación." *Cuba in Transition* (papers and proceedings of the fifth annual meeting, Association for the Study of the Cuban Economy [ASCE], Miami, Aug. 10–12, 1995), 269–87.

———. "Economic Factors in Selecting an Approach to Confiscation Claims in Cuba." In ASCE, *Cuba in Transition* (papers and proceedings of the fifth annual meeting, Association for the Study of the Cuban Economy, Miami, Aug. 10–12, 1995), 227–43.

Castro, Fidel. "Discurso pronunciado en la sesión conmemorativa por el 50 aniversario de la creación del sistema multilateral de comercio, Palacio de las Naciones, Ginebra, Suiza, 19 de mayo de 1998" (electronic circular no. 194). Havana: Dirección de Información del Ministerio de Relaciones Exteriores, 1998.

Centeno, Miguel Angel, and Mauricio Font. *Toward a New Cuba? Legacies of a Revolution.* Boulder, Colo.: Lynne Rienner, 1997.

Center for International Policy. "A Discussion of Some of the Perplexing Questions Raised by the EU-U.S. Understanding on Expropriated Property." Washington, D.C., 1998.

———. *Helms-Burton: A Loose Canon?* Washington, D.C., Feb. 9–11, 1997.

Central American Parliament and the Latin American Parliament. "Resolution of the Central American Parliament and of the Latin American Parliament," July 1996.

Christopher, Warren. Circular to All Diplomatic and Consular Posts. September 1993.

Clagett, Brice M. "The Expropriation Issue before the Iran–United States Claims

Tribunal: Is 'Just Compensation' Required by International Law or Not?" *Law and Policy in International Business* 16 (1984): 813–91.

———. "Present State of the International Law of Compensation for Expropriated Property and Repudiated State Contracts." *Private Investors Abroad*, 1989, 12–27.

———. "Protection of Foreign Investment under the Revised Restatement." *Virginia Journal of International Law* 25 (Fall 1984): 73–98.

———. "A Reply to Professor Lowenfeld: Title III of the Helms-Burton Act Is Consistent with International Law." *American Journal of International Law* 90, no. 3 (July 1996): 434–40.

———. "Title III of Helms-Burton: Who is Breaking International Law—The United States, or the States That Have Made Themselves Co-Conspirators with Cuba in Its Unlawful Confiscations?" *George Washington Journal of International Law and Economics* 30 (Fall 1997).

Clagett, Brice M., and Daniel B. Poneman. "The Treatment of Economic Injury to Aliens in the Revised Restatement of Foreign Relations Law." *International Lawyer* 22 (Spring 1988): 35–68.

Clinton, Bill. "President Clinton's Statement on the Helms-Burton Waiver." January 3, 1997.

Cohn, Evelyn F., and Alan D. Berlin. "European Community Reacts to Helms-Burton." *New York Law Journal* 218, no. 24 (August 4, 1997): S2.

Colomer, Josep M. "Después de Fidel, ¿qué?" *Encuentro de la Cultura Cubana* (Madrid), nos. 8–9, (Spring–Summer 1998): 77–90.

Communist Party of Cuba. "The Meaning of Helms-Burton." *Political Affairs* 75, no. 7 (July 1996): 11–12, 35.

Congreso de los Diputados. Comisión Mixta para la UE. "Acuerdo entre los Estados Unidos y la UE." *Boletín oficial de las Cortes Generales* no. 107 (June 3, 1998): 2211–27.

———. Pleno del Congreso. "Efectos del acuerdo entre la UE y los Estados Unidos." *Boletín oficial de las Cortes Generales* no. 167 (June 10, 1998).

———. Proyecto de Ley. *Boletín oficial de las Cortes Generales* (March 3, 1998): 1–3.

"Constitutional Law—Grandfather Clause in International Emergency Economic Powers Act Permits the President to Ban Travel to Cuba without Declaring an Emergency, *Regan v. Wald,* 104 S. Ct. 3026." *Vanderbilt Journal of Transnational Law* 17 (Fall 1984): 977–93.

Consuegra-Barquín, Juan C. "The Present Status Quo of Property Rights in Cuba." In ASCE, *Cuba in Transition* (papers and proceedings of the fifth annual meeting, Association for the Study of the Cuban Economy, Miami, Aug. 10–12, 1995), 207–26.

Consultores Asociados (CONAS). *Inversiones y negocios.* Informe 1995–96.

Cotman, John Walton. "Cuba and the Caricom States: The Last Decade." In Donna Rich Kaplowitz, ed., *Cuba's Ties to a Changing World,* 145–64. Boulder and London: Lynne Rienner Publishers, 1993.

Cova, Bruno. "Extra-Territorial Reach of the U.S. Iran-Libya Sanctions Act of 1996." Parlement Européen, Commission des Relations Economiques Extérieures. Public hearing concerning "Les lois extraterritoriales comme sanctiones unilatérales," June, 24, 1998.

Cruz, Alberto. "Dos aspectos de la política española hacia Cuba: Derechos humanos e intercambio comerical." *Cuadernos Africa, América Latina* 14, (1994): 85–104.

Cuba. Decreto Legislativo no. 50 (February 15, 1982). Press release.

———. "Ley de reafirmación de la dignidad y soberanía cubanas." Ley no. 80, Dec. 24, 1996. Press release.

———. Ministerio de Economía y Planificación. Informe económico (1997).

Cuomo, Mario M. "Helms-Burton Bill: A Sound Solution?" *New York Law Journal* 215, no. 33 (Feb. 20, 1996): 81.

Dattu, Riyaz, and John Boscariol. "GATT Article XXI, Helms-Burton, and the Continuing Abuse of the National Security Exception." *Canadian Business Law Journal* 28, no. 2 (April 1997): 198–209.

David, Clara. "Trading with Cuba: The Cuban Democracy Act and Export Rules." *Florida Journal of International Law* 8 (Fall 1993): 385–89.

De Falco, David S. "Comment: The Cuban Liberty and Democratic Solidarity (LIBERTAD) Act of 1996: Is the United States Reaching Too Far?" *Journal of International Legal Studies* 3, no. 125 (1997).

Del Rosario Hernández, Vivian. "España-Cuba: Empresas mixtas, nuevos lazos, nuevas realidades." *Estudios Europeos* 6, no. 23 (July–Sept. 1992): 54–71.

De Paz-Sánchez, Manuel. *Zona rebelde: La diplomacia española ante la Revolución Cubana (1957–1960)*. Tenerife: Taller de Historia, 1997.

Díaz Briquets, Sergio. "Emigrant Remittances in the Cuban Economy: Their Significance during and after the Castro Regime." In ASCE, *Cuba in Transition* (papers and proceedings of the sixth annual meeting, Association for the Study of the Cuban Economy, Miami, Aug. 1996).

Dodge, William S. "The Helms-Burton Act and Transnational Legal Process." *Hastings International and Comparative Law Review* 20, no. 4 (Summer 1997): 713–28.

Domínguez, Jorge. "U.S.-Cuban Relations: From the Cold War to the Colder War." *Journal of Interamerican Studies and World Affairs* 39, no. 3 (1997): 49–73.

Donner, Laura A. "The Cuban Democracy Act of 1992: Using Foreign Subsidiaries as Tools of Foreign Economic Policy." *Emory International Review* 7, no. 1 (Spring 1993): 259–67.

Eisenstat, Stuart. "Testimony of Under Secretary Eisenstat on Sanctions." *U.S.A. Text* (Brussels), June 3, 1998.

Erisman, H. Michael. "Cuba and the Caribbean Basin: From Pariah to Partner?" *Journal of Inter-American Studies and World Affairs* 40, no. 1 (Spring 1998): 87–94.

Erisman, H. Michael, and John M. Kirk, eds. *Cuban Foreign Policy Confronts a New International Order*. Boulder and London: Lynne Rienner, 1991.

European Union—Commission. "Communication of the Commission to the Council and the European Parliament." June 28, 1995.

———. "Information Note for the Attention of Delegations: Helms-Burton/ILSA: EU/U.S. Summit on 18 May 1998." June 25, 1998.

———. Memorandum of Understanding. April 11, 1997.

———. "Understanding with Respect to Disciplines for the Strengthening of Investment Protection." *European Union News,* May 18, 1998.

European Union—Council. "Declaration on Cuba." January 23, 1992.

———. "Declaration on Cuba." December 22, 1992.

———. Regulation (EC) no. 2271/96. *Official Journal of the European Communities* (Nov. 29, 1997).

European Union—European Parliament. "Note on the Political Situation in Cuba and Its Relations with the European Union." January 30, 1995.

———. "Recommendations on the MAI." Session Documents, February 26, 1998.

———. "Resolution on Cuba." September 16, 1990.

———. "Resolution on Cuba." March 14, 1996.

———. "Resolution on Relations with Central America, including Cuba." February 22, 1991.

———. "Resolution on the Communication from the Commission to the Council and the European Parliament on the Relations between the European Union and Cuba." January 18, 1996.

———. "Resolution on the Current Situation in Cuba, Particularly on Human Rights." December 15, 1988.

———. "Resolution on the Embargo against Cuba and the 'Torricelli Law.'" September 16, 1993.

———. "Resolution on the Executions and Violations of Human Rights in Cuba." February 13, 1992.

———. "Resolution on the Obligations of the Member States Regarding GATT." June 10, 1996.

———. "Resolution on the Relations between the European Community and the Non-European Countries Members of COMECON." October 31, 1988.

———. "Resolution on the Restrictions to International Trade Imposed by the United States (Cuban Democracy Act)." December 17, 1992.

———. "Resolution on the Situation in Cuba." September 29, 1994.

———. "Resolution on the Situation of Human Rights in Cuba." March 11, 1993.

———. "Resolution on the Situation of Political Prisoners in Cuba." October 29, 1987.

European Union—Presidency. "Declaration of the European Union on the Destruction of the Two Civilian Aircraft by Cuban Authorities." February 26, 1996.

———. "Declaration of the Presidency of the European Union on Cuba." April 5, 1995.

———. "Declaration of the Presidency on the Project of the Helms-Burton Law." October 11, 1995.

———. "Note from the Presidency of the European Union to the U.S. State Department (March 1996), the European Parliament (May 1996) and the General Affairs Council of the EC (October 1996)."

Fábregas i Guillén, Dídac. *La ley de la inversión extranjera y la situación económica actual en Cuba.* Barcelona: Viena, 1998.

Fairey, W. Fletcher. "The Helms-Burton Act: The Effect of International Law on Domestic Implementation." *American University Law Review* 46, no. 4 (1997): 1289–1335.

Falcoff, Mark. "America's Culture War and the Cuban Revolution." In *A Culture of Its Own: Taking Latin America Seriously,* pp. 169–86. New Brunswick and London: Transaction, 1998.

———. "Reflections on a Dying Revolution," *Orbis,* Fall 1998, 565–74.

Falk, Pamela S. "Broadcasting from Enemy Territory and the First Amendment: The Importation of Informational Materials from Cuba under the Trading with the Enemy Act." *Columbia Law Review* 92, no. 1 (Jan. 1992): 165–91.

———. "Eyes on Cuba: U.S. Business and the Embargo." *Foreign Affairs* vol. 75, no. 2 (March–April 1996): 14.

———. "The U.S.-Cuba Agenda: Opportunity or Stalemate?" *Journal of Inter-American Studies and World Affairs* 39, no. 1 (Spring 1997): 153.

Fauriol, George, and Eva Looser, eds. *Cuba: The International Dimension.* New Brunswick, N.J.: Transaction, 1990.

Fidler, David P. "LIBERTAD v. Liberalism: An Analysis of the Helms-Burton Act from within Liberal International Relations Theory." *Indiana Journal of Global Legal Studies* 4 (Spring 1997): 297–354.

Fiszman, Sula. "Foreign Investment Law: Encouragement versus Restraint—Mexico, Cuba, and the Caribbean Basin Initiative." *Hastings International and Comparative Law Review* 8 (Winter 1985): 147–83.

Florentino Graupera, Francisco R. "Cuba and Germany in the 1990s: Towards a New Opening?" *Revista de Estudios Europeos* 41 (Jan.–March 1997): 19–51.

———. "Cuba y la política alemana de ayuda al desarrollo tras la unificación." *Revista de Estudios Europeos* 12 (1992): 143–57.

Fogel, Jean-François. "La transición económica en Cuba: Eludiendo los caminos europeos y asiáticos." *Encuentro de la Cultura Cubana* 6/7 (Fall/Winter 1997): 142–55.

Font, Mauricio, and Francisco León. "Cuba and Latin America: The Political Dimension." In Font, ed., *Reintegration into World Society: Cuba in International Perspective.* New York: City University of New York, in press.

———. "Friendly Prodding and Other Sources of Change in Cuba." *Social Research* 65, no. 2 (Summer 1996): 573–602.

"Foreign Investment in Cuba: A Preliminary Analysis of Cuba's New Joint Venture Law." *Law and Policy in International Business* 15 (1983): 689–710.

Foster, Frances H. "Restitution of Expropriated Property: Post-Soviet Lessons for Cuba." *Columbia Journal of Transnational Law* 34 (1996): 621–56.

Foster, Peter. *Family Spirits: The Bacardi Saga, Rum, Riches, and Revolution.* Toronto: MacFarlane, Walter & Ross, 1990.

Freer, Robert E., Jr. "Helms-Burton Myths and Reality." *Cuba in Transition* (papers and proceedings of the fifth annual meeting, Association for the Study of the Cuban Economy [ASCE], Miami, Aug. 10–12, 1995), 429–47.

Freres, Christian L. "The Role of the European Union and Its Member States in Promoting Political Change in Cuba." Paper presented at the Latin American Studies Association conference, Chicago, Sept. 24–26, 1998.

Gallo, Samuel. *Bacardí, 1862–1962.* Miami: Bacardí Co., 1962.

García Amador, Francisco. *La cuestión cubana en la OEA y la crisis del sistema interamericano.* Coral Gables, Fla.: Institute of Interamerican Studies/Graduate School of International Studies, University of Miami, 1987.

Gerke, Kinka. "The Transatlantic Rift over Cuba: The Damage Is Done." *International Spectator* 32, no. 2 (April–June 1997): 27–52.

Gierbolini, Luisette. "The Helms-Burton Act: Inconsistency with International Law and Irrationality at Their Maximum." *Journal of Transnational Law and Policy* 6 (Spring 1997): 289–321.

Giuliano, Maurizio. *El caso CEA: Intelectuales e inquisidores en Cuba. ¿Perestroika en la isla?* Miami: Universal, 1998.

———. *La transición cubana y el bloqueo norteamericano.* Santiago de Chile: Ediciones CESOC, 1997.

———. "The United States Embargo and Cuba's Foreign Relations: Missed Opportunities for Democratization." *Democratization* 5, no. 3 (Autumn 1998): 181–99.

Gorham, Richard V. "Canada and Cuba: Four and Half Decades." In Donna Rich Kaplowitz, ed., *Cuba's Ties to a Changing World,* 201–14. Boulder and London: Lynne Rienner, 1993.

———. "Canada-Cuban Relations: A Brief Overview." In H. Michael Erisman and John M. Kirk, eds., *Cuban Foreign Policy Confronts a New International Order,* 203–6. Boulder and London: Lynne Rienner, 1991.

Grabendorff, Wolf. "European Community Relations with Latin America: Policy without Illusions." *Journal of Interamerican Studies and World Affairs* 19, no. 4 (1987–88): 69–87.

———. "Germany and Latin America." In Susan Kaufman Purcell and Françoise Simon, eds., *Europe and Latin America in the World Economy,* 85–112. Boulder, Colo.: Lynne Rienner, 1994.

———. "The Relationship between the European Community and Cuba." In Donna Rich Kaplowitz, ed., *Cuba's Ties to a Changing World,* 89–116. Boulder and London: Lynne Rienner, 1993.

———. "The Relationship between the European Union and Cuba." In Joseph S. Tulchin, Andrés Serbín, and Rafael Hernández, eds., *Cuba and the Caribbean: Regional Issues and Trends in the Post–Cold War Era,* 207–42. Washington, D.C.: Latin American Program, the Woodrow Wilson International Center for Scholars, 1997.

Granell, Francesc. "Conflicto y cooperación entre Europa y EE.UU." *Política Exterior* 60, no. 11, (Nov.–Dec. 1997): 35–53.

————. "Cuba y la UE: Del encuadre latinoamericano al ACP caribeño." *Revista Española de Desarrollo y Cooperación* no. 3 (Fall–Winter 1998): 85–97.

Greenberg-Traurig Law Partners. "New U.S.-Cuba Related Law Creates Statutory Cause of Action for Confiscated Property." *Alert,* March 25, 1996.

Grenier, Guillermo, and Hugh Gladwin. *FIU Cuba Poll.* Miami: Institute for Public Opinion Research, Florida International University, 1997.

Gutiérrez, Nicholas J., Jr. "The De-Constitutionalism of Property Rights: Castro's Systematic Assault on Private Ownership in Cuba." *Yearbook of International Law* (University of Miami Law School) 5 (1996–97): 51–64.

————. "Righting Old Wrongs: A Survey of Restitution Schemes for Possible Application to a Democratic Cuba." In ASCE, *Cuba in Transition* (papers and proceedings of the sixth annual meeting, Association for the Study of the Cuban Economy, Miami, Aug. 1996), 406–24.

Haass, Richard N., ed. *Transatlantic Tensions: The United States, Europe, and Problem Countries.* Washington, D.C.: Brookings Institution, 1999.

Hagelberg, Gerry, and Tony Hannah. "Cuba's International Sugar Trade." In Alistair Hennessy and George Lambie, eds., *The Fractured Blockade: West European–Cuban Relations during the Revolution,* 137–62. London: Macmillan, 1993.

Hans, Rupinder. "The United States' Economic Embargo of Cuba: International Implications of the Cuban Liberty and Democratic Solidarity Act of 1995." *Journal of International Law and Practice* 5 (Summer 1996): 327–46.

Harper, George R. "The Helms-Burton Bill, if Enacted into Law, Would Increase the Significant Financial Risks Investors Face When They Attempt to Conduct Business in Cuba." *National Law Journal* 18, no. 11 (Nov. 20, 1995): B6.

Jatar-Hausmann, Ana Julia. "What Cuba Can Teach Russia." *Foreign Policy* 113 (Winter 1998–99): 87–103.

Hebert, Marc C. "Unilateralism as Defense Mechanism: An Overview of the Iran and Libyan Sanctions Act of 1996." *Yearbook of International Law* (University of Miami Law School) 5 (1996–97): 1–28.

Helander, Robert C. "Creditors' Rights: Claims against Cuban Confiscated Assets." In Jaime Suchlicki and Antonio Jorge, eds., *Investing in Cuba: Problems and Prospects,* 37–50. New Brunswick: Transaction, 1994.

Helms, Jesse. "What Sanctions Epidemic?" *Foreign Affairs* (Jan.–Feb. 1999): 2–8.

Hendrix, Steven E. "Tensions in Cuban Property Law." *Hastings International and Comparative Law Review* 20 (Fall 1996): 1–101.

Hennessy, Alistair. "Cuba, Western Europe and the U.S.: A Historical Overview." In Hennessy and Lambie, eds., *The Fractured Blockade: West European–Cuban Relations during the Revolution,* 11–63. London: Macmillan, 1993.

Hennessy, Alistair, and George Lambie. "Future Scenarios." In Hennessy and Lambie, eds., *The Fractured Blockade: West European–Cuban Relations during the Revolution,* 336–41. London: Macmillan, 1993.

————, eds. *The Fractured Blockade: West European–Cuban Relations during the Revolution*. London and New York: Macmillan, 1993.

Henze, Gerhard. "Agenda Item 24. Necessity of Ending the Economic, Commercial and Financial Embargo Imposed by the United States of America against Cuba. Explanation of Vote." Press release, New York, October 26, 1994.

Herd, Julia P. "The Cuban Democracy Act: Another Extraterritorial Act That Won't Work." *Brooklyn Journal of International Law* 20 (1994): 397–442.

Hernández Truyol, Berta Esperanza. "Out in Left Field: Cuba's Post–Cold War Strikeout." *Fordham International Law Journal* 18, no. 1 (Nov. 1994): 15–117.

Hoffman, Bert. "La ley Helms-Burton y sus consecuencias para cuba, Estados Unidos y Europa." Paper presented at the Latin American Studies Association conference, Chicago, September 24–26, 1998.

Horowitz, Irving Louis. "The Cuba Lobby Then and Now." *Orbis,* Fall 1998, 553–63.

Howland, P. Kimberly. "Radio Martí and the U.S.-Cuban Radio War." *Federal Communications Law Journal* 36, no. 1 (July 1984): 69–94.

Huber, Jürgen. "The Blocking Statute of the European Union." *Fordham International Law Journal* 20, no. 3 (1997): 699–716.

Huntington, Samuel. "The Erosion of American National Interests." *Foreign Affairs* 76, no. 5 (1997): 28–49.

Ibero-American Summit. "Final Declaration of the Sixth Ibero-American Summit," November 1996.

Instituto de Relaciones Europea-Latinoamericanas (IRELA). *Cuba: Apertura económica y relaciones con Europa*. Madrid, 1994.

————. *Cuba: Economic Transformation and Cooperation with the European Union*. Conference report no. 9/95. Havana, December 4–7, 1995.

————. *Cuba in Crisis: Processes and Prospects*. Dossier no. 50. September 1994.

————. *Cuba y la Unión Europea: Las dificultades del diálogo*. June 17, 1996.

————. *Europa–América Latina: Veinte años de documentos oficiales*. Madrid, 1996.

————. *Inversión extranjera directa en América Latina (Direct Investment in Latin America)*. Madrid, 1998.

————. *La posición común de la UE sobre Cuba: Debate interno, reacciones y repercusiones. Informe*. Madrid. Dec. 13, 1996.

————. "The Strengthening of the U.S. Embargo against Cuba." Papers presented at seminar held in Sitges (Barcelona, Spain), July 8–10, 1996.

Jatar-Hausmann, Ana Julia. "What Cuba Can Teach Russia." *Foreign Policy* (Winter 1998–99): 87–103.

Jenkins, Gareth. "The Effects of Extraterritorial Laws: Their Impact on External Investment in the Case of Cuba." Public Hearing on Extra-Territorial Sanctions of the Committee on External Relations of the European Parliament, June 24, 1998. Press release.

———. "Trade Relations between Britain and Cuba." In Donna Rich Kaplowitz, ed., *Cuba's Ties to a Changing World*, 117–27. Boulder and London: Lynne Rienner, 1993.

———. "Western Europe and Cuba's Development." In H. Michael Erisman and John M. Kirk, eds., *Cuban Foreign Policy Confronts a New International Order*, 183–202. Boulder and London: Lynne Rienner, 1991.

———. "Western Europe and Cuba's Development in the 1980s and 1990s." In Alistair Hennessy and George Lambie, eds., *The Fractured Blockade: West European–Cuban Relations during the Revolution*, 312–35. London: Macmillan, 1993.

Jenkins, Gareth, and Lila Haimes. *Cuba: Prospects for Reforms, Trade and Investment*. London: *The Economist*/The Economist Intelligence Unit. December 1994.

Joffe, Josef. "How America Does It." *Foreign Affairs* (Sept.–Oct. 1997): 13–27.

Johnson, Cecil. "Congress, Isn't This a Parody? Helms-Burton Law Takes Foolish Approach to International Trade." *Los Angeles Daily Journal* 109, no. 214 (Nov. 4, 1996): 6.

Jones, Kirby. *Opportunities for U.S.-Cuban Trade: A Study from Johns Hopkins University School of International Studies*. Washington: Alamar Associates, 1988.

Kaplowitz, Donna Rich. *Anatomy of a Failed Embargo: U.S. Sanctions against Cuba*. Boulder, Colo.: Lynne Rienner, 1998.

———, ed. *Cuba's Ties to a Changing World*. Boulder and London: Lynne Rienner, 1993.

Kaye, David. "The Helms-Burton Act: Title III and International Claims." *Hastings International and Comparative Law Review* 20, no. 4 (Summer 1997): 729–46.

Kelso, Robert. "Espousal: Its Use in International Law." *Arizona Journal of International and Comparative Law* 1, no. 1 (Winter 1982).

Kircher, Allen. "The Act of State Doctrine and the Antitrust Laws: Time to Retreat from Sabbatino?" *Saint Louis University Law Journal* 25, no. 4 (Oct. 1982): 867–89.

Kirk, John M. "Cuba's Canadian Connection." In H. Michael Erisman and John M. Kirk, eds., *Cuban Foreign Policy Confronts a New International Order*, 207–14. Boulder and London: Lynne Rienner, 1991.

———. "Descifrando la paradoja: La posición del Canadá respecto a Cuba." *Estudios Internacionales* 107–8 (1994): 570–85.

———. *A la redécouverte de Cuba: Cinquante annés de relations canado-cubaines*. Ottawa: Les Cahiers de FOCAL, 1997.

Kirk, John M., and Peter McKenna. *Canada-Cuba Relations: The Other Good Neighbor*. Gainesville: University of Florida Press, 1997.

Kirk, John M., Peter McKenna, Julia Sagebien, and Demetria Tsoutouras. "Canada, Mexico and Helms-Burton: The Diplomacy of Defiance." Paper presented at the 21st International Congress of the Latin American Studies Association, Chicago, September 24–26, 1998.

Kleinberg, Howard. "U.S. Should Lift Cuba Embargo, Let Castro Hang Himself." *Los Angeles Daily Journal* 106, no. 14 (Jan. 21, 1993): 6.

Kneale, John. "Tightening the U.S. Embargo: Talking Points." Paper presented at the seminar on "The Strengthening of the U.S. Embargo against Cuba." Sitges (Barcelona, Spain), July 8–10, 1996.

Krenzler, Horst G., and Gunnar Wiegand. "EU-U.S. Relations: More Than Trade Disputes?" Paper to be published in *European Foreign Affairs Review* (Leicester University) and the *SAIS Review*.

Krinsky, Michael. "U.S. Embargo of Cuba: An Overview: What Activities Are Prohibited, Permitted?" *New York Law Journal* 215, no. 33 (Feb. 20, 1996): S2.

Krinsky, Michael, and David Golove, eds. *United States Measures against Cuba: Proceedings in the United Nations and International Law Issues.* Northampton, Mass.: Aletheia Press, 1993.

Lambie, George. "Anglo-Cuban Commercial Relations in the 1960s: A Case Study of the Leyland Motor Company Contracts with Cuba." In Alistair Hennessy and George Lambie, eds., *The Fractured Blockade: West European–Cuban Relations during the Revolution,* 163–97. London: Macmillan, 1993.

———. *Cuba-European Relations: Historical Perspectives and Political Consequences.* Cuban Studies Association Occasional Papers 3, no. 4 (May 15, 1998).

———. "De Gaulle's France and the Cuban Revolution." In Alistair Hennessy and George Lambie, eds., *The Fractured Blockade: West European–Cuban Relations during the Revolution,* 197–233. London: Macmillan, 1993.

———. "Franco's Spain and the Cuban Revolution." In Alistair Hennessy and George Lambie, eds., *The Fractured Blockade: West European–Cuban Relations during the Revolution,* 234–75. London: Macmillan, 1993.

———. "Western Europe and Cuba in the 1970s: The Boom Years." In Alistair Hennessy and George Lambie, eds., *The Fractured Blockade: West European–Cuban Relations during the Revolution,* 276–311. London: Macmillan, 1993.

Lamore, Jean. *Cuba.* Paris: Presse Universitaire de France (PUF), 1970, 1997.

Leigh, Monroe. "Sabbatino's [*Banco Nacional de Cuba v. Sabbatino,* 84 S. Ct. 923 (1964)] Silver Anniversary and the *Restatement*: No Cause for Celebration." *International Lawyer* 24 (Spring 1990): 1–20.

Leiseca, Sergio A. "Foreign Investors' Property Rights and Legal Guarantees against Non-Commercial Risks in Cuba." In ASCE, *Cuba in Transition* (papers and proceedings of the sixth annual meeting, Association for the Study of the Cuban Economy, Miami, Aug. 1996), 155–62.

LeoGrande, William. "Enemies Evermore: U.S. Policy towards Cuba after Helms-Burton." *Journal of Latin American Affairs* 29, no. 1 (1997): 211–21.

———. "From Havana to Miami: U.S. Cuba Policy as a Two-Level Game." *Journal of Inter-American Studies and World Affairs* 40, no. 1 (Spring 1998): 67–86.

León, Francisco. "La negociación de la transición." *Encuentro de la Cultura Cubana* (Madrid), no. 6/7 (Fall/Winter 1997): 74–86.

Leyva de Varona, Adolfo, ed. *Propaganda and Reality: A Look at the U.S. Embargo against Castro's Cuba.* Miami: Cuban-American National Foundation, 1994.

Lisio, Stephen A. "Helms-Burton and the Point of Diminishing Returns." *International Affairs* 72, no. 4 (1996): 691–711.

Locay, Luis, and Cigdem Ural. "Restitution vs. Indemnification: Their Effects on the Pace of Privatization." In ASCE, *Cuba in Transition* (papers and proceedings of the fifth annual meeting, Association for the Study of the Cuban Economy, Miami, Aug. 10–12, 1995), 246–52.

Long, Susan. "A Challenge to the Legality of Title III of LIBERTAD and an International Response." *Indiana International and Comparative Law Review* 7, no. 2 (1997): 467–96.

Losman, Donald L. *International Economic Sanctions: The Cases of Cuba, Israel, and Rhodesia*. Albuquerque: University of New Mexico Press, 1979.

Lowe, Vaughn. "Helms Burton and EC Regulation 2271/96." *Cambridge Law Journal* 56 (July 1997): 248–50.

———. "U.S. Extraterritorial Jurisdiction: The Helms-Burton and D'Amato Acts." *International and Comparative Law Quarterly* 46 (April 1997): 378–90.

Lowenfeld, Andreas F. "The Cuban Liberty and Democratic Solidarity (Libertad) Act." *American Journal of International Law* 90, no. 3 (July 1996): 419–34.

Lucio, Saturnino E. "The Cuban Liberty and Democratic Solidarity LIBERTAD Act of 1996: An Initial Analysis." *Inter-American Law Review* (University of Miami School of Law) (Winter 1995–96): 325–42.

———. "Impact of the Helms-Burton Law (the Cuban Liberty Act) on Cuban Tourism." In ASCE, *Cuba in Transition* (papers and proceedings of the seventh annual meeting of the Association for the Study of the Cuban Economy, August 8–10, 1997), 131–36.

Luzarraga, Alberto. "Castro Must Open Regime before U.S. Opens to Cuba." *New York Law Journal* 215, no. 33 (Feb. 20, 1996): S1.

———. "Castro's Self-Imposed Embargo." *New York Law Journal* 214, no. 118 (Dec. 20, 1995): 2.

MacDonald, Scott. "Cuba's Relations with Europe and Canada: Accommodation and Challenges." In Fauriol and Looser, *Cuba: The International Dimension*, 233–54.

Mack, Jonathan. "Constitutional Law—Grandfather Clause in International Emergency Economic Powers Act Permits the President to Ban Travel to Cuba without Declaring an Emergency." *Vanderbilt Journal of Transnational Law* 17, no. 4 (Fall 1984): 977–93.

Maier, Harold G. "Extraterritorial Jurisdiction and the Cuban Democracy Act." *Florida Journal of International Law* 8 (Fall 1993): 391–400."

———. "Making Cuba Pay: Satisfaction of Nationalization Claims against Cuba: *First National City Bank v. Banco para el Comercio Exterior de Cuba* [103 S. Ct. 2591]." *Brooklyn Journal of International Law* 10 (Summer 1984): 515–42.

Mallett, Nick. "The Application in the United Kingdom of the Cuban Liberty and Democratic Solidarity Act (Libertad) Act of 1996." Paper presented at the seminar on "The Strengthening of the U.S. Embargo Against Cuba." Sitges (Barcelona, Spain), July 8–10, 1996.

Marcus, Noreen. "Attorneys Capitalize on Anti-Castro Law: Helms-Burton Sparks Suits." *Legal Times* 18, no. 47 (April 8, 1996): 2.

McKenna, Peter, and John Kirk. "Canada and Helms-Burton: The Politics of Extraterritoriality." Paper presented at the 21st International Congress of the Latin American Studies Assn., Chicago, Sept. 24–26, 1998.

Meron, Theodor, and Detlev F. Vagts. "The Helms-Burton Act: Exercising the Presidential Option." *American Journal of International Law* 91, no. 1 (Jan. 1997): 83–84.

Mesa Lago, Carmelo. *Are Economic Reforms Propelling Cuba to the Market?* Coral Gables, Fla.: North-South Center, University of Miami, 1994.

Mesa Lago, Carmelo, and June S. Belkin. *Cuba in Africa.* Pittsburgh: University of Pittsburgh Press, 1982.

Messina, William A. "Agriculture and Cuba's Reintegration into the Global Economy." Paper presented at the symposium on Cuba, City University of New York, September 28, 1998.

Mexico. "Posición de México sobre la 'Ley Helms-Burton' y la cuestión de Cuba" [Position Taken by Mexico on the Helms-Burton Law and the Question of Cuba]. Press release, Secretaría de Relaciones Exteriores, August 28, 1996.

———. Press release, August 28, 1996. Official text in English published in the *Hastings International and Comparative Law Review* 10, no. 4 (Spring 1997): 809–14.

———. Resolution of Congress, May 29, 1996.

Michalec, Laura A. "Trade with Cuba under the Trading with the Enemy Act: A Free Flow of Ideas and Information?" *Fordham International Law Journal* 15 (1991–92): 808–38.

Migdall, Carl. "Mexico, Cuba, and the United States: Myth Versus Reality." In Donna Rich Kaplowitz, ed., *Cuba's Ties to a Changing World*, 201–14. Boulder and London: Lynne Rienner, 1993

Miller, Mark M., and Tony L. Henthorne. *Investment in the New Cuban Tourist Industry.* Westport, Conn.: Quorum Books, 1997.

Moncarz, Raul, and Leonardo Rodríguez. "Cuba: An Economy in Transition?" *Florida Journal of International Law* 9 (Fall 1994): 401–20.

Montaner, Carlos Alberto. *Cuba hoy: La lenta muerta del castrismo.* Miami: Universal, 1996.

Morici, Peter. "The United States, World Trade, and the Helms-Burton Act." *Current History* 96, no. 607: 87–88.

Moss, Ambler. "Vino nuevo en cueros nuevos: Buscando fórmulas para una política nueva hacia Cuba." Paper presented at the symposium on "Una nueva política hacia Cuba." Fundación Diálogos, Madrid, Nov. 20–21, 1996.

Mujal-León, Eusebio, and Jorge Saavedra. "El postotalitarismo carismático y el cambio de régimen: Cuba en perspectiva comparada." *Encuentro de la Cultura Cubana* 6/7 (Fall/Winter 1997): 115–23.

Müller, Jorg Paul, and Thomas Cottier. "Estoppel." In Rudolf Bernhardt, ed., *Encyclopedia of Public International Law*, 116. Amsterdam / New York: North-Holland Publishing / Max Planck Institute for Comparative Public Law and International Law.

Muse, Robert L. "The Ins and Outs of the Helms-Burton Act: Implications for Canadian and United States Business. Helms-Burton and International Business: Legal and Commercial Implications." The House of Commons of Canada, Standing Committee on Foreign Affairs and International Trade, hearing on Foreign Extraterritorial Measures Act, remarks. Ottawa, September 26, 1996.

————. "Legal and Practical Implications of Title III of the Helms-Burton Law." Presented at the seminar on "The Strengthening of the U.S. Embargo against Cuba." Sitges (Barcelona, Spain), July 8–10, 1996.

————. "The Libertad Act: Implementation and International Law." Hearing before the Subcommittee on Western Hemisphere and Peace Corps Affairs of the Senate Committee on Foreign Relations, prepared statement, 104th Congress 62 (1996): 62–76.

————. "The Nationality of Claims Principle of Public International Law and the Helms-Burton Act." *Hastings International and Comparative Law Review* 20, no. 4 (Summer 1997): 777–98.

————. "A Public Law International Critique of the Extraterritorial Jurisdiction of the Helms-Burton Act (Cuban Liberty and Democratic Solidarity [Libertad] Act of 1996)." *George Washington University Journal of International Law and Economics* 30, nos. 2–3 (1996–97): 205–70.

Nuccio, Richard. "Cuba: A U.S. Perspective." Paper presented to the conference on "Transatlantic Tensions: The Challenge of Difficult Countries," Brookings Institution, Washington, D.C., March 9–10, 1998. In Richard N. Haass, ed., *Transatlantic Tensions: The United States, Europe, and Problem Countries*, 7–28. Washington, D.C.: Brookings Institution, 1999.

Nuttall, Simon J. *European Political Co-operation.* Oxford: Clarendon Press, 1992.

O'Brien, Janet L. "Beyond Sabbatino: The Exception That Consumes the Rule?" *University of Toledo Law Review* 17, no. 1 (Fall 1985): 295–312.

Ondetti, Gabriel A. "Western European and Canadian Relations with Cuba after the Cold War." Cuba Briefing Paper Series no. 9. Washington, D.C.: Georgetown University, Center for Latin American Studies, November 1995.

Oppenheimer, Andrés. *Castro's Final Hour: The Secret Story behind the Coming Downfall of Communist Cuba.* New York: Simon and Schuster, 1992.

Organization for Economic Cooperation and Development (OECD). "Multilateral Agreement Investment: Consolidated Text." Paris: OECD, 1998.

Organization of American States (OAS). Opinion of the Inter-American Juridical Committee following the mandate of the Resolution AG/DOC.337/96 of the General Assembly of the Organization of American States, titled "Freedom of Trade and Investment in the Hemisphere." August 23, 1996.

————. Resolution of the General Assembly of the OAS (June 1996), on the Opinion of the Interamerican Judicial Committee (August 1996).

Pagan, María L. "U.S. Legal Requirements Affecting Trade with Cuba." *Tulsa Journal of Comparative and International Law* 2 (Spring 1995): 289–317.

Peña, Lázaro. "El comercio bilateral Cuba-España y sus afectaciones luego del ingreso de España a la comunidad económica Europea." *Temas de la Economía Mundial* 24 (1988): 7–55.

Perera Gómez, Eduardo. "Cuba and the European Union: Factors of Stagnation." *Revista de Estudios Europeos* 40 (Oct.–Dec. 1996): 78–116.

———. "Cuba en la política exterior de Francia." *Revista de Estudios Europeos* 12 (1989): 91–118.

Pérez, Louis A. "Between Meanings and Memories of 1898." *Orbis,* Fall 1998, 501–16.

Pérez-López, Jorge F. "Foreign Direct Investment in the Cuban Economy: A Critical Outlook." Paper presented at the symposium on Cuba, City University of New York, September 28, 1998.

———. "Foreign Investment in Socialist Cuba: Significance and Prospects." *Studies in Comparative International Development* 31, no. 4 (Winter 1996–97): 3–28.

Pérez-Stable, Marifeli. "Democracia y soberanía: La nueva Cuba a la luz de su pasado." *Encuentro de la Cultura Cubana* 6/7 (Fall–Winter 1997): 189–99.

Porotsky, Richard D. "Economic Coercion and the General Assembly: A Post–Cold War Assessment of the Legality and Utility of the Thirty-Five-Year-Old Embargo against Cuba." *Vanderbilt Journal of International Law* 28, no. 4 (Oct. 1995): 901–58.

Powell, Charles. "La transición política española (y su posible interés como modelo para la cubana)." *Encuentro de la Cultura Cubana* 6/7 (Fall–Winter 1997): 87–100.

Purcell, Susan Kaufman. "U.S. Policy toward Cuba: Has the Time Come to Lift the Trade Embargo?" *Focus Americas,* Nov. 1995, 5–7.

Purcell, Susan Kaufman, and Françoise Simon, eds. *Europe and Latin America in the World Economy.* Boulder, Colo.: Lynne Rienner, 1994.

Quickendon, Christine L. "Helms-Burton and Canadian-American Relations at the Crossroads: The Need for an Effective, Bilateral Cuban Policy." *American University Journal of International Law and Policy* 12, no. 4 (1997): 733–67.

"Radio Martí: Meeting on the Need for Uncensored Information in Cuba." *New York University Journal of International Law and Politics* 19 (Winter 1987): 433–55.

Radu, Michael. "Don't Reward Castro, Keep the Embargo." *Orbis,* Fall 1998, 545–52.

Ratchik, Jonathan R. "Cuban Liberty and the Democratic Solidarity Act of 1995." *American University Journal of International Law and Policy* 11 (1996): 343–73.

Reiff, David. "Cuba Refrozen." *Foreign Affairs* 75 (July–August 1996): 73–83.

Reinicke, Wolfgang H. "Global Public Policy." *Foreign Affairs* 76, no. 6 (Nov.–Dec. 1997): 131.

Remiro Brotons, Antonio. "Cuba, las amistades peligrosas." *Política Exterior* 55, no. 15 (Jan.–Feb. 1997): 5–20.

Restrepo, Daniel A. "Helms-Burton: The Political Context." In IRELA, "The Strengthening of the U.S. Embargo against Cuba," 1996.

Rio Group. "Declaration of the Tenth Summit of the Rio Group," September 1996.
————. Final Declaration of the Summit held in La Paz, Bolivia, September 1996. Press release.
Robaina, Roberto. Intervención ante el 51 Período de Sesiones de la Asamblea General de las Naciones Unidas, New York, Sept. 30, 1996. Archivo Central, Ministerio de Relaciones Exteriores, Havana.
————. Intervención ante las Comisiones de Relaciones Exteriores y Cooperación y Desarrollo y la Delegación de México, Cuba y América Central del Parlamento Europeo. Havana: Ministerio de Relaciones Exteriores, Oficinas del Ministro, 1998.
Rodríguez, José Luis. "Economic Relations between Western Europe and Cuba since 1959." In Alistair Hennessy and George Lambie, eds., *The Fractured Blockade: West European–Cuban Relations during the Revolution,* 100–115. London: Macmillan, 1993.
Roque Valdés, Nelson. "Italian-Cuban Relations in the 1990s." *Revista de Estudios Europeos* 42 (April–June 1997): 69–85.
Ross, Susan Kohn, and John W. Shi. "Sovereignty Matters: The Expanded Embargo against Cuba." *Los Angeles Daily Journal* 109, no. 185 (Sept. 24, 1996): 7.
Roy, Joaquín. "Auge y caída de la ley Helms-Burton." *Leviatán* (Madrid) 68 (Summer 1997): 33–42; *Archivos del Presente* (Buenos Aires) (April–June 1997): 117–30; *Encuentro ed la Cultura Cubana* (Madrid) 4/5 (Spring–Summer 1997): 68–77.
————. "Consecuencias internacionales de la ley Helms-Burton." *Estudios Internacionales* (University of Chile, Santiago) 30, no. 118 (April–June 1997): 117–94.
————. "Cuba: Des inconnues pour l'avenir." *L'Espagne et l'Amérique Latine, Documentation Française* (Paris) no. 595 (Nov. 11, 1988): 24–28.
————. *Cuba y España: Relaciones y percepciones.* Madrid: Biblioteca Cubana Contemporánea, 1988.
————. "España, la Unión Europea y Cuba: La evolución de una relación especial a una política de gestos y de presión." Occasional paper. Miami: University of Miami, Cuban Studies Association, 1996.
————. "España y Cuba: Una relación muy especial." *Revista Afers Internacionals* (Barcelona) no. 31 (1996): 147–66.
————. "España y Cuba: Una relación muy especial." In Joaquín Roy and Juan Antonio March, eds., *El espacio iberoamericano: Dimensiones y percepciones de la relación especial entre España y América Latina,* 185–227. Miami / Barcelona: Instituto de Estudios Ibéricos / Centro de Estudios Internacionales, 1996.
————. "European Alternatives to the Helms-Burton Law." *Collegium* (College of Europe, Bruges, Belgium) 10, no. 3 (1998): 3–7.
————. "Europe: Cuba, the U.S. Embargo, and the Helms-Burton Law." In Richard N. Haass, ed., *Trans-Atlantic Tensions: The United States, Europe, and Problem Countries,* 29–47 Washington, D.C.: Brookings Institution, 1999.
————. "The Helms-Burton Law: Development, Consequences, and Legacy for

Inter-American and U.S.-European Relations." *Journal of Inter-American Studies and World Affairs* 39, no. 3 (Fall 1997): 77–108.

———. "The Helms-Burton Law: EU's Perceptions and Reaction." *European Union Review* (Associazione Universitaria di Studi Europei, University of Pavia, Italy) 3, no. 2 (1998): 29–50.

———. "El impacto de la ley Helms-Burton en la Unión Europea y España." *Papel Político* (Universidad Javeriana, Bogotá) no. 6 (Nov. 1997): 61–90.

———. "La ley Helms-Burton: Desarrollo y consecuencias para las relaciones interamericanas y europeas." *Relaciones Internacionales* (Universidad Autónoma de México) no. 74 (May–August 1997): 89–107.

———. "La ley Helms-Burton: Origen, desarrollo y consecuencias para las relaciones internacionales." *Revista de Derecho Comunitario* (Universidad de Salamanca) 1, no. 2 (July–Dec. 1997): 487–510.

———. "Origen, desarrollo y consecuencias de la ley Helms-Burton." In *Anuario Iberoamericano '96*, 439–47. Madrid: EFE, 1997.

———. "El regreso al triángulo: La ley Helms-Burton." In Roy, *La siempre fiel: Un siglo de relaciones hispanocubanas (1898–1998)*, 137–66. Madrid: Instituto Universitario de Cooperación y Desarrollo, Universidad Complutense de Madrid / Los Libros de la Catarata, 1999.

———. "Las relaciones actuales entre Cuba y España." *Política Exterior* 1, no. 3 (Summer 1987): 282–86.

———. "Las relaciones actuales entre Cuba y España." *Afers Internacionals* (Barcelona) no. 12–13 (1988): 5–19.

———. "Las relaciones Madrid–La Habana." *Política Exterior* 2, no. 6 (Spring 1988): 275–79.

———. "Lawyers Meet the Law: Criticial U.S. Voices of Helms-Burton." *International and Comparative Law Review*, in press, 1999.

———. "Relaciones y percepciones entre España y Cuba: Trasfondo de la 'Crisis de las embajadas.'" In Carlos Robles Piquer, ed., *Cuba 1990: Realidad y futuro*, 27–47. Santiago de Compostela: Fundación Alfredo Brañas, 1991.

———. "Spain and Cuba: A Special Relationship." In Roy and Galinsoga, eds., *The Ibero-American Space*, 205–65.

———. "Spain's Relations with Cuba: One Hundred Years after 1898." In Mauricio Font, ed., *Reintegration into World Society: Cuba in International Perspective*. New York: City University of New York, Cuban Project, in press, 1999.

———. "La Unión Europea y España ante la ley Helms-Burton." *Ibero-Amerikanisches Archiv* (Ibero-Amerikanisch Institut, Berlin) 24 (1998): 213–45.

———, and Albert Galinsoga, eds. *The Ibero-American Space: Dimensions and Perceptions of the Special Relationship between Spain and Latin America.* Miami/Lleida: University of Miami/University of Lleida, 1997.

———, and Juan Antonio March, eds. *El espacio iberoamericano: dimensiones y percepciones de la relación especial entre España y América Latina.* Miami/Barcelona: Instituto de Estudios Ibéricos/Centro de Estudios Internacionales, 1996.

Ruiz Bravo, Hernán de Jesús, and Manuel Morán Murillo. "La Ley Helms-Burton: Líneas de acción para contrarrestar sus efectos extraterritoriales." Paper presented to the seminar on "El refuerzo del embargo de EE.UU. contra Cuba," Sitges (Barcelona, Spain), July 8–10, 1996.

Sahagún, Felipe. "Cuba: Un asunto interno español." *Meridiano CERI* (Madrid, Centro Español de Relaciones Internacionales), August 1996, 4–9.

Salinas, José O. "Radio Martí: Meeting the Need for Uncensored Information in Cuba." *New York University Journal of International Law and Politics* 19, no. 2 (Winter 1987): 433–55.

Scherlen, Renee G. "The Politics of Helms-Burton: Explaining a Cold War Policy in the Post–Cold War Era," Paper presented at the International Studies Association annual convention, March 17–21, 1998.

Schild, Georg. "Tensions in American Foreign Policy between President and Congress," *Aussenpolitik*, 49, no. 4 (1998): 56–66.

Schoultz, Lars. *Beneath the United States: A History of the U.S. Policy toward Latin America*. Cambridge: Harvard University Press, 1998.

Schwab, Peter. *Cuba: Confronting the U.S. Embargo*. New York: St. Martin's Press, 1999.

Shelzi, María. "Making Cuba Pay: Satisfaction of Nationalization Claims against Cuba." *Brooklyn Journal of International Law* 10, no. 2 (Summer 1984): 515–42.

Shifter, Michael. "United States–Latin American Relations: Shunted to the Slow Track." *Current History* 97, no. 616 (Feb. 1998): 49–54.

Shneyer, Paul A., and Virginia Barta. "The Legality of the U.S. Economic Blockade of Cuba under International Law." *Case Western Reserve Journal of International Law* 13 (Summer 1981): 451–82.

Silverson, Kyle A. "Act of Sate Doctrine: Determining Its Viability in a Suit Involving an Expropriation by Cuba of Foreign-owned Assets." *Lawyer of the Americas* 14, no. 2 (Fall 1982): 337–53.

Sistema Económico de América Latina (SELA), Secretaría Permanente. *Implicaciones jurídicas y económicas de la Ley Helms-Burton*. Report of the Secretariat presented to the 22d Latin American Council, Montevideo, October 1996.

Smagula, John W. "Redirecting Focus: Justifying the U.S. Embargo against Cuba and Resolving the Stalemate." *North Carolina Journal of International Law and Commercial Regulation* 21 (Fall 1995): 65–109.

Smith, Wayne S. *The Closest of the Enemies*. New York: W. W. Norton, 1987.

———. *Cuba after the Cold War: What Should U.S. Policy Be?* Washington, D.C.: Center for International Policy (CIP), March 1993.

———. "Cuba's Long Reform." *Foreign Affairs* 75, no. 2 (March–April 1996): 99–112.

———. "The Helms-Burton Law: Danger Signal for the Future." Paper presented at the seminar "The Strengthening of the U.S. Embargo against Cuba," Sitges (Barcelona, Spain), July 8–10, 1996.

———. *Our Cuba Diplomacy: A Critical Reexamination.* Washington, D.C.: Center for International Policy (CIP), October 1994.

———. "Our Dysfunctional Cuban Embargo." *Orbis,* Fall 1998, 533–44.

———. "Shackled to the Past: The United States and Cuba." *Current History* 95, no. 598 (Feb. 1996): 50–54.

———. *The Travel Ban to Cuba.* Washington, D.C.: Center for International Policy, May 1994.

———. "The U.S.-Cuba Imbroglio: Anatomy of a Crisis." *International Policy Report,* May 1996.

———. "Waving the Big Stick: The Helms-Burton Affair." *NACLA Report on the Americas* 31, no. 2 (1997): 27.

Solís, Anthony M. "The Long Arm of U.S. Law: The Helms-Burton Act." *Loyola of Los Angeles International and Comparative Law Journal* 19, no. 3 (1997): 709–41.

Sorel, Julián B. *Nacionalismo y revolución en Cuba (1823–1998).* Madrid: Fundación Liberal José Martí, 1999.

Stoner, Lynn. "Recent Literature on Cuba and the United States." *Latin American Research Review* 31, no. 3 (1996): 235.

Suchlicki, Jaime. "The US Embargo of Cuba: Important Considerations." CSA Documents Series no. 3, Cuban Studies Association, University of Miami, March 1, 1998.

———, and Antonio Jorge, eds. *Investing in Cuba: Problems and Prospects.* New Brunswick, N.J.: Transaction Publishers, 1994.

Sumner, Bret A. "Due Process and True Conflicts: The Constitutional Limits on Extraterritorial Federal Legislation and the Cuban Liberty and Democratic Solidarity LIBERTAD Act of 1996." *Catholic University Law Review* 46 (Spring 1997): 907–61.

Torres Hurtado, Nicolás, and José Limia González. *Orígenes de la Compañia Ron Bacardí.* Santiago de Cuba: Editorial Oriente, 1982.

Torres Macchiavello, María Soledad. "Antecedentes de la ley Helms-Burton." *Diplomacia* no. 71 (Dec. 1996): 54–66.

"Trading with Cuba: The Cuban Democracy Act and Export Rules." Symposium. *Florida Journal of International Law* 8 (Fall 1993): 335–446.

Travieso-Díaz, Matías F. "Estado actual de la implementación de la 'Cuban Liberty and Democractic Solidarity LIBERTAD Act of 1996' y posibles efectos del Acuerdo EE.UU/U.E. de mayo de 1998." Paper presented to the seminar "Cuba: Nuevas perspectivas tras el acuerdo sobre la Ley Helms y el relajamiento del embargo," Cuba Negocios, Madrid, July 3, 1998.

———. *The Laws and Legal System of a Free-Market Cuba: A Prospectus for Business.* Westport, Conn.: Quorum Books, 1997.

———. "Some Legal and Practical Issues in the Resolution of Cuban Nationals' Expropriation Claims against Cuba." *University of Pennsylvania Journal of International Business Law* 16 (Summer 1995): 217–58.

Travieso-Díaz, Matías F., and Steven R. Escobar. "Cuba's Transition to a Free-Market Democracy: A Survey of Required Changes to Laws and Legal Institutions."

Duke Journal of Comparative and International Law 5, no. 2 (Spring 1995): 379–421.

Travieso-Díaz, Matías F., and Alejandro Ferraté. "Recommended Features of a Foreign Investment Code for Cuba's Free-Market Transition." In ASCE, *Cuba in Transition* (papers and proceedings of the fifth annual meeting, Association for the Study of the Cuban Economy, Miami, Aug. 10–12, 1995), 207–26; reprinted in the *North Carolina Journal of International Law and Commercial Regulation* 21 (Summer 1996): 511–60.

Tulchin, Joseph S., Andrés Serbín, and Rafael Hernández, eds. *Cuba and the Caribbean: Regional Issues and Trends in the Post–Cold War Era.* Washington, D.C.: Latin American Program, the Woodrow Wilson International Center for Scholars, 1997.

United Kingdom. "Protection of Trading Interests (U.S. Cuban Assets Control Regulations) Order," No. 2449, Oct. 14, 1992. Press release.

U.S. Congress. "Cuban Liberty and Democratic Solidarity (LIBERTAD) Act of 1995." Pub. L. 104–114, March 12, 1996; 110 Stat. 785. 22 U.S.C. [Sections] 6021–6091, 16431; 28 U.S.C.

———. *Cuba Liberty and Democratic Solidarity (Libertad) Act of 1996.* Pub I No. 104–14, 110 Stat. 785 (1996).

U.S. Congress. House of Representatives. Subcommittee on International Policy and Trade, Hearing, March 12, 1998.

U.S. Congress. Senate. Committee on Foreign Relations and the Committee on International Relations of the U.S. House of Representatives. *Cuba at the Crossroads: The Visit of Pope John Paul II and Opportunities for U.S. Policy.* Washington, D.C., March 1998.

U.S. Congress. Subcommittee on Western Hemisphere and Peace Corps Affairs of the Senate Committee on Foreign Relations. "Cuban Liberty and Democratic Solidarity Act: Hearings." 104th Cong., 1st sess., 1995.

Vázquez Díaz, René. "La extraña situación de Cuba." *Encuentro de la Cultura Cubana* (Madrid) 6/7 (Fall–Winter 1997): 46–51.

Vázquez Montalbán, Manuel. *Y Dios entró en La Habana.* Madrid: Aguilar/El País, 1998.

Vera, Esther, and Josep M. Colomer. "El nacional-catolicismo de Fidel Castro." *Claves de la Razón Práctica* (Madrid), 81, April 1998, 14–19.

Viñas, Angel. "La Unión Europea y Cuba: Historia de una acción de estrategia exterior en la post guerra fría." In Teodoro Flores Gómez, ed., *Temas de economía internacional: Volumen de homenaje a Rafael de Juan y Peñalosa,* 311–59. Bilbao: Universidad del País Vasco, 1996.

Warner, Mark A. A. "Cutting Ourselves on Cuban Politics." *Legal Times* 18, no. 43 (March 11, 1996): 26.

Watson, Alexander. "The Cuban Democracy Act: One Year Later." Foreign Affairs Committee of the House of Representatives, November 18, 1993, *U.S. Department of State Dispatch,* December 6, 1993.

Welke, Brian J. "GATT and NAFTA v. the Helms-Burton Act: Has the United States Violated Multilateral Agreements?" *Tulsa Journal of Comparative and International Law* 4 (Spring 1997): 361–78.

Werlau, María C. "Foreign Investment in Cuba: The Limits of Commercial Engagement." In ASCE, *Cuba in Transition* (papers and proceedings of the sixth annual meeting, Association for the Study of the Cuban Economy, Miami, Aug. 1996), 456–95.

Wilner, Gabriel M. "International Reaction to the Cuban Democracy Act." *Florida Journal of International Law* 8 (Fall 1993): 401–14.

Wolf, Manfred. "Hitting the Wrong Guys: External Consequences of the Cuban Democracy Act." *Florida Journal of International Law* 8 (Fall 1993): 415–20.

Wong, Kam S. "The Cuba Democracy Act of 1992: The Extraterritorial Scope of Section 1706(a)." *University of Pennsylvania Journal of International Business Law* 14, no. 4 (Winter 1994): 651–82.

World Trade Organization. Declaration of the Council of Mercantilism (March 1996) and of the General Council of the World Commerce Organization (April 1996). Establishment of the Special Group about the Law on the Panel of Solution of Differences of the WTO, a Petition of the EU (Nov. 1996).

Yáñez-Barnuevo, Luis. "Cuba en la década de los noventa." *Encuentro de la Cultura Cubana* 6/7 (Fall–Winter 1997): 44–45.

Yoo, John. "Federal Courts as Weapons of Foreign Policy: The Case of the Helms-Burton Act." *Hastings International and Comparative Law Review* 20, no. 4 (Summer 1997): 747–76.

Zimbalist, Andrew. "Dateline Cuba: Hanging On in Havana." *Foreign Policy* no. 92 (Fall 1993): 151–67.

Zipper, Arnold M. "Toward the Termination of Licensed U.S. Foreign Subsidiary Trade with Cuba: The Legal and Political Obstacles." *Law and Policy in International Business* 23, no. 4 (1992): 1045–69.

INDEX

ABC (newspaper), 119
ACS (Association of Caribbean States), 97, 163
Adams, John Quincy, 42
advertisements, in Mexico, 94
African-Caribbean-Pacific (ACP) group, 97, 107, 168, 169, 170, 190, 198
aging, 190
agriculture, 10, 12, 15, 179
airplanes: Concorde's visit, 164; shot down, 2, 19, 30–31, 102, 116, 188. *See also* Iberia Airlines
ALADI (Asociación Latinoamericana de Integración), 96, 189–90
Alarcón, Ricardo: on CDA, 27; on compensation for expropriation, 48; H-B denounced by, 44, 45, 103; Mas Canosa's debate with, 204; on new hardline efforts, 169; on 1998 compromise, 155; on 1999 proposal, 194, 238n.57
Albania, on embargo, 102
Albright, Madeleine, 39–40, 148, 156
Alcatel (company), 111
Alemán, Arnoldo, 95
Algeria, independence of, 110
Allende, Isabel, 169
Almunia, Joaquín, 157
Altozano, Hermenegildo, 74
Álvarez-Mena, Sergio, 70, 72–73
American Bar Association, 53
American Journal of International Law, 62, 176
American Law Institute, 24, 64, 69

American Sugar Bill (1960), 10
American Sugar (company), 15
Angolan civil war, Cuba in, 11, 19, 110
annexation, suspicions of, 44
Ardanza, José Antonio, 137
Argentaria (company), 165, 166
Argentina: Cuba's relations with, 109, 158, 189; on embargo, 103; investments in, 165; visit to, by Juan Carlos, 132
Arias, Ricardo Alberto, 96
Arthur, Owen, 163
ASCE (Association for the Study of the Cuban Economy), 29–30, 49
Asociación Latinoamericana de Integración (ALADI), 96, 189–90
Associated Press, 40
Association for the Study of the Cuban Economy (ASCE), 29–30, 49
Association of Caribbean States (ACS), 97, 163
Atlantic Council, 27
Australia: on embargo, 103; investment by, 14
Axworthy, Lloyd, 87
Aznar, José María: ambassador's appointment and, 157; Castro pressured by, 140–41, 145, 148, 160; Castro's name for, 132, 140; conservatism of, 134; criticism of, 143; E.U. relations and, 150; PSOE and, 139, 145–46

Bacardí, Emilio, 205
Bacardí, Facundo, 205

Bacardí company: concerns of, 54–56; description of, 205–6; expropriation of assets of, 52–53
Bacardí Moreau, José, 205
Bacardí y Masó, Facundo, 205
banana market, 179
Banco de Bilbao-Vizcaya (BBV), 165, 166
Banco Nacional de Cuba v. Sabbatino, 75
Bangor Punta Company, 15
Barbados: Castro's visit to, 169–70; Cuban investment of, 171; Cuban links with, 163; Ros-Lehtinen's proposal and, 98
Barrios, Cristina, 226n.59
baseball, cultural exchanges in, 195
BASF (company), 112
Basulto, José, 236n.10
BAT (company), 161
Bayer (company), 112
Bay of Pigs invasion, 9, 10
BBV (Banco de Bilbao-Vizcaya), 165, 166
Belgium: Common Position and, 123; on 1998 compromise, 153
Benedí, Claudio, 228n.18
Benetton (company), 112
Bermuda, Bacardí company incorporated in, 54
Bernell, David, 186, 187
Berrios, Rubén, 97
Beta Gran Caribe (company), 161
Betancourt, Ernesto F., 29–30, 65–66
Bingaman, Jeff, 32
blockade, use of term, 221n.38. *See also* embargo
BM (company), 115
Boeing (company), 107
Bonne, Félix, 195
Bonsor, Nicholas, 109
Borbón, Juan Carlos de, 47
Borotra, Franck, 110
Borrell, Josep, 146, 157–58
Bosch, Pepín, 206
Bow Valley Industries, 161
Brazil: on embargo, 103; investments in, 165
British Airways, 164
British Borneo Petroleum (company), 109
Brittan, Leon: 1997 compromise and, 5, 127, 128; 1998 compromise and, 153,

185; "side letter" of, 227n.15
Brookings Institution, 154
Brothers to the Rescue, planes shot down by Cuba, 2, 19, 30–31, 102, 116, 188
Buñuel, Luis, 185–86, 189
Burns, Nicholas, 89
Burton, Dan: biographical sketch of, 205; H-B introduced by, 29–30, 32; H-B's legacy for, 160; on 1997 compromise, 128; on 1999 proposal, 194
Bush, George H., 18, 26, 42, 136
Bush, Jeb, 188
businesses (Cuba): increase in, 17–18; registered brands of expropriated, 55–56; U.S.-owned, 49–50. *See also* foreign investment (in Cuba); tourism (Cuba); *specific companies*
Byrne, Brendan, 204

caballerito, use of term, 132, 140
Cable News Network (CNN), 40, 149
Cabrera Infante, Guillermo, 149
Campbell, Kim, 26, 89–90
Canada: autonomy of, 187; blocking statute and, 122, 138; confrontation by, 88–90; coordinated action in NAFTA, 91–93, 94; criticism of, 32; Cuban relations with, 158, 176, 181, 189; Cuban tourism and, 18, 90; Cuban trade with, 17, 85–87, 90, 108; diplomatic and legal motions by, 87–88; on embargo, 103; foreign investment by, 12, 14; H-B criticized by, xi, 2, 7, 9, 86, 87; H-B's legacy for, 159; international position of, 90; on 1997 compromise, 128; on 1999 proposal, 194; reaction to H-B, 31, 58; response to CDA, 26; visa issues and, 71, 88–89, 164–65
CANF. *See* Cuban-American National Foundation (CANF)
Cárdenas, José, 128
Caribbean Basin: Castro's tour of, 169–70; Cuban trade in, 161–64; Cuba's current role in, 184; nationalism in, 183; reaction to H-B, 97–98; Ros-Lehtinen's proposals and, 98, 163–64. *See also specific countries*

Caribbean Council for Europe, 163
CARICOM (Caribbean Community and
Common Market): Cuban links to, 97,
190; Cuba's membership in, 163–64;
proposed sanctions against, 97–98;
reaction to H-B, 31
CARIFORUM (Caribbean Forum), 161–64,
170
Carnival Cruise Line, 220n.23
Carter, Jimmy, xi, 4, 11, 58
Castañeda, Rolando, 49–50
Castilla, Octavio, 170–71
Castro, Fidel: accusations against, 35, 51;
ambassador's appointment and, 157;
apology of, 150; attitudes toward, xiv,
20–21, 136, 195; on Aznar, 132, 140; on
Caribbean politics, 170; clothing of, 140;
communications of, 95, 169; compadres
of, 191–92; on compromises, 155, 168;
cooperation aid agreement and, 116–17;
on elections, 140; on 1492 discovery,
132; Franco's relations with, 131; H-B as
positive for, 29–30, 41, 58–59, 65–66,
81, 100, 173; H-B's legacy for, 146–47,
159; on investment, 190; photo op for,
164, 231n.90; recommendations for
dealing with, 46–47, 81–82; on
Revolution, 192; survival of, xiii, xv, 18,
47, 74, 101, 147, 174, 182–83; on
trademark issues, 56; travel of, 110, 114,
132, 139, 166, 169–70, 193; UN speech
of, 102; Vatican efforts and, 156; in
Who's Who, 196
Castro, Raúl, 46–47, 149, 191
Catholic Church: on dissidents' trials, 195;
on 1999 proposal, 194; pope's visit and,
3, 114–15, 140, 149–50, 172, 180;
reassessment of, 183; Spanish-Cuban
relations and, 131; U.S.-Cuban relations
and, 155–58
CDA. See Cuban Democracy Act (CDA,
1992)
Cementos Mexicanos (CEMEX), 93, 94
Central Bank of Cuba, 124
Centro de Estudios sobre América (CEA), 99
Cervantes Prize, 149
Chávez, Hugo (Venezuela's president), 193

Cheysson, Claude, 110
Chile: Cuban relations with, 189; investments in, 165; reaction to H-B, 98–99
China. See People's Republic of China
Chirac, Jacques, 110, 189, 193
Chrétien, Jean, 181
Cigar Aficionado (magazine, U.S.), 193,
238n.57
citizenship: Cuba's perspective on, 100–
101; definitions of, 51–54, 62–63, 70;
estoppel principle and, 67–70; H-B's
impact on, 113–14; legal opinion on, 65–
67; nationality of claims principle and,
67; reinstatement of, 47–48; waiting
period and, 70
Clagett, Brice, 63, 65, 69, 70, 76
Clinton, Bill: aid offered by, 147;
"calibrated response" of, 60, 73;
contradictory actions of, 178; criticism
of, 109; on Cuban policy, 125, 126;
Cuban response to, 101; downed planes
and, 30–31; H-B and, 1, 5, 34, 152, 160;
impeachment proceedings against, 160;
motivation of, 5, 18, 26; 1999 proposal
of, 193–95; Title III suspended by, xiii, 3,
17, 31, 56–57, 61, 70–71, 79, 80, 101,
114, 119, 125, 127, 129. See also Helms-
Burton Law (H-B)
CNN (Cable News Network), 40, 149
Coderch, Josep, 132, 141
coercion, 80, 92, 102. See also embargo
Cold War: continuation of, 186; Cuban-
Europe relations in, 107–8; Cuban-
Mexican relations in, 91; legacy of, 7–10,
82–83; U.S.-Spanish dispute over Cuba
in, 134–35
Colombia: Cuban relations with, 189;
human rights vote and, 158
COMECON (Council of Mutual Economic
Assistance), 11
Commission of Political Parties (Mexico), 93
Committee on Inter-American Affairs (New
York Bar Association), 23, 24
Committees for the Defense of the
Revolution, 45
Common Foreign and Security Policy
(E.U.), 107, 123, 168

Communist Party (Cuba), 100–101, 195–96
compensation/restitution: amount of, 64–
65, 66; H-B and, 48–50; lack of well-
defined, 14–17; legal opinions in, 62–
65; undermined hope for, 113–14; U.S.
rejection of, 14, 171. *See also* citizenship; nationalization/expropriations
CONACEX (Consejo Nacional de
Comercio Exterior, National Council on
External Commerce), 92–93
Concorde (French-British plane), 164
Confederación Patronal de la República
Mexicana (Employers Confederation of
the Mexican Republic, COPARMEX),
92–93
confiscated, use of term, 37. *See also*
nationalization/expropriations
Consejo Nacional de Comercio Exterior
(National Council on External
Commerce, CONACEX), 92–93
coordinating official, concept of, 44
COPARMEX (Confederación Patronal de la
República Mexicana, Employers
Confederation of the Mexican Republic),
92–93
COREPER, 234n.165
Corporación Cuba Ron, 54
Costa Cruise Line, 220n.23
Costa Rica: Cuban relations with, 170; H-B
criticized by, 96
Council of Europe, 164
Council of Ministers (E.U.), 120–22, 141
Council of Ministers of Economy and
Finance (ECOFIN), 123–24
Council of Mutual Economic Assistance
(COMECON), 11
Council on Foreign Relations, 173, 192, 193
Coverdell, Paul, 31–32
Crane, Daniel A., 70, 72–73
criminal activities, 50, 190–91
Cuba: accusations against, 35–36, 156;
constitution of, 11; criticism of, 115–16;
demographics of, 190–91; domestic
politics reform in, 116–17; H-B as
blueprint for changing, 40–50; H-B's
legacy for, 167–73; international role of,
7–8, 10, 178–79; on 1998 compromise,

155; political reform in, 3, 44–45, 141–
42; pope's visit to, 3, 114–15, 140, 149–
50, 172, 180; reaction to H-B, 9, 33, 84,
99–102, 172; Ros-Lehtinen's proposal
and, 98; as security threat to U.S., 21, 36,
77, 122, 156, 175; Spanish Cultural
Center in, 148, 149; survival of, xiii, xv,
18, 47, 74, 101, 147, 159, 174, 182–83;
U.S.-Spanish dispute over, 134–35; U.S.
trademarks registered in, 56. *See also*
E.U.-Cuban relations; nationalization/
expropriations; Spanish-American War
(1898); Spanish-Cuban relations; U.S.-
Cuban relations
Cuba Business (U.K.), 154, 161
Cubalse (company), 115
Cuban Air Force, planes shot down by, 2,
19, 30–31, 102, 116, 188
Cuban-American Bar Association, 53
Cuban-American exile community:
adjustments in, 4; on aid package, 147;
attitudes toward Cuba of, 20–21, 187–
88; CDA and, 25–26, 28–29; divisions
in, 180; fears of, 7–8; foreign policy
influenced by, xvi–xvii, 1, 3–4, 6–9, 118;
on humanitarian aid, 180, 233n.129;
leadership of, 156; legal option for, 52,
65–67; legal response to concerns of,
213n.28; on 1999 proposal, 194; pope's
visit to Cuba and, 115; reaction to H-B,
41, 70, 113; reassessment of, 183–84;
remittances and travel to Cuba by, 40; on
Spanish politics, 135–36. *See also*
citizenship; Mas Canosa, Jorge;
nationalization/expropriations
Cuban-American National Foundation
(CANF): Castro's opposition to, 141,
146; formation of, 204; H-B supported
by, 32; influence of, xvii, 19; on ITT-
STET deal, 113; leadership of, 3; on
1997 compromise, 128; Spanish relations
with, 157–58; victims' rights in
expropriations and, 54. *See also* Mas
Canosa, Jorge
Cuban Assembly of Popular Power, 140
Cuban Assets Control Regulations Act, 10
Cuban Claims Act, 15, 99

Cuban Democracy Act (CDA, 1992): "calibrated response" and, 60, 73; certified vs. uncertified claims and, 17; codification of, 33–35, 60, 62, 71–73, 100; components of, 11, 18, 21–22; cost of, 173; criticism of, 115–16; evaluation of, 22–23; extraterritoriality and, 24–25; H-B's origin in, 7; legality of, 24–27; limitations of, 28–29, 53; motivations for, 24, 167–68. *See also* embargo
Cuban Electric Company, 15
Cuban Land Reform Law (1959), 10
Cuban Legislature, 101–2
Cuban Liberty and Democratic Solidarity (LIBERTAD) Act. *See* Helms-Burton Law (H-B)
Cuban missile crisis (1962), xiii–xiv, 9, 10
Cuban National Assembly, 204
Cuban Revolution: anniversary of, 3, 189–90; legacy of, 182–84; political links and, 110; roots of, 134; Spanish fascination with, 137
Cuomo, Mario M., 58
Czech Republic, human rights vote and, 158

Daily Gleaner (Jamaica), 98
D'Amato, Alfonse, 111, 160. *See also* Iran-Libya Sanctions Act (ILSA)
Dausá, Rafael, 101
Declaration of Viña del Mar, 139
de Falco, David S., 74
Delaney, Ian, 88–89
Democratic Party (U.S.): Cubans' dislike of, 8–9, 160; H-B critiqued by, 32; influence of, 29
democratization: declarations on, 123–24, 139–40; Germany's expectations and, 112; H-B as inconsistent with, 59–60, 73, 92; measures to promote, 80–81, 86, 95, 116, 125, 127, 168, 185, 202; pope's visit to Cuba and, 114–15; in Spain, 131–32. *See also* transition government
Diario de la Marina, El (newspaper, Cuba), 146
Díaz-Balart, "Fidelito" Castro, 203
Díaz-Balart, Lincoln: background of, 194,

203; on H-B and executive power, 32; H-B's legacy for, 160; on humanitarian aid, 180; on 1997 compromise, 128; politics of, 8
Díaz-Balart, Mirta, 203
Discovery Channel, 231n.90
dissidents, trial of, 192, 195
Dissidents' Working Group, 169
Dodd, Christopher, 32, 58, 195
Dodge, William S., 78–79, 176
Dole, Robert, 30, 31
Domínguez, Jorge: H-B criticized by, 6, 19–20, 29, 42, 50; on "mobilizing incidents," 29; on U.S.-Cuba relations, 18, 154, 186
Dominica (island), foreign investment in, 12
Dominican Republic: in ACP group, 168, 170; Castro's visit to, 169–70; foreign investment in, 12; normalization and, 161–62
Domos company, 93, 113, 165, 217n.31
Durán Lleida, Josep Antoni, 137

ECHO (European Community Humanitarian Office), 124
ECOFIN (Council of Ministers of Economy and Finance), 123–24
Economist, The (weekly, U.K.), 108–9
economy (Cuba): credit status and, 171–72, 190; exports and, 40; food rationing and, 10; H-B's goal for, 6, 70; H-B's impact on, 170–73, 190–91; private enterprises in, 12; reason for poor, 3, 99; reforms in, 11–12, 171, 180–81, 201; Spanish relations and, 143–44. *See also* foreign investment (in Cuba)
education, 191
Egypt, Cuban commerce with, 17
Einaudi, Luigi, 188–89
Eisenhower, Dwight D., 10
Eisenstat, Stuart, 5, 122, 128, 179
elections: H-B's legacy for, 160; oversight of, 45–46; push for democratic, 139–40
Elorza, Antonio, 146
El Salvador: Cuban relations with, 170; H-B criticized by, 96; human rights vote and, 158

embargo: codification of, 33–35, 60, 62, 71–73, 100; cost of, 14, 173; defensive action against, 108; definition of, 38–39; evaluating rationale for/against, 158–59, 161–62; failure of, xv, 173, 183–84; humanitarian aid vs., 172–73; international impact of, 26–27; John Paul's impact on, 180; legality of, 24–27; motivations for, 24, 192; opposition to, 114–16, 131, 175, 195, 200, 202; origins of, 9–10; political conditions for lifting, xiv, 3–4, 22, 32, 33–35, 41, 45; renewal/reinforcement of, 1, 18–24, 38–39; replaced with reconciliation, 81–82; restitution as expected result of, 62; UN condemnation of, 102–3, 103; use of term, 221n.38. *See also* Cuban Democracy Act (CDA, 1992)

Empresa de Teléfonos de Cuba (ETECSA), 165

Erisman, H. Michael, 97

Escarré, Gabriel, 166

espousal, concept of, 69

estoppel: principle of, 67–70; state doctrine and, 62–63

Etchegaray, Roger, 114

ETECSA (Empresa de Teléfonos de Cuba), 165

European Community Humanitarian Office (ECHO), 124

European–Latin American summit, 193

E.U.-Cuban relations: E.U.'s approach to, 115–16; France's role in, 109–11; Germany's role in, 111–12; increased trade and, 107–9; Israel's role in, 115; Italy's role in, 112–14; lack of understanding in, 117–18; nature of, 106–7; pope's visit and, 114–15

European Union (E.U.): autonomy of, 187; blocking statute and understanding of, 116, 118–22, 168; Common Position of, 116, 118–19, 123–24, 159–60, 169, 185; compromises of, 119, 152–59; cooperation aid agreement and, 2, 116–19; coordinated action and, 91; Cuban agreement and, 110–11; Cuban relations with, 178, 200–201; Cuban trade with, 13, 86, 107–8, 111, 124; on embargo,

103; foreign investment by, 12, 152; foreign policy in, 118, 153; H-B criticized by, xi, xv, 2, 7, 73–74, 115, 116; H-B's legacy for, 146, 159; human rights voting of, 126–27; Permanent Representations to, 151, 227n.14; reaction to H-B, 9, 31, 58, 105–6; recommendations for, 82; social democratic parties in, 185; understanding of, 199. *See also* E.U.-Cuban relations; U.S.-E.U. relations; World Trade Organization (WTO)

executive branch (U.S.): eliminated in foreign policy decisions, 34, 60, 71–73; nationality of claims principle upheld by, 68; role of, in H-B, 43–45; Title III waiver and, 56–57. *See also* Clinton, Bill

Express (Trinidad), 98

Exterminating Angel, The (film), 185–86, 189

extraterritoriality: Canada's perspective on, 88; embargo's legality and, 24–25; H-B's impact on, 5, 92; legal issues on, 51, 58, 62–63, 74–76, 95, 120–21

Fairey, W. Fletcher, 81

Falcoff, Mark, 20, 191

FCSC (Foreign Claims Settlement Commission), 15, 16, 56, 114

Federal Republic of Germany (FRG): caution of, 111–12; Cuban link with, 107

Feinberg, Richard, 205

FEMA (Foreign Extraterritorial Measures Act, Canada), 26, 88

Fernández Albor, Gerardo, 119

Fernández de Cossío, Carlos, 172

Fernández-Revuelta, Alina, 203

Ferradaz, Ibrahim, 110, 169, 170, 173, 190

Ferreiro, Francisco Javier, 147–48

Fidelity (company), 109

Fidler, David, 81–82

Florida: boycott against tourism in, 89; citrus industry in, 161; victims' rights in, 53. *See also* Cuban-American exile community

follón, use of term, 145

Food Security Act (1985), 38

Foreign Affairs (journal, U.S.), 179

Foreign Assistance Act (1961), 10, 22, 38, 75

Foreign Claims Settlement Commission (FCSC), 15, 16, 56, 114

foreign currency, in Cuba, 11–12, 124

Foreign Extraterritorial Measures Act (FEMA, Canada), 26, 88

foreign investment (in Cuba): announced vs. committed, 13; banned, 6, 22, 39, 73–74; as "collaborationism," 29, 32; 1998 compromise on, 152–59; encouragement of, 114; evaluation of, 27; from expropriations to, 14–17; H-B's impact on, xi, 161–62, 165–67, 170–73; legal recommendations on, 79–82; opportunities for, 8; protection for, 110, 127, 128, 138; punishment of, 50–58; sources of, 12–14; U.S. corporations' desire for, 175, 195. See also specific countries

foreign policy (U.S.): assessment of, 199–200; codification of, 22, 33–35, 60, 62, 71–73, 100; contradictions in, 159; criticism of, 85, 189; Cuban-Americans' influence on, xvi–xvii, 1, 3–4, 6–9, 118; domestication of, 72; failure of, 183–84, 187; legal recommendations on, 79–82; motivations in, 42–43, 186; as unilateral, 174. See also specific acts and laws

Foreign Relations Law of the United States, 64, 69, 75

Fraga Iribarne, Manuel, 137

France: change of government in, 117; Common Position and, 123; coordinated action and, 91–92; Cuban relations of, 107, 109–11, 220n.17; Cuban trade with, 17, 110–11; leadership of, 106; on 1998 compromise, 153

Franco, Francisco, 131, 134, 184, 186–87

Freeport-MacMoran Company, 88

Freer, Robert, 66

Freixenet (company), 165

Fuentes, Carlos, 118

Galeote, Guillermo, 119

Galliano, Ralph, 228n.18

García Márquez, Gabriel, 30, 118

GATT (General Agreement on Tariffs and Trade), 24, 58, 76–77, 96. See also World Trade Organization (WTO)

Gaviota (company), 143, 166

Gencor (company), 161, 224n.30

Gerke, Kinka, 176–77

German Democratic Republic (GDR): Cuban debt to, 190; Cuban relations with, 107, 111–12

Germany: Common Position and, 123; Cuban tourism and, 18, 112; Cuban trade with, 17; social democratic party in, 185; trade agreement of, 110. See also Federal Republic of Germany (FRG); German Democratic Republic (GDR)

Geyer, Georgie Anne, 174

Ghana, Cuban diplomatic relations with, 189

Gibbons, Sam, 32

Gierbolini, Luisette, 62, 79–80

Gilman, Ben, 154–55, 194

Gingrich, Newt, 32, 156

Giuliano, Maurizio, 99, 200

globalism: Castro's denunciation of, 192; commerce and, 5, 17–18; economic issues in, 78–79, 81, 82–83, 130; public interest in, 174–75

glossary (H-B), 37–39

Godfrey, Peter, 89

Goizueta, Roberto, 204

Gómez Manzano, René, 195

González, Felipe: on Aznar, 142–43; on businessman's arrest, 148; criticism of, 146; NATO and, 135; U.S. relations of, 135–36, 141

Gore, Al, 160

Gortari, Salinas de, 91, 94

Gortázar, Guillermo, 138

Graham, Bob, 55–56, 180

Gramm, Phil, 30, 32

Gran Caribe (agency), 143, 166

Granell, Francesc, 106

Granma (Cuba): on H-B, 100; on Robaina's dismissal, 196–97, 198; on Ros-Lehtinen's proposal, 98; on Spain's foreign minister, 132

Great Britain. See United Kingdom

Grenada: Castro's visit to, 169–70; Cuban links with, 163

Groth, Carl J., 158
Guardans, Ignasi, 153
Guardia Civil (Spain), 135
Guatemala: E.U. agreement with, 124; H-B criticized by, 96; human rights vote and, 158
Guitart (company), 161
Gunn, Gillian, 173
Gurría, José Ángel, 128
Gutiérrez Menoyo, Eloy, 32, 191–92

Haas, Richard, 201
Haig, Alexander, 135
Haiti: Cuban investment of, 171; Cuban relations with, 189; immigration from, 162, 191
Halperin, Morton, 205
Hans, Rupinder, 81
Havana Ambassadors Human Rights Working Group, 169
Havana Club (rum), 55–56
Havana International Fair (1996), 171
H-B. See Helms-Burton Law (H-B)
Heenan Blakey (company), 161, 224n.30
Helander, Robert, 14, 16
Helms, Jesse: biographical sketch of, 204; on Cuba, 192; H-B introduced by, 4, 29, 30, 32; H-B's legacy for, 160; initiatives of, 163; on investment impact, 161; on 1997 compromise, 128; on 1998 compromise, 154–55; on 1999 proposal, 194; obstructionism of, 193; victims' rights in expropriations and, 54
Helms-Burton Law (H-B): approach to, xiii–xvi; background of, 5–6; as blueprint for changing Cuba, 40–50; as codification of policy, 33–35, 60, 62, 71–73, 100; commerce/tourism and, 17–18; components of, 1–2, 33–40, 65; compromise over, 2–3, 5–6, 110–11, 119, 125–29, 168; compromise reaffirmed on, 151–59, 169–70, 184; consequences of, 77–83; constitutionality of, 62–63, 70–71; criticism of, xi, 1–5, 7, 29–30, 73–74, 164; development of, 6–9, 40, 106; economic realities of, 173–79; from expropriations to investment, 14–17; future of, 184–89; historical context of,

9–12; legacy of, 159–73, 189–96; midterm review of, 155–59; nicknames for, 52–53, 81; objectives of, xi, 36–37, 54, 73–74, 104, 113; passage of, 29–31; policy suggestions and, 199–202; political commentaries on, 59–60; positive results of, 82–83; staff time allocated to, xiv, 78. See also citizenship; international law; legal opinions; nationalization/expropriations; Title II (H-B); Title III (H-B); Title IV (H-B)
Helsinki Agreement, 139
Hennessey, Alistair, 108
Henze, Gerhard, 115–16
Hermanos al Rescate planes, shot down by Cuba, 2, 19, 30–31, 102, 116, 188
Hernández, Francisco, 228n.18
Hernández, Jorge, 228n.18
Hickenlooper Amendment, 75
Ho Chi Minh, 131
House Committee on International Relations, 29, 228n.18
House Foreign Relations Subcommittee, 205
House Subcommittee on International Policy and Trade, 228n.18
Huber, Jürgen, 121–22
Human Development Index, for Cuba, 190
humanitarian aid: Cuban exile community on, 180, 233n.129; embargo vs., 172–73; from E.U., 124; rejection of, 156–57; from Spain, 144; from U.S., 147, 156, 180, 229n.33
human rights: Common Position and, 123–24; Cuban improvement in, 170, 202; Cuban violations of, 36, 115, 156, 158, 195–96; declaration on, 46; E.U. supervision of Cuban, 168, 169; E.U. voting on, 126–27; expropriations and, 69; Germany's expectations and, 112; measures to promote, 80–81, 86, 95, 116, 125
Huntington, Samuel, 6–7, 174

Iberia Airlines, 131, 162
Ibero-American summit: boycott of, 197, 198; Castro at, 132, 139, 166; sites for, 95, 189, 192

IDB (Inter-American Development Bank), 76
ILSA (Iran-Libya Sanctions Act), 111, 113, 222n.52
IMF (International Monetary Fund), 76, 171
immigration: from Cuba to U.S., 191; from Haiti, 162, 191; H-B's repercussions for, 71; from Spain to Cuba, 133. *See also* Mariel boatlift
Indonesia, Cuban investment of, 171
infant mortality rate, 190
information gathering: legislation on, 162–63; as problematic, 39–40, 78
ING-Barings (company), 94
Inter-American Development Bank (IDB), 76
Inter-American Dialogue, 29, 188–89
Inter-American Juridical Committee, 94–95, 96–97
Inter-American System. *See* Organization of American States (OAS)
interdependence, shift to globalism, 174
Interest Sections (Cuba-U.S.), 11
internal matter, use of term, 135–36
International Claims Settlement Act (1949), 15, 52, 56, 67
international community: CDA's impact on, 26–27; Cuba's role in, 7–8, 10, 178–79; H-B criticized by, 1–2, 58–60, 73–74, 195; H-B's legacy for, 62–63; H-B unanimously opposed in, 3, 171, 173–74; from interdependence to globalism in, 174–75; internal structures of, 199; reactions to H-B, 31, 104; on traffickers barred from U.S., 57–58; U.S. interests in, 174–75. *See also* foreign investment (in Cuba); traffickers; *specific countries*
International Court of Justice, 68, 76, 94, 96
International Labor Organization, 46
international law: compensation/restitution process and, 63; embargo evaluated in, 24–27; estoppel in, 67–70; on extraterritoriality, 51; H-B as violation of, 2, 4, 62–63, 76–77, 92, 95, 96, 101; H-B's legacy for, 176–78; H-B's use of, 64; importance of, 82–83; nationality of

claims principle and, 67; 1998 compromise and, 154; political consequences of violating, 77–79; state violation of, 65; theft definition and, 66; visa denials and, 71. *See also* citizenship; extraterritoriality; sovereignty
International Monetary Fund (IMF), 76, 171
International Telephone and Telegraph (ITT), 15, 112–14, 165
intrahistoria, use of term, 186–87
Investment Promotion and Guarantee Agreement (German-Cuban), 111–12
Iran: European interests in, 151, 152; French investment in, 111, 113
Iran-Libya Sanctions Act (ILSA), 111, 113, 222n.52
Iraq, sanctions against, 152
Israel: Cuban investment of, 115; on embargo, 102, 103; E.U. agreement with, 124
Italy: citizenship in, 48; Common Position and, 123; Cuban tourism and, 18, 112; Cuban trade with, 17, 112–14; foreign investment by, 12, 14, 15; social democratic party in, 185; trade agreement of, 110
ITT (International Telephone and Telegraph), 15, 112–14, 165
Izquierda Unida (United Left, Spain), 135, 138

Jamaica: Castro's visit to, 169–70; Cuban links with, 163; normalization and, 162; Ros-Lehtinen's proposal and, 98
Japan: Cuban trade with, 17; on embargo, 219n.78; reaction to H-B, 31
Jarmin, Gary, 53
Jay Treaty (1795), 89
Jiang Zemin, 189
Joffe, Josep, 179
John Paul II (pope): Cuban visit of, 3, 114–15, 140, 149–50, 172, 180; diplomatic messages from, 189. *See also* Catholic Church
Johnson, Lyndon B., 9
Joint Corporate Committee on Cuban Claims, 53

Joint Political Declaration on Canada-E.U. Relations (1996), 89
Juan Carlos I (king of Spain): Cuban visit delayed, 157, 167, 181, 189, 192, 197; Latin American visit, 132, 149, 150
judiciary: establishment of independent Cuban, 46; foreign policy codification and, 71–73; on H-B, 62–63; interpretive role of, 81; nationality of claims principle upheld by, 68. *See also* international law; legal opinions
Junco, Eduardo, 157
Juventud Rebelde (Cuba), 198

Kaplowitz, Donna Rich, 9–10, 24, 183
Kaye, David, 77
Kennedy, John F., 9, 10, 42
Kirk, John, 85, 86
Kirkpatrick doctrine, 159
Kneale, John, 87
Kosovo, as context, 197

labor restructuring, 12
Lage, Carlos, 102, 164, 167, 171
Lagos, Victor, 96
Lake, Tony, 34
Lambie, George, 131
Lares (company), 115
Latin America: autonomy of, 187; Cold War relations in, 91; Cuban relations with, 11; nationalism in, 183; political characteristics of, 182; reaction to H-B, 9, 98–99; response to CDA, 26–27; Spain's relations with, 145–46, 167; U.S. attitudes toward, 42–43. *See also* U.S.– Latin American relations; *specific countries*
Latin American Parliament (PARLATINO), 93
Law for the Protection of Trade and Investment (Mexican), 93–94
legal action: contradictions in language on, 48–50; H-B's authorization of, 1–2, 7, 29, 33–34, 56; resistance to, 61–63; victims' rights in expropriations and, 53–54
legal opinions: on citizenship issues, 65–67; estoppel concept and, 67–70; on extraterritoriality, 51, 58, 62–63, 74–76,

95, 120–21; foreign policy recommendations in, 79–82; H-B criticized in, 61–63, 76–77; on H-B's consequences, 77–83; on H-B's objectives, 73–74; overlooked, 199; policy codification and, 71–73; on property and compensation issues, 62–65; sources on, 212n.2
LeoGrande, William, 19, 34, 60
Leyland (company), 109
Libya, European interests in, 151, 152
Lisio, Stephen, 59–60
Lojendio, Pablo de, 141
Lomé Convention: as alternative, 118; Common Position and, 168, 169; Cuba's observer status in, 170; Cuba's possible inclusion in, 163–64; trade guidelines and, 107
Lone Star (company), 53
Long, Susan, 75
Los Angeles Daily Journal, 61
Lowe, Vaughn, 74–75, 77, 78
Lowenfeld, Andreas F., 63–64, 72–74
LTU (company), 112
Lucio, Saturnino, 73
Lufthansa (company), 112

Maastricht Treaty, 153
Mack, Connie, 55–56
MAI (Multilateral Agreement on Investment), 111, 152, 178, 179–80, 200
Maine (ship), 42, 133–34
Mallett, Nick, 73
Malvinas/Falkland Islands, 109
Mao Zedong, 131
Mariel boatlift, 11, 19
Marín, Manuel, 116–17
Marquis, Christopher, 161
Mas, Jorge L., 204
Mas Canosa, Jorge: Aznar supported by, 141; biographical sketch of, 204; death of, 3, 4, 156, 188; goal of, 29; Spanish investments of, 165; victims' rights in expropriations and, 54
Matos, Huber, 191–92
Matutes, Abel: on Aznar-Castro exchange, 145; on foreign investment, 166; media appearances of, 226n.60; on 1998

compromise, 154; papal visit and, 149; Spanish-Cuban relations and, 141, 142, 150

May Day rally (Cuba), 100

McCarry, Caleb, 230n.68

McCollum, Bill, 162

McDonnell Douglas, 107

McKinley, William, 42, 133, 147

media: Cuban offices of, 40, 149; on Title III's suspension, 125. *See also specific magazines, newspapers, and journals*

medical resources, 190

Meliá (company), 166

Menem, Carlos, 140, 158, 181

Menéndez, Robert, 8, 41, 160, 205

Mercedes-Benz (company), 112

Meron, Theodor, 62, 76, 176

Mesa Lago, Carmelo, 173

Mexican Congress, 91–93

Mexico: blocking statute and, 122; Castro's criticism of, 136; "clawback" law of, 93–94; Cuban relations with, 91, 176; Cuban trade with, 17, 90, *91,* 91–93; foreign investment by, 14; H-B criticized by, xi, 2, 7, 58, 91–93; H-B's legacy for, 159; human rights vote and, 158; on 1997 compromise, 128; reaction to H-B, 9, 31, 98

Miami Herald: on Clinton's proposal, 194–95; on Cuba's value, 178–79; on investment impact, 161; on property confiscation issue, 89; on Robaina, 197

Michell, Keith, 163

Middle East war, 115

Milliken, Peter, 89

millitary (U.S.), pressure for compromise from, 175

Mirapeix, Eudald, 141

Mitchell, James, 163

Mitterrand, François, 110

Moa Bay Mining (company), 15, 88–89

Mondale, Walter, 204

Monroe, James, xv, 42

Monroe Doctrine: development of H-B and, 6; embargo as continuation of, xiv–xv, 9, 20, 24, 42; motivation for, 106

Montalván, Plinio, 49–50

Montaner, Carlos Alberto, 141

Monte Barreto (joint venture), 115

Morocco: agreement with, 124; Spanish military in, 133–34

mover pieza, use of term, 140

Mujal León, Eusebio, 185

Mulroney, Brian, 85

Multilateral Agreement on Investment (MAI), 111, 152, 178, 179–80, 200

Muse, Robert: on citizenship issues, 66, 67, 69; on H-B's implications, 89; on H-B's political cost, 77–78; on international law, 82–83; recommendations of, 79, 80

NAFTA (North American Free Trade Agreement): actions against H-B in, 87–88, 91–93, 94; Chile and, 98–99; as context, xvi, 6; Cuba's value vs. maintaining, 178–79; H-B critique and, xi, 31, 98; H-B's legacy for, 164–65, 178; H-B's violation of, 58, 76, 92–93, 96; opposition to, 176; trade war threats in, 179–80. *See also* Canada; Mexico; United States

Namibia, Cuban investment of, 171

Naranjo, Fernando, 96

narcotics, terminology of, 64

Nation (Barbados), 98

Nation, The (magazine, U.S.), 106

National Association of Manufacturers (U.S.), 175

National Bank of Cuba, 11–12

nationalism, persistence of, 183

nationalization/expropriations: areas of, 10–11, 85; certified claims for, 15, 16, 17, 53; Cuba's perspective on, 100–101; financing related to, 39; trafficking and, 37–38, 50–52; U.S. rejection of negotiations on, 14, 171; victims' rights in expropriations and, 53–54. *See also* citizenship; compensation/restitution; foreign investment (in Cuba); traffickers

National Union of Cuban Lawyers, 33

Native Americans, property confiscation and, 89

NATO (North Atlantic Treaty Organization): E.U.-U.S. disagreements on, 107; France's role in, 106; intervention of, 197; Spain's role in, 135

Netherlands: Common Position and, 123; Cuban trade with, 17
Netherlands Antilles, foreign investment by, 14
New York Bar Association, 23, 24
New York Law Journal, 61
New Zealand, on embargo, 103
Nicaragua: Castro's policies and, 95; Cuban relations with, 189; FDR on, 158–59; U.S. confrontation with, 76
North American Free Trade Agreement. *See* NAFTA (North American Free Trade Agreement)
North American Sugar (company), 15
North Atlantic Treaty Organization. *See* NATO (North Atlantic Treaty Organization)
North Korea, sanctions against, 152
Nuccio, Richard: background of, 205; on cooperation aid agreement, 221n.42; on Cuba as security threat, 21; on H-B's passage, 34; recommendation to president, 181; on Title III waiver, 57; on U.S.-Cuba relations, 154, 184, 189
nuclear threats, H-B compared to, 179–80, 234n.165

OAS. *See* Organization of American States (OAS)
Obligatory Diplomatic Protection, 138
Occidental Hoteles, 143, 166
OECD (Organization for Economic Cooperation and Development), 119, 179–80
"offensive intervention," use of term, 174
oil industry, 10, 15
Olympics (Barcelona), 132
Oppenheimer, Andrés, 178–79
Ordóñez, Francisco Fernández, 135, 136
Organization for Economic Cooperation and Development (OECD), 119, 179–80
Organization of American States (OAS): Canadian efforts to reinstate Cuba in, 158; Cuba suspended from, 10, 39, 139; embargo evaluated in, 24; extraterritoriality issues and, 25; opposition to H-B in, 93, 94–97; sanctions lifted by, 11

Organization of Caribbean States, 97
Ortega, Jaime, 156–57

Paemen, Hugo, 107
País, El (newspaper, Spain), 140
Panama: Cuban relations with, 189; H-B criticized by, 96
Panetta, Leon, 34
Paradores de España (company), 143, 166
Paraguay, on embargo, 102
Parent, Gilbert, 158
PARLATINO (Latin American Parliament), 93
Partido de Acción Nacional (Party of National Action, PAN), 93
Partido Popular (PP, Spain): agreement's failure and, 118; attitudes toward, 135; Aznar vs., 157; CANF support and, 146; compromise and, 119; Spanish-Cuban relations and, 137–38, 141, 150
Pastors for Peace, 172
Pastrana, Andrés, 193
Patterson, P. J., 163
Pemex (company), 161
Pentagon report, on Cuba, 156
People's Republic of China: Cuban trade with, 17; E.U. agreement with, 124; U.S. trade with, 159
Perera Gómez, Eduardo, 118, 124
Pérez, Lisandro, 21
Pérez Roque, Felipe, 196–98
Pernod-Ricard (company), 55–56, 111
Perry, William, 34
Peru: human rights vote and, 158; investments in, 165
Pierre Cardin (company), 111
Pinochet, Augusto, 197
Piqué, Josep, 167
Platt, Orville, 43
Platt Amendment: effect of, 43; H-B compared to, xiv, 9, 41, 100, 101; justification of, 35
Poland, human rights vote and, 158
Portugal, Cuban trade with, 17
PP. *See* Partido Popular (PP, Spain)
Prado, Juan, 206
Presidential Proclamation 3447, 10
Presidential Review Directive (PRD) 21, 21

prisons, investigations of, 45
property, legal opinions on issues of, 63–70. See also nationalization/expropriations; traffickers
protectionism, consequences of, 174. See also embargo
Protection of National Independence and the Economy of Cuba, 192
Protection of Trading Interests Act (U.K.), 26, 138
PSOE (party, Spain): accusations against, 134; leadership of, 146, 157–58; Spanish-Cuban relations and, 117–18, 135–36, 138, 141, 145
public opinion (U.S.): on Castro and Cuba, 20–21, 136, 195; on embargo, 19; on H-B, 20–21, 58–60; on international relations, 174–75; on Latin America, 42–43
Puerto Rico: normalization and, 162; reaction to H-B, 97; status of, 44
Pujol, Jordi, 137
Putnam, Robert D., 19

Quickendon, Christine L., 79, 80

Radio Martí: continuation of, 39; Cuba's transition and, 46; establishment of, 204; funds for, 193; Helms on, 161; Mas Canosa's death and, 3
Rangel, Charles B., 25
Ranneberger, Michael E., 228n.18
Rapid Response Brigades (Cuba), 45
Rasco, José Ignacio, 58–59
Reaffirmation of Cuban Dignity and Sovereignty (1996), 101–2
Reagan, Ronald: attitudes toward Latin America, 42; background of, 204; Cuban policy of, 19; Grenada invasion and, 169–70; Spanish relations of, 136; travel restrictions imposed by, 11
reconciliation: H-B as inconsistent with, 60; legal recommendations on, 81–82. See also democratization; U.S.-Cuban relations
Redpath (company), 161
Registry of Claims, 152
Reinicke, Wolfgang H., 174

Remírez de Estenoz, Fernando, 219n.78
Reno, Janet, 34
Republican Party (U.S.): Cuban-Americans' alliance with, 8–9, 26; H-B and, 31–32, 127; as minority, 29
Restatement (Third) of Foreign Relations Law of the United States, 64, 69, 75
Revista de Estudios Europeos, 118
Rhone-Poulenc (company), 111
Richardson, Bill, 30–31
Rio Group, 93, 94–95, 96–97, 192
Robaina, Roberto: on Clinton, 101; fall of, 196–98; on H-B, 33, 102, 155; on human rights, 139; on Matutes, 142; on new hardline efforts, 169; travel of, 95, 196; on Vatican efforts, 156
Robles Fraga, José María, 157
Robles Piquer, Carlos, 119
Roca, Vladimiro, 195
Rodríguez , José Luis, 194
Rodríguez de la Vega, Eduardo, 142, 143–44, 148
Romania, on embargo, 102
Romero, Peter, 193, 194
Roosevelt, Franklin D., 42, 158–59
Roosevelt, Theodore, 42, 43
Roosevelt Corollary, 6
Roque, Marta Beatriz, 195
Ros-Lehtinen, Ileana: biographical sketch of, 203; CARICOM sanctions proposed by, 97–98; Cuban report and, 228n.18; election of, 8; on H-B motivations, 122; on H-B's effects, 89, 155, 161; H-B's legacy for, 160; on humanitarian aid, 180; on 1997 compromise, 128; on 1999 proposal (Clinton's), 194; politics of, 8
Rothschild (company), 109
Rubert de Ventós, Xavier, 118
Ruiz Jiménez, Joaquín, 149
rum industry, 52–56, 205–6
Russia: cooperation with, 106; Cuban trade with, 17; H-B criticized by, 164

Sabbatino v. the National Bank of Cuba, 100
Safont, Francisco, 3, 114–15, 140
Saint Lucia, anniversary of, 193
Saint Vincent, Cuban links with, 163

Salafranca, José Ignacio, 119
Sánchez, Ignacio, 70
Sánchez Santacruz, Elizardo, 110, 191
San Gil, José Antonio, 141
Schoultz, Lars, 42–43, 186
Schueg, Enrique, 205
Schumer, Charles, 160
Schwenninger, Scherle R., 106
Secretaría de Comercio y Fomento
    Internacional (Secretariat for Business
    and International Development,
    SECOFI), 93
Senate Foreign Relations Committee, 29,
    228n.18
separation-of-powers doctrine, 71–73, 75,
    189
Serrano, José, 162
Seward Johnson (research ship), 231n.90
Shalikashvili, John Malchase David, 34
Sheehan, Gen.John, 229n.38
Sherritt International (company), 88–89,
    164–65
SINTEL (Sistemas e Instalaciones de
    Telecomunicacíon, S.A.), 165
Sistema Económico de América Latina
    (SELA) Council, 96
60 Minutes (television program), 89
Smith, Wayne, 60, 191, 197
Soberón, Francisco, 124
social class, 20, 191
social policy (Cuba), 46, 190–91
Società Telefònica e Telegràfica (STET), 15,
    112–14, 165
Solana, Javier, 196–97
Solís, Anthony: on domestication of foreign
    policy, 72; H-B criticized by, 62, 73;
    recommendations of, 80, 82; on state
    doctrine, 74
Sol Meliá (hotel chain), 165
Somoza, Anastasio, 159
Sorel, Julián (pseud.), 47
Sotillo, Alberto, 119
South Africa, foreign investment by, 14
South Korea, Cuban investment of, 171
sovereignty: citizenship definition and, 66;
    compromises and, 153–54, 168, 169;
    embargo and, 24–25; H-B as affront to,
    59–60, 92; as justification for H-B, 77;

Ros-Lehtinen's proposal as violation of,
    98. *See also* extraterritoriality; state
    doctrine
Soviet Union: Cuban relations with, 9–10,
    183; demise of, 11, 19, 106, 170, 188;
    U.S. relations with, xiv
Spain: aid priorities in, 149; Castro's visit
    to, 132; citizenship in, 48; Common
    Position and, 123; coordinated action
    and, 92; Cuban-Spanish foundation in,
    141; Cuban tourism and, 18, 142, 143–
    44, 148, 166–67; Cuban trade with, 17,
    115, 133, 143–44, 146, 148, 165–67,
    167, 171; democratization in, 131–32;
    domestic politics in, 117, 118, 134, 136–
    37, 143, 184; foreign investment by, 12,
    14; H-B criticized by, 113; H-B's legacy
    for, 146, 159–60, 165–67; immigrants
    from, 133; internal structures of, 199;
    intrahistoria and, 186–87; on 1998
    compromise, 153–54; on 1999 proposal,
    194; reaction to H-B, 9, 105, 137–38,
    150; role of, xi, xv; trade agreement of,
    110; transition government and, 47. *See
    also* Spanish-American War (1898);
    Spanish-Cuban relations
Spanish-American War (1898):
    commemoration of, 124, 130, 149;
    impact of, 133–34, 145; U.S. role in, xv;
    Yugoslavia compared to, 197
Spanish Chamber of Deputies, 132
Spanish Civil War, 134, 145
Spanish Congress, 132, 135
Spanish-Cuban relations: balance for, 146–
    47; context of, 133–34; contradictions in,
    131–32; de-Hispanization of, 142;
    diplomatic issues in, 124, 126, 141–43,
    157; economic relations and, 143–44; as
    family relationship, 134–38, 141;
    globalization of, 139–43; possible truce
    in, 148–50, 157, 181; tensions in, 139–
    43, 145–48; U.S. role in, 130
Spanish Cultural Center (in Cuba), 148, 149
Spenser (judge), 68
Standard Oil (company), 15
state doctrine: estoppel concept and, 62–63;
    extraterritoriality and, 74. *See also*
    sovereignty

State Security Department (Cuba), 45
Stein, Eduardo, 96
Stephanoupoulis, George, 34
STET (Società Telefònica e Telegràfica), 15, 112–14, 165
Suárez, Adolfo, 47
Sudan, sanctions relaxed for, 152
Summit of the Americas, 53–54, 98–99
Sunday Herald (Jamaica), 98
Syria, Cuban support for, 115

Tabacalera (company), 165–66
Tamayo, Juan, 194–95, 197
Tate and Lyle (company), 161
tax laws: Cuban, 12; U.S., 14–16, 162
Tejero, Antonio, 135
telephone system, 15, 112–14, 164–65, 188, 236n.10
TELMEX, advertisements for, 94
Texaco (company), 15
Thomas, David, 235n.1
Thomas, Hugh, 190
Title II (H-B): audience of, 51; author of, 8; on changing Cuba, 40–46, 194; on citizenship, 47–48; as codification of policy, 33–35; components of, xiv, 30; on confiscation issue, 48–50; on Cuban leadership, 46–47; language of, 40; public opinion on, 21; as separate law, 40–43
Title III (H-B): activation of, 56–57; audience of, 51; components of, 30, 67; language of, 40; moderation of, 126; on punishing foreign investment, 50–58; rationale for, 65; suspension of, xiii, 3, 17, 31, 56–57, 61, 70–71, 79, 80, 101, 114, 119, 125, 127, 129; as threat, 147, 159; waiver of, 153, 155, 162
Title IV (H-B): components of, 30; constraint of, 126, 127–29; enforcement of, 78; impact of, 161–62; invocation of, 71, 159; suspension of, 185; traffickers barred from U.S. by, 57–58; waiver of, 152–53, 155
Torres, Esteban, 180
Torres, María Soledad, 99
Torricelli, Robert, 18, 160, 162, 203–4
Torricelli law. *See* Cuban Democracy Act (CDA, 1992)

Total (company), 111, 113
tourism (Cuba): airplane travel and, 164; Canadian interest in, 18, 90; criminal activities and, 191; cruise lines and, 220n.23; currency in, 124; German interest in, 18, 112; hotel bombings and, 148; increase in, 17–18, 171, 172; Italian interest in, 18, 112; Spanish interest in, 18, 142, 143–44, 148, 166–67
trade: in bananas, 179; Canadian-U.S., 85; H-B's impact on, 7, 62–63, 175–76; H-B's violation of agreements on, 76–77, 92; maintaining balance in, 106–7, 179–80. *See also* GATT (General Agreement on Tariffs and Trade); NAFTA (North American Free Trade Agreement); World Trade Organization (WTO)
trademarks, suits over, 55–56
Trading with the Enemy Act (TWEA, 1917), 10, 25, 38, 39
traffickers: legal action against, 1–2, 7, 29, 33–34, 56; punishment of, 50–58; shift to "legal," 113–14; in "stolen" property, 63–65; U.S. entry visas for, 71
trafficking, meaning of, 37–38, 62, 64, 95
transition government: concept of, 44–45; as goal, 3, 44; people excluded from, 46–47. *See also* democratization; human rights
travel: to Cuba by Cuban-Americans, 40; H-B's repercussions for, 62–63, 71. *See also* visas; *specific individuals*
Treaty of Paris (1783), 89
Trinidad, Ros-Lehtinen's proposal and, 98
Turkey, E.U. agreement with, 124
TVE (Spanish television), 149, 226n.60
TV Martí, 3, 46, 193
TWEA (Trading with the Enemy Act, 1917), 10, 25, 38, 39

Unamuno, Miguel de, 186
Underhill v. Hernández, 74
UNESCO (United Nations Educational, Scientific, and Cultural Organization), 110
Unión de Centro Democrático (UCD) governments, 134–35, 145
United Fruit Sugar (company), 15

United Kingdom: blocking statute and, 122, 138; Common Position and, 123; coordinated action and, 92; Cuban debt to, 190; Cuban relations of, 107, 109; Cuban trade with, 17; H-B criticized by, 2; on 1998 compromise, 154; reaction to H-B, 105, 108–9; response to CDA, 26; trade agreement of, 110

United Nations: embargo condemned in, 23, 102–3, 174; E.U.-U.S. disagreements on, 107; extraterritoriality issues and, 24–25; H-B condemned by, 33, 96; H-B's violation of charter and resolution of, 76, 96; Mexico's request to, 94

United Nations Commission on Human Rights, 36, 126–27, 158, 170, 196, 197

United Nations Educational, Scientific, and Cultural Organization (UNESCO), 110

United States: constitution of, 62–63, 70–71; Cuban trademarks registered in, 55; Cuba's value for, 178–79; domestic politics in, 8–9, 19–20, 26, 29, 31–32, 127, 136–37, 160; H-B's legacy for, 159, 160; ideology of, 41–43, 174; isolation of, 102–3, 180, 189, 197; leadership of, 106, 118; negative image of, xi–xii, 78, 174, 187; in new world order, 7–8, 84; potential economic impact on, 5–6; property confiscation in, 89; separation-of-powers doctrine in, 71–73, 75, 189; theft defined in, 66. See also foreign policy (U.S.); U.S.-Cuban relations; U.S.–Latin American relations; U.S.-E.U. relations

U.S. Chamber of Commerce, 175

U.S. Commerce Department, 195

U.S. Congress: anti-Cuban initiatives in, 136, 162–63, 169; attitudes to international law in, 82–83, 189; as "enemy," 151; on expropriated companies' brands, 55–56; H-B passage and, 29–31; Hispanics in, 8–9; nationality of claims principle upheld by, 68; on 1998 compromise, 154–55

U.S.-Cuban relations: approach to, xv; businessman's arrest and, 147–48; CDA's impact on, 27; compensation issues and, 63; context of, 185–86;

contradictions in, 188–89; cultural exchanges in, 195; decline of, 10–11; development of H-B and, 6–7; H-B's impact on, 2–3; *intrahistoria* in, 186–87; legal recommendations on, 79–82; literature on, 207n.4; pattern of, xi–xii, 154, 184–89, 193–96; Spanish investments and, 148; Vatican's efforts in, 155–58. See also embargo; Helms-Burton Law (H-B)

U.S.–Latin American relations: in Cold War, 91; as context, xvi, 9; termination of (1964), 10; U.S. attitudes in, 42–43

U.S.-E.U. relations: compromise on H-B, 2–3, 5–6, 110–11, 119, 125–29, 168; compromise reaffirmed in, 151–59, 169–70, 184; cooperation aid agreement and, 117–18; frustration over H-B in, 167–68; H-B compared to nuclear threats and, 179–80, 234n.165; paramount importance of, 177–79; policy differences and, 106–7. See also World Trade Organization (WTO)

U.S. Justice Department, 188

U.S. Permanent Representation to the European Union, 151

U.S. State Department, 39–40, 78, 160

U.S. Supreme Court, 24, 74–75, 100

Universal Declaration of Human Rights, 46

Uruguay, visit to by Juan Carlos, 132

USSR. See Soviet Union

usucapion (ownership based on length of occupancy), 50

Uzbekistan, on embargo, 102, 103

Vagts, Detlev F., 62, 76, 176

Vajpayee, Atal Behari, 189

Vatican.See Catholic Church

Vázquez Montalbán, Manuel, 137

Venezuela: Cuban trade with, 17; human rights vote and, 158

Villalonga, Fernando, 139, 141

Villamil, José Antonio, 233–34n.147

visas: for Canadians, 71, 88–89, 164–65; for Cuban nationals, 39, 158; for E.U., 138; lottery for, 191. See also work permits

Vitro (company), 161, 224n.30

Wallace, David, 53
Wal-Mart (company), 88–89
Watson, Alexander, 135
Western Europe. *See* European Union
 (E.U.); *specific countries*
West Indies Sugar (company), 15
White, Robert, 31, 131
Wijdenbosch, Jules, 193
Wilhelm, Gen.Charles, 175
William, Benjamin, 164
Wilson, Woodrow, 42
Wiltel (company), 161, 224n.30
Wood, Gen. Leonard, 43
work permits, 94
World Bank, 76, 171
World Health Organization, 190
World's Fair (Seville), 132
World Trade Organization (WTO):

Canada's threat of complaints to, 87;
Castro at, 155; 1997 compromise and,
125–28; divisions in, 176–78; function
of, 7; H-B condemned in, 119–20, 122–
23; H-B's impact on, 2, 5–6, 31, 58; H-
B's violation of, 76–77; leadership of,
107; trade war threats in, 179–80

Y Dios entró en La Habana (Vázquez
 Montalbán), 137
Yoo, John, 72
York Medical (company), 161, 224n.30
Yugoslavia, Spanish-American War
 compared to, 197

Zedillo, Ernesto, 140
Zhu Rongji, 189
Ziff, Soren, 233n.129

Joaquín Roy is professor of international studies and director of European studies and the Iberian Studies Research Institute at the University of Miami Graduate School of International Studies. He was born in 1943 in Barcelona, Spain, where he graduated from law school. He holds master's and Ph.D. degrees from Georgetown University and is the author or editor of 23 books, over 150 scholarly articles and reviews, and more than 900 essays and columns. Among his recent books are *Cuba and Spain: Relations and Perceptions*, *Latin American Christian Democratic Thought*, *The Reconstruction of Central America: The Role of the European Community*, *The Ibero-American Space*, and *The Ever Faithful Island*.